Migration, Terrorism, and the Future of a Divided Europe

Migration, Terrorism, and the Future of a Divided Europe

A Continent Transformed

CHRISTOPHER DELISO

Praeger Security International

BLOOMSBURY ACADEMIC
NEW YORK · LONDON · OXFORD · NEW DELHI · SYDNEY

BLOOMSBURY ACADEMIC
Bloomsbury Publishing Inc
1385 Broadway, New York, NY 10018, USA
50 Bedford Square, London, WC1B 3DP, UK
29 Earlsfort Terrace, Dublin 2, Ireland

BLOOMSBURY, BLOOMSBURY ACADEMIC and the Diana logo
are trademarks of Bloomsbury Publishing Plc

First published in the United States of America by ABC-CLIO 2017
Paperback edition published by Bloomsbury Academic 2024

Cover design by Silverander Communications
Cover photo: People queue for buses behind a policeman in Brussels, Belgium, March 22, 2016.
(AP Photo/Martin Meissner)

Library of Congress Cataloging-in-Publication Data
Names: Deliso, Christopher, 1974- author.
Title: Migration, terrorism, and the future of a divided Europe: a continent
transformed / Christopher Deliso.
Description: Santa Barbara, California: Praeger Security International, [2017] |
Includes bibliographical references and index.
Identifiers: LCCN 2017011042 (print) | LCCN 2017018388 (ebook) |
ISBN 9781440855252 (eBook) | ISBN 9781440855245 (hardcopy: alk. paper)
Subjects: LCSH: European Union countries—Emigration and immigration. |
European Union countries—Emigration and immigration—Government policy. |
European Union countries—Emigration and immigration—Social aspects. |
Refugees—European Union countries. | Terrorism—European Union countries. |
National security—European Union countries.
Classification: LCC JV7590 (ebook) | LCC JV7590 .D456 2017 (print) |
DDC 325.4—dc23
LC record available at https://lccn.loc.gov/2017011042

ISBN: HB: 978-1-4408-5524-5
      PB:979-8-7651-1981-5
      ePDF: 978-1-4408-5525-2
      eBook: 979-8-2161-1741-4

Series: Praeger Security International

Contents

Introduction

The match was a friendly one, and symbolic, too; France and Germany, once mortal enemies, but for 70 years and more, firm allies, the indispensable pair that held together the entire European project. Among the enthusiastic crowd at the Stade de France that Friday evening was the country's president, François Hollande and his special guest, German foreign minister Frank-Walter Steinmeier. The explosions were somewhat muffled by the din of the game; the crowd was not informed that two suicide bombers had just detonated outside the stadium, in the space of three minutes. Only the attentiveness of one security guard had prevented the first terrorist from entering the stadium, where the carnage would have been much greater.

Meanwhile, in the center of Paris, the other parts of a methodically organized paramilitary attack were unfolding. Six minutes after the stadium explosions, shooters opened fire on people out for the evening at cafés on the Rue Bichat, leaving 10 dead and 15 critically injured before escaping by car. The lightning raids continued, as terrorists firing Kalashnikovs sprayed restaurant-goers, killing another 24 innocent people. Then, just as a third suicide bomber injured 15 at a café on the boulevard Voltaire, terrorists stormed the Bataclan theatre. The gunmen methodically fired into the crowd of 1,500 concert-goers and tossed grenades before taking hostages. A full 35 minutes had elapsed by the time elite police units finally ended the carnage in a hail of bullets and explosions.

In the aftermath of the attacks, a shocked France learned that 137 people were dead, and another 368 wounded. The media said that it was the deadliest event in France since World War II; that same date had been haunting Europe for months, in the context of the simultaneous refugee crisis emerging from the Mediterranean basin. The worst humanitarian catastrophe since World War II, it was said; leaders called for solidarity. In the confusion and chaos of that night of Friday the 13th of November in Paris, the German national soccer team slept on mattresses inside an empty silent stadium. The French team joined them, in the spirit of solidarity.

Less than a week later, the suspected ringleader of the attacks, Abdelhamid Abaaoud, was killed in a police assault on a north Paris apartment. Abaaoud had been one of Europe's most wanted men and was suspected of involvement in "four of the six terror plots that French intelligence services had foiled" in 2015; however, Interior Minister Bernard Cazeneuve reportedly admitted that "no EU intelligence service had alerted France that he was on European soil."[1] It was a stunning admission: France's most wanted terrorist had been hiding in plain sight.

The Paris attacks had been planned in Syria and communicated through closed channels to cells in Belgium. They involved young Muslims with European passports, veterans of Islamic State's devilish war in Syria. It was quickly established that some of the attackers had reached France via the "Balkan Route" refugee corridor, a route that Germany's Angela Merkel had inundated with souls after welcoming "unlimited numbers" of refugees, on her own volition. For the countries along the way, like Greece, Macedonia, and Serbia, managing the flows had been nearly impossible, due to the sheer volume of travelers. And not only that: the European Union had not been particularly interested in intelligence collected on the migrants by these Balkan states.

Cumulatively, it was a security policy failure of the highest order, though no one would ever be held responsible for it. What the Paris attacks would do, however, was to irrevocably end Europe's general sympathy for the refugee cause, and open the way to a longer period of introspection and political infighting during which neither migration waves nor terrorism would cease. The Continent lurched from one crisis stopgap deal to the next, with each acrimonious resolution matched by another sensationalistic media depiction of violence, protests, or tragedy involving migration and security. It was the beginning of Europe's new phase of existence, and, just as with the previous one (the breaking of the Berlin Wall), no one knew how it would end. The old Chinese proverb seemed to hold true: "May you live in interesting times."

2015 MIGRATION CRISIS: THE TURKISH-BALKAN-CENTRAL EUROPEAN CORRIDOR

Map showing the 2015 Migration Crisis corridor, with refugee and migrant flows from the Middle East and SE Asia routed through Turkey, Greece (Lesvos, Athens), Eidomeni, Belgrade, Vienna, Munich, Frankfurt, and Berlin.

CHAPTER 1

The Migration Explosion: Europe's Rude Awakening

All great historical events are marked by great myths. In the case of Europe's 2015 migration crisis, the greatest, and most accepted, myth is that this event was fundamentally a humanitarian disaster. However, although this perception was relentlessly pushed by the media, various politicians, and international organizations, it failed to present the crisis at the level of its primary reality.

To be sure, the perilous peregrinations of millions of people seeking a safer or more prosperous life in Europe have been marked by tragedy; from death at sea and disease to assaults and robbery, the people making this cross continental journey have often fallen victim to great hardship, suffering, and danger. Yet this has been a risk inherent to all human travel since the beginning of time; what differentiates individuals, and individual journeys, is the amount of risk in which travelers are willing to put themselves. Today's illegal migration to Europe has been going on for at least three decades, under identical conditions, and has always been marked by the same risks. That it did not become a major talking point until 2015 owes not to the realities of migration risk in general.

What was different about 2015, then? The answer is simple: volume. The numerical rise in migrant flows increased the probability that more individuals would be affected negatively by unsafe methods of transport along with the multiplied interactions with strangers. The spike in migration also guaranteed that the existing structural capacities to receive this "unprecedented" volume of newcomers would be overwhelmed, leading to further tragedies. And, with the unwillingness of countries (especially Germany) to provide direct transport to the masses they had so enthusiastically and recklessly invited, the range of risks was multiplied by geographic distance. What could be a three- or four-hour plane ride instead became an Odyssean journey of weeks or months through a dozen or more countries.

From this perspective, the 2015 migration crisis was first and foremost a logistical issue. In 2015, everything else that would be given symbolic meaning, or manifest in reality, from political and intercultural perception to security outcomes and financial aspects, ultimately derived from the basic fact that the migration phenomenon was essentially a logistical problem—and one that was, and is, encouraged by different actors having their own distinct interests.

This ground reality must be considered when assessing the multifaceted dimensions that the crisis would acquire, in terms of politics, diplomacy, security concerns, socioeconomic challenges, organized crime, and more. Increasingly heated debates within (and indeed, beyond) Europe were perpetuated by sharply divided political rhetoric that was amplified by the media, in both its traditional forms and "new" incarnations. Thus, when assessing the almost two-year period of drama and decision making that bookend the crisis, certain symmetries become discernible. This represents a pattern of problem–reaction–solution that constantly repeats during the period in question; understanding the likely perpetuation of this pattern in the future requires understanding the specific events that marked the 2015 crisis.

Although a wider span of time could be examined, the pattern remains the same. Thus, a narrative of events following this crisis reaction model can be established and assessed between January 2, 2015, and September 19, 2016—a period during which the seminal events and decisions shaping the migrant crisis occurred. On the former date, a human-trafficking "ghost ship," the Ezadeen, was rescued off the Italian coast, after having drifted for weeks with 360 Syrian refugees on board. On the latter date, the United Nations formally adopted a charter on refugees, under the guidance of American president Barack Obama and supported by some of the world's most powerful and influential private corporations and organizations.

The chronology of migration-related events between these two dates—very roughly, between the problem and the solution—is unsurprisingly long. In the broad scope, what occurred during the period was a continual shifting of migrant travel routes due to outside factors, such as wars, national economic and political crises, security events, and institutional decisions. Little wonder, then, that this supercharged climate was pervaded by a marked sense of unreality, of an opaque but enormous system change occurring, without anyone seeming to be overtly in control of the process, though there were in fact powerful entrenched interests that did help steer the crisis from the background.

Although many have tried to find a "root cause" for the sudden spike in migrant numbers in 2015, no simple answer exists. The ongoing civil war in Syria—a frequently cited "root cause"—had after all been raging for four years by 2015, with millions of refugees already settled into camps in Turkey, Jordan, and Lebanon. The argument for the Syrian conflict also does not account for increasing numbers of migrants from countries not affected by war, such as Pakistan, Bangladesh, Eritrea, and other African countries. Indeed, UN statistics revealed that ethnic Albanians from the Balkans—who certainly suffered no security risks at home, and were thus promptly returned there—comprised the second-largest percentage of all asylum seekers in Germany during 2015.[1] Thus rather than trying to identify causes of the 2015 migration explosion, it should suffice to just take a good look at the actual events that occurred during the period of peak crisis, and their geographic distribution over time.

Until 2015, illegal migration to Europe had followed a more or less predictable seasonal pattern, relying on good weather for sea transport between North Africa and Italy as well as between Turkey and Greece. Although less restricted by weather conditions, illegal land crossing between Turkey and Greece had dramatically decreased due to the Greek erection of a border fence in 2012—a great irony in itself, considering how the Greek government would criticize other European countries throughout 2015 when they likewise built border fences to protect their own territory. Even back in 2011, when the Greek fence was proposed following a massive increase in illegal crossings, some senior European Union (EU) officials and the German mainstream media had criticized Greece's plan to secure the European Union's external border.[2]

At the beginning of 2015, illegal migration into Europe was essentially an Italian problem. The maritime route between Turkey and Greece had not yet become the major phenomenon that it would by spring. Spanish cooperation with Moroccan leaders, and Spain's beachhead on the Moroccan coast, had always kept migrant numbers to a minimum. The European Union's first operational reaction to migration was therefore geared toward Italy's needs. Situated on the European Union's soft Mediterranean underbelly, Italy had always been a prime destination for illegal immigrants from Africa and the Middle East, due to the proximity of the Italian mainland (and, especially, the island of Lampedusa) to Libya. The 2011 NATO intervention there that plunged the country into anarchy following the overthrow and murder of longtime dictator Muammar Qaddafi created ideal conditions for human trafficking to flourish. Qaddafi had blocked trafficking, even before the 2008 deal with then Italian prime minister Silvio Berlusconi. This was envisioned within a broader range of Italian–Libyan cooperation measures, driven largely by Italy's interest to maintain the historically privileged position of state-owned energy giant, ENI, in Libya.[3]

A month after the January 2, 2015, rescue of the Ezadeen, the year's first large-scale migration accident to take on humanitarian overtones occurred on February 9, when 300 migrants drowned off of the Libyan coast. On March 3, the Italian Coast Guard rescued almost 1,000 migrants from a capsized vessel off the coast of Libya. In the same maritime zone on April 13, roughly 400 people also drowned while about 150 were picked up by the Italian Coast Guard. This pattern of events continued to repeat in the Central Mediterranean, with the single most dramatic one being the drowning of about 650 migrants, south of the Italian island of Lampedusa, just days later. It would be the largest loss of life from a single maritime accident during the period in question.[4]

The outcry from political blocs and international humanitarian organizations over such maritime migrant deaths in the Central Mediterranean prompted the European Council to hold an emergency meeting, on April 23, 2015. Although a similar maritime influx of migrants from Turkey to Greece was also occurring, the sheer scale of the tragedies—as well as Italy's larger size and closer proximity to Western Europe—influenced the European Union's decision to focus security assets and research on the Libya–Italy route. This decision was not necessarily a mistake, but in hindsight it does appear that European officials had still failed to understand the size and geographic scope of the crisis that would unfold in the months ahead.

Indeed, the April 23 European Council meeting offered relatively modest solutions. Funding for rescue operations aimed at migrant vessels would be tripled, with several EU member states pledging additional ships and resources to an Italian-led naval effort to deter migrant smugglers. The possible deployment of European immigration officers to non-EU states was also discussed. The cumulative result was the first of two major 2015 maritime missions, combining humanitarian operations at sea with intelligence-gathering and risk assessment regarding traffickers and their operations.

Even before the April 23 meeting, tensions over migration had been building up in the Eastern Mediterranean. In January 2015, elections in Greece had elevated to power an odd coalition of the far-left Syriza party, led by the charismatic but untested Alexis Tsipras, and the right-wing Independent Greeks (ANEL) of nationalist politician Panos Kammenos. That government had been elected by a public long frustrated with the political establishment's never-ending concessions to the German-backed Troika (the International Monetary Fund, European Central Bank, and European Commission) and its policy of austerity measures and tax hikes in return for financial bailouts.

The Greek government that faced the 2015 migrant crisis was thus marked by a populist and antiestablishment character, an eccentric combination of the fringes of left and right, as the traditional political center had collapsed. This phenomenon was, and would continue to be, witnessed widely in Europe (as will be discussed in detail in other chapters).

Although the ruling parties in Greece had diametrically opposing views regarding migration, they did agree on the following: Greece was a victim, and the crisis should therefore be used to extract concessions from the European Union. The targets of this policy would change over the coming months to keep up with events, but the general outlook was always the same: that a small country on the southernmost frontiers of the European Union was a victim, not only of unfair European financial policies, but of the refugee burden, due to its unenforceable maritime border with Turkey.

In spring 2015, when a political game of chicken was unfolding between the Greek government and the Troika over new bailout conditions, some Greek politicians saw what leaders from other countries (most notably, Turkey) would soon realize: migration could be weaponized for political goals. Most flamboyant was ANEL leader and defense minister Panos Kammenos. "If Europe leaves us in the crisis, we will flood it with migrants, and it will be even worse for Berlin if in that wave of millions of economic migrants there will be some jihadists of the Islamic State too," Kammenos warned.[5]

Although it would hold a referendum against the Troika's new bailout terms and austerity measures, the Greek government blinked first in its own showdown with Brussels and Berlin. By early summer, Greece was implementing capital controls, amid fears of bank runs and total economic meltdown. The government conceded to onerous new bailout terms, including ever more taxes, pension cuts, and other policies that Syriza and ANEL had specifically opposed during their successful election campaigns. Yet despite the contradictions, these parties again formed a government, following snap elections in September 2015. Already disillusioned, the Greek electorate did not have any faith in mainstream political parties either.

During that summer of political and economic unrest in Greece, the country would also overtake Italy as the main transit route for refugees and illegal migrants entering the country primarily by sea from Turkey and passing north through the Republic of Macedonia and Serbia (the so-called Balkan Route) toward Central Europe. Since ancient times, this corridor has been favored as the faster and most direct corridor for armies and merchants traveling between the Aegean coast and Central Europe. Modern-day migrants too had always favored the Balkan Route, but never in such massive numbers as in 2015. As such, transporting illegal migrants through Macedonia and Serbia—countries that were not part of the European Union or its "borderless" internal Schengen Zone—had previously been considered a crime.

However, the sheer volume of migrants arriving daily forced the Macedonian government to decriminalize this transport and to allow migrants free passage onward to EU countries that were readier to receive them. The policy was implemented after tragic incidents, such as when 14 Somali and Afghan migrants were killed by a train near Veles, in central Macedonia. Contemporary reports suggested that traffickers had instructed them to simply walk north along a railway track that actually passes through canyons and over steep ravines. The dissemination of similarly false information by traffickers and pro-migrant activists would repeatedly lead to unnecessary deaths and injuries along the Balkan Route in the months to come.

In the spring of 2015, when the European Union had set its sights on tackling migration into Italy and was still primarily regarding Greece as an economic problem child, it was also preparing initiatives that would, if successful, increase its own powers—a trend that the bloc has historically embraced and one that has fueled considerable Euroskepticism over the years. During this period, controversial policies were being debated in Brussels that would further incorporate the migration crisis into overall EU policy. Most notably, on May 11, 2015, the European Commission proposed a quota scheme, according to which EU member states would be required to take in a proportional number of refugees and asylum seekers.

More than any other single policy proposal during the migration crisis, the quota scheme suggestion caused outrage across Europe. It exacerbated existing differences between governments and peoples. Countries that had traditionally received the most migrants and asylum applications and felt unfairly burdened due to their geographic location (such as Italy, Malta, and Greece) were supportive of the idea, as was Germany, which under Chancellor Angela Merkel and her advisers saw incoming migrants as a way of bolstering productivity and as a pension fund base in an aging country intent on maintaining its leading economic position.

However, other countries like Austria, Estonia, and the powerful Visegrad Four (V4) group of Hungary, Slovakia, Poland, and the Czech Republic opposed what was seen as unwarranted interference in internal affairs by Brussels, and as the imposition of a German agenda that disrespected state sovereignty. Hungary's prime minister, Viktor Orbán, became the leading voice against Merkel's open-borders policy, basing his arguments not only on state sovereignty and security concerns, but also on the perceived inability and unwillingness of migrants from largely Muslim countries to assimilate and respect their host countries' cultural norms. Although Orbán was continually savaged by liberal leaders and media throughout the crisis, his basic arguments would be upheld by most opponents to the quota scheme; further, Hungary's preventive security measures (such as border fences, military deployment, and information campaigns designed to deter migrants from coming to Europe) would later be adopted by other European countries and even copied by a European Council desperate to keep the EU from breaking apart due to Merkel's adventurism.

The public backlash against mandatory quotas caused Brussels to pause and recalibrate its position for a softer, but similar, policy suggestion. By

June, UN figures revealed that 63,000 migrants had arrived in Greece and 62,000 more had reached Italy during the year's first half. These numbers were alarmingly high, but still seemed manageable to Brussels. On June 26, after long negotiations, the European Council agreed to relocate just 40,000 migrants from Italy and Greece to willing EU member countries.[6] Although the call for mandatory quotas had been dropped, the European Council did also agree to absorb a further 20,000 refugees from non-EU states.

However, simultaneously with this agreement, the potential security dangers of uncontrolled migration were being witnessed in France, at the notorious Calais "Jungle" migrant camp, near the English Channel. In the last week of June, a ferry-workers' strike created a bottleneck, with vehicles bound for Britain backed up in heavy traffic jams. With trucks defenseless and immobile, hundreds of migrants from the radicalized camp tried to break into trucks, threatening drivers with knives and iron bars. The police were forced to respond, leading to clashes and the temporary closure of the Channel Tunnel. Such events would fuel Euroskepticism in Britain, one year before the successful Brexit referendum on leaving the European Union for good. On June 27, British authorities announced their plan to construct a security fence stretching for over two miles, near the Channel Tunnel port in Calais.

Similar measures were under way elsewhere in Europe. On July 13, the Hungarian government began fortifying its southern border with Serbia, in response to the increasing migrant wave from Greece and the Balkan Route. Although it was situated east of the main regional corridor, Bulgaria responded to the escalating situation similarly, building the final section of a fence begun in November 2013, along its southeastern border with Turkey.

Unlike Britain, Hungary, and Bulgaria, Macedonia was neither a European Union nor a NATO member—the result of a perpetual veto by its southern neighbor, Greece, which also has a province named Macedonia. Greece refused to recognize the Republic of Macedonia under its constitutional name after it declared independence from Yugoslavia on September 8, 1991. Thereafter began a Greek state policy of blocking Macedonian EU and NATO accession unless the country changed its name. In 2009, the International Court of Justice ruled that Greece's ongoing veto violated a 1995 Interim Accord, in that it continued to block Macedonia from joining international organizations. Nevertheless, the ruling was not binding and Greece has always used its diplomatic and strategic leverage to keep Macedonia excluded from the Western security architecture and political bloc.

Although the results of this have largely been negative for Macedonia and its people, during the 2015 migration crisis, nonmembership in the European Union actually had some benefits. As a "third country" (like

Turkey, Serbia, and other non-EU countries), Macedonia was not obliged to participate in any pan-European quota systems or similar migrant redistribution arrangements. With a population of only two million and insufficient infrastructure for dealing with migrant inflows, Macedonia understood illegal migration as a threat to national security, as it compounded an existing crisis. The year 2015 had already seen a faux political crisis over opposition allegations of governmental wiretapping, and a terrorist plot by ethnic Albanian paramilitaries organized from neighboring Kosovo that was foiled in a dramatic police operation on May 9, 2015. Although the details of these events are not well understood even by specialists, let alone the world public, it is undeniable that Macedonia's ability to survive through a time of security threats and political paralysis changed the course of history. Had Macedonia broken down—as many had expected, and indeed, hoped for—the continued inflow of illegal migrants would have increased, with unpredictable results for the entire continent.

By early August, Macedonian security planners were casting a wary eye on Greece—the source of approximately 3,000 incoming migrants per day—as well as on the north—where the public remained, for the time being, at least, favorable to Merkel's "refugees welcome" policy. However, being a non-EU, non-NATO country meant a considerable lack of leverage, which, even in the best of times, would adversely affect national abilities to preserve internal security. Therefore, by August 2015, Macedonian leaders had (privately) established a timeline for action: when Austria closed its borders to migrants, Macedonia would do the same, to prevent a "migrant bubble" from forming on its territory.

Poor security relations with the European Union's local delegation during the 2015 political crisis had carried over to the migration one, with Macedonian leaders seeing the bloc as obtuse and slow to help, in comparison to the attention and funds lavished upon Italy, Greece, and other countries. Further, the national risk assessment determined that, with the migrant influx, all security risks to the country were coming from the territory of the European Union (that is, from Greece). Although it itself was an aspiring EU member, Macedonia had none of the reciprocal cooperation or security guarantees that member states enjoy. It thus decided to enforce its borders with the European Union (that is, Greece) and to possibly seek bilateral police assistance from willing European countries as a sovereign state.

To take control of its fate, therefore, on August 20, 2015, Macedonia declared a temporary closure of the illegal border with Greece. The government declared a crisis situation at both the southern border with Greece and the northern one with Serbia, where migrant backlogs were also apparent. The declared crisis situation brought into effect a special law governing crisis situations. Under the law, the president, Gjorge Ivanov, tasked the army with enforcing police presences on the border following a risk assessment report and multi-institutional response. As Britain, Hungary, and Bulgaria had already done, Macedonia also began to build a security fence on the border with Greece. Athens and Brussels, which had been taken completely by surprise, were shocked.[7]

Although the border closure was temporary, it did force the European Union to at least pay attention to the southern Balkans and the potential for another migrant bottleneck to form in Greece—that is European Union and Schengen Zone territory. At the same time, the general crisis was still generally being considered a humanitarian one. Throughout August, several other high-profile accidents involving migrants killed at sea or due to suffocation in trucks brought increasing pressure on European leaders to act. Nongovernmental organizations (NGOs) large and small were operating in full force across affected areas, such as Greek islands like Lesvos near Turkey, Sicily, and Lampedusa in Italy, on the Macedonian–Greek border, and in many other places on the continent.

Early September 2015 also represented the high-water mark for public perception of the crisis as a humanitarian one with implied European moral responsibilities. On September 2, the bleak image of Alan Kurdi, a refugee child found dead on a Turkish beach, caused a worldwide sensation, putting pro-migrant voices at the forefront of the discussion. None was louder than that of Angela Merkel, who stated on September 5 that there would be "no limits on the number of asylum seekers" Germany was willing to accept. This open invitation would have serious repercussions for Merkel and indeed all of Europe, as it had been made unilaterally by the leader of a single EU member state, and a leader whose weak coalition gave her no mandate for such sweeping decisions. The fact that one leader, even from such a powerful country as Germany, should decide for all of Europe angered many Europeans.

The chancellor justified her "refugees welcome" policy by saying that "as a strong, economically healthy country we have the strength to do what is necessary."[8] For a time, this depiction of a national moral duty appealed to Germans, particularly those from the left. Indeed, as Merkel's words were still resonating, convoys of enthusiastic German and Austrian activists were driving migrants into the country from Hungary, where the government had given up trying to register them following a four-day protest by thousands of migrants determined to go to Germany. The Hungarian government stated that it had been trying to enforce EU law: according to existing legislation (the Dublin Regulation), all refugees must claim asylum at the point of entering the European Union. The disconnect between European law in theory and in reality had already been a major issue for years before the crisis. Indeed, when putting together its campaign platform in October 2014, Greece's Syriza had already been planning to call for an EU summit on revising the Dublin Agreements within six months of taking office. By the time they took power, in January 2015, events had already overtaken them.

The essential dilemma of the Hungarian standoff involved the question of whether an asylum seeker could choose a specific EU country of residence. This issue soon reappeared in Denmark. On September 8, Danish police stopped a train carrying hundreds of migrants from Germany to Sweden. The police were obliged to close a highway and temporarily stop railway services with Germany, when 200 migrants refused to leave the trains, and another 300 set off by foot along the highway to Sweden. These protesters had refused to be registered in Denmark, as Sweden offered more generous social benefits. Along with Germany, Sweden had been most welcoming at that point.

Angela Merkel's announcement that Germany would take in unlimited numbers of asylum seekers immediately caused a spike in migrant numbers on the Balkan Route, causing alarm in those countries most affected. A side effect was the acceleration of individual state reactions that would eventually lead to the closure of that route in March 2016. Indeed, only a week after Merkel's warm welcome, Germany was forced on September 13 to enforce temporary controls on its Austrian border, which included a 12-hour suspension of rail service between the two countries. With more than 13,000 migrants having arrived in Munich in just one day, Germany and 40,000 more the following weekend, the German vice-chancellor announced that Germany was "at the limit of its capabilities."[9]

Unsurprisingly, the German reaction toward Austria had a domino effect—as Macedonian security planners had anticipated months before. Thus, on September 14, Austria sent soldiers to enforce new controls on its border with Hungary, which closed its border with Serbia and declared a state of emergency in two southern counties. Hungary also began fortifying its border with Croatia. The closure of the Hungarian border led Croatia to close most of its border crossings with Serbia following a mass influx of some 13,000 migrants. And a jittery Slovenia, near the northern edges of both the Balkan and Italian migrant land routes, imposed controls on its border with Hungary.[10]

The domino effect on the Balkan Route jolted the European Union, as it threatened not just bilateral relations between neighbors but also the future viability of the passport-free Schengen Zone, the members of which included countries like Greece, Germany, Austria, Hungary, and Slovenia. As with previous moments of emergency during the overall crisis, the instinct of Brussels was again toward expanding its own powers for more centralized decision making and compulsory cooperation. Thus, on September 22, the European Commission proposed that a scheme to relocate 120,000 refugees across the union be mandatory for all EU member states.[11] This had followed a majority vote at the European Union's Justice and Home Affairs Council, despite the objections of Hungary, the Czech

Republic, Slovakia, and Romania. Thus, far from retreating from its position following moments of crisis, Brussels again saw moments of disunity as a chance to impose longer-term ambitions—a tendency that would be consistently reaffirmed throughout the crisis.

The expansion of EU capacities supposedly necessitated by the migrant crisis was hardly limited to simple relocation schemes, however. Common policing and military action under the blue-and-yellow EU flag had already been a reality for years by 2015. The grandest such mission yet was unveiled on October 7, as the continuation and extension of the Central Mediterranean maritime mission begun in spring. Dubbed EUNAVFOR Operation Sophia, the new Italian-led mission would not only rescue migrants and monitor traffickers, but also intercept trafficking vessels smuggling migrants.[12] Further, an EU–Turkey "action plan" was announced on October 15. Despite opposition from many European leaders, the hard reality was that Turkish president Recep Tayyip Erdoğan had all the leverage. As the key migrant exporter, Turkey demanded not only financial assistance, but also expedited visa liberalization for Turkish citizens traveling to the European Union, and renewed EU membership negotiations. With the latter two demands particularly undesirable for many European politicians, the course was set for a long and difficult process of negotiations between two forces with deep divisions, a legacy of mutual mistrust, but also significant shared economic and security interests.

Through October 2015, heavy arrivals of migrants continued into Greece from Turkey, increasing the pressure on the still-open Balkan Route. This spike was due to residual belief among migrants that they were welcome in Germany and Sweden. It also stemmed from the realization that winter was coming (and, with it, more dangerous weather for crossing the Aegean Sea), along with fears that the Balkan Route might close, due to the hasty erection of fences and temporary border closures. In Greece, the same migrant activist groups that had been operating since the early summer were still heavily involved with transporting, feeding, and advising thousands of new arrivals each day, on both the islands nearest to Turkey and at Eidomeni, a small village on the border with Macedonia that would become an infamous flashpoint only a few months later.

The midautumn refugee spike was registered again on October 22, when more than 12,600 migrants arrived in Slovenia in one day, causing the already panicked nation to call for EU assistance. Just a week earlier, Slovenia had said it could accept 2,500 new refugees per day. This decision to set daily restrictions on incoming migrants would later be adopted by other Balkan Route countries. After yet another emergency EU meeting on October 25, the leaders of 11 EU states and three non-EU states agreed to expand migrant intake once more, allotting 100,000 more spaces in refugee centers, while 400 police officers would be dispatched for Slovenian border assistance. Over 9,000 new migrants had arrived in Greece every day during the previous week—matching the total number of 63,000 arrivals Greece had received in the entire first half of 2015.[13]

This stark statistic indicated just how significantly European leaders had underestimated the sheer volume of migrants determined to reach European shores. In this light, the European Union's presentation of September's forced agreement to resettle a mere 120,000 as a great achievement appeared almost ridiculous, considering that it had required months of hard-fought negotiation between diametrically opposed member states. The glacial pace of EU bureaucracy and decision making was well outpaced by events. Indeed, by the end of 2015, more than one million migrants and refugees in all would enter the European Union by sea, with more than 80 percent having arrived in Greece from Turkey.[14]

Only weeks after the decision to help Slovenia, an event occurred that would dramatically change the European public mood concerning migration: the November 13 Paris terrorist attacks carried out by Islamic State militants, which left 130 dead. When it later emerged that some of these terrorists had arrived among the migrant throngs, both public opinion and official security policies dramatically changed.[15] That a terrorist attack with some migration-related element would occur was unsurprising for those security experts and leaders like Hungary's Orbán and Macedonia's Ivanov, who had been predicting this specific threat for months. The March warning of Greek defense minister Kammenos about "flooding" Europe with migrants that included jihadists could no longer be dismissed by critics as mere bombastic rhetoric.

The Paris attacks also prompted specific preventive measures on all sides of the continent. In Macedonia, President Ivanov convened the National Security Council the day after the attacks. Security planners agreed to expand the border fence with Greece and to be prepared to close the border to all refugees when—not if—the countries further north on the Balkan Route also did so. In the meantime, Macedonia planned to restrict passage of refugees to citizens of countries affected by war, specifically Iraq, Syria, and Afghanistan. This created further pressure on Greece, which could only protest what it saw as an unfair and discriminatory restriction. Unlike his coalition partner Kammenos, the leftist Greek leader, Alexis Tsipras, was a solidly prorefugee leftist and consistently echoed the calls of European liberals and foreign globalists that saw the migrant crisis as a chance for expressing "European solidarity" and "common values." In the case of Greece, this meant not being isolated by its northern neighbors as the number of arrivals from Turkey continued to rise.

On November 22, the president of the European Council, Donald Tusk, visited Macedonia's capital, Skopje. There he met with President Ivanov, EU officials, and government security planners to discuss the crisis. According to an official present at the meeting, Mr. Tusk was "shocked and surprised" to learn that a local EU official had failed to pass on to the council an official request for border assistance drafted by the Macedonian foreign affairs and interior ministries, back in September. This meant that for two months, the European Council had been unaware of the emergency needs at a vital point on the migrant route. At the official press conference with President Ivanov, EC president Tusk reaffirmed support for the Macedonian position: "Like any country, you do not only have a right but an obligation to secure your borders," Tusk stated.[16]

Meanwhile, far to the north in Sweden, one of the most liberal of all EU states, the leftist government was finally forced, on November 24, to declare that most refugees could only expect temporary residence permits from April 2016. Sweden's deputy prime minister Åsa Romson memorably burst into tears while announcing the measures on television.[17] Four days later, Finland announced that migrant reception centers were overwhelmed, with over 30,000 asylum claims having been made in the Nordic nation. A similar number of applications had also been lodged in nearby Norway (which is, by choice, not an EU member). In mid-December the newly appointed minister for migration, Sylvi Listhaug, pledged that Norway's new asylum policy would be "one of the strictest in Europe."[18]

The same antimigrant stance that was visible in riots against a planned migrant shelter in the Dutch town of Geldermalsen would harden further with the reaction to a wave of sexual assaults and robberies carried out by migrants against German women in Cologne and other cities during New Year's Eve celebrations. According to the chief prosecutor, "the overwhelming majority" of suspects were asylum seekers and illegal immigrants who had recently arrived from North Africa and the Middle East.[19] Such incidents would stoke a rising (and, again, entirely predictable) backlash from right-wing groups such as Germany's increasingly visible PEGIDA movement, which protested in Cologne on January 9, 2016, clashing with police and calling for Merkel's resignation. As usual, the protest was met with a counterdemonstration by leftist pro-migrant activists.

February 2016 saw accelerated talks with Turkey over limiting the flow of migrants. It also marked the beginning of the end for large-scale movement of people along the Balkan Route. This would cause serious diplomatic turmoil and security problems for countries affected, from Greece all the way north to Austria. The latter became increasingly critical of Greece's handling of the crisis—especially in the context of vetting newcomers and preserving Europe's external borders. This criticism would soon manifest in official EC policy documents.

Sensing opportunity in an increasingly divided Europe wracked by recrimination and one-upsmanship, President Erdoğan threatened on February 11 to send millions more migrants to Greece unless Turkey recent received more aid money.[20] The threat exacerbated panic in European capitals; anyone who had somehow not already been aware now understood that Turkey enjoyed total leverage over the European Union. Greece was the first to suffer from the collateral damage of President Erdoğan's clever stratagem. The very next day, Athens was admonished by the European Council, which adopted several recommendations following an evaluation of Greece's perceived failure to uphold the security of the Schengen Zone. Within the European Union, Austria had provided the diplomatic clout to increase the pressure on Greece, though, behind the scenes, most of the intelligence that had been provided to Austrian, V4, and EU leaders had come from Macedonian and Serbian security officials.

The experience of having processed over one million migrants from Greece in the previous year had provided the opportunity for collecting copious amounts of evidence that indicated Greek failure to correctly register incoming migrants. And the fact that Macedonia had invited mixed policing teams from EU countries to help man the border meant that the ground reality they were seeing was simultaneously being transmitted to EU member state capitals. This meant that any contentions from Macedonian authorities would be instantly corroborated by these partners within the EU. As with everything else in the migrant crisis, the essential problem remain a logistical one: the volume of incoming traffic was simply too much for Greek officials to handle, and in many cases they chose to truck the migrants north, where they would become a problem for Macedonia. Yet the fact that the latter was not a European Union nor Schengen Zone member complicated things tremendously.

The problem for Greece was that it was bordered by two "third countries," in Turkey and Macedonia. Turkey's pressure on the European Union, and the pressure from Austria and V4 countries on Brussels and Berlin, caused a rapid movement toward closing the Balkan Route. This had to be handled in an organized and careful way to avoid any chaotic closure. Although not directly on the corridor, Bulgaria took the first step. Immediately after the February 11 Turkish proclamation, Bulgaria announced the imminent closure of its external EU borders, including with Turkey, announcing that it would be deporting any migrants not matching asylum status criteria.[21] Next, Austria announced a cap on the number of asylum seekers allowed in daily. This decision angered humanitarian organizations, frustrated Angela Merkel's cabinet, and caused panic among Greek leaders, who leaned on Brussels. Although he officially represented the European Union, Commissioner Avramopoulos also defended the interests of his native Greece. He blasted Austria, saying the asylum cap would break EU and international law. Avramopoulos warned soon after that the European Union's migration system could "completely break down" within weeks. On February 25, Athens recalled its ambassador to Austria in anger.[22]

Behind the scenes, Balkan states like Macedonia, Serbia, and Croatia had quietly been planning a concerted strategy with Hungary, Slovenia, and Austria. No one along the Balkan Route wanted to become a "migrant bubble" when the corridor closed. In any case, they argued, under the existing Dublin Regulations, Greece—as first point of entry in the Schengen Zone—was obliged to accept asylum applications, or at least process migrants correctly. Neither was being done. Thus on March 9, following Austria's lead, Balkan countries announced new restrictions: Slovenia, Croatia, Serbia, and Macedonia commonly declared that they would accept only those migrants seeking asylum in these countries, or who were in need of immediate humanitarian care. Those lacking valid travel documents would be returned back to Greek territory.[23] As the southernmost state on the route, Macedonia had the most difficult task, in having to return migrants to EU member Greece. It was not an enviable situation, but Macedonian leaders were prepared for all outcomes. Meanwhile, Hungary declared a state of emergency and sent more soldiers and police to the borders. A very frustrated and increasingly isolated Chancellor Merkel condemned these states for their allegedly "unilateral" closure of the Balkan route.[24] Some help for Greece would come with NATO's February decision to send a maritime patrol to the Aegean to intercept migrants and send them back to Turkey.[25]

At the same time that the Balkan Route showdown was intensifying, a separate front—with similar security risks—was opening far to the northwest, in France. There, on February 29, migrants attacked police trying to dismantle parts of the infamous Calais "Jungle" camp. They were joined by increasingly aggressive activists from the Germany-based "No Border" international movement, who had been organized on social media. No Border activists were frequently deployed to flashpoints in Europe, joining with local anarchist groups in making attacks on police and in defense of migrant causes. French authorities had planned to move Calais migrants to new, official camps, but most stubbornly refused, fearing that their dream of reaching Britain would be endangered. Reactions followed on March 7, when hundreds of Calais citizens marched in Paris against the local "economic catastrophe" caused by out-of-control migrant violence.[26] Five days later in Calais, roads leading from migrant camps to the town center were blocked by over 130 activists from the right-wing Identitarian movement, claiming to defend traditional European identity and values from Muslim migrants. Simultaneously, about 3,000 Germans protested in Berlin against the government, sparking a leftist counterprotest. The next day, March 13, right-wing nationalist party Alternative for Germany (AfD) made strong gains in state elections, running on an anti-immigration platform. It was yet another indicator that the "refugees welcome" euphoria of the previous fall had been a pipe dream shared by few others than Merkel, aid agencies, and the left.

Working under unprecedented pressure, Berlin and the European Council had been bartering for a deal with Turkey—any deal—that would guarantee no repeat migrant deluge in the spring and summer of 2016. For

EC president Donald Tusk and other leaders without personal ties to the most affected countries or rival ideologies, saving the Schengen Zone was necessary for preserving the European Union from implosion. The month before, Hungary had announced its plan for a public referendum on the "migrant quotas" proposal, while the British referendum on leaving the European Union was less than three months away. Clearly, something needed to be done.

The first solution was to close the Balkan Route. On March 9, following months of behind-the-scenes negotiations with various European countries and the European Council, Macedonia, Slovenia, and Croatia announced that their borders would be closed to irregular migrants. EC president Tusk stated clearly that "irregular flows of migrants along the western Balkans route have come to an end." Slovenia's prime minister, Miro Cerar, added that "the so-called western Balkan route for irregular migrants is no more."[27]

Athens, which had underestimated the diplomatic capabilities of its northern neighbors—particularly, Macedonia—was predictably infuriated. It had failed to forcibly export its logistical problem north, and instead the migrant bubble would be formed on its own territory. Tsipras lashed out at the "unilateral actions taken by certain countries" in closing the route. However, Tusk quickly reminded him that the Balkan states had not acted unilaterally, but as part of an agreed EU policy. He specifically thanked Balkan countries "for implementing part of EUs comprehensive strategy to deal with [the] migration crisis."[28] Although Greece had been completely defeated (and had to deal with the over 42,000 migrants stuck on its territory) few in Eastern Europe felt much sympathy: Athens had been promised 750 million euros in EU emergency money earlier in the month. Chancellor Merkel warned that the country could not handle the burden much longer and urged the European Union to finalize an agreement with Turkey.

The breakthrough came on March 18, when the European Union agreed to give Turkey 3 billion euros for refugee-hosting costs, while also promising to allow Turkish citizens visa-free travel in the Schengen Zone by June. In return, Turkey agreed to take back any "irregular" migrants arriving in Greece if they failed to apply for asylum or had their claim rejected there. Although the lavish donation amount and unlikelihood of the plan actually working caused an outcry across Europe, the element of the deal that most rankled critics was the fact that it would not actually reduce refugee numbers: for each Syrian sent back to Turkey, another, more "suitable" Syrian refugee would be resettled in the European Union.

As rival European leaders fought over the relative merits and weaknesses of the deal, two things happened: first, the European Union all but stopped its chronic criticisms of Turkish democratic deficiencies, tacit support for ISIS, and crackdown on the Kurds; and second, both right- and left-wing partisans found the deal objectionable for opposing reasons, adding to domestic polarization trends. By April 18, the inability of Europe to reach consensus on Turkey's stipulated reform program led Ankara to threaten pulling out of the deal. In such a case, it would no longer take back migrants from the European Union.[29] Because of their poor negotiating style, Angela Merkel and her EU cohorts had clearly shown that they had no prior experience in haggling for carpets in Istanbul. They had been totally outplayed by the Turks, who still held all the cards.

In the meantime, the situation was deteriorating along chokepoints like the Italy–Austria border and on the closed Balkan route. Thousands of migrants began to amass at the Greek border with Macedonia, at the village of Eidomeni—fast becoming a second Calais—attracting hundreds of activists and anarchists dedicated to the "cause" of forcing the borders open. Journalists and aid workers were also well represented at Eidomeni. On March 15, mysterious maps and flyers in Arabic and English were being circulated in the camp by unknown activists; these papers called for a mass crossing into Macedonia, evading the border fence by moving northwest across the Suva Reka (Dry River). Although the leaflet promised that the river was dry, it was anything but, and three people drowned in the following disaster, with hundreds of migrants, activists, and journalists being gathered by Macedonian police and army and promptly returned to Greece. The activists had both manipulated ignorant migrants and miscalculated the preparedness of Macedonian border guards. "The border fence is there only for you to think that the border is closed," the activists had promised. "If you come in thousands the police can't do anything with such numbers and they won't send you back."[30] Both claims were proven wrong, and the invading migrants were summarily collected and returned to Greek authorities, who had been unable or unwilling to stop the mass movement from their territory. Smaller attempts to attack the Macedonian border fence would continue during the month.

This turbulent event was quickly overshadowed, however, by the terrorist attacks that shut down Brussels' airport and public transportations system on March 22. The attacks, which left 35 dead and more than 300 injured, were carried out by young immigrants, some of them former fighters in Syria and Iraq, who had ties to the cell responsible for the November 2015 Paris attacks. The Brussels attacks also caused a new wave of alarm over migration and the future of Islam in Europe. These benefited both right- and left-wing activists. On April 3, hundreds of activists protested at the Alpine Brenner Pass, on the Italy–Austria border. Nine days later, Austria began building a fence and registration center at the Brenner Pass, threatening to shut it completely unless Italy stopped the migrant flow there. The European Union (which had a powerful Italian voice in Foreign Affairs Commissioner Federica Mogherini) condemned Austria, as did humanitarian groups. Clashes between activists and police at the Brenner

Pass erupted again in late April. Further clashes at the pass occurred on May 7.[31]

The activists simultaneously were at work in Greece, where nationwide migrant protests were growing over the government's plan to enforce the Turkey deportation deal and move people from improvised camps like Eidomeni to official shelters. The two issues became a cause célèbre for anarchists seeking to overthrow borders across Europe. Another major attack from Eidomeni was organized—in similarly mysterious fashion—and on April 10, hundreds of migrants attacked Macedonian police and attempted to destroy the fences, using new, almost paramilitary tactics. Police drove them back with tear gas. The Greek government spokesman called the Macedonian police actions "dangerous and deplorable." However, the Greek minister of civilian protection also pronounced that the images of angry, rock-hurling migrant attack indicated the "jihadists of tomorrow."[32] A video clip of a Macedonian soldier shouting "I will die for my country" while being taunted by migrants at the fence quickly went viral on YouTube. The overall security event became one of the most-discussed ones of the crisis.

The Greek migration problem was, of course, the logistical impossibility of enforcing a much longer Turkish maritime border dotted with islands and coves. The capacity of social services to handle hundreds of thousands of migrants was also overwhelmed. On the other hand, Greece's socialist leader, Alexis Tsipras and his Syriza party were ideologically natural defenders of the migrant cause; although he had railed against the European Union and Angela Merkel over austerity measures in Greece, Tsipras was allied with the German chancellor on migration. This complex relationship created numerous opportunities for the Greek leadership to essentially incentivize procrastination on slowing the flood of migrants into the country.

This proclivity was reinforced by the fact that Tsipras, like leftist Italian counterpart Matteo Renzi and leaders of major humanitarian organizations, sought to depict migration as a global moral issue requiring "solidarity" and "common solutions." In this regard, Tsipras also had a firm ally in Pope Francis. The outspoken pontiff memorably visited the Greek island of Lesvos—the major point for incoming migrants from Turkey—on April 16, just days after the Eidomeni debacle. The ensuing spectacle saw a devoutly atheistic Greek premier and the head of the Roman Catholic Church compliment each other's humanitarian impulses. The pope reiterated his call for Europeans to accept refugees, making a symbolic point by taking home three whole Syrian families from the island.[33] Nevertheless, the illusion of progress was quickly shattered with renewed migrant rioting at Lesvos's Moria detention center on April 26, following a visit from the Greek and Dutch migration ministers.[34] It was a sign of things to come for Greece's overstretched institutions.

On the opposite end of the ideological spectrum from Tsipras and the pope, the presidential candidate of Austria's Freedom Party, Norbert Hofer, won the election's first round on April 24. The unexpected result reaffirmed simmering anger over migration and caused Socialist chancellor Werner Faymann to resign. Hofer would later be defeated by a razor-thin margin in a second round that was, however, overturned; the planned September rerun of the vote was later delayed due to a strange technicality. (Hofer would be defeated in a subsequent election rerun.) The phenomenon of the "far right" coming to power in Europe, even in a largely ceremonial role like that of the Austrian presidency, became a salacious story for media around the world, which played into the tendency to regard migration as a moral issue.

However, European governments were also taking more practical measures to deal with the logistical impossibilities the migrant waves presented. Non-EU member Norway on April 25 offered a "bonus" of 10,000 Norwegian krone (about $1,250) to 500 asylum seekers willing to leave voluntarily.[35] And, following the earlier example of another non-EU state, Switzerland, the Austrian parliament on April 27 passed a law defining conditions for declaring a state of emergency, along the Hungarian and other models, to deal with any new surge in immigrant numbers. The restrictions would limit entrance to refugees deemed as being under threat in a neighboring country or who had family in Austria.

Despite the perceived defiance of much of Europe, the European Commission on May 4 came out with its most controversial proposal yet—to literally fine EU member states that refused to accept their mandated quota of asylum seekers. With fines of up to 250,000 euros possible for each asylum seeker not accepted, the proposal would have made the European Union essentially the world's best-compensated human trafficking outfit. Under the plan, which caused outrage across Europe and hardened existing opposition to the German-backed "open-door" migrant policy, the fines money would go to Italy and Greece.[36] It was clear that part of the impetus for the proposal had come from internal EU lobbying from these countries, despairing at the multi-billion-euro largesse Brussels had offered to non–member state Turkey. The Visegrad countries all rejected the proposal, with Poland questioning its seriousness and Hungary denouncing it as "blackmail."

The May 4 policy proposal was, in the big picture, part of the ongoing effort to reform the European Common Asylum System while not simply overturning the Dublin Accords. The basic points of the proposal (that had been and would continue to be developed) were the concept of "solidarity" between member states and the redistribution of migrants according to a "fair share" system, while also boosting efficiency and security measures (such as expanding the EURODAC fingerprint database of asylum seekers).[37] The proposal followed a commission letter of April 6, 2016, that listed "options" for system reform, including harmonization of policy and a stronger mandate for the European Asylum Support Office (EASO).[38]

In the meantime, individual countries continued to look after their own interests. In May, a new Austrian law outlined conditions for declaring a state of emergency if the cap number of asylum seekers (37,500 for the year) was exceeded. By the end of July, Austria had already received 24,260 applications. The domestic politics of individual member states and their separate alliances prevented the European Union from making definitive progress on its relocation and quota goals: while it continued to discuss them, much more consensus was found on external security measures, such as extending the maritime EUNAVFOR Operation Sophia's mandate for another year, on June 20. The extension had been previously decided at a May 23 commission meeting.[39]

Despite this apparent progress Brussels was making toward achieving its increasingly centralizing goals, the summer of 2016 was marked by two major events that jolted Europe and for the first time forced the European Union to contemplate its own existential crisis. The first and most serious event was Brexit, the British referendum on leaving the European Union that conservative prime minister David Cameron had promised as a concession to Tory Party Euroskeptics, while campaigning three years earlier. Once the referendum date of June 23, 2016, had been announced, Cameron (and both the right- and left-wing establishment) vigorously campaigned against leaving the European Union. Despite the spirited campaigning and populist appeal of the pro-Brexit United Kingdom Independence Party (UKIP), the smart money was on Britons choosing to remain in the Union.

There was thus almost total shock when, on the early hours of June 24, it was announced that Britain had in fact decided to leave the European Union. Cameron resigned, leaving the messy work of sorting out the European divorce to his successors. The stunning decision was immortalized by numerous images and speeches, perhaps the most memorable being the comments of UKIP leader Nigel Farage at the European Parliament following the vote. "Isn't it funny," Farage said before a group of ashen-faced Euro-parliamentarians. "When I came here 17 years ago and said I wanted to lead a campaign to get Britain to leave the Europeans Union, you all laughed at me. Well you're not laughing now."[40]

The Brexit vote came at a time when larger and larger numbers of Europeans were questioning the wisdom of the pro-migrant policies promoted by the European Union and Germany. A Pew Global research poll released on July 11 found that "in eight of the 10 European nations surveyed, half or more believe incoming refugees increase the likelihood of terrorism in their country." A solid half of respondents also believed that migrants were "a burden" for European countries as they consumed social benefits and might take away jobs from locals. More than half of respondents in Britain, Greece, Germany, Sweden, Holland, Poland, Italy, and Hungary affirmed that migrants increased the risk of terrorism, with Hungarians (at 76 percent) and Poles (at 71 percent) at the highest positions. On the question of assimilation, at least half of all respondents in most countries stated that migrants would refuse to adopt European cultural norms. Here, the long-experienced Greeks had the strongest misgivings, with a full 78 percent of respondents doubting migrants' interest in assimilating.[41]

Another and even more unexpected event took place during the summer that temporarily took the European Union off of its policy track, and perhaps irrevocably changed the geopolitical landscape in Europe's far southeast. On the night of July 15, one of the most dramatic events in modern European history occurred in Turkey, when a reported small group of army and air force officers attempted to pull off the first military coup since 1980. For several perilous hours, the fate of the republic hung in the balance, with incredible images of Istanbul bridges blocked by army vehicles and tanks on the streets flashed across world television screens. Barely escaping assassination while on vacation in the seaside resort of Marmaris, President Erdoğan put down the coup with a single phone call carried on television, imploring his millions of supporters to take to the streets and face down the army. Hundreds of civilians were killed and over 2,000 were injured before order was restored.

Erdoğan quickly blamed archrival Fethullah Gülen, an Islamic cleric based in America, whose movement is linked with a worldwide network of schools, charities, and businesses. Once allies, the two men had fallen out in previous years amid suspicions in the Turkish government that Gülen sympathizers had helped organize 2013 mass protests against the Erdoğan government. The failed coup was followed swiftly by large-scale arrests of military and other officials accused of participating in the coup, the mass closure of antigovernment media bodies, and the dismissal of thousands of teachers, judges, and others. It was the largest single system change in modern Turkish history. In the aftermath of the failed coup, President Erdoğan immediately took steps to restore the relations with Russia that had been destroyed when a Turkish fighter jet shot down a Russian jet over Syria in 2015. With an even stronger grip on power, President Erdoğan was in no mood to concede to EU demands. Yet the Turks kept lines of communication open. Indeed, in an interview published just days after the dramatic events, the Turkish ambassador to the European Union, Selim Yenel, reaffirmed that Turkey would uphold its negotiated agreements over migration, stating that "Turkey and the EU need each other."[42]

Throughout the turbulent summer of 2016, migrants continued to come to Greece and, despite the Balkan Route's continued closure, trickle northward into Central Europe with the help of traffickers and activists. The improved cooperation with Turkey, closure of the Balkan Route, and increasing instability in Libya did, however, mean that the majority of maritime migrants were coming to Italy via North Africa—the same state of affairs that had existed in early 2015. In that year, the greatest success the EU had had in terms of developing institutional capacities was the Italian-led maritime mission that would be replaced by EUNAVFOR Operation Sophia. These were all part of a larger project for a unified European military that had been suggested since the time of Winston Churchill. The migrant crisis gave it, at least on the maritime front, some added urgency among policy makers. As such, on June 21, 2016, the European Council, EU Parliament, and European Commission reached a compromise agreement on a proposed regulation on a European Border and Coast Guard.[43]

Indeed, with the migration crisis the European Union took the opportunity to expand its presence further south. On July 18, the European Union also extended until 2018 its EUCAP Sahel mission to train police in Niger and limit illegal migration from northwest Africa.[44] And, on August 30, the EU's Political and Security Committee authorized Operation Sophia to begin two additional tasks: training the Libyan coast guard and navy; and helping to implement the UN arms embargo off the coast of Libya.[45] Finally, on September 14, the council approved the envisioned European border and coast guard project, for border management at the union's external borders—a further reinforcement mechanism for Greece and Italy. "To save Schengen, we must regain control of our external borders," European Council president Tusk stated at the time.[46]

Yet despite the proclaimed emergency of "saving Schengen," in the big picture the establishment of a more integrated EU coast guard and border service does suit embedded interests on the federalist side. It is another example of the kind of solution to a problem followed by a crisis that was seen during the entire crisis. It would be, perhaps, used also as a precedent for the kind of future full military integration that some of the union's founding fathers had envisioned after World War II. The European Union has always had a hard federalist core, and proponents of the "ever-closer union" formerly evoked were out for vengeance following the Brexit vote. For major business and political leaders with entrenched interests from the "original" European Union—countries like France, Germany, Belgium, the Netherlands, and Luxembourg—the looming loss of Britain was not a moment of defeat, but merely one of recalibration. The short-term defeat, it was thought, could actually strengthen the ambitions of federalists to take more and more power from member states.

The first opportunity for discussion on this issue took place in Slovakia—at the time, holder of the honorary six-month EU presidency—and was conducted largely in secret. The rather inconclusive results of these deliberations were announced during a one-day summit in Bratislava, on September 16, 2016. Although an informal one, it was the first EU internal summit without a British delegation. In Bratislava, EU leaders spoke of a "road map" for regaining public trust and support for the European Union post-Brexit. Chancellor Merkel stated that leaders would use the following six months to "jointly agree on an agenda," and called for solidarity, cooperation, and common values—the buzzwords that had enlivened the entire migration crisis, and the very ones that had been enthusiastically supported by globalist leaders and scrutinized with suspicion by supporters of national and sovereign movements. Hungarian prime minister Viktor Orbán, the major voice from the latter camp, denounced Merkel's migration policies as "self-destructive and naïve," and stated that the Bratislava summit had accomplished nothing new in terms of agreeing on a common stance on migration.[47]

Yet Angela Merkel would receive a more enthusiastic reception at an event three days later—one that neatly bookended the entire migration crisis, and one that brought the entire problem–crisis–solution model to its inevitable conclusion. Speaking at the UN General Assembly's special Leader's Forum on migration on September 19, U.S. president Barack Obama specifically praised Merkel and her pro-migrant policies, while also hinting at her own unpopularity at home: "The politics sometimes can be hard," Obama said, "but it's the right thing to do."[48] Describing the migration issue as "a crisis of epic proportions" and comparing refugee totals (as was done repeatedly throughout the year) to those of World War II, Obama defined the migration crisis in general as "a test of our international system where all nations ought to share in our collective responsibilities," and also as "a test of our common humanity." This sweeping depiction conflated—in the same way that European pro-migration leaders had consistently done—an averred global institutional role with a call to moral duty.

Some 52 countries participated in the refugee summit, which resulted in a further tendency toward management of migrant crises by international organizations: an extra $4.5 billion in donations to the UN over 2015 levels was pledged, as were efforts meant to educate refugees and migrants and expedite their path to obtaining work in newly adopted countries, as well as greater acceptance rates for migrant resettlement. In short, the historic summit was a massive reallocation of financial resources and a movement toward the reorientation of legal systems in sovereign states, toward a globalist agenda and an entirely new economic model.

Under the new agreements, entities like the World Bank would get involved, creating a Global Crisis Response Platform to "provide low- and middle-income countries hosting large refugee populations with access to financing on favorable terms for projects to benefit both refugees and their host communities." Similarly, a U.S.-backed Emergency Resettlement Country Joint Support Mechanism (ERCM) would be run jointly by the International Organization for Migration (IOM) and the UN Refugee Agency (UNHCR), in order to provide "both financial and technical assistance to countries that are interested in establishing or expanding refugee resettlement programs."[49]

But that was not all. The president had also commandeered 51 of America's leading companies, which saw in the refugee crisis a clear way of expanding their core business while helping humanity. Tech leaders like Microsoft, Facebook, TripAdvisor, HP, Accenture, LinkedIn, and Google were all specified as being among those investing, donating, or raising more than $650 million for educating, training, or hiring up to 6.3 million refugees in 20 countries.[50] The Obama plan was followed immediately by an announcement from one of the most controversial and powerful shadow figures influencing the Democratic Party and international leftist causes in general: billionaire philanthropist George Soros, who had always been known for spotting developing business trends. Soros announced on September 20 that he would be investing $500 million into migrant-established business start-ups. Stating that these investments would be run through his nonprofit network of NGOs and foundations—many of which had been instrumental in supporting his influential pro-migrant policy during the crisis—Soros specified targeted sectors, including—unsurprisingly, considering Obama's pledge—"emerging digital technology, which seems especially promising as a way to provide solutions to the particular problems that dislocated people often face."[51] Goldman Sachs and Master Card were among other major American corporations to enlist in the president's program of "aid" to refugees.

The UN itself described the summit as a "historic opportunity to come up with a blueprint for a better international response [and] a watershed moment to strengthen governance of international migration." Tellingly, the UN hinted at creating "a more responsible, predictable system for responding to large movements of refugees and migrants"—a tacit indication that migrant crises as a sort of global business model were here to stay. At the same time, UNHCR anticipated the summit as a "game-changer" for global migration policy. The summit's outcome (the New York Declaration) would contain "annexes on refugees and migrants that will serve as the basis for future compacts," a UNHCR spokeswoman stated.[52] Further confirmation that the migrant issue was on the verge of becoming a major global business came when António Guterres (UNHCR director until 2015, former Portuguese prime minister, and a former leader of the Socialist International) was elected to replace Ban Ki-Moon as the next UN secretary general on October 13.[53]

The seeds of the September UN Summit had partly been planted during the May 2016 G7 Summit in Japan; it had called for "a global response to the migration and refugee crisis." At that earlier event, leaders "called on financial institutions and bilateral donors to bolster their assistance. They also agreed to enhance legal channels for migration and encouraged the establishment of resettlement schemes."[54] Among the EU luminaries taking part in the summit were first vice president of the European Commission Frans Timmermans, Foreign Affairs commissioner Federica Mogherini, commissioner for Migration, Home Affairs, and Citizenship Dimitris Avramopoulos, commissioner for Humanitarian Aid and Crisis Management Christos Stylianides, and European Council president Donald Tusk. "No other global problem is more urgent today than the ongoing migration of millions of people," Tusk stated in his address at the summit. "We hope that today's declaration will mark a new pragmatic approach and a shift toward a global system of more orderly movement, where the responsibility is shared and where no one will bear the burden alone."

After assuring that the European Union would allow no repeat of the mass migration of 2015, President Tusk listed several diplomatic achievements hinting at the European Union's foreign policy goals in relation to migration: new compacts with Jordan and Lebanon, to fund refugee resettlement in those countries, new partnerships with African countries, and continued cooperation with Turkey and with the Western Balkans.[55] As the UN summit showed, while Angela Merkel and friendly Eurocrats may have been on the losing side domestically, they were firmly aligned with globalist agendas for treating not only the migrant crisis, but with global governance in general. Fulfillment of this vision prefers—actually, demands—a stronger and more centralized European Union. And this necessity had already set these leaders on a collision course with those European states and millions of citizens adamantly opposed to further centralization of EU power and globalist social-engineering projects in their native countries.

For there was always still a chance—one that EU leaders knew very well—that another unexpected inflow of migrants could cause an irrevocable split within the European Union, and condemn the federalist project before it had even begun. The countries that had the power to do this were Turkey, and, to a lesser extent, the Balkan ones, the borders of which could never be completely sealed to clever traffickers and stubborn migrants. Thus, at a September 24 migration policy meeting with EU and Balkan states in Vienna, EC president Tusk reiterated that "we need to confirm—politically and in practice—that the Western Balkan route of irregular migration is closed for good."[56]

In the big picture, the twin crises of 2016 for the European Union—migration and Brexit—had already been internalized in the imaginations of those who had always sought a very different kind of European Union, one in which direct democracy was irrelevant and in which the decrees of an appointed bureaucracy would prevail over any opposition from the masses. To understand how deeply rooted this mentality really is, and how it finds natural affinity with the globalist movements of today, we must first examine its intellectual origins—which far predate the Treaty of Rome and establishment of the European Union itself.

CHAPTER 2

The History of a Dream: Ideologies, the European Project, and Outcomes for the Migration Crisis

In August 2016, as the European Union was still reeling from the migration crisis, terrorist attacks, and Great Britain's vote to leave the union, Italian prime minister Matteo Renzi hosted German chancellor Angela Merkel and French president François Hollande on the island of Ventotene, in the Tyrrhenian Sea. They had gathered to lay a wreath at the tomb of Altiero Spinelli, an ideological founding father of the European Union who had penned the famous "Ventotene Manifesto" while imprisoned there in 1941. Noting the symbolic event, media reported that Spinelli and his fellow imprisoned ideologues had expressed "a vision of a free, united, democratic Europe that eventually evolved into the EU."[1]

A member of the Italian Communist Party, Spinelli had written the manifesto to call for the complete federalization of Europe, with the incorporation of all European nation-states. He would spend the rest of his long life trying to realize this dream. The fact that Europe's battered (but not defeated) leaders would choose such a symbolic place for commemoration speaks volumes about the eternal goals of the European Union—goals that have long led conservative parties and countries like Britain and the Visegrad countries to treat the Brussels bloc with great suspicion.

To understand the European Union's response to the 2015 migration crisis, and its plans for dealing with this phenomenon in the future, it is necessary to trace the evolution of the ideologies that both set the foundations of that union and created the conditions by which its migration policy in 2015 would be driven by concerns for "European solutions" and "common values." These ideas have by no means been constants, in the broader sweep of European history. But what is constant is the general development of different ideologies due to cycles of conflict or crisis fueled by wars, plagues, economic volatility, or migration. Europe has thus always been defined by a continuous intellectual ferment, one that both drives and results from periods of crisis. The scientific, artistic, cultural, and technological contributions of European thinkers living under these dynamic conditions are immense and irreplaceable for civilization as we know it.

Today's European Union is a partial—though by no means inevitable—outcome of this general ideological ferment. But it is just one among many politico-economic models that have been attempted (or at least imagined) over the years. Indeed, the air of inevitability about the "European project" that backers of the European Union so often exude continues to provoke intense resentment among Euroskeptics—to a large degree, a factor that has influenced the bloc's contemporary crisis of confidence. Such critics have often singled out influential politicians who seem to personify the perceived arrogant detachment of an elitist group of technocrats. One favorite target in recent years has been Jean-Claude Juncker. One of the more colorful Eurocrats (he is known for greeting fellow leaders with an affectionate slap on the head), Juncker became president of the European Commission in 2014, following the usual backroom negotiations. This consummate Brussels insider had run Luxembourg—the world's last grand duchy, and a leading destination for discreet financial services—for 25 years as either finance minister or prime minister, until a still-murky scandal involving the country's intelligence services forced him from power in 2013. Many years earlier, *The Economist* had recorded one of Juncker's more revealing comments about how EU policy is actually made:

We decide on something, leave it lying around, and wait and see what happens. If no one kicks up a fuss, because most people don't understand what has been decided, we continue step by step until there is no turning back.[2]

Such comments have tended to anger Euroskeptics as they imply a disdain for democracy, arrogance, and a grim preference for technocratic processes, the implementation of policy by stealth. Some would attribute this Eurocratic instinct to personal conditioning and experience: after all, in the case of Juncker, Luxembourg's relative affluence and cozy location between France and Germany means that its citizens are never terribly bothered by politics. Indeed, since the end of World War II, the country has been essentially a one-party state, with the Christian Social People's Party holding power for 64 of the past 72 years. The country's postwar wealth, political stability, and guaranteed security have made it immune to the periodic poverty and conflicts that have always fueled the great battle of ideas across Europe. Indeed, it might be said that Luxembourg is where intellectual ferment goes to die.

However, the bland bureaucratic identity of today's European Union can hardly be associated with any single person or country; after all, EU officials by necessity hail from all across the Continent. But what is so often invoked as a rich diversity of national representation that has influenced national politics has not really "trickled up" to the level of Brussels. There, a tacit ideological conformity means that EU representatives often have more in common with each other than with the citizens of their own countries. And this is where the 2015 migration crisis became such an important test of European cohesion. As a well-oiled bureaucratic machine with precisely calibrated moving parts, in terms of its separate commissions, committees, and agencies, the European Union is an institutional wonder; not a terribly efficient one, but one that very effectively perpetuates its own existence through regulation, legislation, and the recycling of huge amounts of money. European national laws are crafted or influenced in Brussels, where an estimated 30,000 registered corporate lobbyists curry favor and hunt out lucrative contracts.

Yet as the deep divides over migration policy have abundantly shown, the bloc remains weakest precisely where it is meant to be strongest: its search for a common ideological foundation. For despite the ceaseless references to "shared European values" in official documents and public statements, these ideals remain vague and are thus generally taken at face value. And this is precisely because the European Union itself was not set up according to any solid philosophical system, but rather was established through arduous and often contentious processes of negotiations, referenda, and treaties between bitterly divided sides. In the context of this historical reality, the current ferment over immigration policy is not an aberration from the norm.

What is unusual, however, is the degree to which the pro-migrant camp throughout the crisis invoked the need for "shared European values" that have never actually been agreed on by all. The rhetoric and policies that have characterized the EU response to migration do thus indicate that certain ideologies have had more influence than others. But before exploring this fascinating and lesser-known history of the ideas influencing today's debate, it is necessary to take a broader overview of the successive movements that have led to the modern European Union.

Indeed, the concept of a political, economic, and bureaucratic union had been in gestation for 150 years by the time the 1957 Treaty of Rome created the conditions for the modern institutional structure that would create today's European Union, with the Maastricht Treaty of 1992 that followed the Cold War and German reunification. Those who have historically espoused European federalist ideals were always motivated by one or all of three concepts: first, idealism and reactive security tendencies (i.e., the need to prevent future internal wars); second, the perceived need to unite against external security threats; and third, business and logistical goals, such as the desire to strengthen economic cooperation, regulate economic processes in the name of fairness and efficiency, and generally broaden the reach of financial markets.

The movement toward these goals has therefore always been championed most by conservative and left-wing ideologues, defense planners, and captains of industry and their bankers. At different points, the federalist goal has been given further impetus by conflict or economic dislocation. Although not an armed conflict, the 2015 migrant crisis—with its perceived territorial, security, and economic aspects—is just the latest in a long line of conflict events that have driven public discourse and private plans for greater centralization of power on the Continent.

Less than 30 years after the American Revolution, which led to the equally dramatic French Revolution, Napoleon Bonaparte mused that a "United States of Europe" would minimize the chances of internal conflict.[3] Napoleon also envisioned a Continent customs union—one which was, however, meant to be more of an embargo on the British Empire in French interests than a cooperative venture (it is interesting to note that, 200 years later, British opposition to aspects of the European Union's Common Market and perceived French protectionism had become two key points of tension). By 1814, and the Congress of Vienna, some French supporters of a socialist Utopia were already calling for a parliamentary European federation. The congress had been called to restore order following the Napoleonic Wars, according to the dispute resolution process of the time: namely, territorial reallocations between rival Great Powers, which was meant to achieve political balance across the Continent.

One result of the Congress of Vienna was the 1815 German Confederation (*Deutscher Bund*) of 38 sovereign German states—an early and more informal stab at Continental union. The various conceptions of a European federation were historically always augmented by practical goals: movement toward a common trade area—what the European Union today calls the "Single Market"—as was the case with the Deutscher Bund and its 1834 customs union (the *Zollverein*). The concept of a borderless Europe as an international organization under international law was invoked by Polish scientist Wojciech Jastrzębowski in 1831 as a hypothetical guarantor of world peace. Then, in 1843, Italian writer and politician Giuseppe Mazzini called for European republics to unite in a political federation. Four years later, Mazzini organized an International Peace Congress in Paris, where the famed French author Victor Hugo called for a United States of Europe. Mazzini also created the "Giovine Europa" (Young Europe) movement, according to which the future of Europe could only be a confederation of sovereign states created once every European "nation" would be free from foreign rule.

Although his ideas were considered absurd at the time, Hugo's call for a "supreme, sovereign senate" would eventually manifest in today's European Parliament and European Commission. Such peace conferences were held annually between 1843 and 1853, and were organized by international pacifistic Christian groups like the London Peace Society, active from 1816 to 1930. The organization worked with similar groups internationally, such as the Quakers, who supported similar causes, like the abolition of slavery in the United States. A similarly revolutionary (if less pacifistic) character was Italian philosopher Carlo Cattaneo, who participated in an 1848 uprising against the Austrians and was an avowed believer in federalism. Approaching the issue from a rather different orientation, Mikhail Bakunin, the forefather of anarchism and rival of Karl Marx, also favored forms of federalism as opposed to existing state and economic structures. Bakunin spoke at the 1867 Geneva congress of the League of Peace and Freedom, a leading left-wing event at the time that was also attended by novelist Hugo and the influential British philosopher John Stuart Mill. Four years later, France's National Assembly symbolically called for a United States of Europe.

At the same time that left-wing ideologues were promoting the idea of national or Continental federalism as a preventive measure against future armed conflict, the more tangible benefits of closer cooperation were being attempted, such as the German Confederation's 1834 customs union. Later, a somewhat successful system of common financial standards—the precursor to today's euro currency—was established in an 1865 treaty between France, Belgium, Italy, and Switzerland—founding members of the Latin Monetary Union (LMU). It would survive in various forms until 1927. Under the treaty, each state was obliged to mint gold and silver coins according to common specifications (based on the French franc). Containing fixed proportions of gold or silver, such national coinages would be freely exchangeable and thus promote more stable and predictable trade across the Continent.

Although the monetary union only had members from a handful of countries (and their overseas colonies), it did increase the trend toward monetary treaties. One example was the treaty struck bilaterally (as that between the Austro-Hungarian Empire and France in 1867). Although a clever idea in theory, the LMU in practice was sensitive to constant fluctuations in gold and particularly silver prices, which would lead by 1873 to a flood of cheap silver minted advantageously against the fixed gold value, meaning that silver coinage was "essentially upon the same footing as bank notes," according to one historian.[4] Worse, some LMU members would be suspected of debasing their metals to make a profit (which caused the Papal States to be expelled from the LMU in 1870).[5] Similar destabilization occurred when members would issue paper money based on their unreliable national currencies.[6] Despite the LMU's practical shortcomings, some theorists assumed—as they still do today—that the currency problem could be solved through other approaches. In 1888, Polish economist (and abolitionist) Theodore de Korwin Szymanowski laid out a comprehensive plan for a Europe united by a customs union, a central statistical office, a central bank, and a single currency.[7]

In general, the 19th-century movements toward a more centralized Europe were motivated primarily by pacifistic idealism and economic expansionism. Federalist ambitions in the 20th century would become more complex, and more pragmatic, with the rise of Communism as a new competitor for influence against the traditional, Christian-Europe view of Continental unity. Both movements sought, in the carnage and devastation of World War I, to find justification for federalism. Thus in 1923, Austrian count Richard Coudenhove-Kalergi founded the Pan-Europa movement (a Christian conservative project) whereas Leon Trotsky called for a "Soviet United States of Europe."

Coudenhove-Kalergi (1894–1972) is perhaps the most important of modern European history's forgotten figures. Over a long lifetime of advocacy, he would continually agitate for a European constitution, common currency, and full federation. Founder (and president until his death) of the Pan-European Union (today's "Pan-europa"), Coudenhove-Kalergi also decided the future European Union's official anthem, Beethoven's *Ode to Joy*, and "national day" of May 9. Today, the European Society Coudenhove-Kalergi awards a biennial prize to a European leader who has made "exceptional contributions to the European unification process." In accepting the prize for 2010, Angela Merkel averred that the euro currency had created better conditions for "greater European integration." The German chancellor also pledged her support for "social cohesion and a clear foundation of shared values."[8]

Richard Coudenhove-Kalergi's first manifesto for the federalist cause, *Paneuropa*, was published in 1923, coinciding with the creation of his so-called Pan-European Union. The financial support of banker Max Warburg, who the count would later credit in his memoirs, helped the movement develop and gain visibility in high circles in Europe and the United States. By 1926, Coudenhove-Kalergi had organized the First Pan-European Congress in Vienna, attracting great interest among leading European thinkers and politicians. Indeed, Otto Von Habsburg (1912–2011), the son of Austria's last emperor became involved in the movement in the 1930s and served as the European Society's president after its founder's death in 1972. Today, the European Society remains active and continues to push for a federalist agenda based on common Christian values. Otto Von Habsburg's own work in the Pan-Europa movement has been continued by his daughter, Walburga Habsburg Douglas, who married Swedish count Archibald and was elected to the Swedish parliament in 2006 and 2010 with the Moderate Party. Through the federalist cause, there is thus a direct and unbroken line between the old European aristocracy and Europe's modern influencers.[9]

The Pan-Europa movement in the 1980s would support figures fighting Communism like Pope John Paul II, and organized the so-called Pan-European Picnic of August 19, 1989. A form of peaceful protest designed to pressure Hungarian authorities into opening the border to Eastern Germans wishing to travel to West Germany, it was a key event leading up to the fall of the Berlin Wall and end of the Cold War. The 20th anniversary of the picnic was commemorated by a special event at which both Angela Merkel and then Swedish foreign minister Carl Bildt spoke. In comments that directly prefigured the EU policy to the 2015 migration crisis, the latter stated that "we must remain an open Europe of open societies and open minds, open to others beyond our present boundaries."[10]

The influence of Richard Coudenhove-Kalergi extended to French statesman Aristide Briand (1862–1932), a socialist who had led France during and after World War I. The leading roles of these two men in the Pan-European Union would be specifically praised two decades later by Winston Churchill.[11] In 1926, Briand won the Nobel Peace Prize (together with German counterpart Gustav Stresemann) for achieving the Locarno Treaties that normalized relations between the Western allied powers, Germany, and the Central and Eastern European states. Briand's 1927 proposal (with U.S. secretary of state Frank B. Kellogg) for a universal pact outlawing war was followed two years later by his call, before the ill-fated League of Nations, for a European federation based on economic cooperation.

As with many similar past invocations, the federal plan was partly a by-product of idealism (i.e., a countermeasure against potential future wars), but also was motivated by a more pragmatic desire to achieve French security. The proposed economic cooperation concerned heavy industry— Germany's rapid revival of an industry that could sustain a war effort alarmed many—and a political component that would provide safeguards for the Eastern European countries from the new Soviet Union. The plan is laid out in Briand's 1930 *Memorandum on the Organization of a System of European Federal Union*.[12] The idea was also promoted by contemporaneous allies in a book, *The United States of Europe*, written by French politician Édouard Herriot in 1930.[13]

Another work of the same name appeared three years later, by British civil servant Arthur Salter. As an internationalist with broad experience in shipping, transport, and economics, Baron Salter is of particular interest. He participated in both League of Nations and later UN projects, and was also praised by Churchill for his economic acumen. In 1917–1918, Salter had worked with future EU founding father Jean Monnet in the Chartering Committee of the Allied Maritime Transport Council, created to coordinate shipping between the Allied powers during World War I.

This almost entirely forgotten entity can be considered an early exemplification of later EU federalist impulses, in that it was designed to eliminate economic and logistic competition between Allied states, managing prices, allocating tonnage, and coordinating Allied logistics. This shipping council—essentially, a cartel between states—thus prefigured the kind of supranational coordination that would come to define the bureaucratic organizing principles of the nascent European Union.[14]

The European federalist dream was not only shared by aristocrats, politicians, and bureaucrats in the run-up to World War II. On the other side of the spectrum, the pure idealism of poor Communists would have a dramatic effect on the future development of the European Union. The gestation period for this movement similarly occurred during World War I and its aftermath and was based on 19th-century thought. The major contributor to federalist ideology from the Communist camp was Italian activist, and later politician, Altiero Spinelli (1907–1986). Spinelli's lifetime of work for the EU project and total federalism is still celebrated in Brussels. A special European Parliament group exists to further his ideals, while a European Parliament building is named after him. However, average Europeans (and the media) hardly mention Altiero Spinelli; he is, like Richard Coudenhove-Kalergi, Aristide Briand, and Arthur Salter, a forgotten figure from a bygone era.

Spinelli was a protégé of the Sardinian neo-Marxist founder of the Italian Communist party, Antonio Gramsci (1891–1937). Both men were imprisoned by Italy's Fascist dictator, Benito Mussolini in the 1920s. Although not published properly until the 1950s, nor translated into English until the 1970s, Gramsci's collected works (the *Prison Notebooks*) had a huge underground influence among Communists and anarchists. There is a direct line between Gramsci, the European Union, and today's "social justice warriors" of the left, in both ideology and tactics; given the heavy influence of such movements on today's EU approach to migration, it is thus worth understanding his basic ideas.[15]

In his philosophy, Gramsci tried to explain why the worldwide socialist revolution predicted in conventional Marxism had not naturally replaced capitalism by the early 20th century. To do so, he argued that capitalist states did not exert power only through political, military, and economic force, but also through the ideological means of "cultural hegemony"— the concept that the working classes identified their own good with that of the bourgeoisie through unwitting, consensual social processes. For Gramsci, this both explained why the proletariat had not revolted and gave a justification for Communists to achieve revolution through achieving their own rival cultural hegemony. This was to be achieved laterally, through broadening the base of people in society (such as public intellectuals) whose views would align with those of the workers and help create new cultural norms that would eventually triumph over those inherent to the capitalist system. Interpreting all ideologies according to a historicist methodology, Gramsci was thus a cultural relativist. He both denied the universal truths of Christianity (and the Platonic idealism upon which that religion ultimately rests) yet admired the Church's practical system of cultural influence. Thus, Gramsci conveyed a vision by which traditional Marxist praxis could be used to change social and cultural values laterally and from within. Ironically, this process is now used by both leftist, pro-immigration "civil society" activists and right-wing Identitarians opposed to immigration in Europe.

What Antonio Gramsci needed in order to achieve his dream was someone who shared his ideology and was capable of employing his methodology in the real world. That person would be fellow traveler Altiero Spinelli, another political prisoner of Mussolini's. Indeed, Spinelli's personal experience of captivity and World War II fueled his hatred of Fascism and fed his federalist dream, forging a supranationalist, antinationalist worldview that remains prevalent among EU leaders today. While confined to the Ventotene prison, Spinelli and his Communist coprisoners read the works of theorists like Gramsci and others in the Communist milieu. Inspired by their thoughts and by his own perception of the Italian government and the war, Spinelli had completed (with coprisoner and economist Ernesto Rossi) the Ventotene Manifesto by 1941; the work, which was secretly spirited out of the prison and circulated widely among fellow leftists across Europe, calls for a fully federalized Europe.

Officially entitled "Towards a Free and United Europe," the manifesto argued that nationalism was the root cause of conflict in Europe, and that the traditional European system of sovereign nation-states would have to be replaced by a supranational European federation, that would be so tightly integrated that war would become impossible.[16] Thus Spinelli's federalist impulses represented the continuation of similar proposals based on pacifistic ideals, but one also heavily influenced by Communism. In 1943, after being freed, Spinelli created the Movimento Federalista Europeo (MFE; Federalist Movement of Europe). Aware that this idea would be met by widespread popular resistance, Spinelli and his fellow anti-Fascists realized that the MFE could not become a political party. Instead, as with Richard Coudenhove-Kalergi's Pan-European Union, it sought to create influence laterally, working from the periphery of politics, business, and society in order to influence politicians and eventually achieve its goal. Following his mentor Gramsci's vision, Spinelli embarked on a consistent path of challenging the "cultural hegemony" of nationalist, capitalist Europe through the means of lateral social influence and stealth.

Spinelli's creative ability to work laterally to create new consensus with broader parties is indicated by his first target of influence: Alcide De Gasperi, Italian prime minister and foreign minister between 1945 and 1953.

Except for both having been arrested by Mussolini, the two men could not have been more different. Whereas Spinelli was a devout Communist, De Gasperi was a Vatican insider and the founder of Italy's Christian Democrat Party. Further, he owed his government's early budget partly to a propitious U.S. bank loan (along with covert funding from American intelligence) made in order to keep Italy from going Communist. In fact, De Gasperi excluded the Communist Party from his fourth cabinet in 1947, when Italy was still led by the Constituent Assembly and when cooperation among the biggest forces in parliament was needed. He did so to maintain good relations with Truman and the United States—which were about to inaugurate the new Marshall Plan—while Socialists and Communists were alternatively pushing for an equidistant positioning between the Soviets and Americans.

The historical record of U.S. involvement in the whole EU project received new attention during the migration crisis and, particularly, around the Brexit vote of June 2016. Aside from the well-known Marshall Plan for reviving Europe after World War II, a deep political and intelligence effort was made in order to stave off the purported Soviet threat. "US intelligence funded the European movement secretly for decades, and worked aggressively behind the scenes to push Britain into the project," reported *The Telegraph* in April 2016. Citing declassified U.S. government documents, the newspaper concluded that leaders of the "key CIA front" organization, the American Committee for a United Europe (ACUE), "treated some of the EU's 'founding fathers' as hired hands, and actively prevented them finding alternative funding that would have broken reliance on Washington."[17]

Among the important American officials involved in initially pushing the European project were "Wild Bill" Donovan, director of the wartime Office of Strategic Services (OSS), and Allen Dulles, chief of the Central Intelligence Agency (CIA), which followed and replaced the OSS. In fact, the ACUE had sprung into action in 1948 following a funding request from both Churchill and Count Richard Coudenhove-Kalergi, who had used his aristocratic and financial alliances on both sides of the Atlantic to gain influence for his federalist dream.[18] The ACUE funded groups like the European Movement, established in 1948 to support all European integration means and create and work with student groups and like-minded institutes. (Now known as the European Movement International, the group continues its activities as a lobby group in Brussels).[19] It was the final outcome of a 1947 Paris meeting of the so-called Liaison Committee of the Movements for European Unity, set up "to organise and promote a publicity campaign in support of European unity." This meeting led, in November 1947, to the creation of the grandly named International Committee of the Movements for European Unity (ICMEU), which brought together federalist groups from around Europe, including Churchill's

United Europe Movement, the French Council for a United Europe, led by Raoul Dautry, administrator-general of the French Atomic Energy Commission (CEA), Count Coudenhove-Kalergi's European Parliamentary Union, and several others. The ICMEU was chaired by Churchill's son-in-law, Conservative MP Duncan Sandys, and headed by its secretary-general, Joseph Retinger. Georges Rebattet oversaw its Paris operations.[20]

The ICMEU then convened, between May 7–11, 1948, the Congress of Europe in The Hague, a seminal event attended by 800 high-profile participants. Among its goals was "to demonstrate the existence, in all free countries of Europe, of a body of public opinion in support of European unity, to discuss the challenges posed by European unity and propose practical solutions to governments and to give new impetus to the international publicity campaign."[21] On October 25, 1948, the ICMEU changed its name to the European Movement. Its early leaders were all federalists of a sort, and most are considered EU founding fathers. They included Count Richard Coudenhove-Kalergi, Winston Churchill, former French prime minister Léon Blum, Italian prime minister Alcide De Gasperi, Belgian prime minister and foreign minister Paul-Henri Spaak, French foreign minister Robert Schuman, and German chancellor Konrad Adenauer.

The last two leaders (along with Frenchman Jean Monnet) are considered particularly prominent in the conventional understanding of the European Union's founding process. But the official Brussels hagiography of its 11 leading men, detailed on the European Commission's website, is in part mythology, omitting as it does the fundamental organizing and funding role of the U.S. government and others.[22] The fact remains that the European Union's distinguished (and often, divided) founders had been herded under the American umbrella. That the European Movement rapidly metastasized, creating innumerable related nation-level NGOs, institutes, and other supportive groups created the conditions for Gramsci's "cultural hegemony"—though hardly in the grassroots way that the Marxist theorist had anticipated.

This shadow network included innumerable groups, such as Rome's Institute for International Affairs (in Italian, Istituto Affari Internazionali, or IAI). It was founded by Altiero Spinelli in 1965, partly with funding from the Ford Foundation, when U.S. Cold War policy was still heavily invested in supporting profederalist think tanks. The IAI is still active and very influential in Italy today, working with a variety of international partners favoring supranational and federalist agendas. One prominent member is the European Union's Commissioner for External Affairs since 2014, Federica Mogherini, who also served in the CONSIUSA (Council for the United States and Italy, founded in 1983 by the late industrialist tycoon Gianni Agnelli and David Rockefeller).

Of most significance for the long term was that the "new" Europe's "chosen leaders" would manage to overcome constant personal and national differences to forge new common institutions where none had existed and to educate (through CIA-funded youth NGOs under the European Movement's influence) several generations of young Europeans throughout the 1960s and 1970s. This remains significant, since the leaders who were educated in that period are largely the ones who have created or executed the policies leading up to and including the 2015 migration crisis.

Indeed, the ACUE used its money and influence judiciously in the 1950s and 1960s to support European politicians who backed successive agreements leading toward the "ever closer union" that would be affirmed in the 1983 Stuttgart Declaration on European union.[23] Among these selected initiatives were organizations like the Council of Europe, the European Coal and Steel Community (ECSC), and the proposed European Defence Community. By 1951, the ACUE budget was $1 million per year, making it "one of the most expensive covert operations of the early Cold War period."[24]

However, despite concerted early influence and American pressure on various leaders, plans for a full political and military union had collapsed in 1954, as individual states (especially France under Charles de Gaulle, until 1969) objected to various proposals, defending state sovereignty. In the absence of federal union, other founding fathers had realized that economic union could pave the way for an eventual second go at a federalist political project. The most important among them was Dutch banker and politician Johan Willem (Wim) Beyen (1897–1976), who created a plan for a European common market marked by horizontal integration, rather than the important but sector-based earlier example of the ECSC. In April 1955, Beyen proposed his idea of a common customs union—a goal that had proven so elusive since the 19th century *Deutscher Bund* and Latin Monetary Union—to his Benelux colleagues Paul-Henri Spaak (Belgium) and Joseph Bech (Luxembourg). Later that year, a joint memorandum (known as the Benelux memorandum) was sent to CSCE colleagues from France, Germany, and Italy. In the ensuing Messina Conference of June 1955, Beyen's argument prevailed, formed the basis for the 1957 Treaties of Rome and the creation of the European Economic Community and Euratom the following year.

The key role of Wim Beyen revealed another dimension of the nascent EU project: the growing participation of globalist finance. Just as the American Committee for a United Europe had been funded by the CIA, Rockefeller, and Ford Foundations, the Dutch banker was intimately involved with the postwar international financial system change. In 1944, Beyen had been a key player at the Bretton Woods conference that laid the foundations for both the IMF and World Bank, later serving on the boards of both. Even in the 1920s, Beyen had served as secretary of the board of Philips, and led the Dutch East Indies' central bank in its Holland office. He had also run a predecessor of AMRO Bank, and in the late-1930s had a high position in the Bank for International Settlements. He was even director of Unilever.

By 1983, and the Stuttgart Declaration, events had overtaken the European project, in terms of American support for full federalization. That dream had, however, been kept alive by the ideologues, chief among them Spinelli. Disappointed by the slow progress of a full political union, he had realized (like Wim Beyen and others) that economic cooperation through the existing European Economic Community (EEC) treaty of 1958 was the best way to advance his goals. Thus, he served on the European Commission (from 1970 to 1976), in the area of developing a common industrial policy. It was just the kind of trademark EU activity that had been exactly prefigured by the European coal and steel negotiations of the early 1950s, and indeed by the shipping cartel in which bureaucrats like Arthur Salter and Jean Monnet had organized common Allied operations during World War I.

In the European Parliament's first direct elections of 1979, Spinelli ran as an independent candidate, under an Italian Communist Party (PCI) that had become much watered-down since Antonio Gramsci had cofounded it in 1921. True to his beliefs, the newly elected Spinelli immediately proposed a reform that would transform the EEC into a federative European state. To fulfill this mission, Spinelli would use the classic Gramscian tactic of consensus-building laterally. The only difference was that he was not trying to foment a Communist revolution (that would be impossible) but simply a superstate based on the ideological and economic ideals of the founding fathers. Although this goal was unrealistic, owing to internal rivalries and the concerns of many European leaders for retaining their nations' political, diplomatic, and monetary sovereignty, Spinelli saw the implementation of any step that led in the "right direction" as a plus. His method and thinking were precisely those of modern-day Eurocrats like Jean-Claude Juncker.

One battle tactic of Spinelli's was to bring together MEPs (members of the European Parliament) from different political blocs for informal discussions aimed to build consensus and support for profederalist legislation. This was hardly impossible considering that (as has been abundantly demonstrated) the federalist goal had always had adherents from ideological conservatives, technocrats, and globalists—hardly only from the left. Altiero Spinelli's grand plan for building the cultural hegemony of federalism was inaugurated by himself and eight other MEPs on July 9, 1980, at The Crocodile restaurant (located at 10 rue de l'Outre, in the French city of Strasbourg). Spinelli's band of federalists thus became known as the "Crocodile Club." From the beginning, Spinelli made it clear that the group would not produce polemics or actively oppose MEPs on the opposite side, but seek to slowly and methodically create consensus by drawing them into its general ranks—again living out the praxis aspect of Gramsci's neo-Marxism.

The cross-party Crocodile Club soon grew to the point that they could successfully table legislation. The European Parliament quickly approved the bloc's motion to establish a special committee; it would be formalized in January 1982 as the Committee on Institutional Affairs, with Spinelli in charge. The committee's purpose was to draft a proposal for a new treaty—not simply an amendment to the Treaty of Rome—and one that would officially establish a full European Union. After some negotiation and compromise, the European Parliament approved the Draft Treaty Establishing the European Union, on February 14, 1984. Indicating the power federalists had achieved, the bill was passed with 237 votes in favor and 31 against (as well as 43 abstentions).[25]

Spinelli also proposed an increase in European competencies like that of the internal market and coordination in foreign policy, leading to a full "European Union"; these were among other key measures included in the Single European Act of 1986. The constant lobbying of Spinelli (who personally influenced French president François Mitterrand to reverse decades of French prosovereignty policy) created the conditions for the 1992 Maastricht Treaty, by which the European Union was officially established. Following the death of Altiero Spinelli in 1986, his allied MEPs established the "Altiero Spinelli Action Committee for European Union," an interparty group of federalists who backed propositions like a European Constitution and single currency.

These goals received a dramatic push due to Europe's first phase change since the end of World War II: the fall of the Berlin Wall on November 9, 1989, and the ensuing reunification of Germany; it should be remembered that these events were partly influenced by Coudenhove-Kalergi's Pan-European Movement and their "Pan-European Picnic" held on the Austrian–Hungarian border on August 19, 1989. For European states, the Cold War had been a bloodless conflict. This experience of almost a half-century of peace, conditioned by decades of pro-federalist education and propaganda (originally sponsored by the United States) had created several generations of leaders having a unique worldview: they saw (and still see) supranationalism as benevolent and natural, and recognize World War II as the beginning of history. This is the fundamentally flawed contextualization in which EU reactions to today's migration crisis must be understood.

By 1992 and the Treaty on European Union (Maastricht Treaty) policies and opinions regarding migration, and global security, were much different than they are today. The treaty had created a common European security and foreign policy, while creating conditions for the common currency (the euro) that would arrive 10 years later. It was followed by the wider implementation of 1985's Schengen Agreement, which eliminated borders

between many EU member states in the interest of facilitating trade efficiency and freedom of movement. Thus, less than a decade after Spinelli's
death, the federalists had achieved everything they wanted, save for political union and a European constitution. It was a stunning achievement that
had been reached through many years of stealth diplomacy and shadow
networks that ultimately rested on a hard core of left- and right-wing
federalism, funded by a the old European aristocracy, globalist financial
interests, and (for many years) the American intelligence apparatus. That
today's EU officials are generally unwilling to admit this reality, instead
preferring to regurgitate empty platitudes about "common values," goes a
long way toward understanding why the European Union has become so
internally confused, and so intensely resented, by many Europeans who
feel it is out of touch with daily realities.

The Schengen Agreement exemplifies the historic tendency of EU legislation to move, slowly and incrementally at first, readjust to opposition,
and reemerge until (in Juncker's celebrated words) "there is no turning
back." The agreement was first reached on a riverboat near the town of
Schengen in Luxembourg, on June 14, 1985. Signed by only half the members of the then EEC (France, Belgium, Luxembourg, Holland, and West
Germany) it created Europe's Schengen Area. Supporters referenced the
Treaty of Rome's section on freedom of movement to justify the agreement for a borderless Europe. The initial Schengen Agreement was meant
to gradually abolish border checks (and even traffic stops for residents of
border areas) within the five signatory states. It was also meant to harmo-
nize visa policies, but in both cases was signed outside of the larger EEC
institutions, because of strong disagreements with other members such
as Britain and Ireland, nations that in fact would never join the scheme.[26]

In keeping with the European Union's long-attested tendency toward
centralization of power in stages, the Schengen Agreement was read-
dressed in 1990, after the fall of the Berlin Wall. A new Schengen Conven-
tion proposed total abolition of internal border controls, while calling for
a common European visa policy. Brussels's centralization of power continued with the 1999 Amsterdam Treaty, which made the previous extra-
EEC agreement a core part of EU law, with opt-out clauses only existing
for Ireland and the United Kingdom. However, certain non-EU countries
adopted much of the Schengen Zone conditions, such as Norway, Liech-
tenstein, and Iceland (under the European Economic Area) and Switzerland (under the Agreement on the Free Movement of Persons (AFMP),
achieved in 2007 after a public referendum two years earlier).[27]

The Amsterdam Treaty also incorporated the *Schengen acquis*, a set of
criteria that new EU members would need to fulfill before joining. As of
2016, EU members Bulgaria, Romania, Cyprus, Slovenia, and Croatia were
not yet Schengen Area members, though they are legally obliged to eventually join. This process has been slowed by factors including geopolitical

realities and perceived border-control insufficiencies, among others, and the prevailing Euroskepticism and strong reactions caused by the 2015 migration crisis that have put a new emphasis on the future viability—and even desirability—of the borderless travel area. The concept of borderless European travel is something rooted in an earlier and more peaceful time, before mass immigration and the evolution of an ever-increasing terrorist threat. This is also why the very concept of a Schengen Area became so controversial, before and during the migration crisis. The entry of Eastern European countries into the European bloc, and their resulting ability to travel and work freely across the European Union, fostered years of disgruntlement in some countries, effectively lending impetus to the successful Brexit vote in 2016. This added a key aspect of economic competitiveness (i.e., the perceived displacement of local labor forces by foreign workers willing to work for less) that has only been amplified by the arrival of over one million migrants from impoverished countries since 2015.

Arguments over the Schengen Zone have of course gone hand in hand with disagreements over asylum and migration policy since even before the 2015 migration crisis. As will be seen in the following chapters, this argument includes (but is certainly not limited to) the diverging political and ideological blocs in Europe today. The European Union's fundamental asylum policy, the Dublin Agreements, has become a lightning rod for criticism, with numerous calls in recent years for its abolition or amendment. Since the initial Dublin Agreement in 1990 (and initial implementation in 1997), the legislation has gone through three revisions, the most recent having been that of July 19, 2013. However, despite various amendments and clarifications, this "Dublin III" agreement reaffirms the most contentious aspect of the whole system: that the first EU member state to take an asylum seeker's fingerprints and asylum claim is responsible for that individual's asylum claim. This stipulation has of course been heavily criticized by "front-line" countries like Greece and Italy, which have always borne the brunt of migrant waves.

The Dublin Regulations were originally intended to stop a phenomenon known as "asylum shopping," by which refugees try to choose their EU country of preference. This practice has historically occurred due to the individual's perception of economic and social benefits in the host country, making Britain, the Netherlands, Sweden, and Germany among favored destinations. However, Angela Merkel's extraordinary invocation of the Dublin "sovereignty clause" allowed her to specifically invite refugees to Germany—despite the many European borders they would pass along the way, in violation of the established agreement.[28]

The demand of Merkel and EU allies such as Jean-Claude Juncker and Dimitris Avramopoulos for mandatory migrant resettlement quotas was another "innovation" to existing legislation that infuriated many

Europeans, and was particularly opposed by the strong Visegrad Group (V4) of Hungary, Poland, Slovakia, and the Czech Republic. Merkel's policy proposal has been criticized not only for the perceived security and integration risk factor, but also, fundamentally, because it is impractical: in a borderless Schengen Zone, there is simply no way to force asylum seekers or migrants to stay where they are told. EU asylum policy has never been geared up to the challenges of economic migration disguised asylum seeking. The "free movement of people" from one EU country to another was controversial to some, but sustainable, whereas mass migration from non-EU countries is impossible to manage, both legally and practically. What is under scrutiny now is what the enshrined value of "freedom of movement" actually means, and under what conditions it should apply.

To understand this issue, it is necessary to go back to the origins of the concept. The Dublin Accords and EU migration policy in general are rooted in supranationalist projects, like the UN and European Movement, that were implemented after World War II but that drew from the decades of idealism that had preceded it. The United Nations' Universal Declaration of Human Rights (1948), often taken to be the basis of EU law, states that "everyone has the right to freedom of movement and residence within the borders of each State. Everyone has the right to leave any country, including his own, and to return to his country."[29] The UN's 1966 International Covenant on Civil and Political Rights (ICCPR) further adds that "everyone lawfully within the territory of a State shall, within that territory, have the right to liberty of movement and freedom to choose his residence."[30] As for today's European Union, according to the European Parliament, "freedom of movement and residence for persons in the EU is the cornerstone of Union citizenship."[31]

Indeed, both the 1951 Treaty of Paris, which established the European Coal and Steel Community, and the 1957 Treaty of Rome granted rights for the free movement of workers. However, over time there has been an unhelpful conflation of the abstract and idealistic principles of the UN with those of negotiated, internal agreements (such as the Treaties of Paris and Rome) that granted limited rights of movement to workers within certain industries and under certain conditions. However, by 2015 and the European migration crisis, these distinctions had become inseparable, so that it sufficed for EU officials to merely invoke the names of decades-old treaties as sacrosanct, without exploring what they had actually stated. And, as with European leaders' August 2016 trip to Ventotene to lay flowers on the grave of Altiero Spinelli, a certain pious mythology, one top-heavy on symbolism, had become the fundamental aspect of EU public discourse. When asked whether the worst result of possibly ending the Schengen Zone would be economic costs, or merely traveler inconvenience, a German parliamentarian replied (in all seriousness) that the "symbolic value" of the Schengen Zone was its most important role.[32]

In Brussels today, federalists and ideologues remain—as has been the case for over a century—those most determined to expand the European project, continue centralization of power, and preserve the Schengen Zone. But this is for far more than "symbolic" reasons. Supranational organizations like the UN, European Union, and global financial, technology, and health care interests have an intertwined role in an increasingly globalized economy. At the same time, legislation is increasingly being influenced by the involvement of "civil society" organizations; not incidentally, the most prominent such groups frequently partner with the private sector. There are also huge amounts of money to be circulated through the EU bureaucracy for initiatives of import, with the migration crisis becoming the one of greatest importance for the medium to long term.

Considering the apparent sound and fury of political infighting surrounding the 2015 migration crisis, appreciating the history of European federalism that sustained and created the European Union is helpful. As was the case almost a century ago, federalists have hailed from the old European aristocratic right, from the socialist left, from the captains of industry and finance, and from a hard bureaucratic core that has constantly sought to "rationalize" processes and as such create ever-tighter cooperation between states, under centralized technocratic control. In the summer and fall of 2016, in the aftermath of Brexit and with the migrant crisis still rumbling on, many pundits speculated that the European project was in peril. It was true that Merkel, Juncker, and the rest of the core EU inner circle were on the defensive; but with only six months to plot until the 60th anniversary of the Rome Treaty in March, they had to reassess not only EU policy, but what made it appealing to the residents of Europe in the first place. Clearly, there was a public crisis of confidence in the European Union, but this was also part of a wider European identity and values crisis.

Although the 2015 migration crisis sparked sharp opposition from anti-federalist forces in Central and Eastern Europe, Britain, and elsewhere, it would be naive to think that the movement that has essentially run the EU project since the beginning will just admit defeat. Indeed, it is most likely that the migration crisis will continue to be manipulated for ideological, political, and economic gain—and not only from the right- and left-wing parties, but especially from the federalist elite that has always guided the European Union project from its earliest iterations. Philosophically, the union's roots in 19th-century German idealism and the Marxist historicist approach to events has led the European Union to consider itself an inevitable outcome of historical progress; in reality, the political union of today exists not out of some abstract necessity, but because the prevailing conditions during its formation were favorable for its specific development.

Thus, if historical patterns—rather than historical preferences—are anything to go by, we will see in coming years more determined efforts by federalists representing traditionally mixed, but overwhelmingly elitist interests to use all global trends toward centralization of European power within the Brussels bloc. This involves harmonizing agendas with major international organizations (like the UN, World Bank, and IMF) and with major global corporations. The migration issue is going to be the one where achieving this harmonic convergence will prove most fruitful, even if it ultimately means that a smaller and more centralized core of EU political forces participates. An early confirmation that federalists were mounting a new offensive in Brussels came when the European Parliament on September 9, 2016, announced its "representative" for the Brexit negotiations: the former Belgian prime minister and MEP, Guy Verhofstadt. The appointment of this "arch-federalist" from the left-wing parliamentary bloc Alliance of Liberals and Democrats for Europe (ALDE) was announced by the parliament's leftist president, Martin Schulz, immediately causing a "furious row" between rival political blocs. It was another indication that the profederalist center of power in Brussels was looking to maximize the results of negotiations with Britain.[33]

Not incidentally, Verhofstadt (a leading figure in the Union of European Federalists that Altiero Spinelli had founded) had already created, in September 2010, the European Parliament's "Spinelli Group." Meant to promote federalization and continue the work of the Crocodile Club of the early 1980s, the group sought to utilize Spinelli's method of achieving a broad, cross-party consensus through activities led by a steering committee and a parliamentary group of over 100 MEPs. It similarly stresses the input of NGOs, academics, and think tanks supporting the federalist cause.[34] Other prominent members of the Spinelli Group include the cochair of the Green Party–European Free Alliance parliamentary group, Daniel Cohn-Bendit, a German-French politician and radical anarchist during the 1960s and 1970s. In addition to strong profederalist views, Cohn-Bendit showed himself to be very sympathetic to the migrant cause. His close friend, former German foreign minister Joschka Fischer (similarly an anarchist activist in the 1970s long converted to mainstream politics), is a Spinelli Group supporter, as is Jacques Delors, the legendary three-time European commissioner who presided over developments like the single market negotiations in the 1980s.

In the aftermath of Brexit, the migrant crisis, and lingering unrest over austerity measures meant to save the euro in Greece and other countries, Europe's leaders have sought new ways to revive the "European dream." But, as history reveals, it was always just a dream: the trajectory of every process in the European project after World War II was driven by a narrow (but powerful) series of groups with overlapping interests—the old-Europe aristocracy and right, the ideologists from the left, the American political and intelligence establishment, and international banks and corporations.

What is most likely to occur, as the aftershocks of the 2015 migrant crisis rumble on, is a slow but steady retrenchment of influence at the hard bureaucratic core of European federalism, occupying a centrist position as the various right- and left-wing parties and factions across Europe vie for power and attack one another. In this scenario, the European Union—which will almost certainly defer its full Balkan enlargement plans further—will simply have to be less incompetent than national-level forces. With its existential capacity for survival never having truly been tested, the European bloc will draw on its most dependable, most established, entrenched interests—which are inevitably in some form or another, federalist—to weather the storm. This time around, the operative conditions in which Europe finds itself are different than in previous phase changes, such as World War I, World War II, and German reunification. The migration crisis is modern Europe's next moment of change, and a whole new range of influencers—from global think tanks and NGOs to corporations, states, and asymmetric threats—will have great influence in defining how the Continent's next phase will be.

Yet although the European Union appeared weak and confused in the aftermath of the crisis, it is wise to remember an old adage that may be applicable: "the house always wins." In short, an established order of concentrated wealth and power is not simply going to be overthrown because of the crisis. It will instead use that crisis to its own advantage. Whether this will translate into increased power for the European Union, itself supported by so much of these interests, remains to be seen.

CHAPTER 3

Media Coverage and the European Migration Crisis

Even before the 2015 migration crisis exploded, the media had been the central point of convergence for all interests and activities related to this crisis. Everything—ideological and political perspectives, activism, ground activity, policy formation, and financial accumulation—has been both recorded for posterity and amplified to advance specific goals through different forms of media.

It would therefore be insufficient to judge the media in the context of the migration crisis simply through a traditional lens of relative qualitative coverage analysis. Rather, it must be acknowledged that media (and general communications) has become an all-pervasive and intrinsic element of the crisis and its perpetuation, and will remain the key factor in all of the developments and outcomes affecting the course of events, for all of the above-mentioned interests.

For many people, the defining image of the 2015 migration crisis was that of Alan Kurdi, a three-year-old Syrian refugee who drowned when the boat he was on capsized, off the Turkish coast. The boy was photographed after having washed ashore on September 2, 2015, his body resting dead in the sand. The anonymity of this bleak photograph had an instant and global impact. The image elicited an overabundance of commentary, from the general public, newspaper columnists, and world leaders. The picture proved to be a trigger for (brief) mass public emotion on the Internet. For media pundits and advocacy groups, it provided a platform for (often self-righteous) condemnation of Europe's failure to act in the crisis. And for all the global humanitarian organizations and nongovernmental organizations (NGOs), the tragedy proved to be a windfall for fund-raising and rhetorical projection. In Britain alone, *The Guardian* reported that Kurdi's image brought a 70 percent donation increase within a day to global charity Save the Children, while in the same period another British charity, The Migrant Offshore Aid Station, took in over $200,000 from approximately 2,000 donors. "A day after shocking pictures were published of Alan Kurdi, the three-year-old Syrian boy whose lifeless body was washed up on a Turkish beach," the newspaper reported, "tens of thousands of people across the country were signing petitions, donating to NGOs, preparing to drive truckloads of supplies to Calais or volunteering to take asylum-seekers into their homes."[1]

Although this initial wave of public humanitarian enthusiasm soon subsided, as the crisis continued the tragic photo would become a key point of reference in the greater public dialogue. As such, it became internalized; a much-referenced driver of public opinion, and eventual shaper of policy. And it trickled all the way up to the speeches of world leaders, from the French president's initial call for global cooperation to the September 2016 UN Leader's Summit on refugees, where President Barack Obama himself referenced the picture in justifying his migration policy. Obama referenced tragic images of refugee victims, specifically that of "little Alan Kurdi from Syria, lifeless, face down on a Turkish beach, in his red shirt and blue pants." This rhetorical compounding of implied meanings was used to provide emotional weight to Obama's policy promises. "Starting next week," the president said, "the United States will welcome and resettle 110,000 refugees from around the world—which is a nearly 60 percent increase over 2015." According to Obama, the UN summit marked "the beginning of a new global movement where everybody does more."[2]

Photography is at once the most immediate and compelling form of media for creating tacit consensus. Since the development of modern media, almost every conflict or crisis situation has been characterized by such emotive images. How specific images become the most memorable and defining owes to a collective and often unconscious creation of consensus. The process that creates this consensus is defined by factors such as the degree to which the image is proliferated (a quantitative value), the written record that accompanies it (an interpretive one), the audience in which the image is circulated and, crucially, the specific persons and groups within the social or political hierarchy who endorse it (an identitive function). In the case of the ill-fated Alan Kurdi, his image was circulated globally, documented profusely, and personally endorsed by some of the most powerful leaders in the world. In short, it ticked all the boxes to be nominated as the migration crisis's defining image.

Although these three characteristics of public consensus creation have always prevailed, the great difference today is that the ever-increasing decentralization and the displacement of traditional media by "citizen journalists" and the general pace of technology have widened the number and quality of media creators. Many idealists had hoped that the Internet age would mark the end of the mainstream media's traditional "gatekeeper" function and the development of a more democratic and varied media landscape—though experience has not borne out this dream.

Indeed, while the Internet has created the conditions for a much more varied range of sources, and while whistle-blowers and independent media still do make an impact, the general tendency is and will be toward a total consolidation of media ownership and influence, one tightly integrated with corporate and governmental interests. And, with the rise of social media, the general public has become the driving force behind this process of consolidation. True, major corporations can and do simply purchase or invest in large media groups, but the fundamental shift toward social media reporting has increased the power of a select few tech corporations to the extent that they can shape—and calculate—public opinion in ways so subtle that they often cannot even be noticed. This factor too has characterized the migration crisis in Europe.

Another key aspect about the new and ever-expanding space of traditional and social media is that it favors trends toward what can only be described as total information warfare. As conventional conflicts diminish, particularly in the developed world, cyberattacks are but the most extreme manifestation of the constant confrontations between individuals, groups, and governments meant to influence behavior, belief, and participation in events. Concerning the migration crisis, the information war that has played out across the Internet especially has been highly charged, emotive, and abetted violent rhetoric and actions. It has also resulted in backlashes, censorship, and self-censorship of unpopular viewpoints and an increasingly extremist opposition between already antagonistic sides.

In this light, it is unsurprising that major media corporations have colluded with politicians to "manage" the migration crisis toward particular outcomes. A particularly egregious example occurred in September 2015, when German chancellor Merkel was caught speaking with Facebook founder Mark Zuckerberg on an inadvertently "open" microphone, during a UN development summit. Merkel was anxious to know whether the company was making progress on policing its German-language website after "recent xenophobic outbursts"—user commentary which, of course, opposed her open-door migration policy. Zuckerberg replied that "we're working on it."[3]

Indeed they were. A few weeks earlier, on September 14, Facebook had announced it would work with a German nonprofit "Internet watchdog," Voluntary Self-Monitoring of Multimedia Service Providers, the purpose of which was said to be monitoring "suspected hate postings."[4] And, a full year before the UN refugee summit that cemented Facebook's multi-billion-dollar "investment" in refugees, the social media giant's policy was clearly more expansive than one specific issue. "We are committed to working closely with the German government on this important issue," a company spokeswoman said. "We think the best solutions to dealing with people who make racist and xenophobic comments can be found when service providers, government and civil society all work together to address this common challenge."[5]

The story caused a minor uproar at the time regarding its implications for free speech and the collusion of corporate and governmental interests. However, it was almost immediately forgotten in the endless stream of text, images, and video that companies like Facebook are built on. It was simply another story among millions and had no effect on a modern global online public marked by its diminished attention span and disinterest in any topics beyond a narrow sphere of personal and group interests. Second by second, media users are flooded by an overwhelming stream of data. This media phenomenon has incessantly neutralized the human capacity for logical interface with the world.

Reactions to the new media reality, therefore, seem largely driven by emotional and subconscious factors of influence. Industry moguls, and others who wish to benefit from it, have realized this long ago. In July 2014, Facebook was forced to apologize for having run a secret psychological experiment meant to see how its own users could be manipulated emotionally. According to *The Guardian*, Facebook researchers "decided after tweaking the content of peoples' 'news feeds' that there was 'emotional contagion' across the social network, by which people who saw one emotion being expressed would themselves express similar emotions."[6] This scientific conclusion would seem self-evident to anyone who has used social media in any manner involving news consumption. Although the Facebook experiment was modeled to determine the financial return that could be expected from a future venture, the overlap with general emotional manipulation among users concerning other topics is obvious.

As it turns out, social media itself has a radicalizing effect, in that it increases the speed of information received and processed by the brain, as well as the propensity for people to instantly react to any perceived provocation in language that would normally not be used, in an earlier and more reasoned time. To put it briefly: social media puts people in a bad mood, and negative sustained incidents like the migrant crisis perpetuate and worsen the results of this collective ill will. Indeed, according to a behavioral research example noted by Stanford University, social media users who had been confronted by symbols of negative emotions tended to spent more time reading and looking for further negatively focused content.[7]

In a collective event such as the migration crisis, which was heavily influenced by all sorts of negative impulses in media, it is no surprise that social media helped foster a more polarized atmosphere in Europe. Across the world, by 2015, "Twitter wars" between rival politicians, athletes, and everyone else had become the norm, and traditional media were increasingly using "tweets" as sources of public information, and in place of typical quotes both from public figures and from regular people. (This pro-clivity peaked with the contentious 2016 U.S. presidential campaign, when the unorthodox and ultimately successful candidate, Donald Trump, used Twitter to his advantage, communicating directly with the people and cir-cumventing a generally hostile legacy media.)

Further, the growing global tendency for people to choose and tai-lor their sources of online news also added to the polarization of public opinion and radicalization of views. As CNET reported in August 2016, regarding the mood on migration in Scandinavia, "Sweden's humanitar-ian identity is at risk of shattering—in part because the social media echo chamber broadcasts a growing hostility toward immigrants."[8]

The migration crisis clearly showed how supporters of opposing sides could use social media to attack one another over current events. But added into this mix too were international NGOs and humanitarian agencies, which had begun to use the platforms not only for reporting their activities, but for political advocacy. For example, through the crisis, international organizations like Médecins sans Frontières (Doctors with-out Borders) would take to Twitter to excoriate the Greek government, European Union, and anyone else over migrant deaths at sea. Because of the speed of events, and the brevity of speech on the platform (Twitter limits users to 140 characters), it was not clear whether this was part of a clearly organized public relations campaign launched from headquar-ters, or simply represented the view of the local officer who had posted the data. This kind of activity repeated over time tended to blur the lines between humanitarian work, news reporting, and advocacy.

The crisis also provided a textbook case of how the news media could be weaponized to amplify and propel public unrest, without the will of any central entity; it was just the structural result of the platform. During the migrant crisis, it thus became possible for lone actors or small online groups to have a disproportionate result on specific local outcomes. At the same time, on the other end of the spectrum—the corporate exploita-tion of "big data"—concerns have been raised, due to the potential for mass manipulation. The "tweaking" of a search algorithm to return (or not return) certain results or search phrases has been noted and widely criti-cized, especially with highly charged events like the migrant crisis, Brexit, and the 2016 presidential campaign in the United States.

The issue became of such concern that it would be noted in 2016 by German chancellor Merkel and by the European Parliament. In one draft document of October 2016, the European Parliament's Committee on Civil Liberties, Justice, and Home Affairs argued that "biased algorithms and other analytical tools, low quality of data, spurious correlations, errors, the underestimation of legal, social and ethical implications and the mar-ginalization of the role of humans in these processes can trigger flawed decision-making procedures." In keeping with the European Union's legalistic and rights-driven approach, the report added that "information revealed by big data analysis is only as reliable as the underlying data permits, and that strong scientific and ethical standards are therefore needed for judging the results of such analysis and its predictive algorithms." The advisory report also stressed that "the prospects and opportunities of big data can only be fully enjoyed by citizens, corporations, governments and institutions when public trust in these technologies is ensured by strong enforcement of fundamental rights and legal certainty for all actors involved."[9]

In 2015, the media in general used several talking points when interpreting the migration crisis, which fundamentally shaped its interpretation in global media. And the existence of certain cultural norms and mainstream beliefs—in short, the contemporary discursive context—in Europe meant that these interpretations remain uniform. Oftentimes, we can tell as much about a society from its discursive absence as from its presence. Thus, the media's interpretation of the 2015 migration crisis essentially revealed (or simply, reconfirmed) about polite society that it is limited by short memory and a political correctness based on assumed shared values. The mass of media and social media commentary, therefore, did not compare the migration crisis (as a historian might) to the fourth-century barbarian invasions or the sixth-century Slavic migrations. And it certainly did not compare the migrant deluge (as the perceived ideological outliers on the right did) to the Ottoman Muslim invasion of Europe starting from the 14th century.

Rather, the global media's historical contextualization of the migration crisis was delimited to an emotionally and symbolically charged event: World War II. Thousands upon thousands of articles and videos defined the crisis as the worst mass movement of people in Europe "since the Second World War." This was an extremely important descriptor. It essentially set the event in a historical context that the modern world order, and particularly today's European Union, considers as being for practical purposes the beginning of history: the end of European colonialism and empire, the beginning of the UN and European Union, the Holocaust and the creation of the state of Israel, the ascendancy of the United States as undisputed global superpower, and the rivalry of the latter with Russia (then, the Soviet Union). All of these aspects would become vital to sustaining a media narrative that favored certain outcomes.

Indeed, the historical association with World War II would prove very convenient for advocacy groups and policy makers as it evoked images of the Holocaust and Nazism, bringing back to public life other pictures just as harrowing as that of the dead refugee infant on the Turkish beach. Thus although certainly not the only competing narrative that characterized the migration crisis, it is clear that the prevailing one that would define policy and institutional reactions was based on the historical context of World

War II, and all of the perceived connotations that provided for modern-day "moral Europe" to act.

What the reference to World War II did was to simplify the many complexities and contradictions of the migration crisis, leading to easily digestible, black-and-white generalizations. The cumulative effect of this already charged contextualization was a media and political atmosphere self-regulated by concepts such as race, genocide, nationalism, and extremism. For years already, documentary channels broadcasting in Europe had been reinforcing this historical contextualization, with programming about World War II and the Nazis being far more prevalent and pervasive than those covering any other specific historical period or event. To completely conflate the two events, *Time* magazine and others published emotive photographs of World War II refugees alongside those of the current crisis.[10]

European media in various local languages produced articles through the crisis using the World War II reference. Also, among the many examples of influential American media promoting the "worst refugee crisis since World War II" narrative were the *Washington Post* (in April 2015), the *New York Times* (in August 2015), and CBS News (in September 2015). An important fact to note is that since the very earliest days of the crisis, these mass media outlets often took the word association directly from UN aid agencies' talking points.[11] The World War II contextualization in media was sustained and promoted by other organizations that were heavily involved in "branding" the migration crisis, and which generally benefited from it financially. They were active (and remain active) in promoting this mental association. For example, Amnesty International cited the World War II refugee context in a report on the migrant crisis in June 2015.[12] In a press release of December 2015, the IOM also made the word association.[13]

Similarly, in June 2016, CNN pushed the association when announcing the UNHCR's new report on 2015 refugee spikes (at the time, the organization was also launching a social media campaign to influence the UN General Assembly three months later, and the efforts made there by the American president, corporations, and other interested parties).[14] Also, on a more grassroots level, the influential Refugees Welcome network of NGOs also plastered the headline "The World Is Facing the World's Largest Refugee Crisis since World War II" on its homepage.[15] Finally, as was the case with President Obama, European leaders were quick to contextualize the migration crisis in the shadow of Nazism. In an August 2015 speech, EU commissioner Dimitris Avramopoulos stated that "the world finds itself facing the worst refugee crisis since the Second World War. And Europe finds itself struggling to deal with the high influxes of people seeking refuge within our borders."[16] The World War II reference was again invoked by Sergei Stanishev, president of the Party of European Socialists, in September 2015.[17]

Of course, this contextualization had a particularly potent effect in Germany, which became, not coincidentally, the key target and greatest proclaimed supporter of the refugee cause under Angela Merkel. She was sanctified by the American establishment when *Time* awarded her as 2015 "person of the year" under a rather grandiose title that added hints of the Cold War, lauding Merkel as "Chancellor of the free world."[18] Media coverage of refugees suffering also acted as a challenge—and unexpected opportunity—for Germans, burdened since the Holocaust with the lingering sense of "German collective guilt" (*Kollektivschuld*). This concept was first formulated by the famous Swiss psychoanalyst Carl Jung in 1945; he considered that the theory was "for psychologists a fact, and it will be one of the most important tasks of therapy to bring the Germans to recognize this guilt."[19]

Jung's concept became policy for British and American occupying forces in the immediate postwar years and was executed in a publicity campaign meant to shame and humiliate Germans.[20] In short, "German guilt" as a concept was a form of psychological warfare. The concept was influential in the postwar German psyche, subtly influencing foreign policy, but it also emerged as an influential policy for global governance in general. The charge of collective guilt has been levied as a political weapon often since then, in Europe most famously against the Serbs, for the wars in Yugoslavia. As of 2017, this area of study (on which has been emphasized in a great deal of Balkan modern history media coverage) remained a large cottage industry in world universities, with ambivalent results.[21]

In post–World War II Germany's environment of remorse and self-reckoning, new currents in academic research also began to take root. From the 1950s and 1960s, this was dominated by the controversial but very influential writings of Fritz Fischer (1908–1999), widely considered to be Germany's most important historian of the 20th century. His research, amplified in the German media, argued that Germany alone had been guilty for not only World War II, but for World War I as well, out of a plan for sustained hegemony over Europe. Many Germans disagreed, and this became a point of contention across society. However, generations of students and professors in the so-called Fischer School continued these views of Germany as the European nation with the most blood on its hands over the course of half a century.[22]

Thus, in the post–World War II period that gave birth to the European Union movement, Germany was left with many scars and many points of sensitivity in the public discourse. Along with the concept of collective guilt, also promoted was the complementary one of collective responsibility. Although these issues might appear tangential to the subject of media and the 2015 migration crisis, they are actually quite relevant. They help explain why otherwise rational people (the Germans) would accept, without much resistance, a single leader's rushed and autocratic call for an unlimited number of migrants from wildly different cultural backgrounds to move to their country.

In this respect, the twin aspects of collective guilt and responsibility were used with merciless precision in media to target German public opinion, and world perceptions of Germany. A September 2, 2015, *New York Times* op-ed by a German author asked rhetorically whether the country would "succumb to hate" by opposing Merkel. "Many Europeans, and especially Germans, are watching with a sense of helplessness," claimed the author. "Will our urge to help let loose our darkest demons?"[23] Yet accepting suffering refugees also created the conditions for being able to feel—for once—proud of being German, in a way that no one could criticize as dangerously nationalistic. "Never before have Germans been so willing to help," announced German newspaper *Der Spiegel* in July 2015.[24]

At the same time, embarking on the overall adventure also gave Germany a chance to take pride in a European leadership role, a perception that had taken a beating after four years of intense dislike among populations (particularly, the Greeks) who had felt unfairly punished by German-enforced bailout austerity measures. And so arose the initial enthusiasm behind Merkel's "we can do it!" campaign, which, however, proved completely illusory. In 2015, the open-border policy of Merkel won support partly because of its image value associated with the historical self-perception of collective guilt dating from World War II. Images of migrants traveling along the Balkan Route on decrepit and overcrowded trains, their heads and arms thrust out of small windows, were particularly potent. "Seeing that, it made you feel that it would be unthinkable to turn them back," said one German official. "Our history is very difficult, and we must be responsible."[25]

The resurrection of German guilt ensured that domestic critics could easily be blackballed as either hard-hearted or racist—a charge that was given credence in media by a handful of right-wing attacks on migrant shelters. However, the prevailing media argument during the crisis concerned volume—that is, how many migrants Germany could or should accept—and largely ignored the fundamental issue of why Germany, as opposed to any other country, should take in any migrants at all. In the absence of any objective discussion, the trend was to use, or at least imply, Germany's dark modern history as justifying some modern obligation to save the entire developing world.

Predictably, by the time the shift in public sentiment began to occur, after the November 2015 Paris attacks, and especially after the Cologne New Year's Eve attacks on women, the public discourse had become too extreme and partisan for any civil answer to these basic questions. And when anti-migrant and anti-Islam movements like PEGIDA and the

Alternative for Germany (AfD) party started to gain popularity, the pendulum swung back: the media could point to these critical reactions as evidence that Germany was slipping back into its Nazi past. This sort of opinion was raised in far corners of Europe during the period, showing just how deeply the World War II context value was rooted. "The only alternative [to Merkel's refugee policy]," one liberal EU official said, "would be a return to 1930s style nationalism."[26]

The pro-refugee organizations and politicians, supported heavily by the media, had thus set the perfect trap; it was a no-win situation for Germany. Under these conditions, public discourse inevitably favored the left-wing and globalist causes that expressed support for migrants, despite the rapidly accumulating series of terrorist attacks and other violence perpetrated by them throughout 2016—including, for practically the first time ever, in welcoming Germany.

The prevailing media narrative in favor of refugees and migrants was not only created by deliberate historical contextualization and specific national traps, however. It also had simple, practical and industry-specific rationales that have not really been analyzed. The quality of coverage, therefore, was also an outcome of the structural and topical decisions of the actual media editors who commissioned coverage during the period. To cover the phenomenon of a large-scale logistical problem—which is fundamentally what the crisis was—could be done mostly easily, effectively, and profitably by treating the issue as a human interest story first and foremost. In an age in which few had the interest or attention span for cool-headed analysis, firsthand tales of woe and suffering proliferated wildly.

The structure of such media coverage was essentially very simple, and is used throughout the world in similar crisis or conflict situations. The basic formula for such reporting is to find an individual (typically, a person in a refugee camp) who fills the role of victim, from whom color commentary is then taken. In the 2015 crisis, this commentary generally chronicled the hardships of the individual's journey since leaving his or her war-torn homeland, his or her intended destination and life ambitions (that would probably never be fulfilled), and general "message" to the world. This human interest aspect would then be fleshed out by commentary from an aid worker or "experts," ideally, buttressed by statistics from humanitarian organizations that would paint an increasingly grim picture of the crisis.

This model of journalism could be (and was) repeated ad nauseam because it was easy to produce (whether in text or video format), easy to edit, and emotionally driven. In a world of media consumers increasingly driven by irrational behavior and the tendency to "like" or "share" whatever headline or image seems the most extreme, this tactic also meant readership and (if incentivized correctly) money. And it reinforced the fundamental themes that sustained the mass public perception of the crisis, in its alleged historical and moral dimensions.

This cut-and-paste template of journalism did not really do anything to inform audiences about the deeper causes, implications, or realities of the crisis. The prevailing genre also spawned subgenres and innovations. One pattern of journalistic activity, most prevalent in the summer and fall of 2015, was for reporters to embed themselves among the migrants, crossing borders illegally while chronicling the plight of migrants. For a certain period, until the closure of the Balkan Route in March 2016, this kind of reportage also was heavily commissioned by editors seeking the human interest aspect of the crisis. And, for those reporters who wanted a more heroic image, there was also the possibility of joining the refugees at a restive camp like Eidomeni in Greece or Calais in France, or on a dangerous sea voyage. In 2015, migrant-crisis reporting thus became a somewhat safer (but still exciting) subsector of the traditional war-reporting industry.

Of course, within the (primarily, social) media there was a healthy bit of self-criticism or skepticism, even from those wholeheartedly supportive of the migrant cause. Social media users criticized a form of "morality tourism" that journalism and activism had become. The concept of affluent Westerners touring migrant camps evoked unpleasant images of the "human zoos" of the colonialist past, in which Europeans would gape at exotically dressed people from faraway cultures who had been snatched up for public display back home. Several problematic issues emerge from this structure of coverage, from an ethical point of view. The kind of human interest article described above follows a format essentially identical to those of fund-raising articles created by humanitarian NGOs and international organizations like UNHCR and UNICEF. Such articles are specifically created in order to elicit an emotional reaction in the audience to increase the likelihood of financial donations. The migration crisis saw myriad examples of a mutually beneficial relationship between journalists and aid organizations designed to obtain specific results. In order to obtain these results, it was necessary to present the migration crisis (cumulatively and in individual cases) according to the specific worldview that ultimately manifested, on the global stage, with President Obama's announcements at the UN in September 2016.

The power of emotive images and coverage opened room for not only violations of media ethics, but also very problematic examples of ethics among migrants themselves. This was worsened by the presence of media, which was often seen as an opportunity to gain international sympathy—though often in questionable ways. Migrants protesting at camps or border closures would frequently use children (as at protests on the Greek–Macedonian border) in provocative ways, holding them up against border fences and exposing them to tear gas. The images were terrible, but the fundamental question was rarely asked about these intentional attempts to gain sympathy through child exploitation and endangerment. And so such images would feature in publications and NGO fund-raisers, stripped of their actual context, with an implied moral resonance completely at variance with the reality.

In this sense, the "optics" of the migration crisis became, for both media and humanitarian organizations, the ultimate form of product placement. There is a very fine line between crisis reporting and advocacy, and in the European migration crisis this line has become particularly blurred: this was due to not only the historical resonances (i.e., the deliberate contextualization with repeated comparisons to World War II events) and mass emotional triggers (i.e., tragic photos and interviews), but also as a result of the crisis's sheer longevity. With the ranks of desperate migrants in transit being replenished on a daily basis, and camps across Europe remaining open indefinitely, the phenomenon of an uninterrupted and all-pervasive humanitarian presence became a new part of Europe's daily media coverage. And, of course, the humanitarian agencies and NGOs also proliferated their own accounts, stories, and photographs across newspapers, websites, e-mail newsletter campaigns, and social media. What had just a year earlier been a peripheral part of European life had become a constant and accepted part of the greater public discourse.

Because tragedy is their bread and butter, well-funded humanitarian organizations have of course always been keen to use media to their advantage, in both targeted marketing campaigns and in color commentary or provision of statistics for journalists. For close observers, the European migration crisis was full of cases of such organizations going the extra mile to be sure of optimum branding. (One example of which the author is aware was from a Greek refugee camp, where UNHCR officials reprimanded volunteers for not having the agency's logo displayed on the top of a white bucket—in addition to its side—in case someone might come around to photograph it.)

It is easily understandable, and perhaps acceptable, that such humanitarian agencies use, and misuse media as they do. But for objective media coverage of this (or any) crisis, there is a more problematic aspect regarding media engagement that is inherent to such organizations: a total lack of transparency and institutional prevention of employees to speak about their work. To be sure, this is hardly only the case with large international humanitarian bodies (the private sector and government service also come to mind as sectors in which freedom of speech is discouraged), but for the purpose of the present inquiry, the humanitarian agencies present the major groups of interest.

For journalists covering the migration crisis, getting any meaningful commentary beyond the basic talking points and statistics was next to impossible. Because of the restrictions placed on employees at different levels and competencies, interaction with media was frequently marked by excessive caution regarding what employees were able to discuss. The institutional paralysis this creates inevitably leads to simple information requests being referred to a seemingly never-ending chain of other, equally unhelpful colleagues. When official responses from such organizations do come, they tend to be so general as to be almost unusable. As such, the only way of getting any information of substance regarding organizational activities, outlook, and strategy was in off-the-record comments from employees.

Although these dynamics of media relations are not surprising (and, as said, are hardly unique to the humanitarian sector), they will have a key influence on future reporting of the European and other migration crises. This is specifically because of the expected pervasive nature of such organizations, as migrant-related events become a part of Europe's "new normal." Thus, a new layer of non-transparency, in addition to the existing political and governmental classes, is being added. The cumulative result of this silent expansion of "civil society" power will be greater secrecy concerning overall migration policies, which has already fueled anger and protests across the continent, directed primarily at politicians and states.

The above-cited "hot mic" revelation in which Mark Zuckerberg reassured Chancellor Merkel about Facebook's efforts to block negative views of her policy was hardly the only case of perceived collusion to create a specific public perception. After the mass attacks on women and thefts by migrants on New Year's Eve celebrations in Cologne, Germany, local authorities were accused of covering up additional details and victim testimony that would have proven a much wider degree of assault by migrants than had been reported. The media was directly accused of having avoided the story out of political correctness fears, and the police were also criticized heavily. Hans-Peter Freidrich, a former interior minister, "accused the media of imposing a 'news blackout' and operating a 'code of silence' over negative news about immigrants."[27]

In the wake of the Cologne attacks, Swedish police conducted an internal investigation after they were accused of having prevented local media from covering crimes committed by migrants at a music festival the previous August. The investigation was only launched because an internal police memo that detailed the expulsion of 200 violent youths was leaked to the local media in the aftermath of Cologne. Shockingly, a Swedish police official stated that "sometimes we do not really say how things are because we believe it may play into the hands of the [conservative] Sweden Democrats."[28] In February 2017, an outspoken Swedish police officer took to Facebook to claim that a significant percentage of crimes were being committed by migrants, earning him not only considerable support from Swedes but also criticism and promises of an internal investigation for allegedly whipping up racial unrest. (Sweden does not allow crime suspects to be identified by ethnicity, as part of its politically correct policies.)[29]

From the beginning of the crisis, certain states were also accused by pro-migrant groups (and indeed by some EU governments) of influencing negative media campaigns against the migrant cause. Particularly singled out was Hungary, which from early on in the crisis had begun a media outreach campaign in several migrant countries of origin, in an attempt to discourage them from making the long and dangerous journey to the European "promised land" (although this policy was heavily criticized in the beginning, other European states and even the European Union would eventually follow this example as a deterrent to mass migration).

Hungary—and particularly its outspoken leader, Viktor Orbán—was also singled out for allegedly stoking fear and mistrust about the migrants as a security risk, and of promoting "intolerance" ideas in so doing.[30] To a lesser extent, Austrian and British officials were also accused of this practice. Although not the prevailing or politically correct narrative, this sort of coverage did have a political impact in hardening domestic public opinion in several states, as would be seen by the Brexit vote of June 2016 and the Hungarian referendum against EU-imposed quotas for redistribution of refugees to the country held on October 2, 2016 (the latter only failed due to low turnout).

The issue of censorship or self-censorship of aspects of the crisis that affected political and ideological beliefs fueled existing divisiveness within societies, and the politicization of coverage affected diplomatic relations. But these incidents were all considered essentially a family feud, compared to what came to be popularly known as "hybrid war" against the West by Russia during the migration crisis. According to this interpretation, Russia sought to exacerbate differences between European states by highlighting stories that depicted migrants in a negative light. It must be remembered, of course, that this interpretation of Russian media coverage occurred at the lowest point in American–Russian relations since the Cold War. Antagonisms over Ukraine continued to drive American policy, including economic sanctions that were painful mostly for EU countries that could nevertheless not extricate their own policies from that of Washington. And it did not sit well with the Barack Obama administration that Russia's air campaign in Syria from September 2015 had essentially changed the balance of power in the Middle East and saved Syria from falling under complete control of Islamic State terrorists.

In this overall context, cases of Pentagon planners attacking Russia became more and more prevalent. By February/March 2016, Western media outlets were eagerly reproducing a top NATO commander's allegations that Russia and the Syrian government were actively trying to create more refugees, with their air campaign against jihadists, in order to use new waves of refugees to weaken Western unity.[31] Of course, there was no similar Western concern over U.S. bombing in Syria and Iraq, even as the UN in October 2016 warned that the impending battle for Mosul against Islamic State could result in the exodus of hundreds of thousands of new refugees.

Thus, if there was a propaganda war, it was definitely not from one side exclusively. In truth, throughout the migration crisis, Russian state media provided the only English-language coverage of migration-related events that occurred across a wide area of European territory. This is important because such stories were censored or ignored by the Western mainstream media and would have otherwise only been reported in local languages for local audiences, since the relevant events often occurred in provincial and rural areas. With the exception of specialists and activists who sought out such local information as part of their overall mission, the general Western (and particularly American) audience without access to Russian media was largely unaware of migrant-related events that occurred repeatedly across Europe's hinterlands and in its lesser-covered cities.

Certainly, there was to a large degree a policy interest on the part of Russian media in devoting regular coverage to migration. However, this coverage was invaluable for providing an alternative view of events that were otherwise completely ignored, or were reported in rather uniform fashion by Western media conditioned by policy parameters and by the development/humanitarian/academic-industrial complex—not to mention the restraints of political correctness. Remaining as it did detached from both the effects of migration and these limiting conditions, Russian media was able to provide a different view of events that, although not always totally objective or well meaning, was definitely worth following as a corrective to predictable and staid Western reportage.

In the highly charged geopolitical atmosphere that prevailed during the crisis, the general Western criticism of Russian media coverage was consistently associated with alleged Russian "propaganda" coverage of events in Syria and Iraq. By October 2016, when anti-Russian hysteria was in full swing, the Obama administration and the Hillary Clinton presidential campaign officially charged the Russian state with waging hybrid war via the very damaging media revelations Wikileaks was then making, with leaked e-mails of Clinton campaign chief John Podesta indicating a chronic pattern of deceit and cover-ups that infuriated millions of Americans. Russian officials scoffed at the allegations. In a show of bravado, U.S. vice president Joe Biden announced that America would launch a cyberattack against Russia in revenge.[32]

This larger context is necessary to mention in order to understand the global conditions that prevailed and shaped media coverage—and, in the case of Wikileaks, an information war—during a definite "resolution moment" in the crisis, just weeks after President Obama had announced the next phase of refugee assistance programs from the UN. The general pattern of events indicated (and still indicates) that Russian media will continue to play an important role in highlighting not only migrant-related security events, but also the internal political infighting between right- and left-wing blocs across the Continent. It will thus remain fashionable among Western pundits, academics, and defense planners to affirm the need to fight "Russian propaganda." By 2016, this role had already become institutionalized within NATO and several governments, and will thus serve to further expand the relationship of states, security organizations, technology companies, and media in the years ahead. This will simultaneously lead to an increasing tendency toward the perception of migrants, and the overall migrant crisis, in black-and-white terms.

All indicators indeed point to an increasingly institutionalized subjectivity in migration coverage by the media. Although individual cases certainly do exist of objective crisis coverage, the general media approach to the 2015 migration events was even before the 2016 deterioration of relations cumulatively subjective: and this not only because it was in the interest of governments and media producers, but also because it was the preferred coverage type for mass media consumers. An interesting question remains as to whether, even under the best of circumstances, such a crisis could in fact be covered objectively. However, if recent history is any indicator, audiences should not hold their breath.

Despite criticism of EU malcontents like Hungary and Britain, or the alleged danger of rivals like Russia, the type of media coverage that prevailed during the crisis was qualitatively in favor of the migrant cause, and the politicians that supported it. This indicated clearly a deep convergence of political, ideological, and financial interests, one that proved far more powerful in influencing media coverage of the crisis than did that of any critics. The concerted power of this bloc was indicated by the September 2016 decision by the UN, key governments, NGOs, and the private sector to cooperate and "invest" in migration on a global scale. This objective fundamentally must be—and will be—achieved through a deep penetration of all forms of media by supporters of open-border and pro-migrant causes.

This goal is being achieved partly through exploiting the opportunities provided by electronic media. Contemporary information warfare on the Internet includes popular platforms like the Google-owned video platform, YouTube. Through the platform's own advertising system, opposing sides on the migration issue try to hijack one another. For example, in April 2016, the BBC reported that the activist group Refugees Welcome had taken out keyword-specific advertisements, which would be activated when German YouTube users attempted to search for video content by typing in keywords opposed to mass migration.[33]

Indeed, one Syrian refugee who had become a "YouTube sensation," Firas Alshater, said that the activist campaign started after "he realised that a right-wing party used his videos on the platform for advertising." The advocacy group thus copied this tactic, linking their own ads to pro-migrant websites. The irony was that both opposing parties were sending money (in form of ad revenue) to the side they opposed through the clicks generated. It was seen as an ideological investment. "Of course, it's painful that the uploaders are getting money from our campaign, but at the moment they only earn a few cents," said a cofounder of the movement, Jonas Kakoschke. The Refugees Welcome group itself clearly targeted the same method of search term manipulation used for many years by different parties (as was seen with the domain name that was specified in the article: Search-racism-find-truth.com). Thus, although claiming its main goal was to find shared housing for refugees, the group had a "humanitarian conversion" aspect targeting those who disagreed with their ideology through electronic media.

Additionally, what might be one of the most underresearched and most interesting aspects of migrants and the media pertains to their use of social media and technology during the crisis. Far from being the victimized, helpless masses so often portrayed in the media, the migrants were (or soon became) tech-savvy users of social media in several languages. Incongruously with their media-created image, migrants flashed expensive smart phones in the most miserable of ill-maintained camps. They were able to keep in constant contact with friends and family members, to create virtual groups, and to gather real-time intelligence on developments affecting them (such as border closures or expected openings). This new proliferation of technology among migrants also complicated the tasks of police and intelligence services to predict migrant activity, especially when it would manifest in protests or violent attempted border crossings. This challenge was further compounded by the use of closed-channel messaging apps such as Signal, Telegram, and Threema for communicating and planning by migrants, activists, and, especially, human traffickers.

Similarly, both left- and right-wing activist groups used social media to plan their own activities—and to antagonize each other in an increasingly heated atmosphere marked by demonstrations, counterdemonstrations, and violent showdowns. As with the migrant groups, these groups now had the ability to rapidly react, organize, and plot logistical movements that often manifested as security threats for increasingly overstretched police forces across Europe. In addition to traditional crime and regular duties, police and intelligence services now had to deal simultaneously with rival public security events associated with the right, the left, and the migrants themselves. All evidence indicates that this trend will increase in the future, heightening the risks to public safety and even political stability across key areas of Europe.

The migrants' access to technology, which also played a role in stoking and sustaining the various Arab Spring uprisings of 2011, also had an influential role in attracting potential migrants to Europe in the first place. Images of developed and attractive cities, filled with attractive people and described as being both welcome to newcomers and generous with social benefits had a magnetic attraction. For young people with ambitions and no chance to realize them at home, the images—not reality—of life in Europe had a powerful impact on the decision to set out from villages and towns in far-flung places from Morocco to Eritrea to Bangladesh. However, by the time that European leaders had realized the prevalence of economic migrants among real war refugees, the entire media discourse—with its poignant portrayals and all-pervasive contextualization of the crisis with World War II—had restricted the capability for brave and sober decision making.

Social media exploitation of the less cautious local populations also abetted the activities of human traffickers, who used platforms like Facebook to broadcast deliberately misleading information about their "travel services," specifically for financial gain. For example, by January 2015, smugglers were providing details of ship transport from Turkey to Italy, misrepresenting the safety and quality of travel, and providing contact details for how to "book" tickets, as if they were operating a regular travel agency. The frequent accidents and capsizing tragedies that would accompany such dangerous voyages were not mentioned. But it indicated that, from the earliest days of the crisis, even war-ravaged Syria was technologically well connected and that potential refugees could easily organize travel through mainstream social media platforms.[34]

Partly as a reaction to faulty or deceptive information provided by traffickers, pro-migrant activists provided similar online travel and situational intelligence on multilingual websites such as Welcome to Europe, which provided an exhaustive list of NGOs, emergency numbers, and useful information on a country-by-country basis.[35] Such portals gave migrants and activists a touchstone for useful data, which was amassed with considerable effort. And the network also produces hard-copy "travel guides" in Arabic, containing all relevant information for travel and what to expect in various European countries, with emergency phone numbers and a web of partner organizations provided. This was reported during the crisis (as by Britain's Sky News in September 2015); however, as will be further discussed in Chapter 5, intelligence services had discovered these activist efforts going on one year earlier—well in advance of the main crisis, as conventionally understood.[36]

This type of media is where the network function of activist organization became especially significant. But even ad hoc activist groups that were not as expansive and well organized as Welcome to Europe played an outsized role in aiding migrants where no infrastructure existed. Indeed, for much of summer and fall 2015, the most important channel of information and support for migrants at the border of Greece and Macedonia was carried out by an impromptu group of Greek and international volunteers organized simply by one Facebook page.

As the migration crisis moves into future phases, the early emphasis on media coverage of chaotic and tragic transit events will change to reflect the interaction of migrants with their adopted countries. The existing activist networks will emphasize communications concerning "resettlement" projects, legal defense, and migrant rights, highlighting and opposing "hate speech" and other examples of "racism" against migrants. On the other side, those opposed to the migrant presence will continue to use social media to counter these arguments and organize events such as demonstration and political actions. Meanwhile, largely forgotten amid the general hubbub surrounding the migration crisis and its political and social aspects, those with altogether different motives—criminal groups and aspiring terrorists—will quietly continue to coordinate logistics for new plots via closed communications channels, with their deeds inevitably triggering renewed debate in the media as they become more commonplace.

Indeed, the remarkable ability of the European Union to internalize controversial episodes toward fulfillment of a preexisting goal was well attested by its new media–corporate collusion processes that were cemented in 2016. Citing the risk of terrorism, EU commissars announced a greater need for policing the media; unsurprisingly, this would be an effort that expanded the powers of Brussels over those of member states. Equally unsurprisingly, the European Union's new June 2016 legislation would be done in close partnership with "civil society" actors and many of the tech companies most involved with the global "refugee investment solutions" championed by Obama: YouTube, Microsoft, Twitter, and Facebook.

According to an official pronouncement from the European Commission on May 31, 2016, these companies would be working with the European Union to remove any content that violated a 2008 hate crimes law, which covers: "all conduct publicly inciting to violence or hatred directed against a group of persons or a member of such a group defined by reference to race, color, religion, descent or national or ethnic origin." The IT companies would be required to take down content "flagged" by users— and particularly by unspecified "civil society" partners. The European Union also specifies the need to create counternarratives to hate speech and calls on the tech companies to literally create a network of "trusted reporters" from EU member states to work with on the issue.[37]

As is usual with EU initiatives, this paper received relatively little notice in the media. But for those who were paying attention, the ramifications of a small group of elite tech companies, nameless Brussels bureaucrats, and "trusted" partners from the media and NGO worlds was a terrifyingly typical example of Brussels stealth policy implementation at its worst.

"Opponents counter that the initiative amounts to an assault on free speech in Europe," wrote analyst Soeren Kern. "They say that the European Union's definition of 'hate speech' and 'incitement to violence' is so vague that it could include virtually anything deemed politically incorrect by European authorities, including criticism of mass migration, Islam or even the EU itself."[38]

The May 2016 EU Code of Conduct also specified that EU and tech company representatives would meet on a "regular basis," with the goal of discussing "how to promote transparency and encourage counter and alternative narratives." The Code of Conduct memo also stated that a "High Level Group on Combating Racism, Xenophobia and all forms of intolerance" would be set up "by the end of 2016."[39]

Considering the overall worldview of Brussels, the tendencies of past bureaucratic processes, and the specific private sector and "civil society" aspect of the announced cooperation, the suggestion that Brussels was trying to protect Europeans from the terrorists seemed implausible. Much more likely, all historical patterns considered, was that Brussels was planning to create legal mechanisms for reining in criticism of the migration crisis, and the havoc that leaders like Merkel, Juncker, and Avramopoulos had brought to the heart of Europe. Whether or not they would succeed in policing free thought would be a question inexorably tied up with the European Union's continued ability to survive in the aftermath of Brexit and other shocks to the system.

CHAPTER 4

Europe's "Generation Unknown": Terrorism, Intelligence, and an Uncertain Future

In an average year, the middle of December finds most Brussels' Eurocrats leisurely winding down activities before Christmas and New Year's holidays. Drinks with lobbyists, office parties with interns, comparing plans for ski vacations in the Alps—everything, that is, except the tedium of pushing paper in humorless offices. But 2015 was no average year.

Macedonia's no-nonsense president, Gjorge Ivanov, had called the December 16 meeting. From the EU side, the assembled leaders included European Council president Donald Tusk, head of the Frontex border monitoring mission Fabrice Leggeri, and others from the enlargement and home affairs commissions.[1] Although the latter had been expecting a tough meeting, they certainly weren't prepared for what would happen next.

The Macedonian delegation unceremoniously poured out a large bag over the conference table, filling it with Greek-stamped refugee registration cards and forged passports—just a small portion of the 9,000 false documents that their police had seized, since early November, from migrants attempting to transit Macedonia from Greek territory.

"They were shocked," recalls President Ivanov, in his first extended comments on what was perhaps the key meeting for EU security policy during the crisis. "We had registration forms on which dozens of migrants had, for example, all identical birthdates entered. In registering all migrants, our police calculated that Frontex staff in Greece had been processing only eight percent of people sent through to us. Some also had false Syrian passports purchased from organized crime networks, especially located in Athens. There were even Africans with Syrian passports! They couldn't believe it."[2]

This was not supposed to have happened with the multinational Frontex team and Greek police guarding the European Union's key external border. In fact, a key assessment made way back in September 2011 (by the then operations chief of Frontex, Klaus Roesler) was "the need to work on further strengthening activities relating to screenings and debriefings, in order to better contribute to the migration management under national responsibility and to acquire criminal intelligence."[3] Nevertheless, four years later a Greek police force overwhelmed by sheer migrant volume could not cope. Frontex's previous activity at the northeastern land border with Turkey had proven too successful for its own good, as the increasing number of captured illegal migrants had swelled the Greek asylum system to bursting—particularly unhelpful in the middle of a never-ending financial crisis.

One result of the Frontex activity at the Greece–Turkey land border (and ensuing border fence erected there by Greek authorities) was that it shifted the migration route southward to the more dangerous maritime route to the Greek islands, where coast guard services were heavily engaged. Frequently in distress, migrant boats and rubber dinghies could not simply be sent back to Turkish shores but had to be rescued on humanitarian grounds.[4] And this simply encouraged more migrants to make the journey, creating an increasing pileup of refugees on Greek islands like Chios, Samos, and especially Lesvos. Predictably, activists, NGOs, journalists and international organizations all set up shop, adding a whole new complexity to police and intelligence work and causing considerable problems for local residents—who nevertheless did their best to help.

From the islands, migrants were sent by long-haul ferries to the port of Piraeus near Athens, and then bused to the northern Greek city of Thessaloniki. Finally, the migrants were sent to the border village of Eidomeni, where they flooded across into Macedonia. By summer 2015, the government had established special trains running directly up through Serbia and further north to Central Europe. As long as Germany and Austria continued their "refugees welcome" policy, no one had a problem with this organized transport. And the overburdened Greeks, it appeared, did not try particularly hard to determine who was who among the migrant hordes—even after the Frontex reinforcements had arrived.

By early October 2015, this Balkan Route was operating at maximum capacity, with 3,000 to 8,000 migrants crossing daily. The Greeks had largely given up any attempts to formally identify them. One of only three policemen observing the busloads of arriving migrants at Eidomeni was frank. "They are not all Syrian," he admitted, pointing out several men walking through a large tent and on toward the Macedonian border. "That one's a Bangladeshi, and there's an Albanian—and that one's probably an Iranian. What are we supposed to do? There are just too many."[5]

This candid reminder illustrated yet again that the migration crisis had become a humanitarian and security problem primarily because it was, first and foremost, a logistical one. The concept that *there are just too many* migrants coming in was obvious to frontline countries like Greece, Italy, and Macedonia. For Berlin to realize this took a surprisingly long time—a time in which the terrorist infiltration occurred that would be acknowledged in subsequent terrorist attacks.

The European Union's failure to properly screen migrants and refugees entering its visa-free Schengen Zone in Greece had thus led to a nightmarish—but all too predictable—scenario in which intelligence services would be put at a huge disadvantage for the foreseeable future. Over one million migrants had entered Europe in 2015 alone, many of them possessing false or stolen identification, or lacking any at all. This "Generation Unknown" represents the future of European security risks; since such individuals objectively do not exist, they can appear, disappear, and reappear in all sorts of capacities. They could be recruited by terrorist entities or intelligence services, or get pulled into Europe's criminal underworld. The most unlucky could themselves be trafficked further, sold into slavery or killed for their organs. In all cases, no one would be the wiser.

Europe's Generation Unknown became a de facto reality specifically because of poor crisis management from Brussels and Berlin. Today, it is the precise point of convergence between security risks and intelligence challenges. As will be discussed further in this chapter, these challenges confounded some of the most prominent European leaders involved in guiding this crisis, in ways that have never been reported. On the front lines, the divergent security reactions of Greece and Macedonia were caused by political impulses and risk assessment. Greece was a powerful NATO and EU member and had been vetoing Macedonia's NATO and EU accession for 25 years, over the unresolved "name issue" (Greece has a bordering province also named Macedonia and does not respect the Republic of Macedonia's right of self-determination in name, language, and ethnicity). This situation had fostered a chronic arrogance in Athens. Both Greek leaders and Greek officials in Brussels, such as the Home Affairs Commissioner in charge of migration, Dimitris Avramopoulos, assumed they had all of the leverage over a small and weak neighbor.

Further compounding Macedonia's disadvantageous situation, a political crisis over an alleged "wiretapping scandal" had embroiled the government and opposition, causing heavy diplomatic interference from the United States, Britain, and the European Union. Worse, a Kosovo-led Albanian paramilitary cell planned multiple terrorist attacks in Macedonia, but was neutralized by special police in a two-day gunfight in May. The eight policemen who died in the operation were hailed as heroes. Nevertheless, the Western powers would continue to interfere in local matters through

2016, continuing to support a relatively unpopular leftist opposition through creating parallel institutions and using a shady network of NGOs linked with billionaire provocateur George Soros.

With all of the odds stacked against Macedonia during the 2015 political, security, and migration crisis, foreign officials were shocked that the country did not simply fold. But they had underestimated Macedonia's institutional resilience and President Ivanov—the only leader left standing after rival politicians had been tainted by corruption charges. As commander-in-chief of the armed forces and convener of the National Security Council, the president and his cabinet carried out measures to track the situation at the borders, assess risks, and take steps to safeguard national security. In late August 2015, the president declared a crisis situation on the northern and southern borders, putting into place a special law by which security measures could be rapidly executed.

"We were the first country to distinguish the security and humanitarian aspects, and the first to declare a crisis situation," recalls President Ivanov. "In the months before that, our services noted that the majority of illegal migrants were men aged from 18 to 30; some were deserters from army or rebel groups, or trying to escape recruitment. Our services noted small physical details consistent with gun use. In October a summit was held with EU officials via video link. We showed that there was a distinction between legitimate refugees and economic migrants. Aside from people from countries not affected by war, we found, for example, cases of people coming from parts of Syria or Iraq not affected by war or who had come from camps in countries like Iran."

As the European Union scrambled to find a common policy during the fall of 2015, Angela Merkel was stubbornly clinging to her open-border policy, the Visegrad countries led by Hungary were putting up stiff resistance, and the European Union itself was divided. Leading EU officials like Greece's Avramopoulos and Foreign Affairs Commissioner Federica Mogherini of Italy were seeking financial and refugee-quota deals that were best for their own countries. Meanwhile, European Council president Tusk, a Pole, was heavily engaged in negotiations with all sides (including the Balkan states and Turkey) to try and ensure the survival of the European Union itself.

This train wreck of divergent interests predictably meant frustrations and failures. Austria became increasingly alarmed, British Euroskeptics had another reason to justify a future Brexit vote, and Sweden was being overwhelmed with asylum requests. Meanwhile, from September 2015 onward, the Macedonians made repeated requests for equipment such as biometric machines, police vehicles, and financial assistance from the European Union—requests that were either ignored or lost in bureaucracy. By the end of spring 2016, the tiny country of two million people had spent 30 million euros from its budget for police, army, intelligence, and equipment. The latter suffered a high rate of amortization, with 40 percent of vehicles and other equipment being damaged, while over 100 police and army officers had been injured in defending the country's southern border from militant migrants and violent activists.

The December 2015 Brussels meeting was the last straw. The Macedonian delegation had presented their damning physical evidence that proved that both the Greek authorities and the European Union's Frontex mission had deliberately failed to guard the European Union's own borders. Further, as a non-EU member excluded from the EURODAC database system, Macedonia had not been allowed to share intelligence on transiting migrants. Also excluded from the EURODAC system as being non-EU "third countries" were Turkey (the key exporter of migrants), Egypt (a future key exporter), and Serbia (the second-most important Balkan Route state, after Macedonia).

The European Union, through its own structural limitations on the security front, had thus set itself up to fail in a crisis situation involving a wider geographic region. At the December meeting, Ivanov's delegation announced that although cooperation with the European Union would continue, Macedonia also saw cooperation on the bilateral basis as vital, with European countries sending policemen to help patrol the border with Greece. This scenario was deeply alarming for Athens, as it meant that its embedded officials in the EU bureaucracy could no longer hide or minimize evidence of Greece's border security failure from other EU members. The major beneficiaries of Macedonia's bilateral diplomacy would be the Visegrad countries and Austria, which would increasingly press Brussels to close the Balkan Route, which happened only three months later—leaving 60,000 migrants trapped inside Greece when the illegal border was closed. By March 2016, tiny Macedonia was the de facto gatekeeper of the European Union.

EU noncooperation on the security front embittered Macedonians, who nevertheless continued protecting the borders. By spring 2016, EU officials in Skopje could only make vague explanations regarding their botched assistance.[6] Although the assistance requests were lost in bureaucracy, bilateral assistance rapidly arrived. For example, the Czech Republic donated 24 police vehicles, within 20 days of the request, as well as 800,000 euros directly to the Macedonian interior ministry's budget. And Slovenia donated 200 kilometers' of razor wire fence that would be used to safeguard the border with Greece. The disparate reactions "exemplify what is wrong with the EU," notes President Ivanov. "Since it started out as a peace project, it functions well in times of peace. But it is not prepared for times of crisis."

European mismanagement of the migration crisis only compounded the security risks. This phenomenon owed to complex political disagreements within and between European governments, parties, and EU institutions.

But the awareness of German leadership was the biggest enigma. Karl-Peter Schwartz, a senior journalist with German newspaper *Frankfurter Allgemeine Zeitung*, states that the "the closure of the Balkan route saved Germany. It was only this much criticized decision of Austria and the Western Balkan countries which reduced the migration pressure. This is a fact Merkel never acknowledged."[7]

Migration mismanagement was worsened by the reported poor relations between key decision makers and intelligence services. The leading e-xample was the German Federal Intelligence Service (*Bundesnachrichtendienst*, or BND), which was repeatedly ignored, despite its field knowledge in a tumultuous spring that climaxed with the firing of BND president Gerhard Schindler in April. Merkel's alienation from the service owed partly to the 2013 scandal in which BND–NSA collaboration was revealed. The American SIGINT service was famously found to have been tapping into even Merkel's personal telephone. By October 2016, the German *Bundestag* (parliament) had passed new guidelines restricting the BND's capacities. At the same time, the BND was during the year burdened with moving shop from its longtime Bavarian base to new headquarters in Berlin, which required the creation of a whole new sector to manage the tedious but sensitive logistics of the process.

Two senior European officials with close knowledge of the situation claim that Merkel's inherent distrust of her own intelligence service adversely affected her decision making throughout the migrant crisis; one recalls a revealing personal comment, in which the chancellor stated privately that she believed the BND to be only "working for the Americans."[8] Merkel also reportedly relied exclusively on a close circle of advisers like Wolfgang Schauble, the finance minister, and Christoph Heusgen, who was criticized for lacking expertise in security matters.[9] The cumulative result was that by spring 2016, when the situation at the European Union's external borders was becoming increasingly untenable, Merkel's evolving policy became increasingly out of touch with reality and reactive, ignoring input from both the BND and their counterparts in Greece, Macedonia, and Serbia. In short, there was a total disconnect between the Merkel cabinet and the security pros tasked with informing them on the ground, which naturally led to uninformed policy decisions. This would bode ill for citizens' trust in Merkel, as an unprecedented string of failed and successful terrorist attacks involving migrants afflicted Germany throughout the summer of 2016.

Further comment on the general dynamic between the German government and BND is provided by Phillip Ingram, a former senior British military intelligence officer and consultant specializing in international security issues. Earlier in 2016, "a senior BND officer privately expressed his frustration that they were getting nothing done. He was saying that it was very difficult to get any decisions from Berlin." Merkel's upbringing in East Germany, the NSA scandal, and a controversy over BND operations inside Germany (a practice technically illegal), Ingram notes, all influenced her general outlook toward the BND. The former British intelligence officer adds that "politicians in Germany tend to have a morbid historical fear of the intelligence services, going back to WWII."[10] As with the historical concept of "German guilt" discussed earlier in this book, which helped explain part of the government's initial welcoming stance toward refugees, the collective German experience of dangerous intelligence bodies (for example, the SS, Gestapo, and Stasi) has fueled a chronic distrust of the services—one that would become rather unhelpful during a chaotic migrant crisis with security risks.

Yet even though an increasingly volatile situation was building up at the Eidomeni border camp, where thousands of angry migrants refused to leave the closed border, few Northern Europeans had time for the rapidly inflating "migrant bubble" on the Balkan periphery. By March 22, the very heart of the European Union—the Belgian capital of Brussels—was once again on lockdown, following a deadly attack on its metro and airport that killed 32 and left over 300 injured. Police with assault rifles prowled the normally sedate city of technocrats, while the airport remained closed and citizens struggled to come to terms with the unprecedented atrocity.

Investigators rapidly established connections between the cell—based in the Muslim-immigrant neighborhood of Molenbeek—and the one that carried out the Paris attacks the previous November. The next day, French police charged one suspect for plotting an "imminent" terrorist attack with three others detained in Belgium and the Netherlands. The suspect had traveled to Syria and met with Islamic State leaders there in 2015. And just 11 days before the Brussels attacks, police in Paris had arrested four teenagers—all Muslim girls—who were allegedly planning another attack on a concert hall (to copy the November 2015 Paris attacks), communicating via social media and expecting to get money and weapons from known jihadist networks in Belgium.[11] But the arrests in Paris were far from the only European police action preceding Brussels. For one major example, on February 4, 2016, German police had arrested four Algerians, affiliated with the Islamic State, who had been planning a major attack in Berlin. Police raids targeted facilities, including refugee centers where some of the men had been hosted.[12]

The increasing role of women and migrants in Islamic terrorist plots was just one of many worrying developments to emerge from the shift in European terrorism patterns visible since the 2014 emergence of ISIS in Syria and Iraq. The volatile and complex nature of the wars there had created jihadists who were not only hardened and highly experienced, but also very resourceful in logistics, communications, and acquisition of weaponry. They also possessed an ever-widening range of contacts in various countries in and beyond Europe—a fact that was both confirmed and made more dangerous by the multinational identities of ISIS fighters and the similarly varied nationalities represented in the migrant waves.

Although these trends had already existed independent of the 2015 migration crisis, that crisis dramatically increased the risks to Europe in terms of quantity of fighters traveling the Balkan (and, to a lesser extent, Italy–Africa) Route. The crisis also had a generally beneficial outcome for Islamic terrorists because the total quantity of arriving migrants overwhelmed most European logistics systems, creating a fluid and confusing situation in which authorities simply did not have time or capacity to oversee everything and everyone—a fatal flaw that, as has been seen, stemmed from the European Union's failure to control its own external borders.

Europe after the 2015 migration crisis is now entering uncharted territory. It will take some time before it is possible to fully assess the impact that the overall phenomenon means for general European stability and the terrorism threat matrix. Yet, already, the uptick in terrorism and other violent events associated with migrants and asylum seekers is undeniable. A careful and categorical examination of the new trends visible in European terrorism following the rise of ISIS and the migration crisis shows much more dynamism and change than is presently occurring with other known forms of terrorism or organized violence (left-wing anarchist and right-wing extremism, for example). This examination must consider the terrorist threat according to categories such as weaponry used, expanded terrorist targeting and an increasing range of logistical operations. Finally, there is the general issue of violence that involves migrants; while dangerous for public safety, such violent events may not be considered terrorism but are nevertheless keeping police and intelligence services busy due to the religious and social aspects of these events.

The European terrorism pattern also became increasingly dangerous because of the expanded—and increasingly inexpensive—types of weapons used. In addition to small arms, these have included knives, machetes, metal bars, flammable materials, and even vehicles. This indicates a pattern of attacks similar to those seen in places where the offensive capabilities difference between authorities and terrorists is substantial, such as in Israel, where both soldiers and civilians have been targeted by Palestinians wielding knives or driving vehicles into crowds of people, with deadly effect. It is not certain in all cases whether limited access influenced assailants' choices of weapons, or whether there may be an aspect of "copycat" inspiration from attacks elsewhere in the world. It is probably a bit of both, but with today's instant media, news travels quickly and as such terrorist behavior across all theaters has tended to develop resemblances, whether an attack be carried out in primitive or modern conditions, or in cases where terrorists have a minimal or maximal advantage over local authorities in terms of tactical abilities and raw firepower.

However, aside from the major and well-planned armed attacks (such as in Brussels, Istanbul, and Paris) most examples point to the use of very basic, but deadly, weapons in random attacks carried out by immigrants (and new migrants). On December 21, 2014, a man shouting "Allahu Akbar" in Dijon, France, drove a truck into pedestrians, injuring 11 people.[13] A similar attack occurred the following day in Nantes, where a man driving a van plowed into 10 people attending the town's Christmas market. Both attacks had occurred after an Islamic State propaganda video was released, calling on French Muslims to "kill [non-Muslims] and spit in their faces and run over them with your cars."[14] The most infamous such attack was the Berlin Christmas Market attack on December 19, 2016, in which a convicted criminal and failed asylum seeker plowed a truck into a crowd, killing 12 people. The assailant managed to cross several European borders undetected before being shot by Italian police in Milan—a result that they attributed mostly to luck.[15]

Other, more basic weapons have frequently been used. On September 17, 2015, a knife was used by an Iraqi Islamist who attacked and injured a Berlin police officer. And a machete was used in an attack on a Jewish schoolteacher on January 11, 2016, in Marseille, France. The attack was carried out by a teenaged Turkish ISIS supporter. This attack was reminiscent of other similar attacks carried out in Turkey in recent years. And a meat cleaver was used in a January 2016 Paris police station attack by a Moroccan (who was also wearing a fake explosive belt). The attacker was shot dead. Similar basic weaponry (a knife and hatchet) were wielded by a 17-year-old Afghan refugee who injured five people, two critically while on a train near Würzburg in Germany on July 18, 2016. That refugee, too, was shot dead by arriving police officers. The method has become increasingly popular worldwide, with one high-profile case involving an Egyptian radical who was shout outside the Louvre while waving a machete at police on February 3, 2017.

These types of stabbing attacks have proven almost impossible to stop, as such basic weaponry is easily available and can never be registered in the same ways as can firearms, or even tracked (as with the sale of chemicals or fertilizers used to make bombs). The easy concealment and close-quarters usage of such weapons makes it very difficult for either police officers or victims to be aware of such a terrorist situation until it is basically too late. At present, only metal detectors at airports (and some train stations and sports stadiums) are capable of detecting such weapons. It can be expected that European transport systems will attempt to increase their capacities for detecting knives and similar weapons on the general transport grid, but it would be foolish to think that ground transport will ever be secured in the same manner as air transport; in addition to the detection risks, detailed searches would also cause considerable delays and economic losses for services that are, in general, quite safe.

When it comes to preferred terrorist targeting, in the post–9/11 era, Islamic terrorists in Europe have preferred (but are also branching out from) attacks on open public transport networks in major cities. The March 2003 attack on the Madrid metro was the first such atrocity, and was followed by the July 7, 2005, attacks on London public transport. In this respect, the March 2016 Brussels attacks and June 2016 attacks on Istanbul Airport show a remarkable target consistency in the most ambitious cases. However, the motivations were slightly different, as the earlier two were carried out in symbolic retaliation to those countries' participation in American wars in Iraq and Afghanistan, whereas the latter attacks have been attributed to a "terror for terror's sake" motivation.

Public transport targets remain attractive, especially if they have some added symbolic value. For example, a plot to "commemorate" the 10th anniversary of the London 2005 attacks by bombing the metro system there was thwarted by British police on May 28, 2015. Police found large amounts of chemicals and bomb-making equipment in the possession of the arrested would-be terrorists, a couple. Another potential attack on public transport, the target this time being a train station near Notre-Dame Cathedral in Paris, was thwarted by French police on September 8, 2016. Small-scale attacks on public transport have increased since the migrant crisis began, with greater incidents of attacks on trains. In addition to those mentioned above, an Islamic terrorist shot and stabbed passengers on a Thalys train traveling between Amsterdam and Paris on August 21, 2015, injuring five. With public-transport attacks remaining popular, we can expect a continuation of such small-scale attacks. It is also only a matter of time before the next major plot occurs on a larger scale, in the style of the Brussels and Istanbul Airport bombings.

Another traditional target of Islamic terrorism in Europe has been law enforcement and military personnel and facilities. This trend will likely intensify in the future, as European forces (whether under national, European Union, or NATO banners) take an increasing role in security operations in Africa and the Middle East. Leaving aside the many armed incidents in which long-term internal ethnic or sectarian conflicts have occurred (such as Turkey or Syria), several examples can be illustrated in the post-ISIS age. For one, on April 1, 2016, a British court convicted two local ISIS sympathizers (a Pakistani delivery driver and his uncle) for plotting to kill American and British soldiers in England. Interestingly, the plotters had planned to use asymmetric methods (such as staging road accidents) to cause diversions and obstruct police.[16]

Another thwarted attack on security services in Europe occurred in Italy on December 15, 2015. Two Islamists (one Palestinian and one Tunisian) shouting "Allahu Akbar" were arrested after trying to disarm Italian soldiers stationed outside Rome's Basilica di Santa Maria Maggiore. The attack thus had both a clear antimilitary and anti-Christian motivation.

Two other attacks on security services were thwarted in France. One week after the Rome event, French police in Orleans arrested two Islamists plotting to kill police and army personnel in that city. Somewhat earlier, on November 2, 2015, a French citizen who had tried (and failed) to join ISIS in Syria was arrested and charged for plotting to kill sailors at the country's main naval base, in Toulon.

In an earlier attack—one of four in a three-week period—an Islamist brandishing a knife attacked a police station in Joué-lès-Tours, France, injuring three officers before being killed. Two further traditional targets of Islamic terrorism in Europe have been Christians and Jews. Islamists, and particularly returning foreign fighters and young migrants, are increasingly targeting members of these religions—a reflection of the type of sectarian brutality ISIS has emphasized in Syria and Iraq. Indeed, while terrorist attacks against Jews in previous decades often came as retaliation or political statements against the state of Israel, the post-ISIS attacks seem to be motivated by sheer religious hatred. For example, a French-born veteran of the Syrian jihad killed four people at the Jewish Museum in Brussels, on May 24, 2014.[17] Later, on February 14–15, 2015, a lone gunman opened fire on Copenhagen's Great Synagogue, after having attacked a local café, killing two civilians and injuring five others. And on January 11, 2016, a 15-year-old Turkish ISIS supporter attacked a Jewish schoolteacher in Marseille with a machete, as mentioned above.

Historically, the Israeli state has protested such attacks in Europe and has used its security services to protect Jewish communities. However, today this trend may be changing. "In the past two to three years, there were incidents [targeting Jews], particularly in Belgium and France," notes Israeli security expert and journalist Melman. "There was an increase in plots against Jewish populations, but frankly the Israeli intelligence is less and less involved in providing defense on the ground—it's now more a matter for the local authorities and local Jewish communities themselves. Of course, it is still part of Israel's agenda to be involved, to monitor, and to provide early warning, but the involvement is less than in past." In addition, Melman downplays the possibility of future terrorist plots by Iran in Europe. "It is unlikely that Iran, which is preoccupied with its wars in Syria and Iraq and benefits from lifting the sanctions, will get involved in terror attacks on European soil. Nevertheless Iran will continue to plot against Israel via its proxies, such as Hezbollah."[18]

For Christians, several shocking events have occurred since the explosion of the migrant crisis. The worst to date happened on July 26, 2016, in France, when two ISIS terrorists stormed a church in Rouen and ritually murdered an elderly priest by slitting his throat. The terrorists took four nuns hostage before people arrived and killed them. One of these terrorists had already been on the French government's terror watch-list. The murder of a defenseless elderly priest in his own church in France came as a wake-up call—and sparked public criticism of Pope Francis's ardent calls for Catholics to embrace the pro-migrant cause.

For general analysts, the most interesting new development in Islamic terrorist targeting is its expansion to the general leisure sector. This phenomenon was exemplified by the Paris attacks, which covered everything from café to concert hall to sports stadium in November 2015. Another example from February of that year was that of the Islamist gunman had opened fire at the Krudttoenden café in Denmark's capital of Copenhagen, before moving on to the city's synagogue. A similar attack would later be thwarted in Belgium, where on June 18, 2016, police arrested three Muslims plotting to attack a party organized to watch a soccer match.

The increased targeting of leisure-sector places is a major concern for the future in Europe. "Soft targets such as these are easier to attack, and create mayhem in everyday life—thus breaking down the morale of the population," states Ioannis Michaletos, a leading Greek security analyst. "European security agencies can hardly cope and protect myriads of soft targets. We should expect this trend to continue."[19] Within the same category, sports venues and public celebrations are other types of soft targets increasingly being targeted by terrorists. Four days after the Paris attacks of November 13, 2015, a German soccer match in the city of Hanover was canceled after French intelligence warned German police that a bomb plot against the game had been planned by Islamists. And Turkey's New Year's Eve celebrations in Ankara were luckily safeguarded when police there arrested two ISIS militants planning suicide attacks on the capital's busy Kizilay Square, on December 29, 2015.

During Germany's 2016 summer of terror, in addition to the Würzburg train attack, the busy central pedestrian zone of Düsseldorf became the planned target of another plot that was successfully thwarted on June 2, 2016, when police arrested three Syrian ISIS operatives. Soon after, on July 24, 2016, a wine bar in Ansbach was targeted by a suicide bomber, injuring 15 Germans. The intended target of the ISIS-inspired bomber had been the town's large music festival.

Terrorist attacks near tourist attractions and travel destinations in Europe present another notable and disturbing development, which shows clear resemblances with attacks carried out in recent years in places like Somalia, Tunisia, West Africa, Bangladesh, and other Muslim countries with Western visitors. With the ISIS promotion of a global jihadist ideology, the commingling of varied Muslim nationalities in Europe due to the migrant crisis, and the radicalizing effect of social media, there is no reason why tomorrow's tourism-sector attacks could not take place in Cannes, Monaco, an Alpine ski resort, or a luxurious Greek island.

Several examples of terrorist plots on tourism sites in Europe already exist. On January 12, 2016, an ISIS suicide bomber killed 10 tourists and injured 15 more near the Theodosian Obelisk, an attraction near the famed

Blue Mosque in Istanbul's most-visited historic neighborhood, Sultanah-met. This attack—and subsequent ones by ISIS and the Kurdish PKK (Kurdistan Worker's Party)—severely damaged Turkey's tourism econ-omy in 2016 (as did the temporary Russian tourism boycott of the country due to the downing of a Russian fighter plane by the Turkish Air Force over Syrian territory). Modern terrorism thus has a wider ripple effect that, in damaging traditional tourism economies, also helps create conditions for greater local participation in illicit activities to make ends meet. In the case of Turkey, migrant trafficking and related ventures benefited from the lost tourism opportunities in 2015 and 2016. In France, where the terrorism stigma has also heavily affected the all-important tourism economy, police arrested two Islamists carrying weapons and a copy of the Koran outside Disneyland Paris. Far to the south, on Albania's Adriatic coast, where the town of Vlore is becoming a more popular tourist destination, a Kosovar Albanian shouting "Allahu Akbar" attacked and attempted to kidnap sev-eral visitors.[20]

The most concerning aspects of the postmigrant crisis threat spectrum, in part because it is so random, is attacks on individuals by "lone wolf" terrorists. Some of the above-cited examples fall into this category. On June 26, 2015, a French factory worker was also beheaded in Saint-Quen-tin-Fallavier, near Lyon. Some 11 more were injured in an attack marked by Islamist flags, Arabic-language epithets, and a factory fire.[21] And, on June 14, 2016, a French policeman and his wife were stabbed to death in the town of Magnanville, by an ISIS fanatic.[22] In Scandinavia, the conver-gence of terrorism and the migrant crisis hit home on August 10, when two Swedes were randomly stabbed to death by an Eritrean migrant, while shopping at IKEA in the town of Västerås; according to news reports, the attacker (who then stabbed himself) was seeking revenge against Sweden after his asylum request was denied.

In the big picture, when it comes to countries, the present and expected terrorism risk for European states can be divided into several categories. According to security experts like Ioannis Michaletos, three current threat levels exist. At highest risk are Britain, France, Germany, Sweden, Den-mark, and the Netherlands. These countries are "primarily at risk from its existing, domestic jihadist networks." In the group of European countries at secondary risk, the Greek expert lists Spain, Italy, Austria, and Norway. Finally, a third group of countries that face lesser danger from Islamic ter-rorists include Greece, Cyprus, Bulgaria, Ireland, and Portugal.[23]

Why are different countries at greater or lesser risk? It is both a logis-tical and ideological question. For places like Germany and Sweden, which have suffered the largest sudden jump in migrant numbers since 2015, it is largely a volume issue. However, numerous preexisting Mus-lim ghettoes in cities like Malmö, Sweden, have become "no-go areas" for police and represent enclaves guarded by organized gangs who carry out criminal activities and maintain a fetid atmosphere in which extremism can flourish, and in which internal dissent from nonradicalized Muslims is not tolerated. And, the fact that the now-infamous Molenbeek district of Brussels—the neighborhood that cultivated several of the terrorists involved with the Brussels attacks—is within walking distance of the European Union's key institutions and posh urban center shows that such Islamist enclaves are hardly only limited to industrial zones on the outskirts of cities.

As for the second motivation, France—and to a lesser extent, Italy— seems to be targeted due to ideological reasons. In the former, where a long history of colonialism has left a large French-speaking population of North Africans, the fiercely secular character of the republic is itself a call to war. Strong public opinion, and occasional legislation, against wearing of the Muslim hijab and general cultural differences has sparked an aggressive Islamic ideological and terrorist opposition. Major organized attacks like the January 2015 Paris shootings, in which two Islamists sought to "avenge" the Prophet Muhammad by executing cartoonists at the offices of satirical magazine *Charlie Hebdo*, indicate clearly the continuing tension between an Islamist supremacist ideology and republican French values.

In Italy, the main ideological goal—one that was directly espoused by Islamic State propaganda—is the destruction of Christianity, and its perceived major symbol, the Vatican. Although the Catholic Church has a strong worldwide intelligence network that is complemented by Italian state services and other intergovernmental cooperative bodies, the threat will remain for the foreseeable future. However, simply by quantitative comparison to France, "the jihadist breeding ground in Italy is rather limited," attests Marco Giulio Barone, an Italian security analyst at *Il Café Geopolitico*. "The government has been quite effective at tracking and expelling potentially malicious individuals." Although noting that even terrorism-minded migrants see other countries as a more prime target than Italy, Barone, however, adds that the potential for domestic terrorism linked to migration "is expanding, as Italy has serious leakages in managing migrants within its infrastructure. This creates a porosity, which is every day more and more known on the other side of the Mediterranean."[24] In other words, people-traffickers in Libya, Egypt, and elsewhere continually monitor the abilities of social services and immigration programs in destination countries like Italy, in order to exploit the weaknesses of the system.

Another compelling aspect of European terrorism in the post-ISIS world is the ever-widening logistical range of support structures and operational capacities. This terrorist "reach" has indisputably been expanded by the migration crisis. The phenomenon includes both cases of plots within Europe that are planned from beyond its borders, and the widening area of operations within Europe, particularly the Balkans, due to the pull effect that groups like ISIS and Jabhat Al Nusra had from 2014 until early

2016—and the effective networks created by European fighters active in both regions.

The geographic expansion of plot preparation was attested on April 22, when Danish authorities decorated an American soldier in Afghanistan, who had passed on intelligence that helped police uncover a plot to blow up a school in Denmark.[25] Elsewhere, on February 8, 2016, Russian police arrested seven ISIS members who had been planning terror attacks in Moscow and St. Petersburg.[26] They had arrived from Turkey, which has been the central conduit for foreign fighters—as well as refugees and migrants—passing to and from Syria and other countries. This has partly been due to geography and Turkish policy (i.e., supporting those fighting against the Assad regime), but was also an unintended consequence of an earlier, ambitious Turkish foreign policy of "zero problems with neighbors," that began well in advance of the Syrian conflict. In seeking to develop its global stature, Turkey abolished visas for many (especially Muslim) countries, and opened numerous embassies, including 17 new ones across Africa by 2010.[27] This heightened diplomatic presence, as well as a large increase in Turkish Airlines flight destinations, expedited the travel of migrants, and perhaps terrorists, during the past few years. Numerous cases exist of people from African countries who took advantage of the no-visa policy and inexpensive airfare to travel to Turkey before continuing to Greece by sea since 2014.[28]

Another key example of terrorism terrain and logistics expansion is the Balkans, where wars in Bosnia and Kosovo during the 1990s created both jihadist fighting and logistics structures, strong infrastructure, and extremist indoctrination programs led by Saudi Arabia and other exporters of Islamist ideologies. The result of this long-term operation has been the development of a small, but dangerous, number of jihadists from the Balkans who have gone on to fight in Iraq and Syria. The total estimate for these fighters (typically, ethnic Bosniak and Albanian) is around 1,000 persons. Until relatively recently, the Balkan Islamic extremist network was used as a logistical and ideological hub with links in three directions: to Turkey, the Gulf, and MENA to the south; Italy to the west; and Austria, Switzerland, and Germany to the north. In the latter two places, large Balkan diasporas live. Although Bosnia has its own rural villages run by Wahhabi extremists since the 1990s, the Balkans itself was itself never considered a target. But that might be changing.

On April 27, 2015, a Bosniak Wahhabi terrorist attacked a police station in Zvornik (located in Bosnia's Orthodox Christian entity, the Republika Srpska), killing one police officer and injuring two others before being killed by police. Then, on November 18, 2015, another local Islamist killed two soldiers and injured civilians, leaving three dead and five wounded in the capital of Sarajevo. Evidence of Balkan nationals' participation in Middle Eastern jihad led to the passage of special foreign fighters' laws between 2014 and 2015, in line with U.S. policy, in several countries. This provided a legal basis for police to target jihadists and radical imams involved in the logistics and recruitment activities that connect the Middle East and Western Europe theaters of operation. In 2016, the United States also announced a new NATO "center for excellence" would be built in Tirana to help coordinate the fight against violent extremism regionally.[29]

From 2014, the increasing participation of Balkan fighters in the ranks of Al Nusra and Islamic State—which from early on started using the Albanian language for propaganda purposes—caused embarrassment for governments, particularly that of Kosovo. The discomfiture became particularly acute when a Kosovar Albanian, Lavdrim Muhaxheri, became world-famous for acts of cruelty and beheadings captured on YouTube videos.[30] Kosovo was in fact the region's top exporter of jihadists. In August 2014, Kosovar police arrested 40 people suspected of supporting ISIS and other groups.[31] In March 2015, the law against "foreign fighters" was finally passed.[32] In May 2016, police "charged 67 people, arrested 14 imams and shut down 19 Muslim organizations for acting against the Constitution, inciting hatred and recruiting for terrorism," reported the *New York Times*, in a scathing report that highlighted Saudi influence locally.[33] Kosovar authorities jailed an ISIS recruiter and imam, Zekerija Qazimi, for 10 years.[34] Next door, over two-dozen youths from southern Albanian villages had joined the Islamist ranks in Syria after 2011. As of May 2015, approximately 150 of the 500 ethnic Albanian fighters in Syria and Iraq were Albanian citizens.[35] Some, like the alleged head recruiter, former imam of Leshnica village Almir Daci, was reported to have died while fighting in April 2016.[36] Daci had been a key propagandist for a militant brigade composed of Balkan volunteers.[37]

Ethnic Albanians elsewhere in the Balkans have been targeted by police for terrorism links. In early August 2015, while affected by a political crisis and also bearing the full brunt of the migrant crisis, Macedonian police somehow found time to launch Operation Kelija (Cell), raiding mosques, NGO offices, and residences associated with ethnic Albanian recruiters and fighters for ISIS in five cities.[38] Suspects arrested included Rexhep Memishi, a known radical imam; another 27 suspects were believed to be in Syria. The U.S. Embassy in Skopje praised the action as contributing to regional and global efforts against the "evil of terrorism."[39] In March 2016, a court jailed six persons (including the self-proclaimed imam) for seven years.

Balkan diaspora members elsewhere in Europe have also been targeted, particularly in northern Italy, where two operations in 2016 linked Kosovar Albanian émigrés with ISIS. In November 2015, four Kosovar Albanians in the small town of Chiari, Italy, were arrested; according to Giovanni De Stavola of DIGOS, the Italian police's division for general investigations and special operations, "the group was directing its Daesh [Islamic State] propaganda towards people coming from the Balkan region and residing in Italy. The four arrested were members of the group and have documented contacts with jihadist networks in the Balkans guided by Lavdrim Muhaxheri." Kosovar police simultaneously arrested another cell member, in eastern Kosovo.[40]

In addition to personnel networks, the Balkans has also become a conduit for the smuggling of arms that end up in the hands of terrorists. According to Greek analyst Michaletos, "a hybrid form which has emerged is the mix of second-generation Muslims, who are EU citizens with collaborators from the Western Balkans." He cites the example of the Nice attack, in which the Tunisian French driver "had acquired weaponry from Albanians. And, there was the case of the Paris attacks of November 2015, where some of the weapons were most probably imported from Bosnia."[41]

The increasing role of women in European jihad is also very significant, and owes directly to the general increased role of women—which ISIS heavily advertised—in logistics and even fighting for the terrorist outfit. In cases of beating surveillance or border detection, women are useful to terrorists by generally raising less suspicion than men. But what is perhaps most interesting about the phenomenon is the increased enthusiasm and motivation young radicalized women are showing today. In the case of the thwarted Paris train station attack of September 2016, three women (including one described by French police as a "major" ISIS recruiter) played the main role. According to police, another one of them had previously been engaged to two terrorist fighters. Another major example of female participation in terrorism, mentioned above, was the March 11, 2016, arrest of four teenage girls in Paris who were allegedly planning another attack on a concert hall. Further, a 16-year-old girl was among the four aspiring terrorists arrested in February 2017 when police discovered bomb-making materiel in a house near Montpellier, France.[42] These cases indicate the disturbing expansion of terrorism participation beyond traditional gender lines.

Although not every expert (and certainly not every European politician) believes that a net increase in migrants will lead to a similar rise in terrorism, the crisis of 2015 revealed another problem that is fundamental to the clash of cultures being witnessed across Europe today: the increasing number of violent attacks carried out by migrants that are not counted as terrorism, but that inspire public fear, as well as counterattacks from right-wing and other groups. Such violence includes (but is not limited to): "false alarm" bomb threats that cause evacuations of transport and other facilities; the mass assaults on women at celebrations and festivals in Germany and Sweden; attacks on bathers at swimming pools; the burnings of migrant camps and asylum centers (by both migrants and their opponents); random torching of cars in Scandinavia and France; and attacks on truck drivers and motorists driving to the Channel Tunnel in France.

Such violence also includes incidents of a planned and sometimes paramilitary nature that, with some simple upgrades in weaponry, could easily become lethal. One example was that of migrant youths attempting to storm the Greek–Macedonian border on April 10, 2016, who shouted "Allahu Akbar" while hurling stones at police. They also tried to commandeer a railroad car to break the fence. The attackers even spread toothpaste across their faces (to protect against tear gas) and split into smaller groups to tactically widen the perimeter of activity. These tactics, honed in the frustration of an overcrowded refugee camp, can easily be perfected in any number of urban warfare scenarios.

Similarly, as has been seen from the Calais "Jungle" Camp in France and camps across Greece, refugee camps in general are breeding grounds for instability. For another similar example, on January 26, 2016, a gun battle occurred in the Grande-Synthe migrant camp in northern France. Rival human-trafficking gangs fought it amid humanitarian organization reports that Muslim migrants sought to force Christian refugees from the camp.[43]

Taken together, the cumulative result of this pattern of activity is an increasingly complex operational atmosphere, and an increasing backlog of information for security services to pore through. Both successful and foiled terroristic and other violent events are very expensive—not only in terms of damages, injuries, and human lives, but in terms of police, intelligence, and medical-care budgets. In a world where one telephone call can cause massive disruption and paranoia (for example, a false bomb threat to an airport), terrorism has a pervasive effect that cannot be properly calculated. Although there is no quantifying the general fear and malaise that follows terrorist attacks and creates a general social paralysis, economists do try to find some financial approximations. For example, when Brussels was under lockdown for several days in November 2015, following the Paris attacks, the economic losses accompanying this paralysis were assessed at 51.7 million euros per day.[44]

Terrorism trends are notoriously hard to predict and have led to much disagreement. Primarily this is due to varying interpretations of statistics, motives, and groups. Often it does not take into account the many failed plots—most of which the general public never is aware of—that cannot be counted accurately. Comparative statistics that weigh terrorism trends based on casualty numbers are also problematic for similar reasons. And there is also the issue raised by that old adage: "one man's terrorist is another man's freedom fighter." This was seen in Kosovo in the 1990s and most recently in Syria, where the United States came under criticism for failing to bomb (or at least influence) the Jabhat al Nusra group controlling Eastern Aleppo. Russia argued this U.S. inactivity was simply because this group was fighting the Syrian government. An even more complex example, in the same conflict, is that of the Kurdish YPG (People's Protection

Units) in Syria, a key ally of both the United States and Syria, which Turkey considers (along with the Kurdish PKK fighting the Turkish for over 30 years) as terrorists. The modern tendency for such complex local messes to spring up in different conflict zones has made it almost impossible to make accurate tallies of terrorism activity, at least in the Middle East and North Africa.

In Europe, different varieties of terrorism exist, complicating the situation in another way. Along with the most pressing issue—that of terrorism motivated by Islamic beliefs—there is currently a resurgence of left-wing terrorism and right-wing violence. All of this is keeping security services very busy—and multiplying the general confusion and disagreement among and within European publics over terrorism and other organized violence. The heavily politicized nature of the migration crisis has been obvious, of course, in the type of media coverage devoted to it. But as European leaders have grappled with both policy formation and public relations, the future of terrorism—and the effect that migration will have on it—is becoming increasingly difficult to assess.

A large part of this has to do with definitions, methodology, and relative subjectivity of analysis. Arguments about the present and future of terrorism in Europe often have relied on statistics and historical trends that are only valid in certain contexts or that mislead, sometimes deliberately so. The closeness of national and party political leaders in Europe with specific policies, and their endorsement or criticism in the media, have led to a situation in which terrorism discussions have become de facto political. Adding the migration phenomenon into this mix has made it even harder to discern the facts and to provide what is most needed—that is, a sober and unbiased future analysis.

International law enforcement agencies often provide useful statistics, but nonetheless caution must be taken when assessing statistical findings. For example, a Swedish economist in 2011 exposed how Europol had defined "terrorism" rather broadly (to include window-smashing and property damage); this generous categorization allowed Europol to make the rather remarkable claim that over 99 percent of European terrorist attacks from 2007 to 2009 had in fact been carried out by non-Muslims.[45]

In the aftermath of the March 2016 Islamic State terrorist attacks on the Brussels metro and airport, a trickle of reports from media and think tanks attempted to address the general scale of terrorism's risk to Europe. Some contextualized the incident as proof of an increasingly dangerous public security threat. However, others challenged these concerns, while ignoring the widespread belief among many Europeans that terrorism activity had at least some relation to migration policy. These reports pointed to graphs and statistics to make the point that Europe was in fact doing rather well.

For example, the World Economic Forum (host of an annual meeting of top globalist leaders and business tycoons in Davos, Switzerland) concluded that "our perspective may be historically skewed: the data shows this isn't actually the deadliest spate of terrorist attacks the region has seen." The report cited an academic, who rather remarkably claimed that "Western Europe is perhaps more peaceful now than at any point in modern human history."[46] Similarly in July, Britain's left-leaning *Guardian* newspaper announced that the terror threat to Europe was "waning." It cited figures that indicated "Western Europe is experiencing a higher number of attacks but lower death tolls compared to the 1980s."[47] However, the newspaper also admitted the disparity was partly due to a discrepancy created by a few high-profile and geographically limited cases back then, such as the Lockerbie bombing and various IRA operations.

Although the media and interest groups have been quick to make interpretations, the problematic usage of statistics, definitions, and historical examples make any exercise in comparison a somewhat doomed endeavor. Terrorism bean counting can also be counterproductive because too much information is bound to remain forever absent: while perhaps known foiled plots can be counted, there is simply too much intelligence that governments do not share (even between their own services) that, if publicized, could totally change the perception of general risk. Statistical evaluations for comparative purposes also do not generally account for logistical activity carried out on European soil, which might lead to attacks elsewhere. Here, a famous example would be the "Hamburg Cell," which played a key role in plotting the 9/11 attacks, with members traveling between Germany and Afghanistan and later, to the United States.[48] If that single example alone was to be factored in to the general analysis, Europe would be considered a world leader in exporting serious terrorist plots. But, of course, things are not so simple.

Therefore, instead of trying to assess future terrorism trends or judging whether they are increasing or decreasing based on statistics and historical comparisons, it might prove more useful to simply present a composite picture of the wider threat landscape that exists today in Europe because of the convergence of Islamic terrorism and related security events; left-wing and right-wing violence (which will be discussed in later chapters) are only the most prominent of other forms of public unrest. In this light, the oversimplified, political argument over whether migrants cause terrorism, and whether terrorism should be restricted only to Islamic-rooted attacks, is not really relevant. Rather, we should ask whether migration—as a socially and politically divisive phenomenon, one with a definite security aspect—plays a role in enhancing the general process of public violence creation being witnessed today.

Indeed, it is clear that migration not only plays a role in this process, but is in fact the one issue connecting almost all forms of organized violence in Europe today, through its fundamental relationship with concepts like racism, religious and cultural opinions, other ideological causes, and ground actions. Aside from the many known cases of migrants involved (directly or indirectly) with terrorist attacks or other acts of violence, the protests, shootings, and attacks carried out by right- and left-wing groups and others thus all fundamentally intersect with the migration issue, as will be seen in subsequent chapters. This widened threat landscape in Europe today is causing a major securitization trend—one that bases its justification on the need to handle everything from student protests in France to anarchist attacks in Greece and far-right violence in Scandinavia, in addition to Islamic terrorism.

Concerning the contribution of migration to the widened terrorism threat arena, experts see a clear quantitative jump since the crisis of 2015. According to the British former intelligence officer, Phillip Ingram, "Conservative estimates suggest thousands of extremists have managed to slip in through the refugee crisis. And a significant number of them have experience in fighting, and in planning not only simple operations, but the kind of complex ones seen in Paris and Brussels."[49]

According to Greek security expert Michaletos,

The number of radicalized persons in Europe is increasing, as is the number of jihadist fighters returning to EU countries. There are at least 300,000 people, but probably more, with either fake or incomplete identity documents. If we add to this number those migrants who had arrived in Europe before the crisis, plus the ongoing radicalization process from the second and third generation of Muslims in the EU, then we will likely face urban destabilization and terrorism. Security agencies will barely be able to cope with such challenges.[50]

Since Russian involvement in Syria and the migration crisis began, numerous analysts have posited that foreign military intervention against the Islamic State would result in the terrorist group sending its fighters elsewhere as its territorial base began to shrink. With the United States and Iraqi coalition assault on ISIS-held Mosul in October 2016, this process was expected to accelerate. This territorial "squeeze" on the so-called caliphate, in tandem with the refugee crisis, activated a previously decided terrorist plan to disperse fighters not just across Europe, but across the world, security sources say. Also, as territory continued to be lost, ISIS leaders began to discourage fighters from traveling to Syria.

Instead, since about April 2015, ISIS leaders "have urged supporters in Europe to stay home and wait for instructions," says Ingram, who studies jihadist communications on social media, closed messaging services, and the Dark Web. "I have seen intercepts from closed channels where these calls have gone out. Also, ISIS has used these communications channels to disseminate increasingly sophisticated training videos and manuals, teaching people how to set up secure communications channels, and how to carry out military-style attacks using different weapons systems." Beyond simple "educational" purposes, the British expert says, these kinds of closed-channel electronic groups have been used for "command-and-control purposes, to coordinate operations in near real time. As we saw in the Brussels and Paris attacks, information was being passed back into Syria and Iraq during the attacks. This shows a certain level of sophistication. They have been planning this transition for some time. Every insurgency in the past has seen military and political phases, and so with ISIS we are seeing a transition from a ground-holding entity to an amorphous, multinational based terrorist campaign like al Qaeda was."[51]

Different countries have different challenges in fighting this threat. In places like Belgium and Sweden, immigrant neighborhoods that have essentially become ghettoes by choice are openly hostile to authorities, to the extent that the latter are reticent to act locally (the same can be said for some parts of rural Bosnia or Albania). In the case of Italy, which is a frontline migration country, logistics hub, and possibly even target of terrorism itself, the security services have three specific problems. "As the Muslim population increases, the expertise available is limited," notes security expert Marco Giulio Barone. "In particular, police and carabinieri have had trouble finding reliable Arabic-speaking personnel and/or translators. This has slowed down investigations and capacities for deep penetration. Secondly, some officers have been found to have superficial capabilities or become corrupted. And third, in Italy migration and counter-terrorism policies tend to be highly unpopular, and public support for police initiatives is often low. Thus, government efforts are often less than proportional to the challenge."[52]

The result of these realities is a different, and uniquely Italian counterterrorism model of rapid and discreet action. Experts like Edward N. Luttwak, a senior associate at the Center for Strategic and International Studies who has held numerous security posts in the U.S. government, have lauded Italian tactics over the "encyclopedic" method of countries like Britain, France, or Belgium, in which vast amounts of data on potential suspects are collected before anything is done. By contrast, the Italians "take action the moment the very first indication comes in," Luttwak explains. "This is sometimes a phone or e-mail intercept, and sometimes a tip-off from an agent." If an "expert interrogation" indicates that the suspect may be dangerous, authorities minutely examine his record for any petty crime or irregularity. Often such infractions alone warrant deportation. Italy is thus plagued much less than are France, Belgium, or other countries with an overabundance of petty criminals prone to radicalization, because of a conscious effort to reduce the numbers of potentially problematic suspects.[53]

Finally, one of the most fascinating questions to emerge from the migration phenomenon and European security concerns is how both terrorist organizations and foreign intelligence services are targeting Europe's "Generation Unknown" of migrants. From the perspective of both the European security response, and the future architecture of HUMINT operations involving the Continent, this is perhaps the most important intelligence issue for the future. In this regard, a primary security threat has involved refugee camps teeming with angry, isolated, and vulnerable persons of all ages. People trapped in such confined spaces for long periods of time are particularly exposed to terrorist recruiters, who seek to infiltrate and indoctrinate refugees, making contacts and preparations for future activities. Recruiters have tried to win over migrants during their travels, while in refugee camps, and also later upon arrival in the European Union.

As the Islamic State continued to lose territory in the MENA through 2016, their goal was to create sleeper cells that can be activated later. This concern manifested in September 2016, when Germany's GSG 9 special operations unit arrested three Syrian refugees suspected of belonging to an ISIS sleeper cell. According to German officials, they had received military training from ISIS, which then provided money, documents, and telephones for the men to travel the Balkan Route in November 2015 and get to Germany, "with the intention of 'carrying out a previously determined order [from IS] or to await further instructions.'"[54] The arrests came just weeks after senior German police officials had warned that ISIS sleeper cells and "hit squads" had accompanied refugees into the country, while in July, the Federal Criminal Police (BKA) had revealed that it had "information on 410 leads on possible terrorists among asylum seekers in Germany."[55] In the southern region of Bavaria, deputy intelligence chief Manfred Hauser stated that "we have substantial reports that among the refugees there are hit squads. There are hundreds of these reports, some from refugees themselves."[56]

According to experts like Ingram, terrorist recruiters "have a complete pool of people who are disaffected—people who had been told Europe would be like paradise, but then find that the reality is often living in slums, facing discrimination, having health problems, etc. If they have experienced such propaganda from recruiters while also kept cold, wet, hungry and perhaps abused in refugee camps, within a year they will be in a different position, and vulnerable to changes of thinking and mindset, compared to when they started their journey."[57]

Logistically speaking, the dozens of camps and chaotic conditions that characterized the migrant crisis have proven broadly beneficial for infiltration by not only extremist but also criminal and ideological groups. The Israeli security expert Yossi Melman notes that "it is easy to plant terrorists or agents within migrant groups, and I assume this is what ISIS has tried to do. On the other hand, migrant camps are also recruiting grounds for foreign intelligence agencies seeking to infiltrate terrorist networks and get further info about them."[58]

Indeed, the migration crisis has created a sort of renaissance for HUMINT (human intelligence) that is especially interesting considering the modern reliance on SIGINT (signals intelligence) and ELINT (electronic intelligence) by major intelligence services. The migration crisis has in this respect also given an outsized role to smaller services that lack technical capacities but have good levels of ground penetration. "Intelligence agencies have a huge opportunity to get inside the camps and identify potential terrorists coming in," notes Ingram. "And they also can find individuals who could be groomed to move into communities who could gather information. Whether they have properly exploited this is not sure."[59]

An officer with Bulgaria's counterintelligence service, the State Agency for National Security (Darzhavna agentsiya Natsionalna sigurnost, or DANS) explains that the process of engaging with migrants and determining their true intentions requires patience, as well as intuition, to be successful. "Interviewing these people who came in our country, I have had cases where they tried to deceive me about their true identities and beliefs," he states. "It was only after repeating and rephrasing questions and adding other context that I was able to determine if they were trying to conceal something that hinted at support for terrorism."[60]

Indeed, the process of gathering intelligence from the refugee flows must be carefully done, as it can have unwanted side effects—especially considering the natural impulse of intelligence agencies to gather as much information as possible and as quickly as possible. Indeed, history is rife with disastrous consequences resulting directly from intelligence gathered from "refugees" in Europe, like that of Rafid Ahmed Alwan (later codenamed Curveball) who fled Iraq for Germany in 1999. An overly credulous BND passed on his claim's about Saddam Hussein's alleged weapons of mass destruction program to the CIA. The since-discredited "intelligence" went straight into the George W. Bush administration's dossier against Iraq, and was used as evidence justifying the disastrous 2003 invasion. Reporting in 2008, the *Los Angeles Times* noted that although "Curveball" had told an eager BND much, he "didn't disclose that he had been fired at least twice for dishonesty, or that he fled Iraq to avoid arrest. But he did tell some whoppers that should have raised warnings about his credibility."[61]

The penetration of refugee camps and streams by foreign intelligence services "is actually an old method, but indeed one with high risks," states Michaletos:

There have been cases in France, Belgium, Britain, and the Netherlands in the past decade in which double agents were used—but also went 'rogue,' and also dealt with criminal activities, thus causing a boomerang effect. Recruiting a terrorist or an extremist is an extremely sensitive operation that has to be carefully sanctioned and monitored all the way through. Otherwise, the 'agent' acquires sensitive information around the modus operandi of the state forces, plus training that could be used effectively against the state. Further, he would then be able to perform disinformation activities and damage a wide range of operations. In other words, dealing with these people is a double-edged sword.[62]

Above and beyond the binary concepts of promoters and adversaries of terrorism (as represented by terrorism recruiters and state agencies, respectively), there is the considerable gray area in between—an area that can allow for a great deal of mischief to be made by parties with rival agendas. The outcomes, and indeed existence, of such work will never be known to the public. Particularly when covert actors assume the guise of other persons (such as migrant activists, humanitarian workers, doctors, legal advisers, media members, and more), the possibilities are both limitless and virtually untraceable.

The very nature of such shadow operations make them very difficult to prove, let alone identify. Suffice it to say that wherever there are dueling agendas on political, security, or economic grounds (both internally and externally), intelligence agencies will try to press their advantage to achieve "results on the ground." The migration crisis has provided ideal conditions for the instrumentalization of a volatile situation for intelligence purposes, and professionals involved are well aware of this fact. The infrastructure of refugee camps has also had the effect of developing new internal networks that remain intact once the camps are closed, but across a much wider geographic area. For example, after the Greek border camp of Eidomeni was dismantled in early summer 2016, its residents were dispersed to government-controlled camps where the "veterans" of Eidomeni simply diversified their reach and incorporated their networks with those of Greek anarchists actively working for the migrant cause.[63] In October 2016, the French authorities closed the much larger and more long-standing Calais camp, with a similar goal of dispersing people with existing networks all across France. That will likely have serious ramifications for the state's ability to control migrant-related issues well into the future.

In the big picture, the increasingly polarized and divisive Europe of today is unlikely to see great improvements toward the vaunted pursuit of "intelligence sharing" in years ahead. Although there will be (and already are) improvements on an institutional level with experiments like the European Coast Guard service in the Mediterranean, the European Union's restrictive bureaucracy and internal rivalries on the national and interservice levels will continue to complicate HUMINT cooperation and results. The relative ease by which the migration system can be manipulated for intelligence purposes also adds an intriguing factor of unpredictability. This cumulative forecast indicates that the European security atmosphere will be an ever foggier one in the years ahead.

CHAPTER 5

Organized Crime, Organized Chaos, and the General Migration Economy

Under the August sun, surrounded by young helpers, he ran up in the decrepit yard of an abandoned toilet paper factory, SOFTEX, which the Greek military had requisitioned for use as a migrant camp following the forced breakup of the Eidomeni border mess. "Two euros! Two euros!" the Pakistani shouted, pointing down at a bucket emblazoned with a faded UNHCR logo, and bursting with packs of contraband cigarettes.

Although the migrants of SOFTEX had clearly made connections with organized crime in nearby Thessaloniki since arriving two months earlier, the army man in charge was adamant that there were no signs of crime around the camp, where the inmates had taken to eating from a British Pakistani NGO's food truck that would loiter outside the entrance. They were apparently dissatisfied with the army rations that were provided by a local contractor.[1]

In order to understand the general economy that has grown along with the migration phenomenon, and the symbiotic role of both organized crime and the "legitimate" sector in it, we must first define what that general economy is. Thus, we can understand the migration economy as an eco-system that encompasses numerous industries, as a dynamic environment in which the many players are continually obliged to adapt their strategies and positions to match developing situations. The general migration economy is where the local, national, and supranational aspects of migration meet, and where the activities of licit and illicit interests converge. The migration economy is also that realm where the movement of capital outpaces that of state control, and where the very structure of finance is amenable to both classic organized crime and the equally concealed accountancy of the white-collar world. And, in both its legal and illegal aspects, the general migrant economy has become a key part of a global economic consolidation that seeks to continually increase the scope of its activities through constant territorial expansion.

The migration economy will become increasingly important to a world economy that is volatile and sensitive to periodic financial collapse, unsustainable debt, labor displacement, the loss (and automation) of manufacturing in the developed world and so on. In the place of the economic drivers of the past, we are seeing increasingly globalized policies built around concepts like resource depletion, chronic poverty, overpopulation, and climate change. In fact, the rhetoric around these phenomena are essentially identical to that concerning migration: all of them are defined as global challenges requiring continuous emergency funds and action, while also being at the same time depicted as morbidly inevitable and beyond solution.

Sustaining this economy requires, from the illicit side, a continued quantity of persons and goods to be trafficked and, from the "legitimate" side, a continuous injection of public funds, philanthropic donations, and certain types of "investment" on the local, national, and supranational levels. From the latter side, the migration economy is thus somewhat artificial. It is one of several high-profile "created" industries that, while being fundamentally nonproductive, exists to further a mass migration of wealth. The migration economy is essentially a constant recycling of wealth within closed circles of powerful persons and interests, operating both on the "dark side" and in the light—and, quite often, together.

The perpetuation of such a scheme requires both an aspect of chaos in migration affairs and the ability to control this chaos. There is thus a need for managing both volatile forces (like migration waves, organized crime, terrorism, and other violence), through authoritative, official means, in order to control and guide this chaos toward a preferred policy result that is beneficial for those who organize the overall economy. This preferred policy result, in the big picture, is the control by elite supranational organizations over problems that individual states have unsuccessfully tried to confront on their own. In this light, the 2015 migrant crisis in Europe was a sort of "stress test" for states, similar to the ones that banks underwent just a few years before, during the global financial crisis. The two crises are in fact directly intertwined. For Europe's crisis is, fundamentally, just a territorial extension of a global development sector that is more associated with other and poorer parts of the world.

The general migration economy's licit, white-collar aspects intersect with myriad industries and ultimately are controlled by the most powerful leaders of global finance and politics and can affect geopolitical outcomes. This dimension is arguably more interesting and definitely more important than the illicit sphere of the migration economy. However, the latter is (on the ground level) the fundamental drivers of the entire migration economy, and its visible face. Thus the aspects of organized crime and the generally illicit sectors of the migration economy have been discussed much more frequently in the media than have the white-collar ones. Such coverage deflects public attention from high places, and redirects it on the lower-level, criminal element of the general migration economy. And here the role of the media has been critical.

Throughout the migrant crisis, the mass media tended to concentrate on the alluring, salacious, and photogenic tales of criminal deeds that control and guide the movement and activities of migrants. The most prominent criminal sector, in this regard, has been human trafficking. This was unsurprising, considering that the human interest aspect of the crisis was from the beginning the primary focus of global media. As was discussed in the third chapter of this book, such an approach tended toward poignant depictions that manipulated the emotions and opinions of the public, building an unconscious consensus that would lead over time to the preselected supranational "solution" for the crisis.

Although this media activity itself is thus a central pillar of the whole white-collar migrant economy (as will be discussed below), it also has served a key purpose by obfuscating the totality of that economy. Indeed, the human interest–driven media coverage of the crisis helped create a simplistic dichotomy of criminals and victims that would abet the definition and identification of the "good guys"—supranational organizations and liberal, pro-refugee leaders like Angela Merkel, Pope Francis, and President Obama. Yet the media has never been particularly interested in exploring the deeper economic connections of the migration economy, which lead directly to the financial and political interests of the world's most powerful leaders and companies.

To be sure, the illicit activities associated with the migration crisis are fundamental and critical to any assessment, but these lead again right back to the top of global power structures. "In making her invitation to refugees, without providing them at the same time any safe and direct transport, Angela Merkel activated every single illegal network between Syria and Germany," pondered one senior European intelligence officer. "Why did she do this?"[2] This is a question that has captivated many professional observers of the crisis, but it is one that the international media has been reluctant to ask.

A key point of coordination for EU law enforcement in the fight against human trafficking has been Europol's European Migrant Smuggling Centre. National police efforts assisted from the center have helped the successful capture of human traffickers involved in some of the most high-profile cases of the crisis. One example occurred on August 27, 2015, when 71 migrants were found dead in the back of a 7.5-ton refrigerated truck on the Hungarian–Austrian border. The case was reported widely in world media, resulting in political condemnation and further calls for aid from the NGOs and pro-refugee lobby.

Eleven "key facilitators," most from Bulgaria and Afghanistan, were arrested in the ensuing multinational police operation. Europol's specialists traced this group's involvement in 24 different incidents between June and August 2015. The ring had recruited drivers from Bulgaria to operate trucks and minivans procured in Hungary. This system transported Balkan Route–migrants who had reached Serbia, and made daily runs to Germany. According to the Europol investigation, much of the profit "had been transferred to Afghanistan, where it was invested into real estate businesses. The criminals used underground bankers to move the money from the EU to Afghanistan." Robert Crepinko, Head of Europol's European Migrant Smuggling Centre, noted that the case exemplified "how ruthless the criminal gangs can be" in pursuit of their financial interests. "We are confronted with multinational criminal networks that smuggle human beings and carelessly disregard the dangers they are exposing them to," stated Crepinko. "Money is all that matters to them."[3]

In a more detailed report of February 2016, Europol provided an overview of the migrant trafficking industry as supported by its official statistics and other data. In it, the organization claimed that it "holds intelligence on more than 40,000 individuals suspected of being involved in migrant smuggling." In 2015 alone, some 1,551 investigations targeting networks were undertaken in the European Union. The criminal revenues from migrant smuggling (both to and within the European Union) were estimated at being between 3 and 6 billion euros for 2015 alone. According to Europol, among the 100 different nationalities of traffickers it had encountered, most suspects came from Bulgaria, Egypt, Hungary, Iraq, Kosovo, Pakistan, Poland, Romania, Serbia, Syria, Tunisia, and Turkey.[4]

On the structural level, Europol notes that smuggling networks are usually led by a chief organizer, who coordinates activities from a key migration hub, but who remains apart from the core activities. Under him, local or regional leaders arrange transport prices and connections, such as ground or air transport. These local chieftains and their cells operate within a fixed territory, and pass on their migrant customers to the next cell along the line. At the bottom of the ladder are low-level contacts who "are used as drivers, crew members, scouts, or recruiting agents. These contacts typically operate as part of a network only for a limited time and are exchanged regularly."[5]

Human trafficking, not only in Europe but worldwide, has become an increasingly important issue for global law enforcement. At an October 2016 conference in Switzerland that brought together over 200 investigators and specialists from 55 nations and international organizations, Interpol discussed new approaches and went over its large-scale Operation Spartacus, which had targeted human trafficking in South and Central

America in June, leading to 134 arrests and "the dismantling of at least seven organized crime networks." At the event, Simonetta Sommaruga, Head of Switzerland's Federal Department of Justice and Police, criticized unnamed politicians who seek "national solutions" to the problem. "When crimes happen on an international level, they must also be investigated on an international level," she stated.[6] The activities of Europol, Interpol, and the European Union in 2015 and after indicate that this broader tendency toward supranational law enforcement solutions to migration crime will continue.

This international acknowledgment of the problem also attests to the increasingly multinational composition and fluid organization of migrant smuggling in Europe. The crisis has introduced "new players into the human trafficking game, divided by ethnicities, territory and tasks, and sometimes involved in other illicit industries too," states Greek security and organized crime expert Ioannis Michaletos. "The human trafficking boom has brought many new, loosely-organized groups into the sector, composed partly of immigrants from Iraq, Syria and Pakistan." Groups now active in Southeast Europe include "the traditional pyramid-type groups present in Istanbul and Izmir [in Turkey], plus Balkan groups— Bulgarians, Albanians and Greeks mostly—who were not previously human traffickers per se, but who dealt with other sectors and got involved with human trafficking because of the new opportunities for profits presented by the migrant crisis."[7]

In addition to activities coordinated by entities like Europol and Interpol, the European Union has become more involved with efforts against human smuggling. Several operations at sea, culminating with the European Union's Operation Sophia in 2015, also provided law enforcement a fuller picture of smuggling trends at sea, as an internal report of January 29, 2016, later released by WikiLeaks indicates. The report summarized the operation's achievements and challenges during the first six months of its mandate, and offered recommendations on future courses of action. At the time it was released, the most "exciting" revelation was that the European Union sought the formation of a "reliable" Libyan government, that would then invite the EU fleet into its territorial waters and even land, to police human trafficking.[8]

After an initial period of largely intelligence gathering and rescue operations, the European Council (on September 28, 2015) approved Operation Sophia's transition to phase 2A (High Seas) interdiction of smuggling craft. This practice had only been allowed following a UN Security Council resolution on October 9, 2015.[9] The report provides many interesting insights regarding trafficking and smuggling patterns in the Central Mediterranean during the crisis. It notes that most of those trafficked by sea from Libya in 2015 came from Eritrea, Somalia, Nigeria, Syria, Gambia, Senegal, Sudan, Mali, the Ivory Coast, and Ethiopia (with another

15 percent unknown). This effectively shows that the media depiction of the migrant crisis as a specifically war-driven phenomenon was partly a myth; most of the countries cited would have been, during the period in question, considered as "safe" countries, with people coming from them clearly being economic migrants.

In the same period, the report reveals, more than 400 smugglers were arrested and some were tried, though this process was problematic due to the lack of legal clarity, given Libya's failure to create a government. Most migrant craft (both old wooden vessels and rubber dinghies) departed from the Libyan ports of Zuwarah, Sabratah, Garabulli, and Misrata. The migrant smuggling business was described as "very profitable" for Libya, bringing in an annual revenue of 250–300 million euros. The "more valuable" wooden boats could carry more passengers and were more seaworthy than the dinghies, some of which were reportedly imported legitimately from China via Malta.[10]

However, as predicted in the report, the expansion of Operation Sophia to the "high seas" also meant the interdiction and resulting loss of such vessels. As the January 2016 report already confirmed, the European Union's own humanitarian and policing action made the journey more dangerous for the trafficked persons, as cost-averse smugglers simply dispatched them in cheaper craft and with less rations and fuel than they had provided before. In addition, the Operation Sophia report indicates other types of dangers encountered by migrants during sea crossings. Escort boats from competing smuggling groups were seen to be "stopping migrant vessels for extortion . . . from a smuggling perspective, migrants can generally be considered as highly valuable assets as they carry money both for the crossing and for the eventual arrival in Europe."[11]

Diversification of activities and use of ports by organized crime has also been witnessed during the crisis. Because maritime human (and other) smuggling "inevitably includes criminals specialized in sea smuggling operations involving weapons, counterfeit items, drugs, tobacco, and so on, certainly we have a convergence," says the Greek expert. "In the case of Italy, for example, the local mafia has been involved with both sectors since the crisis with Libya started in 2011, selling weapons to Libya and also assisting the flow of migrants back to Europe."[12]

Weapon trafficking is indeed one of the existing illicit businesses that has rapidly increased in volume and profit due to the migrant crisis, instability in the Middle East and North Africa, and terrorist demand in Western Europe. Indeed, the traffic goes both ways and is again abetted by the same gangs that run human trafficking and related businesses. The trade in arms received new attention following the Paris attacks, when it was discovered that weapons used by terrorists had come from the Balkans, a region where migrants were also heavily crossing. Germany's *Deutsche Welle* reported that "the majority of the illegal weapons in the European

Union have been smuggled via the Balkan countries." In addition to an overabundance of guns left over from the wars of the 1990s there, the cost aspect is also a factor: "while a Kalashnikov can cost between 300 and 500 euros ($325–$540) in the Balkans, the price goes up to 2,000 euros in some countries."[13]

Since 2010, weapons used by Islamist militants in Western European terrorist attacks "originated from the Western Balkans, particularly from Serbia and Bosnia and Herzegovina," according to a March 2016 report from *Jane's Terrorism & Insurgency*. "The routes used to smuggle the weapons from the Western Balkans are similar to those established and operated by organised crime syndicates for drugs and people trafficking, and smuggling migrants."[14] Interpol grew concerned enough to coordinate an action in April 2016, Operation Balkan Trigger, in which some 5,000 officers seized weapons and made arrests in Bosnia, Croatia, Macedonia, Montenegro, Serbia, and Slovenia. "With increased concerns over the illicit trafficking of weapons from the Balkans region into Europe for use in terrorist attacks, a key factor," Interpol noted, a key factor behind the operation was "establishing a strong network to more effectively interdict this flow."[15]

Drug smuggling is another criminal enterprise that has been abetted by migration, as new sources and routes are being established. According to the United Nations Office on Drugs and Crime (UNODC), "The total value of illicit heroin and opium trafficked from Afghanistan to Western Europe through the Balkans amounts to some $28 billion every year. Sixty-five percent of this total ($18 billion) is generated in Western and Central Europe. The four largest European markets for heroin—France, the United Kingdom, Germany, and Italy—account for nearly half of the gross profits, as the major heroin benefits are made by traffickers on the retail markets." Some 155 tons of heroin per year were being shipped through Iran from Afghanistan. In November 2016, the UNODC started a three-year Regional Programme for South Eastern Europe meant to counter trafficking and transnational organized crime and improve international legal cooperation regarding criminal justice prevention, treatment and care. According to UNODC executive director Yury Fedotov, the body's research activities "can strengthen our evidence base for effective action in South Eastern Europe."[16]

An interesting, and perhaps unexpected, aspect of narcotics and migration has been the influence of drugs on migrant health and behavior. "During the crisis, some of our colleagues specialized in the issue noted that some Afghan refugees were displaying erratic behavior consistent with heroin withdrawal," notes Phil Evans, an Englishman who volunteered with a Christian charity at Macedonia's Tabanovce border camp near Serbia.[17] The deprivation of opiates to such people, who had previously been addicted in their home countries, could in some cases explain their aggressive or unusual behavior. But given such large numbers and a dearth of trained specialists, many such cases were likely missed during the crisis.

Another type of organized crime that has been going on for years along the main migration routes, but that has become particularly infamous with the rise of the Islamic State, is antiquities theft. Although the barbaric terrorist group enjoyed blowing up "infidel" sites (like Syria's ancient city of Palmyra) for the media and ideological value, it was keenly aware of the value of movable treasures; in fact, the caliphate's so-called government departments administered an organized system for extracting, selling, and transporting such goods.[18] In the migrant crisis, small items could be sent undetected via special couriers, including among the migrant flows. Antiquities can also be a sort of payment or barter for various types of trafficking and underground banking services. But, fundamentally, their sale goes back into the same criminal-terrorist economy that sustains the same chaotic situations that lead to migration in the first place.

Here the borders between the illicit and licit sectors, between criminality and polite society become impossibly blurred. Although the looted antiquities come from the Middle East and Balkans primarily, their end buyers are wealthy Western customers; even before the migrant crisis began, stolen items ended up disappearing into "untouchable" territory—the private auctions held in the closed quarters of Europe's moneyed classes.[19] This has been a perennial problem, even in peacetime, in poor but archeologically rich places where ancient relics are plentiful.

According to Mark Vlasic, a leading expert in the field, the rise of ISIS led to the intensified trade in what he termed "blood antiquities"—a reference to the illicit trade in "blood diamonds" by warlords during the 1990s African conflicts. Acknowledging the reality of a wealthy, white-collar buyer's class, Vlasic has also proposed greater international cooperation on developing certification methods for antiquities stolen from conflict zones such as Syria.[20] Institutions like the University of Chicago have begun special programs to try and document and assess Islamic State's plundered treasures. Thus in a perverse and unexpected way, the criminal economy has also created conditions for economic growth among those studying its outcomes.[21]

At the very heart of the illegal migration economy is the business of documentation. The sale of real and fake documents is another type of organized crime that is both highly lucrative and highly dangerous for security officials. European leaders were embarrassed when a Dutch journalist in Syria showed just how easy it was to obtain a fake Syrian passport—in fact, he had one printed up with the photo of the Dutch prime minister on it.[22] But the truth is that due to geopolitical decisions, EU antiterrorism leaders were always working from a disadvantage throughout the crisis: they had alienated the Assad government and Russia, and could hardly be expected to verify paperwork with the Islamic State. Meanwhile, as has been recounted, key "third countries" like Turkey, Serbia, and Macedonia were excluded from the EURODAC database, while the Greek authorities (and Frontex officers with them) did a poor job of registering migrants. All things considered, the 2015 crisis offered ideal conditions for this type of criminal enterprise to flourish.

In general, "criminal experts in document fraud or recruitment often work for several migrant smuggling networks at the same time," noted Europol in its February 2016 report. "The false documents used by irregular migrants originate mainly from Athens, Istanbul, and Syria as well as Asian hubs such as Thailand." The report also discloses a fascinating 2015 investigation into a "state-of-the-art counterfeiting print shop in Albania, with equipment worth millions of dollars." The shop's operator had been tasked by smuggling networks in Greece to produce counterfeit documents that were then sent by courier to migrants gathered in Greece. According to Europol, the Albanian forger worked closely with criminal networks in Bulgaria and Turkey. His arrest "led to the seizure of thousands of blank visa documents, residence permits, ID cards, security gelatines, passports and driving licenses for various EU countries."[23] Similarly, in early September 2015, a German newspaper reported that Bulgarian police had seized a box of 10,000 fake Syrian passports in the mail as it was being sent to Germany.[24]

The multibillion dollar profits generated from all of these subsectors of the criminal migrant economy need to be laundered somehow, and there are several ways in which this is done. As seen from the Europol investigation into the migrant deaths in a Hungarian truck, laundered profits can be reinvested in real estate, in such distant and unlikely places as Afghanistan. However, Europol also notes that there is much still unknown about migration black finance: "there is only limited intelligence available on the criminal proceeds, illicit financial flows or money laundering processes associated," it noted in the February 2016 report. "In 2015, less than 10% of the investigations into migrant smuggling activities produced intelligence on suspicious transactions or money laundering activities."[25]

The Islamic Hawala banking system is another popular means of circulating money across borders. Unlike conventional money transfer methods, it is anonymous and without records, and thus ideal for money laundering. The system—hardly only used by criminals—allows anyone to pay a local vendor (known as a *hawaladar*) in one location, so that another person can recover that amount from another such vendor, anywhere in the world.[26] Interpol considers this one example of what it calls an Informal Value Transfer System (IVTS). In a 2015 report on money laundering, Interpol noted Hawala banking's increasing popularity due to new restrictions on traditional banking; it defines an IVTS as "any system, mechanism or network of people that receives money for the purpose of making the funds or an equivalent value payable to a third party in another geographic location, whether or not in the same form."[27]

The Hawala system in Europe alone is estimated to involve 30,000 *hawaladars* who process some 300,000 million euros monthly. Officials in countries like Bulgaria believe that "most of the transactions of money of refugees and migrants are settled by the Hawala system, not by the traditional remittance systems," notes Dr. Gergana Yordanova, a researcher and banking expert with Bulgaria's National Defense College. "Hawala operations are with no payment orders, names of sender/receiver, nor an amount value. All the transactions are processed anonymously and with no paper records." However, although the system has proven popular during the crisis, Dr. Yordanova also notes that "migrants and refugees do not use the Hawala system when they do not have cash. When they need money in cash, they are forced to find new sources." Among these she lists goods such as gold, products, and even the sale of human organs, as well as prostitution.[28]

Established global money transfer systems such as Western Union are a longtime favorite of itinerant immigrants in Europe, but are less known to newly arriving migrants, the Bulgarian expert believes. These services have also been used both for remittances to the migrant's home country and for receiving funds to pay expenses and fees locally. This has been a profitable method: during the crisis, one branch alone in Athens was moving 20,000 euros per day.[29] It is unclear to what extent emerging cryptocurrencies (like Bitcoin) are being used by migration-related crime groups, though we can expect this to increase or decrease in line with the relative use of such alternate currencies by the general public.

Throughout the crisis, European media reported constantly (and sometimes for political reasons) on the massive increase in street crime and general violence accompanying migration; the complaints were particularly loud in countries most affected by migrants, such as Austria, Germany, Holland, and Sweden. As such, the rise of urban crime in Europe is very likely to emerge as a defining and lasting feature of the illicit migration economy—one that challenges the operational capacities and budgets of Europe's already overstretched police and intelligence services.

An indication of what may occur with future migrant-related organized crime is provided by Gavin Slade, a criminologist and lecturer at Glasgow University. Having studied patterns of activity in established Balkan and Georgian organized crime networks in Europe, he notes that "contrary to what some criminologists find regarding the multi-ethnic character of organized crime, there is an ethnic distinction to be made. Recruitment based on kin, ethnicity and locality is preferred . . . though people do work across ethnicities."[30]

In research on what he calls the "chain networks" of diaspora gangs, Slade has also found that for criminals trying to start operating in Europe, "violence is a suboptimal strategy for establishing market position and has all sorts of negative [results], particularly for migrants." Instead of emphasizing violence, his case studies have revealed that competitive advantage is "based on human resources and the ability to replenish positions in the chain, whenever law enforcement disrupts activities." In the case of crime groups from Georgia, this "replenishment" was done through "recruitment outside refugee and asylum centres in Germany as well as in the home country. The advantage of this type of recruitment is based on the combination of proximity and ease of access to Western Europe through established migration routes and diaspora communities firstly." The second advantage, the criminologist notes, is "the relative deprivation and lack of employment in these countries, relative to that of the '[European] countries'—as well as the perceived weak punishments for the intended crimes in these latter destination countries."[31]

This general structural element may be applicable to some migrant-related organized crime groups, but a key difference is that diasporas from the Balkans and Caucasus tend to integrate more easily, and suffer less travel hardship, than do migrants from Muslim countries in the Middle East, Asia, and Africa. The extreme violence and duress to which the latter have become accustomed—both before and after traveling to Europe—is forging a tough new generation of criminals with street smarts and adaptability. "We can predict turf wars, increase in rival gang violence and religious radicalization," predicts Greek analyst Michaletos. "This will be the link between organized crime and the urban terrorism issues that we are going to face in the years ahead." Michaletos anticipates that new structures of organized crime will be established in Europe due to the migration crisis, according to these distinctions:

The newly-arriving elements can be split into categories of ethnic gangs—a phenomenon we have already witnessed for decades—while others will become subordinated to stronger, established groups, like religious ones. EU authorities should be very concerned because they will have a new set of challenges that interact with politics and terrorism, something that inevitably will have geo-political ramifications. Also, many of the "new" criminals brought by the migrant crisis will have had military experience in the vicious wars of the Middle East; they are thus both battle-hardened and have direct access to dark networks across that region. Taken together, these factors increase the chance that Europe's new criminal gangs are going to be even more violent, more complex, and constitute a serious new threat.[32]

One example of an impending turf war between old and new organized crime groups is Palermo, Italy, where the ancestral Sicilian Mafia had to "declare war" on the immigrant gangs in April 2016 because of the latter's increasing prominence in local illegal activities. This has occurred with demographic change and, if such a turf war can happen in the literal heartland of the Mafia, it can happen anywhere in Europe. According to a contemporaneous report, the Mafia is resorting to violence as it faces unprecedented challenges to core businesses like protection rackets and smuggling. The mayor of Palermo, Leoluca Orlando, stated in 2016 "Palermo is no longer an Italian town. It is no longer European. You can walk in the city and feel like you're in Istanbul or Beirut. The Mafia has not understood that the city has changed. We are now a city of immigrants, and the Mafia bosses no longer sit in the mayor's chair."[33] Ironically, part of the reason for why Palermo's historic city center has been reclaimed by migrants is because the Mafia itself ravaged the area from the 1950s to the 1980s.[34]

The migrant crisis of 2015, it must be remembered, abetted not only migrants from war-torn and far-off lands. This fact is, however, often ignored. In addition to the nationalities of trafficked persons stated above in the European Union's Operation Sophia report, there is the general case of Greece. In spring 2016, after the Balkan Route had been shut, both media and officials consistently reported that over 60,000 migrants had been left trapped in Greece. Yet this was not exactly true, as it counted only new arrivals. In the big picture, Greece's population of 11 million has, over the past 25 years, accumulated roughly one million immigrants. These economic migrants have come from the Balkans to Africa, from Bangladesh to Ukraine, and everywhere in between. All of these groups have brought their own ethnic Mafia connections (the Georgian and Albanian ones being among the most celebrated).

What we are seeing now with the migrant crisis is the transference and expansion of these Mafias north, as (particularly Muslim) longtime immigrants in Greece have sought to "blend in" with the newly arriving migrants traveling on. This is leading to odd cases, like Afghan "refugees" in Austria, who somehow speak impeccable Greek. Although most economic migrants (whether longtime residents or newcomers) are not aspiring criminals, those who are will create unique new synergies on the local and international levels, due to their ethnic background, linguistic knowledge, and experience of different locations and cultures. These groups will also fight among each other; the rampant knife fights between, for example, Afghan and Syrian migrants presage the chaotic new conditions we can expect on Europe's streets.

Media accounts of violent crime in Europe associated with migration during the crisis often overlapped with the urban areas of congregation (so-called hot spots) discussed by Europol in February 2016. In European Union countries, these include Athens, Berlin, Budapest, Calais, Copenhagen, Frankfurt, Hamburg, Hoek van Holland, London, Madrid, Milan, Munich, Paris, Passau, Rome, Stockholm, Tornio, Thessaloniki, Vienna, Warsaw, and Zeebrugge. "The hotspots channel migratory flows, act as pull factors and have grown exponentially in the last years," the report adds. "Migrants gather in hotspots where they know they will have access to services during their travel to their preferred destination."[35] Quite obviously, the congregation of itinerant migrants in such chokepoints increases the likelihood for crime and violent events, and for established urban criminal enterprises to use the newcomers for various illicit purposes.

When migrants are congregated not on their own but in refugee housing, opportunities arise for other types of crime, such as drug dealing and prostitution. However, another type, executed by existing "Old Europe" enterprises like the Italian Mafia, is tender corruption and graft associated with local officials who solicit donor funds for migration-related projects. In Catania, Sicily, authorities opened a case on suspicions that the Mafia and public officials were working together in "overseeing" local migrant camps. "In raids in June, Italian police arrested 44 known criminals and senior government workers," reported VOA News, "saying that the mafia was involved at various levels of migrant management—from registration to the running of the camps and the settling of migrants in Italian towns and villages."[36]

Further, police claimed also that the Sicilian Mafia was involved with the forced prostitution of migrant women, while concerns remained for the almost 5,000 migrant children who had disappeared from reception centers across the country in the previous year. In a July 2016 update from Catania, Britain's *Observer* described the island's sprawling Cara di Mineo migrant camp as "an open-air hub for smugglers, operating with the blessing of the mafia; a massive holding pen from where criminals take orders for human traffic." The disappearance of unaccompanied minors in particular was a pervasive phenomenon in this and other Sicilian camps. The report also noted that Italian investigations had linked the Cara di Mineo contracts corruption case to the larger "Mafia Capitale" scandal, in which it was "alleged that organised crime infiltrated public-service contracts on a grand scale," the report chronicled. One notorious underworld figure, Salvatore Buzzi, ran a vast cooperative that provided food and language courses for migrants and his combined business was said to be worth £30 million. In a wiretap recording, Buzzi, who has reportedly denied the allegations, is caught admitting: "Do you know how much we earn off migrants? Drugs are less profitable."[37]

Such examples show how organized crime and corruption can work symbiotically within the local and national power structures. Examples of international corruption and organized crime involve opportunism in the migration economy get more complex and more sophisticated the higher up they reach the legitimate sectors of public life. One simpler example of this trend would be that of corruption in diplomatic missions. Various illicit schemes have been carried out to exploit the migrant crisis. One case of illicit practices at one Muslim-majority country's Athens embassy is revealed by a former employee:

It worked like this. A lot of the migrants from [the embassy's home country] arriving in Lesvos didn't have any passports or other documents. Many of them, they wanted passports. So an important official in the embassy figured out how to make a good business from their problem. He had a Turkish guy on the island who would talk to the new migrants, find out who wanted passports, and for 1,000 euros they could buy a real passport, printed for them in the embassy. He offered me a commission from this money if I would go and bring the passports for the migrants who ordered them. But I didn't want to be involved in any illegal activities. So I quit. But I'm sure they are still doing this business.[38]

The convergence of criminality and international white-collar crime reaffirms the existence of a system of accommodation. Power is not centralized but diffused; as such, the migrant crisis allows the ideal system structure of both illegal business and parapolitics. Throughout the crisis, special projects, camps, and NGOs came and went with no record of ever having existed; just as hundreds of thousands of migrants passed through Europe's borders unidentified, similarly unknown was the massive amount of money circulating through the licit and illicit migrant economy. Numbers are impossible to confirm. One example, in Serbia during the height of the crisis, was that the migration business and presence of migrants in the country was responsible for six million euro per day passing through the local economy.[39]

Although terrorists, criminals, and smugglers in persons and goods will be relentlessly hunted by increasingly well-equipped police and intelligence forces in Europe, they are only a part—and the less important one— of the overall migrant economy. Today, the global migration economy is run by a close network comprised of powerful people, corporations, NGOs, and institutions, comprising a sort of shadow government (this will be discussed in detail in Chapter 9 of this book). Whether or not terrorism is, as various European politicians have said, "the new normal," the migration industry certainly is becoming an increasingly integrated part of the larger world economy, because of the interests of those controlling both. A migration-oriented society will bring more and more Europeans into nonproductive sectors like assistance, bureaucracy, NGO activity, and other such work that is essentially social welfare. (A preview of this phenomenon was seen in 2015, when the traditional, productive tourism economy of Eastern Aegean islands like Lesvos was displaced by the artificial economy of donations and NGOs.)

The white-collar migration economy helps solve one problem facing today's Europe: unemployment for young and educated native Europeans. This is particularly ironic in light of the fact that German leaders like Merkel and Schauble had argued that the migrants themselves were crucial for powering Europe's economy, in both skilled and unskilled labor roles. Demographic statistics, which point to low European birthrates and increasing life spans, have been presented by German leaders as constituting a direct threat to the pension fund sector and sustainability of state welfare budgets. This may be true, and Europe does need workers, but the West has discouraged such workers from countries with common European values (like Russia, Belarus, Moldova, and Ukraine) from coming. Indeed, the anti-immigration platform of the Brexit campaign played on negative stereotypes about Romanians and Bulgarians—actual EU members with a Western culture—who allegedly impact Britain negatively. For whatever reason, Merkel and the European Union have preferred to import Muslims who cannot or will not assimilate. In the long term, the costs created by this reality may outweigh the economic benefits migrants will supposedly bring to Europe.

But, fundamentally, the labor question lurking behind the migration debate does not infer a lack of workers; it infers a lack of interest in working. Young Europeans increasingly lack the desire and often the training to do jobs that their forefathers had done, from manual labor and the service sector to highly skilled jobs that required extended periods of diligent study (such as medicine or engineering). Indeed, at a time of constant terror threats and other public violence, it was somewhat strange (and a bit quaint) to see French protesters take to the streets in defense of the beloved 35-hour workweek and against the government's planned introduction of other market-friendly measures. And it has been particularly surreal (though predictable) to see thousands of migrants come to Europe, expecting to receive social benefits from the state and specifically avoid seeking work.

Thus, one of the European Union's most vaunted achievements—the "Single Market"—has now also become a key point of weakness. The phenomenon of "brain drain" preceded the migrant crisis and will now increase because of it. This is largely the result of disparities within and between local and national economies, which cumulatively results in an overabundance or dearth of labor in different sectors owing to differences in local wages.

Despite the confident beliefs of supporters, this is something that the migration "solution" cannot fix. The wealthier EU countries will always have a suction effect on both skilled and unskilled labor, because of the real or perceived wage disparities in different European countries. This was seen very clearly from the 2015 crisis, when migrants refused to live in specific countries, instead demanding that they be settled in a country of their choice. This, of course, caused indignation from native Europeans who had assumed these people should be grateful for having been allowed to come in the first place. But as critics of the European Union's "quota system" rightly pointed out from the beginning, guaranteeing that a migrant will stay in the country to which he or she is assigned is impossible in a European Union that sees "freedom of movement" as a fundamental right and that is also determined to preserve its borderless interior (the Schengen Zone).

In the big picture, some white-collar subsectors are emerging as the most prominent beneficiaries in the general migration economy. Substitutes for a real economy that is disappearing along with Europe's shrinking manufacturing and market base, these sectors are becoming a sort of refuge for educated native Europeans and the point of convergence with migrants and their causes. The first such sector is essentially real estate: housing and servicing for migrants across Europe. This business has amassed huge fortunes that will be reinvested across other sectors as the numbers of newcomers ebb. Although these operations are mostly more legitimate than the Italian Mafia model of collecting state contracts, there have still been complaints at the quality of care and facilities in certain cases, as well as complaints of abuse. But the governments (and European Union) that do not have alternatives have had to commission these for-profit ventures that include everything from classic camps to retrofitted Scandinavian hotels.

Indeed, as of 2016, for-profit companies were providing about 90 percent of Norway's refugee housing. One particular company, Oslo-based Hero Norway, had become "the leader of a burgeoning Scandinavian industry that charges the Norwegian and Swedish governments a fixed fee—$31 to $75 per person per night in Norway—to house and feed refugees," reported Bloomberg. Started by two Norwegian brothers, the company expected "revenue of $63 million, with profits of 3.5 percent." An even larger European for-profit accommodation provider, Switzerland's ORS Services, generated $99 million in profit in 2014, "caring for refugees in Switzerland, Austria, and Germany. (ORS won't disclose its 2015 profits.)"[40]

ORS is a perfect example of how truly globalized the migration housing business has become. It has been criticized for alleged inferior conditions, but part of this may be due to sour grapes: international organizations like the Red Cross have failed to win tenders from the Swiss government for the same services, because they cannot beat ORS's rates. Since opening in the 1990s, the company has been bought and sold several times by private equity companies. In 2013, it was purchased by London-based private-equity firm Equistone Partners Europe Ltd. According to another report, the company raised "close to $4 billion for two buyout funds since spinning out of British bank Barclays PLC in 2011. Equistone's investors include American public pension funds California State Teachers' Retirement System and Maryland State Retirement and Pension System, and the General Organization for Social Insurance of Saudi Arabia."[41]

The second key sector is the media, which is currently undergoing a harrowing and historic period of transition globally. This has been most painful for the traditional (and especially print) media, which is finding it increasingly difficult to survive according to traditional business models. As a free and increasingly diverse quantity of online content becomes available, and as consumer preferences for audio and video media content becomes more pronounced, the "dead tree" media is scrambling to find novel ways of survival, such as reader donations and paywalls that few will pay for.

This increased media vulnerability has resulted in evermore political and business influence on media, as traditional advertising and subscription revenue dries up. But this is a perilous path. Although (for now) less pronounced in Europe than in the United States, establishment media is being challenged by the rise of social media, Wikileaks, and alternative news websites. In Europe, politicians are also disturbed by new media trends that they do not properly understand. In October 2016, Angela Merkel (who was infamously caught reprimanding Facebook chief Mark Zuckerberg over "racist" posts on the platform) demanded Google release its algorithms, as they allegedly promoted search results opposed to her cause. Ironically, the woman who had marched in solidarity with European leaders under the slogan "Je Suis Charlie" (after the *Charlie Hebdo* attacks) seemed to have become as irritated with free speech as was her ally/rival, Turkish president Erdoğan. He had also criticized social media when it was against his interests, but embraced the medium when it could forward those interests.

Traditional media today can only adopt less overtly political relationships if it can replace them with other ones that contribute to new business models. As such, the migrant crisis—with its human interest aspect and simplistic moralistic depictions—has become the ideal platform for media that want to get clicks and sell papers based on tragic photos and sordid stories of despair and abuse. In this model, financial support comes from philanthropic organizations and other bodies depicted as essentially altruistic. Everyone wins: the media get much-needed revenue and some increased political cachet, while the donors get increased visibility and public approval for their good efforts in solving the world's migration problems.

In Europe, an interesting case study would be British newspaper *The Guardian*, which is slightly unusual in being a company run by a trust. With out-of-control printing costs and declining sales, the newspaper has been "hemorrhaging money," as one contributor privately commented in 2016. The newspaper has thus sought new ways to prop up its flagging fortunes. One source of income has been outside funding for migration-related coverage. Typically in Western journalism, subsidized reportage has been considered ethically off-limits, with special advertorial sections clearly marked and separate from news coverage. But with migration, the industry has found a topic less prone to criticism from the ethical standpoint.

This has brought the media ever more in the warm embrace of the major global philanthropic organizations; together with the big banks, corporations, and international organizations, they are intimately involved with steering the migrant crisis. In the example of the British newspaper, this link is specified under special series like the "Global Development" article section. As of October 2016, cited examples of funding "partners" included the Bill and Melinda Gates Foundation and the Rockefeller Foundation—both of which are heavily involved at the global level in shaping migration policy.[42] Another example of funders that popped under the newspaper's "content funding" model on some articles was Crown Agents, a former British governmental body that now operates as a private company, doing things like advising on customs reforms in places like Bulgaria, Macedonia, and Albania. Some security sources consider it an MI6 front.[43] Comparing specific coverage of migration in such media with its "sponsors" definitely raises questions about media ethics and conflicts of interest, even if the published content itself is interesting and valuable for readers.

Not only newspapers are finding a business model within the migration economy. Broadcasters are involved, too, as with CNN's "Freedom Project" on "ending modern-day slavery."[44] The series, which includes European migration issues in addition to larger global trends, has provided valuable coverage of stories on topics like the trafficking of child migrants.[45] And as of October 2016, it was also sponsored by the Swiss-based Essam and Dalal Obaid Foundation, which supports other entities like the Red Cross and Mayo Clinic. This CNN relationship with the wealthy Saudi Obaid family is not particularly scandalous, but considering the Obaid oil dynasty's vast economic and diplomatic influence, it does reinforce the increasing tendency for big media and big players to join forces, in ways that promote their common interests in the general migration economy.[46]

As explained in the beginning of this study, the 2015 European migrant crisis represented a quantitative, not qualitative, expansion that caused a logistical problem to intensify across a wide area. Since the development industry benefits from all forms of instability, the migrant crisis provided an unprecedented opportunity to expand the territory of development and charity operations. Distracted by colorful and disturbing images of masses of refugees migrating across the continent, the average European could be forgiven for overlooking the mass migration of influence, activities, and finance going on as well from the side of the international development industry.

From this perspective, the political and financial reactions of various parties in the 2015 migrant crisis become highly revealing. Supranationalist organizations like the European Union and UN, and politicians aligned with their agenda, were quick to criticize countries and leaders that took a sovereignty-first attitude to the crisis. Countries like Hungary and Macedonia were criticized on humanitarian grounds to cover for what was essentially an economically driven agenda: by refusing to open their territories to mass migration, such countries became an impediment to the new business models. In September 2015, the Macedonian government rejected a UNHCR private offer of financial assistance if the country would resettle 30,000 migrants in camps on state territory.[47] Did the rejection affect future EU aid policy? We will probably never know. All that can be said for certain is that the European Union provided Macedonia very little assistance in handling the crisis, and channeled what funds it did—in contravention of national law—to the union's "contracting partner," the IOM.[48]

Another subsector of the general migration that will see promising growth is academia. Here, an increased focus on refugee and migrant issues will help address some of the financial and attitudinal challenges faced by the media. As with the latter, the higher education industry will discuss migration from perspectives that appease external donors and prevailing social beliefs. At a time of debate over the value and expense of higher education in general, this can be a clever way to cover for loss-making programs. Most such programs are in the humanities, a field often lamented as in danger of "dying." The increasing perception that once-core humanities courses are "useless" (in having no direct relation to well-paying jobs) is affecting decision making regarding general course offerings.[49] This trend is much less pronounced in Europe than in the United States, but it will continue to grow as technology continues to affect societies and economic need.

One of the major grievances regarding higher education in America—its staggering cost—is much diminished in the European debate, as education there is much more affordable (though countries veering toward the American model, like Britain, have seen student protests over costs). However, what is not different between the two continents is a shared sense of cultural norms and political correctness, which have had serious and perhaps irreparable impact on the types and teaching of humanities courses. This tendency was isolated, in the American context, by a senior Hoover Institution fellow, military historian Victor Davis Hanson. In a trenchant essay of 2014, Hanson charged that "the humanities have been exhausted by a half-century of therapeutic 'studies' courses: Peace and Conflict Resolution Studies, Post-Colonial Studies, Environmental Studies, Chicano Studies, Women's Studies, Black Studies, Asian Studies, Cultural Studies, and Gay Studies. Any contemporary topic that could not otherwise justify itself as literary, historical, philosophical, or cultural simply tacked on the suffix 'studies' and thereby found its way into the curriculum."[50]

The same disease has infected most of Europe's most prestigious universities, as well as others that, while of lesser renown, also have political clout in that they turn out graduates who go on to attain influential positions within academia, NGOs, and governments. A good example from the latter category would be Budapest's Central European University (CEU), established in 1991 by Hungarian American billionaire, activist, and philanthropist George Soros—himself a key stakeholder in the general migration economy and "global governance" movement (the relevant activities of Soros will be discussed in Chapter 9).

Essentially the education branch of Soros's Open Society Foundation, CEU bills itself as a graduate-level university where students come to "address some of society's most vexing problems." In October 2015, CEU announced that it offers "more than a dozen graduate courses in seven different departments that address the issue of migration and refugees, directly or indirectly." These courses, the university advertised, would allow students "to learn about the origins and possible solutions to the crisis"; as events had shown, migration was "more relevant than ever before."[51]

Thus, the migrant crisis is providing a golden opportunity for universities to create or expand humanities courses involving some aspect of "migration studies," through the lens of the prevailing worldview of liberal cultural relativism that has gripped Western European and North American education over the past few decades. Recent years have seen a rapid proliferation of "refugee studies" and "migration studies" centers at European and world universities, institutes, and think tanks. Given the sensitive social, racial, and religious nature of the subject, it is hardly likely that any of these are going to be fundamentally geared up to opposing migration. This means that critics of migration policies in Europe will be moved further still toward the edges of polite society, adding to the polarization on the issue already witnessed by the behavior of opposing political parties in Europe.

The general long-term result of such educational programs will thus be the reinforcement of a consensus on migration, as future graduates begin to enter the ranks of paid experts, media members, and policy makers. The areas of study that benefit most from the migrant crisis include sociology, social anthropology, gender studies, "hate speech" studies, language learning, racial studies, conflict studies, and intercultural studies. Within the confines of the general migration economy, a degree in such subjects is one way to gainful, white-collar employment in an academic, institutional, political, or development sector capacity, for students lacking the interest or ability to engage in other areas of learning or training.

Additional academic fields benefiting from the migrant crisis include law (asylum law, human rights law, and so on), and the whole human rights industry (including education, practice, advocacy, communications, and policy making). In the absence of specific departments, degrees related to migration are bundled under social sciences and similar schools.[52] The global migration economy, with all of its patronage schemes and agendas, will play an increasingly important role in the general European economy. In a way, the migration crisis of 2015 thus simply extended the development sector's territorial reach, following over two decades of similar operations due to wars in the Balkans, Africa, Afghanistan, and the Middle East, while also broadening its presence laterally across society, through deeper penetration into academia and the media.

In addition to bolstering the above-stated fields of higher education, the migration economy also requires persons educated in fields like psychology, counseling, and psychiatry. Everyone agrees that migrants and war refugees have undergone incredible hardships, physical depravations, and emotional suffering; now it is up to the Europeans to diagnose these experiences into disorders, conduct research, and quantify the data into something "useful." An October 2016 study quoted German clinical psychologist Thomas Elbert of the University of Konstanz as saying that "more than half of those [migrants] who arrived in Germany in the last few years show signs of mental disorder, and a quarter of them have a PTSD [Post-Traumatic Stress Disorder], anxiety or depression that won't get better without help." The study cited various other European psychologists, all of whom were running their own mental experiments on migrants and compiling statistics, for studies that "will help them to deal with other displaced populations, and help policymakers to accommodate the current influx."[53]

The integration of such activities into the local, national, and supranational migrant support mechanisms is well under way. European governments and international agencies are spending heavily on psychological assistance and research programs, not to mention the emergency action sector. (As a brief Internet search revealed, on a single day in October 2016 there were 157 such job vacancies with UN and other aid agencies for psychologists dealing with the European migration crisis.) It is clearly going to be a growth industry in the years ahead.

In a November 2015 position paper, the European Psychiatric Association (EPA) claimed that "the permanent increase in the number of refugees will result in a situation that will overstrain the possibilities of the current psychiatric health care structures in Europe. Recent investigations show that about half of the asylum seekers suffer from mental illness like post traumatic stress disorder, depression [and] anxiety." The EPA, which has almost 80,000 professional members across Europe, called for a broader investment in refugee mental health, and announced that it would be putting its knowledge and expertise at the disposal of the European Commission, by advising the Directorate General for Health and that for Migration and Home Affairs, "on specific psychiatric aspects affecting refugees and mental health systems. In particular, local collaboration could be fostered in the frame of the European Migration Network, by creating synergies between the EMN National Contact Points and the EPA National Psychi-atric Associations."[54] It goes without saying that where there is psychiatric research and lobbying, the big pharmaceutical companies are never far behind.

There is a final point to be made about the general migration economy. Whether in peak crisis time or long-term planning periods, the industry is essentially underpinned by a certain organizational structure and network function. Whether established international aid organizations or fly-by-night NGOs, all such organizations are fundamentally geared up toward growth and expansion, whether or not it conforms to ground reality. For example, in late 2016, one prominent international aid agency operating at a camp along the Balkan Route (which housed 50 migrants) had the same number of employees as it had earlier, when the camp held 1,500 people. In general, any business model dependent on grants and donation rather than efficiency and profit will never obey the model of capitalist econ-omies. Once fulfilled, initial funding requests simply provide a staging ground on which further funding can be acquired, irrespective of actual need. And, when government and the private sector get involved—as they are doing now, on a massive scale—the potential for sectoral growth becomes almost infinite.

These observations add a new dimension to the above-cited comment that Angela Merkel had "activated" every criminal network along the migrant route with her invitation. That was only half of the truth: in fact, as has been seen, with one *wilkommen* the chancellor launched a trillion-dollar industry that crossed all sectors, enriching many individuals and groups, then, now, and well into the future. In this context, the expected increased prominence of migration as a global issue will help shape the future interaction of global politics, finance, and social norms. With the shock of 2015, the migration issue became fundamentally and perma-nently tied to the drivers of public opinion, education, big business, and political leadership.

CHAPTER 6

The Challenge from the Left

European politics were, as the British would say, in a bit of a state well before the migration crisis and historic Brexit vote of June 2016. But the temporal convergence of these events, wedded with the simmering unrest arising from years of economic austerity, fears over electronic surveillance, and other issues affected the creation on the left of both a common outlook and common methods, most visibly, street protests and demonstrations in numerous countries in support of migrant causes.

In order to assess the state of affairs in European left-wing parties during the migrant crisis, and the issues that most gained traction within leftist movements, we must discuss them within three distinct but overlapping categories: first, at the top level, European Union left-wing structures; second, the trends and issues involving national-level parties; and third, local movements and generally grassroots blocs (such as minor parties, anarchist groups, and activists), which despite their informal character have had a disproportionate influence on established parties. This precisely mirrors the trend on the right, as the center has increasingly caved in at every level.

However, unlike the orientation of similarly categorized right-wing movements, the European left's orientation toward migration is fundamentally homogeneous. This is not to say that the issue itself is of equal concern to all such leftist parties and movements. But what is striking is the essential uniformity of leftist views concerning migration. Unlike the situation on the right, where one can find examples of parties that either support or oppose migration, on principle or by degree, it would be hard to find a leftist movement in today's Europe that does not support at least the principle of migration. Whether various leftist blocs advocate taking in a greater or lesser number of migrants, or whether they are more or less vocal on the issue, the difference is in degree.

As such, there is a certain tendency toward ideological totalitarianism on the European left; this reflects these parties' Marxist–Leninist roots and their often federalist tendencies. At the same time, this makes their behavior conducive to the current global tendencies regarding corporate–political control of information technology and supranational action. These latter trends appear irreversible. In the big picture, leftist movements are thus generally favored. However, this long-term trend does not also mean that leftist parties in Europe will find it easy to govern or come to common agreements, with either their own ranks or with the movements that oppose them. However, before discussing Europe's left-wing movements categorically, it is necessary to explain just why the essential uniformity of opinion exists regarding migration—and why this view has taken a greater importance in self-definition and depiction of opposing parties.

It can be argued that left-wing support for migration is both ideologically based and historically conditioned. The fact that left-wing ideology was created and honed in Europe well before World War II is often ignored, as that event tends to be (as was discussed in Chapter 2) considered the "beginning of history" for today's Europe in the popular imagination and political process. However, it is of fundamental importance to recall that European leftism has its roots in movements originating from the late 19th and early 20th centuries; the aftermath of World War II simply saw the resurrection and reorientation of preexisting movements toward a desired goal which, as we have discussed, was European federalism based on a sense of unity and "common values" that had always been largely imaginary. Of course, this fantasy conjured up from 1945 also required the cooperation of right-wing idealists. The inherent shortcomings of the postwar "united Europe" ideology tend only to manifest in times of crisis, however, and the lack of defensive warfare in Europe since 1945 has abetted the slow decay of these supposedly lasting ideals.

As has been argued, the 2015 migrant crisis marked Europe's first phase change since the fall of Communism and reunification of Germany. As occurred then, Europe is undergoing a reappraisal of its values and self-orientation. For the left wing especially, conditioned by its ideology and the implicit context of World War II, the migration crisis has proven a unifying and mobilizing force for all fellow travelers. The proclaimed concept of "racism" is what has most effectively defined the debate and united apparently disparate and even single-issue movements to make common cause in favor of migration. The perception that anyone opposed to mass migration was inherently a racist or neo-Nazi was particularly effective in stifling dissent in Europe because of the Continent's modern history. The concept served the left very well; support for migration served as an opportunity both for demonstrating moral superiority and for depicting critics in the worst possible light. Indeed, when trying to understand the political decisions and rhetoric surrounding the migrant crisis, the central place of the concept of racism in the historical context of World War II cannot be overstated.

Viewing the 2015 migrant crisis in the highly specific context of Nazi Germany was effective because it framed the issue in a way that moved the mainstream (if not majority) public discourse further toward the humanitarian left. This public discourse had an overwhelmingly powerful influence; it both endorsed the views of migrant advocates, and created the conditions for literal self-censorship (such as the government-enforced nonreporting of crimes committed against women by migrants in Sweden and Germany). In the 2015 migrant crisis, terms like "nationalism" or "populism" or "Islamophobia" all became conflated and were used to define and denigrate opponents of the prevailing leftist public discourse. As such, a much wider swathe of European society was affected by leftist rhetoric than just those who identified with some sort of liberal or "progressive" outlook.

The tacit consensus over a liberal migration viewpoint was most demonstrable at the top level of the European Union, which is itself fundamentally leftist in being a supranational organization the mandate of which is to take competencies and funds from sovereign states, and reorganize and redistribute them for a supposedly common good. The consensus-based approach extends to how the EU institutions divide these powers. Members of the European Parliament are members of national parties elected by their domestic voters, but become parts of larger blocs within the European Union in order to redistribute power and pass legislation. This consensus model allows powerful positions (EU commissioners and so on) to be negotiated between party blocs.

After 2014 elections, such negotiations brought conservative Jean-Claude Juncker to power as head of the European Commission, while also making the left-wing Martin Schulz head of the European Parliament. During the migrant crisis, Schulz was known for his forthright and dismissive attitude toward critics of EU migration policies. For example, he condemned the Hungarian government's February 2016 announcement of referendum on the European Union's mandatory migrant quota scheme as a "populist and nationalist response to a global challenge." This represented the general leftist view of conservative challenges to Brussels's planned migration policies.

In the European Parliament today, national-level leftist parties can join into four major left-wing blocs that exist along with the major right-wing blocs. The Progressive Alliance of Socialists and Democrats (known in short as S&D) bloc, led by Gianni Pittella, won a total of 189 Member of European Parliament (MEP) seats in 2014, constituting the largest left-wing block. The Alliance of Liberals and Democrats for Europe (ALDE) group, led by Guy Verhofstadt of the Netherlands, won 69 MEP seats in those elections. Further to the left are two other blocs, the European United Left-Nordic Green Left (GUE-NGL) with 52 MEPs and the Greens-European Free Alliance (Greens-EFA) with 50 MEPs in 2014. There are also smaller sub-groups such as the Initiative of Communist and Workers Parties.

The most prominent national-level parties in EU countries find a place in such groupings when their candidates are elected to Brussels. But the blocs have little influence on national elections directly. It has often been said that the average citizen could not name their countries' own elected MEPs—let alone what parliamentary blocs they belong to or what their roles may be in Brussels. There are also several European countries that are not EU members, either by choice (Norway, Switzerland, Iceland, and, soon, Britain) or by being frozen out (much of the Balkans and Turkey). Of course, all of these countries are democracies with their own more or less ideologically established parties, and in this sense it can be said that all affect or are affected by positions and attitudes in Brussels.

In the bigger picture, the migrant crisis has accentuated a general trend in which traditional ideological distinctions and political platforms are changing rapidly, to keep up with new perceptions and needs of society. This is equally true for both right and left. In 2015, migration was just one issue—albeit the most dramatic—of many important to European populations. However, the quantitative and logistical dilemmas that accompanied the unprecedented wave of migrants affected a wide range of existing issues, from borders and security to human rights and the economy, thus making it unusually relevant to a variety of different causes.

Throughout the crisis, the left seemed to be on the defensive; the rise of right-wing parties opposed to migration led them to reactive stances and to accuse critics of various forms of xenophobia and racism. But more so than for any other ideology, liberalism in Europe is facing a moment of reckoning. With each new terrorist attack or crime committed by migrants, the left's support for migration and multiculturalism will increasingly be criticized as self-contradictory and hypocritical by opponents. The left has typically dismissed the highlighting of such events as "scaremongering," but there are very real concerns that they have failed to address, which are vital for Europe's future.

The most obvious is the continued leftist support for migrant populations coming from social worldviews that are fundamentally opposed to their proclaimed European values. An interesting phenomenon during the crisis has been that leftist groups tend not to respond—or to make incoherent accusations—when contradictions are bought up. The types of reaction can also vary by country. But when violence against women or homosexuals is carried out by the same Muslim migrants whose causes they have championed, left-wing ideologues become very easy targets for criticism. The fundamental charge of the right, that leftists betray traditional European values by proclaiming their tolerance for societies that do not reciprocate has become one of the major issues in today's Europe. And it seems to be having a radicalizing effect. The left usually responds to such accusations by avoiding them, or by claiming that such arguments tacitly indicate the accuser's lurking racist, neo-Nazi and populist proclivities. This attitude has further limited the capacity for Europe's divided political factions to communicate—a problem that has only been compounded by the echo-chamber effect created by today's social media. And the lack of critical self-examination on both sides will lead to increasing polarization and rhetorical attacks over what concepts like "European values" and "racism" do or should mean.

Thus increasingly unpopular establishment left parties tended, during the migration crisis, to justify their own grip on power by pointing to the alleged danger represented by the other side. If right-wing parties' concerns about Muslim migrants amounted to mere "scaremongering," it could be said that the same fear tactics were used by the left in order to keep the other side out of power. As such, both opposing blocs began to increasingly identify themselves not in terms of their own positive attributes, but in terms of the dangers allegedly represented by the other side.

The countless examples of this rhetorical trend included the significant media attention that accompanied Norbert Hofer's candidacy for the presidency of Austria in 2016. The media reaction was similar to that of 2002, when France's right-wing Front National founded Jean Le Pen made it to the second round of voting in the French presidential election. In both cases, the media went into overdrive regarding the "shocking" possibility of a European state electing the first far-right candidate since World War II. Yet while in 2002 the disparate French electorate rallied against Le Pen, giving his rival Jacques Chirac a landslide win, the Austrian election 14 years later ended somewhat differently. Amid unrest over migration, Hofer lost by a razor-thin margin to Alexander Van der Bellen (an independent close to the leftist Green Party), though the result was later annulled. A planned election rerun for September 2016 was postponed— allegedly, due to faulty ballot envelopes, but more realistically because timid Austrian officials did not want to be tarred by a right-wing victory. Van der Bellen finally won and assumed office to the largely ceremonial post in January 2017.

The problem for the left with the migration crisis is that it does not benefit—at least not immediately—from it. As elections in countries like Greece and Spain have shown, the establishment left has been gutted due to a lack of public confidence and years of austerity measures. In Greece, the dynastic establishment left PASOK party (which had ruled for much of the previous three decades) essentially left for dead in the 2015 elections. But also in Britain, which was not affected by austerity measures, the 2016 election of liberal ideologue Jeremy Corbyn to lead the opposition Labour Party indicated a bold break with tradition. Throughout Europe, there was a general feeling that the establishment had stagnated, had nothing to offer, or had veered too far from its liberal roots. This, too, in part explains the tendency of left-wing parties to act defensively and reactively on migration, preferring to highlight the alleged dangers of their opponents instead of offering a positive program of their own on the issue.

The migrant crisis thus especially affected countries that had elections, or were expecting major elections in the next year. It is impossible to understand general European posturing or policies concerning migration without also considering the strategizing going on, for example, in preparation for the Dutch, French, and German elections of 2017. The potential for new leaderships that could upend previously decided migration, trade, and other policies had a powerful influence on the decisions and leverage of both government and opposition.

In this climate, it also became tempting for ground-level political forces to try and use migration for demographic benefit. This is, of course, a stratagem increasingly encountered globally, including in the United States. It thus seemed entirely sensible that incoming migrants would vote—in the cases that they could—for those parties or leaders that had abetted their arrival. In 2016, there was news that the French government was "rushing citizenship" for new migrants in order to add votes for a highly unpopular Socialist party. French investigative journalists claimed that "the number of people given French citizenship this year is likely to soar 45 per cent from 2015's figure, with the vast majority of 'new French' from North Africa. The spike follows a concerted push by the ruling Socialist Party to naturalise 100,000 people a year."[1]

Why were such overtures necessary? It was a crisis year in the making, but by 2016 a series of events had cumulatively damaged the Socialists. The increasing polarization of society had been attested all year long by protests against government reforms, fears of yet more terrorism, and the chaotic breakup of the Calais "Jungle" migrant camp, which led thousands of migrants to take their turf war and tents to the streets of Paris. For Hollande, most damaging was the publication of a book by journalists from *Le Monde*, in which Hollande spoke dismissively of allies, rivals, and celebrities, and even laid bare private concerns about Islam at odds with official policy. By the end of October 2016, Hollande's "record unpopularity" of 4 percent had thrown the party into disarray; Reuters cited Benoit Hamon, a former education minister under Hollande, as saying "this is what happens with policies that bewilder left-wing voters, those who once backed François Hollande."[2]

By late January 2017, the leftist party had voted in Hamon as its new leader; critics compared him unflatteringly to the British Labour Party's Jeremy Corbyn, insinuating that both were pushing their similarly flailing parties even further to the left. And this would thereby reduce even further the likelihood that a Socialist Party candidate would win France's national elections in May 2017. Many more centrist members were reported to be leaning toward the "independent," Emmanuel Macron.[3]

The 39-year-old Macron had served as a banker with the Rothschilds, and joined the Hollande government's economic ministry, only to depart in August 2016, just in time to launch a grassroots campaign known as "En Marche!" ("on the move"). As a young and charismatic speaker, Macron was compared by media to a young Tony Blair or Barack Obama. He was depicted as "an unashamed liberal globaliser" with a pro-EU, centrist position.[4] Macron campaigned with speeches that offered more style than substantive policy; he offered "not an ideology or a program," stated Philippe Marliere, a French politics professor, but "more an attitude, a way of addressing people," he stated.[5] Macron's background in high finance was instantly targeted by antiglobalist, right-wing opponent Marine Le Pen. But as the 2017 elections drew nearer, the smart money was on a milquetoast Macron defeating Le Pen, as leftists would rally to his side simply to thwart the right-wing candidate.

However, Macron offered no solutions for an increasingly flammable security situation, as massive riots against police again engulfed Paris in February. Naturally, public safety issues such as this benefited the candidates on the right. This depleted state of affairs on the establishment left guaranteed that migration and religion would take a major role in France's political future, before and after the 2017 elections. The left would seek to depict the right, naturally, as Islamophobic and xenophobic; but not only was this an ideological issue for the average French leftist, it had also become a strategic one for the Hollande–Valls alliance. The behavior of the French leadership in 2016 appears to have been part of their long-term strategy to influence demographics for election purposes through encouraging migration. In 2012, France's interior minister (and later, prime minister) Manuel Valls reportedly "took a wrecking ball to the previous centre-right government's naturalisation criteria"; justifying the decision by chiding France's alleged xenophobia, Valls eliminated multiple-choice tests on French culture and values for aspiring citizens, while no longer requiring candidates to have permanent contracted work. The Socialist politician declared that 100,000 new French citizens should be minted each year, and voiced his wish that naturalization by marriage would happen for 20,000 spouses of French citizens annually.[6]

Such rhetoric and policies have given the right-wing plenty of room for growth, under the banner that France (which historically has had large populations of nonassimilated Muslims) was losing its cultural identity and secular constitutional bearing. In its discovery of the massive post-crisis increase in citizenships being given, investigative journal *Causeur* reported in October 2016 that it was an "open secret" that the department managing French citizenship procedures had been "a machine that is naturalising in full swing." Some 78 percent of the total "New French" citizens come from Morocco, Algeria, Tunisia, Turkey, and Senegal, with an unprecedented backlog of applications ready to be approved before the election.[7] Naturalizations increased massively following Valls's 2012 legal innovations. In 2015 alone, 113,603 people were naturalized, and the 2016 numbers were expected to increase this trend significantly.[8] Some 93 percent of Muslims had supported Hollande's 2012 presidential campaign, because of his promise to amnesty an estimated 400,000 illegal Muslim migrants.[9] Indeed, it was the 1.7 million Muslims voters who made the difference for Hollande, "who beat incumbent president Nicolas Sarkozy by just 1.1 million votes."[10]

Considering this recent history, it is certain that the Socialists will remain keen supporters of the migrant and Muslim vote for the foreseeable future. All parties even further to the left will do the same. However, in the longer term, and not only in France, migrants will not simply vote for the leftist or other parties that had originally abetted their arrival and naturalization. With the passage of time and development of a presence, it is more likely that they will establish Islamist parties than that they will assimilate into European cultures. In whatever case, it is clear that the migration crisis will in the long term increase the role of Islamism in politics and further exacerbates internal ideological divisions between traditional rival parties and factions of society.

The situation in Spain was even more fractious through 2016, though migration is less of an issue because Spain is not seen as a destination country and has had good cooperation with Morocco to the south, effectively cutting off the flow of migrants that was more prevalent in the 1990s. However, this could change in the case of instability in Morocco or Algeria. This is not implausible, considering the instability of Libya and Islamist movements in Mali, Nigeria, and other countries. For now, the King of Morocco—a personality, not an institution—is the main guarantor against migrant floods into Spain. This was the same role that Qaddafi played for the Italians before his demise in 2011. Italy has since then paid a heavy price as a result of "regime change" in North Africa. However, the Strait of Gibraltar is seen as too vital to international commerce to allow unrest, and Spain has a small beachhead in Morocco (the enclaves of Melilla and Ceuta) that it uses to block most migrants from crossing. However, two concerted attacks on the border fencing there in February 2017 showed that security risks still remained for EU migration routes in the western Mediterranean.[11]

As in Greece, public unrest over the economy and austerity measures was the major factor that allowed a populist left-wing movement to challenge the establishment left. The Spanish leftist movement Podemos gained importance, first as a grassroots antiausterity movement and then more generally as a party. In October 2016, partisan commentators bemoaned the "implosion" of Spain's Socialist Workers Party (PSOE) "a 137-year-old party that at one point claimed the allegiance of half of Spain's people. It's now reduced to fratricidal infighting. The PSOE's embattled General Secretary Pedro Sánchez was forced to resign when party grandees and regional leaders organized a coup against his plan to form a united front of the left."[12] The farce became "street theater" when PSOE coup supporter Verónica Pérez was blocked from the party's headquarters by Sánchez supporters, and was forced to hold a press conference on a sidewalk. Even Pablo Iglesias, the leader of rival Podemos, was not relishing in the Socialist self-destruction, deeming it "the most important crisis since the end of the civil war in the most important Spanish party in the past century."[13]

Outside observers have looked with dismay and perhaps, too dramatically, at the deleterious situation on the Spanish left, with British left-wing newspapers deeming the country's leftist parties as the last hope against an allegedly dangerous right wing on the march across Europe.[14] The problems on the left owe to a larger and more general problem: the decline of a traditional system of two major parties. It echoed a similar phenomenon across Europe, in which new players on the margins of left and right had diluted the vote to the extent that strong coalitions became impossible to form after elections. As of October 2016, Spain had been unable to form a government for nine months despite multiple elections. An era of minority governments with weak mandates has thus arrived in Europe, with the migration crisis a major issue exacerbating the tendency of implosion of the traditional center, as Europeans become more divided over how to tackle economic problems, terrorism, and integration of migrants and minorities.

In the case of Spain—as in some other countries—the issue of ethnic Basque separatism compounded the political disharmony, with the controversial and perennial demand for Catalonian independence referendum further complicating the parties' ability to form a national coalition following December 2015 elections. Spain's wealthiest province, Catalonia, already enjoys substantial local government privileges, but many still demand a binding referendum on independence—something the major parties oppose. Podemos also opposes Catalan independence, but supports the locals' right to a referendum on principle. (Catalonia became incorporated into Spain during the War of the Spanish Succession in 1715.)

The European electorate's trend toward third-party options was visible in the December 2015 national elections, in which both the conservative People's Party (PP), led by Prime Minister Mariano Rajoy, and Sánchez's Socialists lost parliamentary seats in parliament. The PP lost 63 seats (and its parliamentary majority), while the PSOE lost 20 seats. From the margins, Podemos took 69 seats while right-wing nationalist party Ciudadanos won 40 seats. Yet despite political haggling, no coalition could be formed to reach a governing majority in the 350-seat Spanish parliament.

The effect was potential neutralization of the new left-wing contender, Podemos (which is strongest in Catalonia). If it joined an offered PSOE-Ciudadanos alliance, Podemos would lose credibility with its base. In a second election, in June 2016, Podemos did slightly worse than expected, though the PSOE fared much worse, leading to the infighting that characterized the year.

In the June 25, 2016, elections, the right-wing People's Party improved its numbers—partly due to the aftershock of the Brexit vote two days before—but could still not form a government. PP leader Rajoy offered PSOE a place in a new government with Ciudadanos. Sánchez refused, surmising that Podemos would be the ultimate beneficiary in that the establishment left would be discredited. "There is a good deal of precedent for that conclusion," recounted a partisan commentator, pointing to similar outcomes elsewhere in Europe. "The Greek Socialist Party (PASOK) formed a grand coalition with the right and was subsequently decimated by the left-wing Syriza Party. The German Social Democratic Party's alliance with the conservative Christian Democratic Union has seen the once mighty organization slip below 20 percent in the polls. England's Liberal Democratic Party was destroyed by its alliance with the Conservatives."[15]

Also as in Greece, where former PASOK prime minister George Papandreou suffered the ill-timing of presiding over a looming financial collapse in 2009, the Spanish Socialists had been blamed for abandoning their economic policy when running an austerity program in 2010. The establishment left is also vulnerable to geographic divisions, and so it was with the Sánchez coup, which began when the party's Andalusian branch withdrew support for the party leader amid fears that he would change policy on a Catalan referendum to win over Podemos. Andalusian coup leader Susana Díaz, poised to take over the PSOE general secretariat, even announced she would let Rajoy form a minority government. "First we need to give Spain a government," she said, "and then open a deep debate in the PSOE."[16] Ultimately, however, she had simply displaced the unpopular Sánchez and conceded to the right-wing's earlier demand, which would ultimately allow Podemos to become the main left-wing party.[17]

Indeed, with this outcome, the Catalan separatist issue will become more prominent—in domestic politics, more polarized—something that is part of a general trend toward regional separatism in Europe today. In February 2017, analysts were anticipating further internal division if the conservative government used the " nuclear option" (a never-used constitutional provision meant to prevent autonomous regions from declaring independence) ahead of an expected referendum in September.[18]

However, as has happened in Greece, the upstart leftist party also moderated its stance on socioeconomic issues, alienating fellow travelers like Spain's United Left (or Izquierda Unida, IU), a coalition that includes the Communist Party. And, as in Greece, the immediate effect of this for left-wing voters was political disillusionment. To rectify this situation, Podemos held a party congress in February 2017. It saw ideals win out over pragmatism, as founder Pablo Iglesias fended off a leadership challenge from party secretary Irigo Errejon. The party had decided to "return to the streets" and stick to its far-left ideology, rather than try to appease the PSOE-centrist public.[19]

This course correction provided more potential for cooperation with pro-refugee activists, but only among some Podemos factions; the party in general remained focused on economy and social welfare. The complexity of the Catalonian independence issue also meant that the massive February 18, 2017, pro-refugee rally in the Catalan capital of Barcelona sparked cynicism among even farther-left Trotskyites, who accused the city's pro-Podemos mayor, as well as more conservative pro-secessionist parties, of falsely supporting refugees for their own, often divergent, political goals.[20]

Indeed, the fact that Spain was relatively unaffected by the 2015 migrant crisis made the size of the February 18 rally even more unusual; drawing more than 150,000 pro-refugee protesters, it was Europe's largest to date. Marchers in Barcelona demanded the government more fully implement the EU migrant redistribution quota scheme.[21]

Spain's Mediterranean neighbors had borne the brunt of the migrant crisis, which of course influenced leftist politics more so than in Spain. Both Italian prime minister Matteo Renzi (who resigned in December 2016, following a failed referendum on institutional changes) and his Greek counterpart Alexis Tsipras made identical calls for "European solutions" and "solidarity" with their countries over migration. And this also led them directly to more visibly exploit their representation in Brussels. Both countries had surprisingly powerful commissioners: Italy's Federica Mogherini was the commissioner for external affairs, while Greece's Dimitris Avramopoulos headed the home affairs and migration commission. These direct connections were crucial to getting special attention reserved for both countries—as well as funds—during the migration crisis.

Ironically, the Greeks had won such a high position at the commission partly due to their role in the internal horse-trading that followed 2014 EU elections, when conservative prime minister Antonis Samaras had helped fellow conservative Angela Merkel get Jean-Claude Juncker appointed as head of the commission. In fact, Tsipras himself had shot to prominence domestically after a strong debate performances against Juncker (he had been selected as the EU Socialist bloc's candidate for EU Commissioner, despite being in opposition in Greece at that time). Tsipras capitalized on his new international visibility to win mass support for his upstart Syriza party—a motley collection of far-left parties and special-interest groups—to prevail in January 2015 elections against Samaras's New Democracy (ND) party, on a platform that was dominated by opposition to the austerity measures championed by Merkel, Juncker, and Samaras and implemented by Papandreou before him.

As mentioned, the main immediate political casualty of Syriza's victory was the collapse of traditional bastion of the left PASOK, which saw mass defections. Previously run by George Papandreou, and his famous father Andreas Papandreou before him, it too had started as a somewhat revolutionary leftist party in 1974, one that would, in its long years in power, enjoy a long and comfortable slide into the overspending, corruption, and bureaucratic bloat that indirectly fed the Greek financial crisis from 2009 on. But in summer 2015 it was leftist successor Tsipras who would blink first in a stare-off with the Troika (the IMF, World Bank, and European Central Bank) of foreign lenders responsible for continuing Greece's bailout program. After the temporary imposition of capital controls amid fears of massive bank runs, Tsipras caved in to the lenders' demands for policies like higher taxation, more privatizations, and pension cuts that Syriza had specifically opposed in winning their mandate.

This capitulation siphoned off public support for Syriza to some degree, and led to a split within the party, as the far left broke off to form new blocs. But Greek voters did not see traditional conservative New Democracy as offering anything better. Thus the coalition that Syriza had made with the new right-wing "third party," the Independent Greeks (ANEL) of Defense Minister Panos Kammenos, survived a second round of elections later in the summer. Mirroring a phenomenon encountered elsewhere in Europe, the two new faces on the left and right were diametrically imposed on important social, cultural, and national issues, but were united by the major issue of the economy and opposition to austerity measures. And, in the Greece of 2015, this was sufficient for forming a government, albeit a weak one. By the second election, Tsipras had also realized that his government—which had few members experienced in turning the wheels of bureaucracy—needed more capable hands, and he thus incorporated a few old-guard PASOK members who had had prior administrative experience. As in Spain, the new left had veered further toward the center. Tsipras was forced to reshuffle his cabinet again toward the center in October 2016, to forestall another early election.[22]

Given its lack of leverage on big economic issues, Syriza (and Tsipras personally) actually benefited tremendously from the refugee crisis, even if the country as a whole did not. The Syriza government enjoyed institutional support from the European Union and influential Greeks in the UN aid structures in New York, as well as a liberal Barack Obama administration, and even the Vatican. Tsipras, himself a devout atheist, added to his image as an outstanding supporter of the humanitarian cause in April 2016, by appearing with Pope Francis on Lesvos, along with the Orthodox Patriarch, Bartholomew, and the Archbishop of Athens. He took advantage of the chaotic situation on the northern border, where Macedonian police had just days before been forced to push back migrants attacking the border; on Lesvos, Tsipras tried to contrast himself against such allegedly less enlightened European leaders.

In reality, however, the migrant crisis had little effect on most Greeks. The Tsipras government was exceptionally good at complaining—a time-honored and endemic national trait—and this proved clever politically, as it heightened Greece's visibility as a "victim" of the crisis, while winning the government hundreds of millions of euros from Brussels and aid organizations. In the few places where the tourism economy had been damaged, like the Eastern Aegean islands of Samos, Lesvos, and Chios, a new "NGO economy" helped offset the losses. But in general, 2015 and 2016 saw massive tourism increases, due to cheaper prices and perceived security risks at traditional Turkish and North African destinations. And with the exception of migrant-heavy areas of central Athens, migrants did not tend to congregate throughout the country, as they were either kept in camps or sought to transit it as quickly as possible. In any case, Greek society had been accustomed to a community of itinerant economic migrants for 25 years already, a presence that has largely been mutually tolerable. So with the expectation of sporadic violence involving migrants and far-left and far-right groups, the crisis did not translate into the kind of violence seen in destination countries like Germany, Sweden, France, and Belgium.

This reality of a generally safe home environment has allowed leftists in southern Europe to indulge heavily in the key concept that racism and xenophobia are the only explanations for public opposition to mass migration. The quality of activism on behalf of "refugee rights" was thus strong in these countries, ones where migrants were essentially just passing through. Yet in pondering abstract values and cherished dreams of a "European solution," such supporters generally did not account for the fact that the effects of travel and reality of location would change the outlook, behavior, and expectations of migrants during their journey. For both locals and migrants, the idea of what was both desirable and acceptable differed dramatically in different parts of Europe. But the rhetoric of the many dedicated activists from Western Europe who volunteered to help migrants in places like Greece and Italy did not confirm this reality; rather, they obscured it further.

As has been seen, the Italian experience has, like Greece, involved volatility at southern borders (where migrants enter) and at northern ones (where standoffs with Austrian officials seeking to block migrants were frequent). But also as in Greece, the majority of Italian citizens have been relatively unaffected by violence due to migrants. Despite threats from ISIS, which sees the Vatican as a ripe, symbolic target, Italy is essentially a transit country and is thus less of a terrorist target than are the countries to its north. Both Greece and Italy have, therefore, been relatively immune from the terrorism threat associated with migration, and through the crisis this allowed migration to be regarded domestically as a humanitarian rather than a security issue. The reactions of Italy's former prime minister, Matteo Renzi were thus essentially similar to those of Tsipras.

A former mayor of Florence, Renzi came to power in 2014, at the age of 39 becoming the youngest premier in Italian history. Renzi's center-left coalition Democratic Party (PD) emerged in 2007 from a grouping of other leftist parties; however, unlike the cases of Syriza or Podemos, the PD brought under one roof blocs that included Catholic leftists and establishment fixtures such as the centrist Democrats of former EU commissioner and prime minister, Romano Prodi. The PD won the largest representation in Italy's Chamber of Deputies and Senate in 2013 national elections. In 2014 European parliamentary elections, the PD became the largest leftist party in Brussels (which certainly helped it win the prestigious external affairs commission for party member Federica Mogherini). In 2015 local elections, the Democratic Party won 15 out of 20 local regional governors.

This relatively stronger mandate allowed Renzi to implement more classically leftist policies such as justice reforms, tax relief, and legislation meant to benefit labor and employment, as well as to boost growth. The Italian premier was able to introduce reforms of the public administration and intelligence services after several scandals, while even introducing same-sex civil unions in a traditionally socially conservative bastion of Catholicism. But with the arrival of Pope Francis, the most liberal pontiff in history, Renzi had found a natural ally in the Vatican—and one who has been firmly committed to the pro-migrant cause.

The Italian leader surely owed some of his achievements to the lack of restraints that have affected Spain and Greece, specifically, austerity measures. But throughout the migrant crisis finance was consistently presented as an area of potential concern, with questions about the stability of Italy's banking system often being raised. Economists consistently warned that Italy's relatively larger economy and banking sector means that, unlike Greece, no bailout could be attempted in the case of a financial sector collapse. This should be taken into consideration as a factor affecting Renzi's decision making during the migrant crisis, and his constant appeals to Brussels for more funding and implementation of the refugee quota system.

The migrant crisis has influenced leftist parties in destination countries like Germany and Sweden, where antimigrant movements are more powerful than in Southern Europe. The cultural differences between the two regions have also led to different styles of reaction from leftist leaders. Thus while leaders in the more demonstrative cultures like Italy and Greece have made vociferous protests—with Renzi event threatening to block the EU budget for 2017 unless he got more migrant assistance—the more subdued Northern Europeans have tended to speak and act in a quieter and more subtle manner.

When the migrant crisis erupted, leftists were also running the show in Sweden, which was (with Germany) initially very welcoming to migrants, in keeping with its long-standing generous policy of social benefits for asylum-seekers. Indeed, the newcomers were attracted to the Scandinavian outpost not for the cold weather or warm welcome, but for the quasi-Socialist country's financial and social benefits. This would lead to tremendous burdening of the system and an eventual reversal of migration policy. However, in the beginning of the crisis, asylum seekers could not have dreamt of a more receptive government. Sweden's 2014 election had brought the Social Democrats (SD) to power. The country's oldest and largest political party, the Social Democrats had dominated until the 1990s, laying the foundations of Sweden's celebrated welfare state. After defeats in 2006 and 2010, the party reclaimed power following the general election in September 2014 (when it formed a coalition with the Green Party).

The SD's new prime minister, Stefan Löfven, had previously headed one of Sweden's most powerful trade unions, IF Metall. His coalition partner, the Greens (which had never been in government until 2014), ran on a platform of fighting climate change and supporting general environmental initiatives. After the migrant crisis began, Sweden made controversial decisions like recognizing Palestine, while miffing Saudi Arabia in 2015 with its advocacy for a feminist foreign policy. (However, relations in Scandinavia are ultimately more pragmatic, as was seen by the visit of a Swedish arms dealer to the kingdom later the next year, during Riyadh's war on Yemen.)[23]

Further to the left, the Left Party has Communist roots and offers the classic ideological platform, opposing privatizations and calling for higher taxation to prop up the welfare state. Although it has never been in power, the Left Party lends informal support to Social Democrat governments and has numerous elected parliamentarians, such as party president Jonas Sjöstedt, a former metal worker, former MEP, and ideologue married to Ann Måwe, a diplomat with Sweden's UN delegation. Finally, Sweden's small Feminist Initiative (which has similarly never enjoyed power) mobilizes against gender and racial discrimination, and also opposes military spending and arms exports by Swedish companies.

With a government and general left primarily motivated by issues like these, it was no surprise that the country was completely overwhelmed by the migrant crisis. Sweden's general outlook, cultural values, and geography have tended to make security a low priority, and the country suffered for that oversight during the crisis. At crucial times, the authorities chose to preserve the country's blissful image at the expense of reality. For example, in January 2016, an internal police investigation revealed that police and media had covered mass sexual assaults by immigrants at a music festival. The government's solution was to prevent police from providing ethnic descriptions of suspects, to avoid accusations of racism against migrants.[24]

This sort of reaction, so predictable in politically correct European countries like Sweden, sparked massive pushback from nationalists, and particularly the right-wing Sweden Democrats. During the crisis, it often seemed that the government was less keen to guarantee public safety than it was to create a positive image of the migrants, in order to limit damage to itself and prevent the opposition from capitalizing on negative events. To this end, media and public figures were instrumentalized to push positive propaganda (or, at least, not report on stories of migrant violence). However, the seething Muslim ghettoes of cities like Malmö and Gothenburg had been flashpoints for years already, and the arrival of tens of thousands of new migrants proved politically and structurally unsustainable. In November 2015, Green Party member and deputy prime minister Åsa Romson—a grown woman—memorably cried on television when announcing that the country could no longer accept a flood of refugees. She hinted that the Greens, and perhaps the coalition, would have been damaged if she had refused to follow the new directive.[25]

Many observers, and hardly just right-wing extremists, have been astonished by the open-door migration policy, lack of security protocol, and self-censorship of hard-left countries like Sweden. In many ways, Sweden is an anachronism to the postwar European dream of peace, harmony, and lavish social spending. For decades renowned for its schools, hospitals, and generally harmonious way of life, Sweden today has experienced severe problems due to a dramatic rise in crime and violence mostly fueled by immigrants. In October 2016, it was reported that a record number of police officers were turning in their badges due to their inability to even work in safety in some "no-go" areas. Yet appeasement seems to be a policy that will continue in Sweden, no matter what it chooses to do with migration numbers, and it may pay a heavy price in terms of future terrorism and organized crime.

Compared to Sweden, liberal countries like the Netherlands have a more celebrated history of interparty acrimony regarding migration and Islam. In the latter, as in France, Denmark, and Britain, the key point defining the issue is that of free speech and cultural tolerance. The feisty debate that has ensued in Holland in recent years has manifested in quite the opposite way from consensus-oriented, censorship-ready Sweden. Instead, the debate has been loud, heated, and tended to end in litigation. Holland is one of the core EU countries, and therefore its leaders undertook a more involved and pragmatic role during the crisis, as they recognized mass migration posed a threat to the very existence of the European Union itself. The leader of the centrist People's Party for Freedom and Democracy (VVD), Prime Minister Mark Rutte, warned, in January 2016 that European leaders "need to get a grip on this issue." Otherwise, the

Schengen Zone could break down "within two months," Rutte warned, citing the need for Turkey to cut refugee numbers to "zero."[26] While the VVD is considered a conservative-liberal party, it has worked with center-right parties like the Christian Democratic Appeal (CDA) in 2010, but later formed a government with the Labor Party (PVDA), in 2012. This social-democratic party is a direct descendent of the postwar restructuring of Europe, formed back in 1946. During the 1970s, it added women's rights, third-world development, and environmentalism to its agenda. Like other center-left parties, PVDA was eviscerated in March 2017 voting.

Nowhere in Europe has the migrant crisis confused the traditional identities of right and left as much as it has in Germany. As we have seen, the country can be considered a special case owing to its history. This makes the state's orientation toward free speech and public organizations very different than in other European countries. In Germany the interior ministry can, and does, shut down organizations deemed to be too far to the right, in addition to occasional far-left organizations. Ironically, in this sense of a heavy-handed approach toward ideologically "dangerous" groups, Germany and Turkey actually have quite a lot in common.

The migrant crisis brought ideological confusion to Germany fundamentally because it was a conservative (at least in principle) government that had invited the migrants to enter. By the time of the crisis, Angela Merkel's Christian Democratic Union (CDU) and the Bavarian Christian Social Union (CSU) coalition had apparently spent all of its conservative capital on belt-tightening austerity measures for the Greeks. Merkel's open-ended invitation to migrants surpassed even that of liberal Sweden. Merkel's weak coalition included Germany's major left-wing party, the Social Democratic Party (SPD), a factor that certainly affected the overall dynamic of the approach to the migrant crisis. SPD has served since 2013 in a "grand coalition" with the CDU and CSU, and Merkel indeed owes her chancellorship to the left's participation. Founded in 1875, SPD is the oldest surviving German party, from the first days of Marxism. Today, it advocates social justice, freedom, and solidarity, as well as a sustainable fiscal policy, open society, and global peace.

Through 2016, the SPD was led by the leftist Sigmund Gabriel, Merkel's economy minister and vice chancellor. However, he stepped aside when former European Parliament president Martin Schulz returned from Brussels to take over the party leadership in January 2017—a dramatic move that injected new life into the leftist party. By February, analysts were widely predicting that Schulz would unseat the unpopular Merkel in upcoming fall 2017 elections. Schulz was seen as a breath of fresh air following 12 years of Merkel's leadership and, however inexplicably for a pro-EU Brussels insider, recasting himself as a "man of the people."[27] The prospect that Germany could go even further to the left, and possibly incorporate even more pro-migrant parties, was a terrifying one for parties and citizens already long fed up with Merkel's "open-door" migration policy.

Nevertheless, barring any unforeseen events, by March 2017 the possibility of a future pro-EU, pro-migrant leftist government ruling Germany seemed very probable. Such a prospect would, of course, guarantee further polarization between the left and far-right in future. Indeed, a taste of what a Schulz-led government was planning was revealed in a February 2017 study commissioned by a party-related think-tank. The report (grandly entitled "Together in Diversity: A Guiding Concept and Agenda for a Society of Immigration"), called for affirmative action, greater migrant privileges, and even the right to vote for non-citizens.[28]

The Alliance 90/Greens is the second major leftist party in Germany, dating to German reunification. In the 2013 federal elections, the party won 8 percent of the vote, making it the country's fourth-largest party at the time. On October 18, 2016, Green Party spokesmen Volker Beck, in an interview, reportedly said that Germans worried about migrants should learn Arabic, just as Americans might learn Spanish. The comment caused a firestorm of criticism, with the CDU's Christina Schwarzer stating that "learning German is the cornerstone of integration." Beck, who had apparently been arrested earlier in the year for a drugs offense, insisted that he had been misunderstood, but the incident did cause some internal dissent among Green Party members.[29]

Germany's smaller opposition leftist parties are more extremist still, and some have had a direct influence on directing pro-migrant activities. Die Linke (The Link) is a radical leftist party with close anarchist ties like Antifa (Antifaschistische Aktion, or Antifascist Action). Such groups supported an existing far-left community in Berlin and other cities that was already active across a broad swathe of social issues, working informally with comrades from across Europe and indeed the world. It is this network aspect of migrant activism that marked a key feature in the general handling of the migrant crisis by Europe's left. Just as Angela Merkel had a key role on the state level in organizing the migrant crisis, German anarchists and other activists were very prominent in coordinating activities at home and across Europe. The so-called No Border activist group and the Welcome to Europe website (which offered detailed information to assist migrants traveling in various European countries) were just two of the many loosely affiliated anarchist groups that coordinated their movements by social media and that had an impact from Britain to Greece and beyond.

The leftist actions ranged from migrant housing (in anarchist squats in several countries) to refugee assistance on Greek islands, and various so-called caravans in which dozens of cars or campers would transport food and supplies to migrants in Greece and Italy. Activists also engaged in protests, sometimes violent, against European border agencies, state structures, and opposing right-wing groups. This activity tended to rise when a new humanitarian tragedy topped the news, when an EU decision was announced, or when a country closed a border or built a border fence. For example, in September 2015, thousands protested outside the prime minister's residence in London, waving signs reading "Open the Borders" and "Refugees In." Roughly 30,000 protesters chanted pro-refugee slogans in one rally outside the Danish parliament in Copenhagen. Other protests were held in Sweden, France, Austria, Greece, Italy, and Holland, among others. Interestingly, far-left protests tended to intensify in the aftermath of terrorist attacks or violent crimes committed by migrants, as counter-protests to demonstrations by right-wing movements. In fact, one often overlooked reality about the migrant crisis was that it represented, for the far left, a renewed reason to wage street battles with the right and with the state. All of the leftist groups united by the "racism" charge against opponents of migration brought their own pet interests and peripheral issues along with them, creating an eclectic set of overlapping interests and relationships.

During the migrant crisis, organized waves of anarchists tended to pass between Germany, Italy, and Greece in order to carry out coordinated protests and sometimes attacks. Thus, in mid-March, activists swarmed to Eidomeni on the Greek–Macedonian border, where they organized a mass invasion through a river crossing, leading to the drowning of three refugees and deportation of several hundred European journalists, activists, and anarchists. Many were banned from reentering Macedonia for six months or longer. The country's exclusion from the Schengen Zone had proved a positive, in that it could safeguard itself from violent extremists who, intelligence information revealed, included some political activists who had planned to engage in a larger plot for state destabilization.

Unlike Macedonia, the anarchists could freely come and go in the Schengen Zone countries. In April 2016, hundreds of "No Border" activists massed at the Brenner Pass, on the Italy–Austria border, to protest Austria's plans for stricter border controls, leading to fights with Austrian police who were forced to use batons, shields, and pepper spray to beat back the attackers. A total of 15 people were injured. Returning to Greece, the activists led the season's major attack on the Greek–Macedonian border, the unsuccessful but much-photographed attempt of several hundred migrants to break through the border fence at Eidomeni. A few weeks later, on May 7, clashes again broke out at the Brenner Pass, where for the third time in a month hundreds of anarchists threw stones and firecrackers at Italian police, who used tear gas to disperse the mob.

Looking at the situation in more depth, it becomes clear that the far-left groups active in the crisis were tightly networked, well coordinated on social media, and global in their outlook regarding migration and the overall need to destroy borders. As was said about the opportunity the crisis provided to make war on the far right, migration also allowed activists a chance to expand their sphere of interest and working partners. Nowhere was this as visible as in Greece where anarchist activities in support of migrants' rights might run the gamut of participation in "anti-racism" festivals, volunteering medical assistance, and working with comrades supporting the armed struggle in Donbass or Kurdistan. The general convergence between anarchists and migrant activists is thus an eclectic one, with a variety of causes and interests represented.[30]

Greece's long and celebrated history of left-wing urban violence goes back to the 1967–1974 military junta, which sparked a leftist resistance movement that would also affect politics and society in general. Anarchist groups grew, proliferating ideology through various publications and activities, while left-wing violence—within acceptable social limits— became a historic phenomenon, particularly in urban Athens. Although far-left violence typically involves nothing more than symbolic vandalism, graffiti, and the occasional Molotov cocktail or protest, extraordinary examples also exist, like the 17 November terrorist group, which killed dozens of people including a CIA station chief, British military officer, and various businessmen and politicians between 1974 and 2002, when it was disbanded. However, the far-left in Greece today seems to have settled down and divided its interests. Compared to the golden age of the Greek "armed struggle," today's anarchists are much less deadly. Former U.S. State Department official John Brady Kiesling, who studied the history of the armed struggle in detail and attended the 17 November trials in Athens, notes that the terrorist group's ability to operate undetected for 27 years "is unlikely to ever be broken." He attributes this to improvements in police surveillance and general technology in a changed world.[31]

In addition to this operational challenge, there is also the issue of intent. The evidence suggests that anarchist groups in popular areas like Exarcheia in Athens, or in the northern city of Thessaloniki, are divided by ideology and interest. Some see helping migrants as a humanitarian issue, while others see it as a challenge to the state. Oftentimes, supporters reveal aspects of both, with opposition to "racism" again being the prime uniting factor in support of migrants-rights cases. Organizing migrant squats is a time-honored tradition, as is making symbolic acts of violence when police shut them down.

Another, more serious bunch support armed robberies, attacks on police, and attempts to free fellow "comrades" from jail. These tend to be associated with more recent left-wing terrorist groups like Revolutionary Struggle or Conspiracy of Cells of Fire. With the exception of a rocket attack against the U.S. Embassy in Athens, such groups have not managed really significant acts—and it is not clear that they are seeking to do so.[32] But of the 80 anarchist groups now believed to exist in Athens, none of them seem particularly interested in assassinating government officials or other figures accused of displaying antirefugee ideologies or engaging in actions detrimental to refugees. Rather than sophisticated and well-timed operations, the Greek far-left groups have limited their ambitions to blunter, more symbolic, and more random attacks in places where they are easiest, chiefly against police, banks and state symbols.[33] Left-wing extremists in Greece more often use the migrant issue as an excuse to attack their favorite enemy—the "Fascists" from the far right. This is a decades-old antagonism, dating ultimately to the Greek Civil War (1946–1949), and for Greece's modern-day far-left, acting on the migrant issue is a natural impulse in the general war on "racist" and "Fascist" forces in the country.

Differences between anarchist ideologies on an inter-European basis were also seen during the migrant crisis. For example, in July 2016 the No Border activist movement occupied Thessaloniki's central university grounds for almost two weeks, with a large contingent of German blackshirted member who insisted on creating internal security peripheries and banned photography. For more relaxed attendees, such behavior was rather absurd.[34] And the isolated incidents of these foreign activists vandalizing parts of the campus irritated the Greeks, as it indicated a lack of cultural awareness; after all, the symbolic importance of occupying a university in Greece lies in the historical connection with the junta's November 17, 1974, attack on students at a university in Athens. The bloody event would help lead to the collapse of the right-wing government; the date would be commemorated by a terrorist group and a national holiday.

The migration crisis showed that the loaded issue of "racism" has resonated with various otherwise unaffiliated groups, and that migration itself is becoming the "glue" that binds all radical leftist groups on the Continent. Leftist groups that would otherwise have little in common have similar views on migration, leading to a cross-fertilization of activist movements. This will have unexpected consequences and will act as an instability and force multiplier for future protests and attacks in support of different far-left causes in the future.

In general, leftist discourse in Europe is increasingly going to keep calling for unity against the alleged threat of the far-right, whether or not these leftist supporters are anarchists, politicians, or armchair intellectuals. Throughout the migrant crisis, numerous party officials and media portrayed this as a dark and sinister future near-inevitability, a force bent on reversing Europe's destined course as a liberal Utopia. This could be seen in dramatic hyperbole, statements like "the left needs to hurry lest xenophobia, racism, hate, and repression—the four horsemen of the right's apocalypse—engulf Europe."[35]

This oft-repeated sense of a predetermined teleological outcome at risk of being violated is very revealing. It betrays the signature weakness at the heart of a movement ultimately based in Marxist–Leninist ideology. The historiographical presuppositions of important thinkers like

Antonio Gramsci have influenced a mass of European society to take for granted a reactive and philosophically unfounded morality based on future outcomes—whether these be a grand triumph of liberalism, or the unimaginable victory of the right. Communal failure or success can only be determined by future outcomes. Traces of this teleological outlook can be seen in, say, European Union reports condemning candidate countries for "backsliding" on reforms. Within the leftist worldview that pervades the European liberal parties and Brussels bureaucracy, there is an ingrained belief in a path of ever-greater forward progress from which any perceived deviation is a dangerous regression toward earlier, and less enlightened, periods of European history.

What the European left does not want to admit, or perhaps did not understand, was that this self-perception of Europe as a liberal example to the world had never been anything more than a myth supported by outside, and often sinister, interests. In the past hundred years, these have included Communists fomenting violent worldwide revolution, bankers and industrialists pushing federalization for economic reasons, and political powers like the United States during the Cold War, scheming about how Europe could be used as a bulwark against the Soviet Union. In reality, the European dream had thus never been anything more than a hobby of aristocrats, the grand ideal of fanatics and interest of bankers, as well as a policy issue for government spooks.

The fact that European left-wing ideology is, according to its philosophical precepts, based on historical relativism devoid of absolutes, means that it can only flourish in specific controlled environments. It did so during the long period of peace following World War II, a time during which occasional violence or political unrest was minor and accepted political models of cooperation, compromise, and establishment parties generally thrived. However, through stagnation, complacency, and the recent shocks of the euro crisis and migrant crisis, this model has broken down. If it is to flourish once again, the European left will do so under a new specific and controlled environment: that of a corporate, technological, and global system geared toward world governance models and supranational initiatives. Such worldviews remain highly unpopular among the majority of European citizens, and will thus require a painful transformation and sharing of power. But as the migrant crisis has revealed, the process is already well under way. Ultimately, resting as it does on a totalitarian view for managing Europe and the world, this model for social engineering and organization is in fact specifically leftist. Perhaps the future will show that some things were in fact meant to be.

CHAPTER 7

The Response from the Right

The most terrifying manifestation of Europe's far right is often portrayed as Anders Behring Breivik, the Norwegian extremist who massacred 77 young leftists at an ideological summer camp in 2011. For the left and much of the world media, the shooting spree symbolized the deadly excesses of the far right, in its war with liberal European values. But these same legally entrenched "values" would allow, five years later, for Breivik to successfully win a court appeal stating that his solitary confinement in a three-room cell equipped with a gym and DVD player violated his human rights.[1]

Such apparent contradictions lie at the heart of today's existential crisis of values in Europe. The continent that reemerged in 1945 from the ashes of war pledged that it would never again repeat the experience. In Germany, the Nazi party was banned. Everywhere, right-wing politics were carefully checked for signs of straying too far from the centrist path, with legalistic and bureaucratic methods being used to keep the more extreme of them from power. This new Europe's bulwark against any future far-right movements rested, however, on the unstable foundations of the vague leftist ideals of "common values." For the approved mainstream, joining the right essentially meant an enthusiasm for disciplined capitalism and collective defense under the NATO umbrella, against an external enemy that in the end never proved much of a threat.

This model of European self-regulation worked fairly well, so long as peace was guaranteed and cultural homogeneity remained relatively solid. But the increasing influx of foreign cultures through immigration from the 1980s, and then the age of Islamic terrorism and the backlash against it, burdened the system with new challenges that it had never been designed to confront. The problem with the European system is that it is no longer relevant for the times. And yet when confronted with this reality, the Brussels bureaucrats continue to expand legislative control.

Regarding migration, right-wing and conservative parties in Europe have shown qualitative differences in their approach and ideology. Theirs is a marked point of contrast with the left, which, as we have seen, tends to support migration in general, with the only internal differences regarding degree of support. This fundamental difference also means that a rich diversity of views and positions exists among European right-wing parties. But just as some have emphasized the worst deeds committed by migrants as representative of all migrants, the same has occurred with the left's tendency to tar all right-wing parties with the same brush when violent protests occur.

Nevertheless, things have slowly changed. Just five years before, the left could point to people like Breivik as the most dangerous manifestations of right-wing extremism. Today, the object of fear has become more pervasive and more political. In future elections, bemoaned one commentator in *The Guardian*, it was "the young, gay people, Jews, feminists" who could not be trusted to stay on board a sinking liberal ship. These people, they bemoaned, "may join the working-class voters who have already abandoned parties of the left to become the new backbone of the populist right."[2]

These parties were allegedly "pursuing a new and devastatingly effective electoral strategy," the newspaper continued. "They have made a very public break with the symbols of the old right's past, distancing themselves from skinheads, neo-Nazis and homophobes. They have also deftly co-opted the causes, policies and rhetoric of their opponents. They have sought to outflank the left when it comes to defending a strong welfare state and protecting social benefits that they claim are threatened by an influx of freeloading migrants."[3]

If such a dynamic "threat" exists, it is certainly not being masterminded from a decrepit establishment right. Europe's decades-old conservative parties (like Britain's Tory Party, Angela Merkel's Christian Democratic Union, the Greek New Democracy, Sweden's Moderate Party, and so on) are either puttering along predictable ideological byways or running on the fumes of legacy. Such establishment parties mostly hail from the postwar European reconciliation period, and are thus based on an outdated model of consensual centrist policies. As such, their criticism of European migration policy has been somewhat tempered.

Additionally, as has already been shown, the vagaries of history—most significantly, in the case of Germany—have influenced conservative parties toward policies conducive to mass migration. As with the European Union's founding liberal values, such parties are to a large extent relics of an earlier time. Voter dissatisfaction with their tired solutions, first and foremost regarding economic and social policies, has damaged their popularity and ability to form strong coalitions. However, these parties remain the best-funded and most established on national and regional levels, with the deepest connections to big business and entrenched power structures. Nevertheless, as noted in coverage of the left, events of recent years have shown voter frustration in several countries. Europe's general unraveling indicates that such parties in Western European countries will continue to rule with weak mandates or even in minority capacities, such as was the case with Angela Merkel's minority government.

A second category of center-right parties includes small Euroskeptic parties that have rose up in recent years but not yet made major inroads. Often, they are probusiness, antiausterity, and noncommittal regarding the big issues. Several originate from some known commodity in local popular culture, as was the case with Greece's To Potami (The River), founded by television personality Stavros Theodorakis. However, although the party won a small handful of Member of the European Parliament (MEP) seats in the 2014 European Parliament elections, it failed to live up to the hype and did not do well enough to enter into either government or become relevant after both of the 2015 elections in Greece.

However, another newly minted centrist party also founded around a cult of personality, Italy's more Euroskeptic Five-Star Movement (M5S), proved more successful than its Greek counterpart. Founded in 2009 by popular comedian Beppe Grillo, the Five-Star Movement came to national prominence when its leader, Virginia Raggi, became Rome's first female mayor in 2016 elections. Although the Socialists of Matteo Renzi remained in control of both national and most local leadership positions, the Five-Star Movement's victory in one of Italy's most important races was seen as a potential step toward a new and different conservative movement. Indeed, following the defeat of a referendum on constitutional reform in December 2016, the party redoubled calls for leaving the euro. The referendum had been supported by leftist prime minister Matteo Renzi, who immediately resigned. "If Europe does not want to implode," said Alessandro di Battista of M5S, "you must accept that you can not go on like this [with the single currency]."[4]

Other conservative Italian movements, like the Northern League, have more of a regional presence but remain important critics of the national migration policy, from a more far-right ideology. This is partly shared with a third sort of alternative right-wing movement (and the one most despised by liberals): the right-wing populists who had become popular even before the migrant crisis began. Germany saw the most important development of a new right-wing movement that owed directly to the establishment right's perceived failure to handle the migrant masses in 2015. From the moment of Angela Merkel's unilateral invitation to migrants, every negative event—from train stoppages to sexual violence and terrorist attacks—became ammunition for the emerging right-wing movements opposed to Merkel's open-door migration policy. Street protests led by the Patriotic Europeans Against the Islamisation of the West

(PEGIDA) movement included one of January 9, 2016, in the aftermath of the New Year's Eve attacks in Cologne.

PEGIDA organized 1,700 people to demonstrate against the assaults, demanding Merkel's resignation. Marchers clashed with police, while far-leftists were also running a counterdemonstration nearby. The event was followed the next day by vigilante attacks on migrants in Cologne. However, "Pegida is simply a radical right-leaning protest movement of regional importance with no distinct political program," says Karl-Peter Schwartz, a senior journalist with the newspaper *Frankfurter Allgemeine Zeitung*.[5] Nevertheless, the PEGIDA protests did aid, and presage big gains by a three-year-old party, the Alternative for Germany (AfD) in local elections. On March 13, 2016, the AfD won up to 25 percent of the vote in state elections, running chiefly on an anti-immigration platform.

The result was seen as a referendum on the Merkel government's "open door" asylum policy. The AfD's very name was a pun on Merkel's "frequent claim that there was 'no alternative' to her policies."[6] Like Merkel's CDU, the AfD was led by a forthright and outspoken woman. Just 40 years old at the time of AfD's big state election gains, Frauke Petry had rallied supporters by saying things considered "shocking" to Germans: for example, that firearms could be used in self-defense by border guards, that Islam did not "belong" in Germany, (an idea shared by two-thirds of Germans in 2016).[7] The AfD has also argued that mosque construction should be banned. Such comments are routinely made by leaders around the world, but they have been taken as particularly unusual in a Germany weighed down by its historical baggage. Indeed, the *New York Times* dutifully eulogized the allegedly dark situation according to the migrant crisis's standard line: in 2017 elections, the AfD could become "the first right-wing party to enter the Parliament since the end of World War II."[8]

The media pushed the alleged symbolic overtones of the migrant crisis that unceasingly depicted it as the modern equivalent of the Holocaust. This decision has had a particularly potent impact on shaping the conventional image of Germany's new right-wing movement. The AfD had narrowly missed passing the 5 percent threshold to enter parliament in 2013, when it was running on an antiausterity platform. But in 2016, it reached 12 percent support, bolstered by the center-right's botched handling of the migrant crisis. The party's call for upholding German identity, culture, and family values have resonated with voters well beyond the ranks of neo-Nazis and xenophobes.

In modern Germany's confined ideological atmosphere, "it is not surprising that a party which argues for a self-conscious nation-state in a Europe of Fatherlands is seen as reactionary," Petry said in an interview. "That only shows how one-sided the discussion in Germany has been for years." She also did not shy away from confronting the issue of "German guilt" for the Nazi past that had been used so pervasively by media and politicians throughout the crisis. "The uniqueness, the singularity of German guilt has stood much too often in the forefront, and distorted the view that there are also enough positive aspects to our history."[9] Although such comments seemed obvious to many Germans fatigued by having to constantly apologize for the sins of bygone generations, it seemed unlikely that Petry and her party would be able to form a coalition with any of Germany's major parties in the coming 2017 election. In any case, by late February 2017, the AfD's poll numbers had slipped to 8 percent, a result that analysts blamed on Angela Merkel's tougher line on immigration and the return of Martin Schulz to the Social Democrat leadership; it was possible, one study contended, that some AfD voters would shift to Schulz simply to push Merkel out of power.[10]

Local experts confirm that Petry's message might be compatible with a public opinion that has been slowly changing over the years. "Moral pressure still works with the Germans but much more with the political class and the mainstream media, and much less with the majority of the people," notes Schwartz. "I think that the 'welcome mood' [towards refugees] of autumn [2015] expressed mainly the simple and spontaneous human sympathy towards people perceived as helpless and poor. As always the desire to atone for the crimes of the Nazi-generation was present in the background but it was not decisive. The mood changed radically after the mass sexual assaults on New Year's Eve in Cologne and other cities." Interestingly, the government's automatic reaction to those disturbing events was to instinctively return to the World War II issue, "Since then the political class repeats the ritual appeal to the eternal guilt of the Germans, but it seems that its impact on the people is rather low."[11]

Just over one month after the German state elections, on April 24, 2016, leftists were dismayed when Norbert Hofer, candidate of the right-wing Austrian Freedom Party (FPÖ), handsomely won the first round of voting in the national presidential election. Remarkably, even this nonresult became a de facto referendum, forcing Chancellor Werner Faymann of the Social Democratic Party to resign. Although Hofer lost by a tiny margin in the second round of voting, the result was later annulled and a rerun was scheduled for fall. However, this was deferred due to alleged technical problems with envelopes. As the ugly effects of the migrant crisis had only grown more obvious in the intervening months, it was clear that Austrian officials were keen to avoid the embarrassment of electing Europe's first "far-right" leader since World War II, as the headlines depicted Hofer. However, the World War II analogy has less potency in Austria, and political experts like Karl-Peter Schwartz do not consider Hofer's appeal to voters as directly mirroring that of the AfD, in regard to migration and the right wing in general. According to Schwartz, Hofer's popularity was "a collateral effect of the increasing frustration with the big coalition, the lack of a real political opposition and the failed attempt to marginalize the FPÖ."[12]

As was the case in France, official German and Austrian governmental migration policies became more restrictive due to the pressure created by the right-wing opposition's political gains. Not only for EU interests, but also out of domestic party interests, European leaders sought to appease the right with slightly tougher security measures, lest the latter win pivotal national elections in 2017. Angela Merkel, in particular, managed to reverse her position without losing the support of her key constituency. This is particularly of concern, as it should not have taken a fear of looming elections for ruling powers to finally start taking responsibility for the chaos that their decisions had unleashed.

Through 2016, the May 2017 presidential election in France was depicted as being among the Continent's most important. There, the Front National (FN) of Marine Le Pen had benefited politically from the terrorist attacks and general social unease that prevailed during the migrant crisis. The unexpected victory of Donald Trump in the U.S. election also fired up Marine Le Pen. In 2016, the National Front was expecting to take 40 percent of the vote in regions nationwide.[13] By February 2017, the conventional wisdom still had it that Le Pen would lose the election in the second round in May against either of her rivals. However, analysts admitted that the anti-establishment, France-first policy that echoed Trump's could indeed have a broader appeal than simply to the far-right. "Fillon and Macron's support of globalisation, the EU, greater European economic integration and immigration increases Le Pen's appeal to French nationalists from both the right and left of the political spectrum," one report noted.[14] Indeed, on balance it could be said that Le Pen's protectionist nationalism hearkened back more to Charles De Gaulle than to Hitler.

De Gaulle, for his part, was after all the major leader whose nationalist concerns slowed the pace of European integration the most through the 1960s. Marine Le Pen's potential to change the political facts on the ground was alarming not only for domestic political rivals, but for the entrenched power brokers in Brussels. Particularly dangerous for them was the party's Euroskepticism. The European Union obviously could not survive without France, and talk of a "Frexit," let alone a real referendum similar to the British one, would cause unpredictable damage for the Brussels elite, for stock markets, and for the general European economy. But given the concerted efforts the leftist government has made to legalize Muslim migrants in the past few years, a future FN president or government would encounter severe resistance if it tried to clamp down on government benefits for immigrants.

As in other countries where liberals are particularly nervous about the new right's image, France's Front National has taken steps to demolish its critics' old arguments. In a 2016 interview, Le Pen stated that "voters see clearly that there's absolutely nothing in our platform that remotely resembles fascism or racism."[15] Even the youth wing was stressing "self-discipline" to avoid charges of racism. In the 2015 regional elections, support among married gay couples exceeded 32 percent—a 13 percent increase over 2012 numbers. These advances had been partly due to Le Pen's inclusion of more openly gay advisers and party leaders. And, although the party had once been associated with anti-Semitism, it now was accepting Jewish voters threatened by Islamic extremism with open arms.

The Front National's Le Pen has played to voter perception that integration has failed. But Germany's chancellor had been saying precisely the same in 2010, before her strange sudden conversion left her a supporter of the migrant cause. Which party leader had been straying from the "center"—if indeed such a position still exists? In France, stabbings, shootings, terrorist attacks and migrant chaos through 2016 caused a backlash against the liberal Valls government and its ineffective handling of security issues. As large-scale rioting continued in 2017, French voters who wanted to see order restored in the Muslim-occupied suburbs were receptive to Le Pen's law-and-order message. These voters also shared, as elsewhere in Europe and North America, a certain nostalgia for an older, safer, and simpler time, when the middle class was more prosperous and the country more homogeneous. Many Le Pen supporters would like to see the return of the French franc, and not only out of nostalgia. (Regarding the last issue, they may get what they want even without her political victory, if economic vicissitudes eventually crash the euro.)

In France, leftist and center-right parties have experience in preventing the Front National from coming to power. Indeed, although the party won 27 percent of the vote in the first round of voting in December 2015 regional elections, it was shut out in all 13 regions after the second round.[16] Although Marine Le Pen was expected to be the party's 2017 presidential candidate, and to make it to the second round of voting, the left was prepared to join forces with centrist parties as it had successfully done in 2002, when preventing Jean-Marie Le Pen (father of the current party leader) from winning. The difference between then and now appeared to be greater local anger over migration—as well as a much larger Muslim and immigrant vote. For the establishment, keeping the latter satisfied will require increased rewards to their causes, in exchange for helping to keep the far-right out. This is a long-term trend that will lead to increased polarization, politicization of the migrant issue, and, eventually, Islamic political parties. That outcome will only further dilute the vote and polarize public opinions.

After Germany and France, Sweden was the European Union country most affected by the aftershocks of migration. There, too, the real political winner from the Social Democratic government's mishandling of the crisis was the right-wing Sweden Democrats, considered by critics as being just as bad as the AfD and Front National. The party, which has distanced itself from its white-supremacist roots, won 13 percent of the vote in September 2014 elections. Slashing immigration by 90 percent was a key point on the agenda.[17] As elsewhere in Europe, the entry of a new player beyond the traditional partisan dichotomy resulted in a diluted vote and a weak leftist coalition. Remaining in opposition during the migrant crisis also allowed the Sweden Democrats, and its leader Jimmie Åkesson, to capitalize on the chaos and advance a platform demanding immigration restrictions, without actually having to implement any policies.

The Sweden Democrats have a marked stylistic difference from both their 1980s iterations and their more acquiescent and milquetoast colleagues in today's establishment parties on the right. These include Sweden's second major party, the establishment center-right Moderate Party, which actually brought the opposition Social Democrat–Green coalition to power after a controversial agreement that staved off a budget crisis in late 2014. Showing the extent to which secularism has taken root, a smaller right-wing party, the Christian Democrats, has even sought to back away "from their religious roots" in order to "build wider support." However, the party barely achieved the 4-percent threshold needed to enter parliament in 2014. The center-right Liberal Party also seemed in trouble after the election, offering an only-in-Sweden platform that combined support for immigration, feminism, NATO membership, and more nuclear energy. With the other parties tentatively standing for everything and nothing, the Sweden Democrats became the only major party with a clearly defined stance. The conditions for this phenomenon were clearly set by the migrant crisis.

However, as in other European countries, the historic stigma surrounding the Sweden Democrats means that it will have a hard time winning suitors for future coalitions. This indicates a future of more weak "national unity" governments with vague, homogeneous mandates, and an angry, excluded right-wing. Because of its uncouth image, the Swedish party has tried to improve its image by expelling racist or neo-Nazi members; however, unlike with France's Front National, this decision has caused "a rift between the mother party and its youth wing which wants to pursue a more radical path."[18] The party's fortunes will depend both on its image-management and, of course, on the social and security impact of the extended migrant crisis. But even if it never enters government, the Sweden Democrats will still have an impact on power; after all, they helped block the center-left coalition's budget proposal after the 2014 election, spawning the crisis that ultimately damaged the center-right Moderates, which negotiated the leftist coalition's rise to power. The case was a direct inversion of what happened to the establishment center-left party in Spain, which lost credibility among its electorate by abetting the creation of a weak right-wing coalition in 2016.

The shock of the migrant crisis allowed the Sweden Democrats to grow from 4 percent support in 2008 to 20 percent just eight years later. Even without an election, this polling jump was interpreted—as in Germany and Austria—as a referendum on the incumbent government, which had already begun restricting migrant numbers and imposing border control checks. Leftists fumed that government policies effectively validated the right-wing's arguments. Yet continuing the same policies that had created the Sweden Democrats in the first place would only have strengthened the party further. For the government, for the left in general, and even for the opposition it was a no-win situation. When the opposition Moderate Party announced it would reach out to the far-right party for its support on economic growth, it led to a drop in the opinion polls and disagreement within the Moderates' own coalition. "We want to shift out Lofven in the next elections," said Annie Loof of the fellow opposition Central Party, "but we don't want to do it with active support from or cooperation with the Sweden Democrats."[19] This comment illustrates perfectly the dilemma Europe's established parties had in dealing with new right-wing parties following the 2015 migrant crisis.

The expansion of migrant street crime from cities like Stockholm to even smaller towns in northern Sweden helped nationalize the Sweden Democrats' support base beyond its original territory. Observers have also noted that the proliferation of social media in a tech-savvy but timid country has abetted the rise of antimigrant sentiment, and thus political allegiances. "Social media has always been the primary platform for the Sweden Democrats," noted journalist and social media expert Emanuel Karlsten. "Their relationship with their voters is built on the fact that they say things that "mainstream media doesn't dare say," and so are able to take the underdog line of being "forced" to use social media. If you compare SD to any other political party, you see how they are much more digitally aware, much more social media friendly, and much more used to online communication" (indeed, Åkesson had the most-liked Facebook page of all Swedish politicians).[20]

A major issue for right-wing parties critical of leftist support for migration and Islamism has indeed been freedom of speech. They have pointed to the violent riots and terrorist attacks following publications of "Mohammed cartoons" by Danish cartoonists and France's Charlie Hebdo magazine when criticizing Islamism in European society. This phenomenon too has been conditioned by local realities, making the Netherlands one of the prime countries undergoing considerable intellectual ferment in the wake of high-profile murders involving Islamism. In 2002, the flamboyantly gay conservative politician Pim Fortuyn, was gunned down by a radical animal rights activist, who blamed Fortuyn for "scapegoating" Muslims. Days after the murder, the Pim Fortuyn List won 17 percent of election returns, becoming the second largest party in the Netherlands.[21] Fortuyn's defense of secularism, gay rights, and progressivism versus immigrant primitivism struck a chord nationally. Fortuyn's "new far-right" approach had been described by *The New Yorker* as "a form of xenophobia ideally suited to a nation that prides itself on its tolerance."[22]

Holland's second galvanizing event was the subsequent November 2004 slaying of filmmaker Theo van Gogh by a young Dutch Moroccan. The murderer, Mohammed Bouyeri, shot van Gogh eight times and slashed his throat before using the knife to pin a letter to his chest. The letter threatened Somali-born Dutch parliamentarian Ayaan Hirsi Ali, who had collaborated with Van Gogh on a short film critical of Islam's treatment of women. These murders and threats shocked the usually placid Netherlands, convincing many that radical Muslims were prepared to act violently against all critics, no matter their ethnicity.

Following the death of Fortuyn and Van Gogh, the right-wing torch was passed to outspoken contrarian Geert Wilders and his Party for Freedom (PVV). As of November 2016, the PVV was polling just behind the Dutch Labor Party. But just weeks before the March 2017 elections, the PVV was leading the polls. The PVV had continuously blamed the establishment for allegedly emphasizing the rights of immigrants over those of its founding demographic, the Dutch working class. As was the case with Marine Le Pen in France, Wilders was galvanized by the victory of Donald Trump in the United States, and leaned heavily on his brand of economic populism, border control, and national values. In a direct nod to the Trump campaign, Wilders promised "to make the Netherlands ours again." Despite the PVV's lead in the polls, most believed it would be unable to form a governing coalition due to its controversial positions on Islam. Yet Wilders felt his message would continue to resonate, regardless of the result. "Even if I lose this election, the genie will not go back in the bottle again," he said in a newspaper interview in February. "People are fed up with the combination of mass immigration, Islamisation and austerity measures that require us to cut pensions and support for health care and the elderly while giving [bailout] money to Greece and the eurozone."[23]

As in other Western European countries, by the time of the migrant crisis the establishment had long seemed out of touch with these changing perceptions, and the state's institutional efforts to rein in Wilders by trying him for "inciting racial hatred" for criticizing Moroccan immigrants in 2014. During the migrant crisis, he had damaged the center-right conservative further by citing the alleged "Islamic invasion" of Europe in September 2015.[24] However, this bureaucratic intercession only emboldened the right-wing figurehead, who dismissed the case by saying he was only voicing what millions of Dutch were afraid to say.[25] This again struck a chord with Holland's critical thinkers and energized the PVV base. Such bumbling state legalistic interference has been witnessed elsewhere in Europe as a sort of punitive measure against the far right; however, in seeming to validate all of the arguments about the insufferable political correctness that had allegedly restricted free expression in polite society, it only emboldened the right-wing even further.

Wilders's PVV had long capitalized on fears of the migrant crisis, presenting slogans like "De-Islamise" as simple solutions to complex national problems. The PVV message fed grassroot efforts to protest government migration policy, block the resettlement of asylum seekers, and attack asylum centers.[26] Public hatred of elites, political correctness, and the European Union technocrats were other potent sentiments that the Wilders party channeled in the March 2017 campaign. And, as with other European "new" right-wing movements like the Sweden Democrats, the PVV mobilized on social media and was supported by popular new alternative news websites like Geen Stijl ("No Style"). In the case of Geert Wilders, this social media outreach was particularly important, as constant death threats from Muslims meant he rarely made public appearances in Holland and lived under constant police protection. Nevertheless, the PVV saw gains in March 2017 elections.

As in Sweden, right-wing use of social media helped liberate speech from the self-censorship of the left. Worse still for the latter, former progressives are also joining the Dutch right out of fears of Muslim intolerance; as has been seen, this is also the case with the new right in France and other countries. Indeed, traditional European political correctness is increasingly being challenged today across the Continent. "For many years it was politically incorrect in Norway to mention any negative facts concerning immigration," notes Carl Schiötz Wibye, a retired Norwegian diplomat and author. "But with the sudden increase in numbers in 2015, the gates were opened somewhat for a more critical attitude towards immigration, especially as it was obvious that the political party that was putting most emphasis on restricting immigration—the Progress Party—gained a lot in popularity. The debate is now much more open and less inhibited by P.C. pressure."[27]

Another Scandinavian country becoming more conservative over migrant crisis fallout and perceived threats to free speech was Denmark. When in 2005 the *Jyllands-Posten* newspaper published cartoons of the Prophet Muhammad, worldwide riots and boycotts of Danish products followed. Public criticism of Islamic extremism since then has only grown, as have the number of migrants coming to the country or trying to pass through to reach Sweden. The main political beneficiary of this situation throughout the migrant crisis was the right-wing Danish People's Party (DPP), which had been steadily chipping away at the establishment right and left alike, due to a wider platform that also emphasizes health care, elder care, and subsidized housing. The DPP also played on anti-immigrant sentiment and, as in other countries, tacitly influenced government to adopt a stricter government policy simply by existing, even if they won just 12 percent of the vote at the latest election. For example,

DPP pressure led indirectly to the January 2016 "jewelry law," by which authorities could confiscate valuables worth more than 10,000 kroner (approximately $1,500) from incoming migrants to fund their costs.[28] It was an appropriately civilized Scandinavian solution that enraged leftist critics from far and wide.

In order to better understand Europe's "new right," it is important to define what precisely is meant by the concept. A common but misleading claim made by liberal critics during the migrant crisis equated all opposition to migration with "nationalism"—a trait then projected as being inherent to far-right belief systems, amenable to Fascism and Nazism. Although many political parties opposed to open-door migration were indeed also nationalist in outlook or origins, there are abundant examples of European nationalist parties that either supported (or did not complain about) pro-migration policies. And nationalist parties with a fundamentally left-wing orientation also exist in various European countries. This contradicts the simplistic narrative spun by a uniformly pro-migration left eager to negatively conflate all perceived rivals according to epithets. In fact, European nationalist and conservative parties today do in fact demonstrate a rich diversity of views. And the migrant crisis did indeed help to reveal this ideological variety.

Specific local realities and historical factors affect some European nationalist parties in their approach to migration. Those that come from countries unaffected by the crisis tend to give it a lower priority on the agenda. Even for countries directly on the migrant path, the crisis revealed nationalist parties that contradicted the all-in-one conflated image of "Fascist" and xenophobic nationalism. For example, while being critical of migration and Islam, Greece's coruling nationalist ANEL party is no friend of Nazism, referring often to the World War II German occupation of Greece. And next door in Macedonia, the largest bloc, the Internal Macedonian Revolutionary Organization—Democratic Party for Macedonian National Unity (VMRO-DPMNE) was never particularly outspoken on migration, paralyzed as it was by an internal political crisis, thus leaving the heavy lifting of security policy up to independent-minded President Gjorge Ivanov.

VMRO-DPMNE had been founded with Macedonian independence from Yugoslavia, as the nationalist continuation of the 1903 VMRO anarchist movement that had fought for an independent Macedonia against the Ottoman Turks and other Balkan powers. But the modern-day party includes various national minorities within its coalition and, although socially conservative and nationalist, since 2006 extended liberal social spending programs similar to the most accomplished of liberal European welfare state. It also associates itself with the mainstream center-right parties of Europe such as Merkel's CDU and the British Tories.

A similarly nationalist party with roots in a turbulent period is Sinn Fein, the political descendent of the Irish Republican Army (IRA). Sinn Fein is as nationalist as a European party can get, with its platform still defined by the dream of a united Ireland. Yet despite this nationalist orientation, Sinn Fein is considered a left-wing party, and its orientation toward migration is again influenced by national history. Indeed, the 2015 migration crisis was privately described as "the greatest humanitarian crisis of our generation," by one Sinn Fein adviser. "There can be no doubt that the world has turned their back." The official criticized the Irish government's response to the crisis, "given that many of our ancestors fled to every corner of the planet to avoid starvation during the [19th century Irish Potato] famine."[29]

Another example of a nationalist-oriented party with left-wing policies and sympathetic views toward migration is the Scottish Nationalist Party, which organized an ultimately unsuccessful independence referendum in September 2014, while also being pro-European Union. "Immigration is essential to the strength of our economy and adds greatly to our cultural fabric," the SNP has officially stated. "We propose a fair, robust and secure immigration system that meets Scotland's social and economic needs."[30]

Further, while conservative in orientation, there is yet another prominent European nationalist party generally supportive of migration. The New Flemish Alliance (N-VA) is an established conservative bloc that seeks to peacefully secede from Belgium. Despite this very nationalist orientation, the party has nevertheless taken a leading role in addressing the migrant crisis, in ways that have angered other parties on the right. In 2012, a government minister from the N-VA provided much-criticized "starter kits" for migrants, including instructions on proper behavior and following local customs, both at home and in countries like Morocco.[31]

Of course, many other parties described as "nationalist" do in fact oppose migration. The more extreme of these do cite racial and religious differences in justifying their views. Interestingly, this has led to a critical reappraisal of some of the long-forgotten forefathers of the European project. The British National Party, for example, has criticized various excerpts from the oeuvre of Count Richard Coudenhove-Kalergi, which appear to show his support for an ideal future Europe of mixed races and Jewish supremacy. Supporters of the Greek Golden Dawn party have made similar criticisms.[32] Such interpretations fit nicely into modern far-right narratives about the dangers of multiculturalism, but possibly are being taken out of context, since the count's musings were affected both by his mixed noble bloodline and by the peculiar atmosphere of the 1920s, in which exotic racial theories were the norm, in a larger context of European colonialism and a historical obsession with the great civilizations of ancient Egypt, China, and Greece. In the current context, however, the veracity of the textual interpretations is less important than the degree to which they are shared by far-right groups.

Perhaps most significant for the future of Europe's migration policy was the reinvigorating role that the 2015 migrant crisis had on conservative parties in countries less affected by political correctness, like the Balkan and former Communist Eastern European states. Many of the conservative parties that sprang up there following the Cold War received lavish Western support in the beginning, simply because they were the enemies of the just-vanquished Communist regimes. But they have also had to remain vigilant due to the heavy presence of outside "reforming" leftist forces (such as the various foundations of Hungarian-born American tycoon George Soros) that through lavish funding became the standard-bearers of the same EU-friendly corporate leftism that is itself being attacked in Western Europe.

Right-wing parties in several Eastern European countries are also worth discussing because they have played specific, significant roles during the migrant crisis: for example, the concerted resistance of the Visegrad Group (Hungary, Poland, Slovakia, and the Czech Republic; V4) essentially blocked Merkel and Juncker from implementing their migrant quota scheme in 2016, altering the course of European history by standing up to an open-door migration policy that was generally supported until the November 2015 Paris attacks.

Conservatives in V4 and Balkan countries believed that their cautious approach to migration was necessary in order to protect Europe from itself. Some of them perceived the migrant waves as representing a sort of barbarian invasion capable of overthrowing Western civilization in the long term. Most associated with this policy was Viktor Orbán, leader of Hungary's Fidesz Party. Orbán became enemy number one of the European liberal elite, UN aid agencies, and George Soros by taking preventive measures against migration on security grounds, erecting a border fence in August 2016 and standing up for the state's right to follow its own sovereign migration policy. Ironically, although Hungary was heavily criticized for its conservative handling of the migrant crisis, almost every European country in the migration firing line has implemented at least some of Orbán's original 2015 policies. For (not only) Hungarians, his policies thus represented a sort of commonsense conservatism rather than a rabid xenophobia comparable to that of Hitler. In this respect, Orbán also benefited from the fact that critics could concentrate their fire on an even "worse" domestic contender, the anti-immigration, populist Jobbik party. Hungary's third-largest party, it voiced support for economic protectionism and a referendum on EU membership. Like other far-right parties, it has reportedly sought to improve its image following accusations of rampant anti-Semitism.

Conservatism based on state sovereignty is strongest in those countries, like Hungary, where it had been largely taken from them during Communist times. Western European leaders and publics living in complacent bliss since 1945 have somehow failed to realize this. Viewing the East through their own cultural lens, they have tended to interpret V4 and Balkan countries' resistance to supranationally enforced immigration regimes as evidence of latent xenophobia and even "Islamophobia." Never mind that some of these countries, like Macedonia, Serbia, and Bulgaria, have historic Muslim populations that do not threaten general society. What such outside observers have failed to understand is that much of Eastern Europe views both Euro-liberal technocrats and Islamic fundamentalists as two sides of the same coin: as representatives of totalitarian worldviews antithetical to human freedom, as sinister forces determined to introduce different social engineering regimes in violation of the nationally based cultures they seek to preserve.

Indeed, during and after the migrant crisis, there were plenty of fevered condemnations of countries like Hungary, Poland, and Macedonia from the mainstream leftist media and political class. The European Union itself went after the Polish government over an internal constitutional court issue, with leftists like then-European Parliament leader Martin Schulz being particularly vocal.[33] German leaders lashed out at Macedonia for being ungrateful for aid that had never actually been given. And everyone criticized Orbán, though his actions prevented countries further north from having to deal with the migrant deluge. Yet such external critics have consistently failed to understand the unique varieties of conservatism in the East. Western countries have often claimed that it is hypocritical of former Communist countries to oppose today's economic migrants and refugees, considering that their own citizens have worked in the West for years. However, this is not the way Eastern European conservatives, who oversaw years of painful reforms to get into the European Union, see the situation.

Indeed, in the view of Eastern European countries that until 1990 endured decades of oppressive rule, the modern European Union had rather started to resemble the old regimes that they finally overthrew, rather than the "classic" Europe for which they had longed. However, the illusory liberal ideals upon which the European Union had been founded meant that by 1990, Western Europe had changed. By the time of the 2015 migrant crisis, the image of a heavy-handed, Brussels-centered bloc perceived as tinkering irresponsibly with multiculturalism and migration had been cemented. And that was something definitely not representative of the "European" union that Eastern European countries had signed up for. This is why the conservatives of the East tend to support a strong Europe—but one that should be based on indigenous European values and geared toward indigenous populations.

Another major phenomenon (albeit a coincidental one) that influenced right-wing sentiment in Eastern Europe during the migrant crisis was, of course, the intensified showdown between the United States and Russia over Ukraine and Syria. This process led both superpowers to increased levels of military buildup unprecedented since the Cold War. This had a tendency to leave some Eastern European right-wing parties divided by the two issues. Although they all tended to support strong antimigrant policies, they differed when it came to Russia. Those countries, which shared a direct border with Russia, like Poland and the Baltic states, stoked up a frenzy of nationalist hysteria regarding the alleged Russian military threat. By October 2016, the government of Lithuania was even handing out instructional brochures, teaching its citizens how to form paramilitary units in order to help defend the motherland, while in Poland, too, a right-wing militia movement was also flourishing, amid hysteria over war with Russia.[34]

Unlike with migration, in such cases right-wing nationalism was actively encouraged by the West, which had made common cause through an increased NATO deployment stretching all along Russian borders, from Norway down through Bulgaria. Romania, which borders on the sensitive countries of Ukraine and Moldova, could afford to back the NATO adventure strongly while remaining relatively quiet on the migration issue, since it had never been on the migrant route and was definitely not considered a desirable destination among the migrants themselves.

However, conservative blocs in countries opposing Russia that were slightly more distant took pains to walk a more cautious line. They viewed Russia more positively than the West did on social and religious issues, but at the same time did not want to anger the Barack Obama administration. In weak countries, like Macedonia, conservatives sought to keep culturally and economically friendly ties with Russia, but did not make military commitments. Countries like Serbia, in a somewhat stronger position, played both sides, even allowing Russian military training facilities on their territory. But only Hungary's Orbán and the Czech president, Miloš Zeman, were open supporters of Russian policy throughout. In Greece, both the left- and right-wing coalition partners (Syriza and ANEL, respectively) were pro-Russian and pro-Western at the same time, using geographic, cultural, and historical linkages to maximum advantage. A German investigative report coinciding with the January 2015 elections that brought the coalition to power even suggested that Russia was strategically funding both parties.[35]

Russia's oft-rumored support for small far-right parties in Orthodox Christian countries, like Golden Dawn in Greece or Ataka in Bulgaria, was also an issue cited in the overlapping contexts of the migrant crisis and NATO's military posturing in 2016. In general, the Russian policy served two purposes. The first was directly political, as it offered an entry point into influencing local elections and other developments. The second, and more sophisticated, goal was part of a larger Russian cultural critique of Europe, one with long-term strategic ambitions. This essentially was intended to show that Russia had retained its traditional (pre-Communist) Christian European values, whereas the West had wavered and would be overrun due to its own liberal weakness. This too has social and political aspects.

The migrant crisis provided a perfect opportunity for Russia to make this critique, one which also had religious bases. "It is surprising that today Russian and European civilizations have exchanged their roles in a certain sense," said a senior Russian bishop, Metropolitan Hilarion of Volokolamsk. "The Soviet Union was the country of the official state atheism, while all of us perceived the West as the Christian region." According to Interfax, the bishop added that "secularism and atheism have in fact become a new ideology of Western Europe." The prelate, however, concluded that eventually Europeans would "start coming back to their Christian roots."[36] Later, on May 29—the historic date on which the Orthodox Byzantine Empire fell to the Muslim Turks in 1453—President Vladimir Putin memorably visited Mt. Athos, a traditional Greek monastic community that has followed strict Byzantine edicts for over 1,000 years. The monks gave the Russian leader a hero's welcome. Finally, in October 2016, Putin slammed European mishandling of migration as a blow to "national values." He cited the shocking case of an Iraqi refugee who had just successfully appealed a conviction for sexually assaulting a young boy at a swimming pool. "A society that cannot defend its children has no future," Putin said.[37]

Just as Europe's easternmost countries have witnessed new anti-Russian national sentiments by calling for citizen self-defense movements on the borders, Russia itself has encouraged such movements when they are directed against the alleged migrant hordes, as in Slovakia. It also publicized such developments in dedicated media coverage of the crisis, emphasizing the idea of a "divided Europe." However, such movements are largely indigenous and would occur without Russian support. Right-wing militias, like Finland's "Soldiers of Odin" (SOO, named for the Norse god of death), arose out of widespread concern that the liberal authorities could not protect citizens (and particularly, women) from violence carried out by Muslim migrants. Since launching in October 2015, the SOO went on to become an international franchise, with offshoots across Scandinavia, and even the United States and Canada.

Although the SOO denied being racist or neo-Nazi, its founder, Mika Ranta, had reported connections to the far-right Finnish Resistance Movement, and Finnish media have claimed that "selected members" of SOO share racist and Nazi views on restricted social media forums.[38] The group denies these charges, and claims to merely organize street patrols and report possible crimes to the police. Their activity has received ambivalent reactions from the authorities; one senior police official called it "a welcome development," while the interior ministry voiced caution over whether the groups actually served a security purpose.[39]

Some SOO members had links to the Nordic Resistance Movement (NRM), a Swedish neo-Nazi political party founded in 1997, later becoming a pan-Scandinavian group. The NRM was also known for handing out propaganda leaflets, attacking leftist and gay pride events, and was linked to several stabbings. It is believed to have rural paramilitary training camps, and members' homes have been raided by security services in recent years.[40] What is interesting about the SOO is that, despite the relatively low number of attacks involving migrants in Finland, the crisis turned it into an international franchise. This was partly due to its preexisting support base among the Nordic white-supremacist movement, but was also indicative of a growing tendency for far-right groups to take the law into their own hands in a climate of fear surrounding immigrants and Islam in general. Less than one year after its formation, the SOO claimed to have 600 members in over 25 different locations across Scandinavia, Poland, Belgium, Holland, Germany, Estonia, Hungary, Ireland, England, Canada, and the United States. "Here will be a war on the streets," predicted one Odin member, "and we are ready to fight."[41]

Simple logistics helped create the SOO during the migrant crisis. Finland has a population of 5.5 million, and received 32,000 migrants between fall 2015 and early spring 2016—more than 10 times the amount of the previous year—and had to open 105 migrant shelters (there had been just three in 2015). At the same time, Finland had less than 8,000 police officers, with further budget cuts expected. Soldiers of Odin claimed to be just filling the gap, and defending women and children from increasingly violent attacks. As of 2016, the group itself had not committed any violent attacks, but police were becoming increasingly concerned that the tendencies of SOO patrols to mobilize in large groups could lead to similar group mobilizations by young migrant men, increasing the potential for open clashes.[42]

Right-wing paramilitary groups tend to arise amid fears of state incompetence after violent attacks and are usually limited to specific "dangerous" urban areas. They also sometimes include criminal elements, such as the Scandinavian biker gangs associated with the drugs trade and with other former criminals. In the case of the Soldiers of Odin, media widely noted that many members had criminal records. The group's leader in Sweden, Mikael Johansson, brightly suggested that by joining the civil self-defense movement, former criminals had the opportunity to atone for their crimes and "give back to the community."[43]

Similarly, Greece's Golden Dawn (founded in 1980) has portrayed itself as the kind of group just there to "help the little old lady cross the street," though its activities have often been somewhat more violent. It too was accused of being a criminal organization when authorities in September 2013 arrested dozens of its members, including elected parliamentarians and the party's leader, Nikos Michaloliakos.[44] Leftists accused the government of having tolerated the group for years, because it reportedly had numerous sympathizers within the security structures. Indeed, the 2013 arrests came only after the public outcry that followed the murder of leftist rapper Pavlos Fyssas by a Golden Dawn supporter. The charge of being a "criminal organization" did not sit well with leftists, who consider Golden Dawn a Fascist terrorist organization—albeit one with sitting members in the Greek and European parliaments. But even during the migrant crisis, Golden Dawn only had influence in certain low-income urban neighborhoods where they offered social assistance to poor Greeks or helped "defend" them from migrant attacks. Meanwhile, their low-scale war with violent anarchists continued, as did their targeting of asylum centers and Islam in Greece.

In future scenarios of lawlessness caused by terrorist attacks, economic collapse, or random violence, such vigilante groups might mobilize and actually temporarily replace the police in specific areas—increasing the risk of fighting between them and anarchist groups or migrants. However, far-right paramilitary groups are easily penetrated by intelligence services, identifiable within their communities and by their propaganda, and clumsy in their violence. The tragic example of Breivik's senseless killings is a good example of the kind of militant menace of traditional right-wing extremists. As conditions between ethnic and religious groups worsen, and as migrant and Islamic leaders become more prominent in Europe, it cannot be excluded that better trained, more secretive and effective subgroups will take part in the "self-defense" movement, through the kind of targeted assassinations carried out (on the other side of the ideological spectrum) by groups like Greece's 17 November in the 1970s and 1980s.

Finally, there is another, more intellectual, movement on the right that gained new prominence due to the migration crisis: the so-called Identitarian movement. Although relatively little-known to the outside observer, this is not a novel initiative, having intellectual roots in movements from the 1960s, particularly in France. Through personnel and ideological overlap with some of the rising right-wing parties, the Identitarian movement could conceivably influence a more mainstream right-wing politics in years ahead.

Founded in France under the name Bloc Identitaire (BI) in 2003, the movement had grown partly out of the former Unité Radicale far-right political group, which had some overlap with the original Front National platform.[45] The BI founder, Fabrice Robert, was a former Front National representative and former Unité Radicale member. Leading colleague Guillaume Luyt had also belonged to Unité Radicale, and once directed the Front National's youth organization. Luyt had also been a member of the monarchist Action Française (AF), a minor far-right movement with a long legacy; dating back to 1899, the AF was originally built along antidemocratic, nationalist values favoring Catholic traditionalism and the pre-1789 French order. Although it has seen much better (and worse) days over the past almost 120 years, AF remains a sort of throwback to the worldviews of the old European aristocracy. In the modern period, it has had most overlap with the Front National.

By the time of the migrant crisis, the Bloc Identitaire had distinguished itself from traditional political party structures, in that it operated as a network of local bodies across France. It was thus most similar to an anarchist group in structure. In fact, in one of the stranger twists in Europe's modern-day intellectual ferment, the Identitarian movement claims inspiration from the same Marxist anarchist—Antonio Gramsci—who influenced Alterio Spinelli's thought, leading to the eventual European Union project, as a left-wing federalist ideal.

However, the BI adopted the left-wing icon's method, if not his Marxist philosophy. In distinction to the allied Front National's battle for the vote, Fabrice Robert has said that the BI had a different goal and method. "We are good followers of Antonio Gramsci," the Identitarian leader stated in a 2012 interview. "Thus, we believe that in order to take the political power in a country, a preliminary and successful conquest of the minds [is needed]. The struggle for the cultural hegemony must be total and therefore take different modes of action: agitprop operations, community network development, creation of alternative media, development of our presence on the Internet, etc."[46]

According to Fabrice Robert, BI classified its identity according to three levels: local (regional), historical (French), and civilizational (European). Its guerrilla media tactics are also more typical of the Anarchist movement. This Identitarian approach to media as a theoretical precept anticipated some of the new communication tactics (executed through social media) that has been noted in the activities of the prominent far-right parties, like Front National, AfD, and Austria's Freedom Party.

The Identitarians, who support local, national, and European traditional identity and culture, are harshly critical of both Islamism and imperialism. This message resonated on the grassroots level with certain types of youth conservative activists during the migrant crisis. As with left-wing activists, the expansion of Identitarian movements across Europe depended on a network-driven approach abetted by social media and provocative events. Examples of such activities include serving "Identitarian soup" that contained pork to the homeless, gathering people to eat sausages and drink wine outside of a mosque, or creating provocative posters. In November 2012 the BI's youth wing, Generation Identitaire, occupied a mosque in the town of Poitiers—symbolic as the site where Charles Martel had in 732 triumphed over the defeated an invading Muslim Moors.[47]

Another important French Identitarian from the movements earliest times, Alain de Benoist, has had a core influence on Identitarianism through intellectual work. In terms of historical influencers, aside from Antonio Gramsci, the BI was fundamentally shaped by Pierre-Joseph Proudhon (1809–1865), the world's first self-declared anarchist, and even by the famed aristocrat who Robert has called "a great European," Richard Coudenhove-Kalergi, as well as by Euro-federalist Yann Fouéré, "who dreamt a Europe of a Hundred Flags, a Europe base on the rich fabric of our different regional identities." In upholding this traditionalist identity-based definition of Europe, the Identitarians considered outside forces to be unnatural and detrimental to the European environment. For example, Robert deemed Islam as being "profoundly inconsistent with the values of European civilization. Islam is a foreign body in our history, our customs and our political culture. We also know that Islam is not a mere faith. Both religion and ideology, Islam leads to totalitarianism."[48]

Identitarian organizations are geared up toward a "guerrilla media" war, using targeted provocations to force media to cover controversial social issues such as immigration. They also have their own official media.[49] They now exist in several countries, such as Austria, Germany, Italy, the Czech Republic, and in Scandinavian countries. The BI has cooperated with political parties like Belgium's Flemish Interest (Vlaams Belang, or VB), a right-wing separatist and anti-EU party with seats in local government. The VB is the direct successor of Vlaams Blok, a conservative anti-immigrant party formed in 1978. Calling for Flemish independence and supporting tougher security, it was consistently blocked by entrenched interests but became one of Belgium's most popular parties by 2004, when a court declared its statutes promoted discrimination. After some modifications and a renaming, it returned to action as the Vlaams Belang.[50] Since the 1980s, the party has gravitated toward similar parties from Scotland to South Africa, with nativism and self-determination being more important than traditional left–right distinctions.

By the 2015 migrant crisis, the VB had developed positive relations with Norbert Hofer's Freedom Party in Austria and the Italian Northern League, which called for substantial decentralization and possible secession from Italy. In many cases, such parties tend to represent wealthier and more homogeneous areas of countries, which are thus naturally adversarial to immigration. It presents what it considers an ideal for the future of European civilization. In this respect, migration was considered a threat to the common project, one that generally resembled aspects of the various conservative pan-European movements that arose after World War I.

Ultimately, the modern Identitarians derived from the New Right (Nouvelle Droite) movement that originated with philosopher Alain De Benoist in 1960s France. The political concepts of identity, direct democracy, regionalism, decentralization, and culture are primary, as is antiglobalism, anticapitalism, and the use of "metapolitics"—the process of introducing and permeating society with an ideology that can change it in their favor, making the ND the "Gramscians of the right."

Although the Identitarian and New Right movement had historically been essentially limited to intellectual activism and the occasional public provocation, it to the movement continued spreading lateral influence (at least in some key countries) due to the the migration crisis. Nevertheless, violence has occasionally plagued the movement, as when 800 assembled Austrian Identitarians were attacked by far-left Antifa activists, leaving one Identitarian in a coma.[51] Europe's current intellectual ferment has, however, resulted in some problematic argumentation (for example, whether religious affiliation should be a core European value and the relative importance of other philosophies).[52] The movement provided an ideological home for many who believed that European cultural and national identities were under siege, but who did not identify as far-right extremists who wanted to participate in violence. What separated the Identitarians from the far-right activist groups like neo-Nazis and civil self-defense militias was not only a preference for nonviolence; the New Right concedes that there is a place under the sun for everyone. However, for Muslims and other nonindigenous groups, Europe is not it.

By 2015, the left had grown alarmed, and, in some way, jealous of such conservative inroads (among young, educated, and middle-class Europeans in particular). Because the activities of these agitators were more subtle than those of the far-right they were long overlooked. *The Guardian*, for example, was thinking not of the Identitarians but of the new "mainstream far-right" parties when lamenting that they had "effectively claimed the progressive causes of the left—from gay rights to women's equality and protecting Jews from anti-Semitism—as their own, by depicting Muslim immigrants as the primary threat to all three groups. As fear of Islam has spread, with their encouragement, they have presented themselves as the only true defenders of western identity and western liberties—the last bulwark protecting a besieged Judeo-Christian civilisation from the barbarians at the gates."[53]

The trickle-up effect of these ideologies, and the political and intellectual environment in which they could develop, should not be forgotten. When such mass media, and the general leftist critic sigh over the explosion of far-right and Europe-first ideologies, they are generally ignorant of the fact that the very same thinkers who shaped the development of the 20th-century European leftist ideologies were also influential among parts of the right—albeit for different reasons—and that the intellectual and policy battles Europe is undergoing today all come from one shared, albeit obscure, philosophical and cultural heritage.

A long-term question remains as to whether far-right parties can ever rule effectively, should they gain power. One major step in setting the foundations was made in 2015, when several far-right parties that generally cannot stand the European Union succeeded in forming an EU parliamentary bloc, which entitled them to European funding for promoting their activities. Known as the Movement for a Europe of Nations and Freedom (MENF), it was formed by six parties: Austria's Freedom Party, France's Front National, the Italian Northern League, the Czech Freedom and Direct Democracy Party, and Belgium's Vlaams Belang.[54] Although they did not join the MENS, several of the other big far-right parties (the Dutch PVV, the Polish Congress of the New Right, and the German AfD) chose to participate in its European Parliament group, ENL. This development was expected to increase the network capacities and ability for such parties to reach common policies, and attempt to influence policy on the EU level regarding migration and other subjects.

Ironically, however, European political dynamics during and after the migrant crisis indicated that the establishment parties still expected to unite (as they had in France in 2002 to keep Jean Le Pen from the presidency) in order to freeze out parties like the Front National and PVV. Speaking several months ahead of the fall 2017 German elections, Karl-Peter Schwartz predicted that the outcome would "weaken CDU–CSU and the Greens, and strengthen the SPD and the rightist AfD. The CDU could be forced to accept a social democratic chancellor in a big coalition including the Greens," the German journalist stated. "In this case Ms. Merkel would probably leave, but German policy would not change significantly. Since Martin Schulz leads the Social Democrats another option became more probable—a coalition of SPD, Greens, and the former communists of Die Linke. It is difficult to forecast the political consequences of such a break."[55]

In the long-term, the simmering unrest caused by with Merkel and her open-door migration policy of 2015 could benefit the new right, though it will take time and could require much more domestic terrorism and economic turbulence to really galvanize voters. "The AfD has a good chance to become a real opposition party but it is still far from being able to govern," says Schwartz. "Maybe in 5–10 years—but only after Merkel [is gone]—a renovated CDU–CSU, together with the AfD could change the course of German politics. But this is more a hope than a realistic prognosis."[56]

Whether or not any of the new right parties can rule on a national level, in a clear majority coalition role, is another story. In one scenario, most such parties would be rendered toothless by social and media pressure, and thus would be blocked from executing the more extreme elements of their agendas once in power. A second scenario, in which such parties are dismissed as essentially protest movements, posits that they would lack the bureaucratic experience and political savvy to rule competently, leading to voter disillusionment and quick defeats. In the third scenario, they could try to enforce strong security measures that would be ineffective, considering the increasing tendency for "global solutions" and the involvement of international organizations and "civil society" in policy making and interface with local populations.

If migration is essentially a problem of volume and logistics, then the popularity of such political parties and groups should rise and fall with the number of migrants, amount and severity of terrorist attacks, and other acts of violence associated with migrants and Islamism. But it is likely that the danger of the right has been overestimated by alarmists on the left. For example, in Norway, home of that infamous executioner of the left Anders Breivik, the political discourse remained broader than one single issue. "The right wing, nationalist parties are obviously doing very well in Norway as in the rest of Europe, against a background of increased nervousness because of the sometimes seemingly overwhelming immigration of people from a completely different culture," notes Ambassador Wibye. "But this fact does not seem to divide society more than other political questions, such as taxes, income distribution etc. It is just one more political question, but a question with an unusually large potential for the parties and movements on the right side of the political spectrum."[57]

In the long term, it is unlikely that far-right parties can really put their full agenda into practice, barring some hypothetical calamity prompting public perception to isolate migration as a major security threat. The presence of an embedded establishment, and the need to cooperate with liberal parties and institutions, means an inevitable compromise or softening of such parties once in power. The transformation of such parties has already been witnessed. The most popular of them have largely disavowed the extremist views that led to their original formation. Thus under Marine Le Pen, France's Front National disavowed the anti-Semitism of earlier years, while the Sweden Democrats party separated itself from its late-1980s origins in the white nationalist movement. Even Geert Wilders had somewhat restricted his proposed regulations on Islam in advance of the spring 2017 elections.

Indeed, as the fruitless efforts of parties like the British National Party (BNP) revealed, the white nationalist platform cannot take a European party very far. But, at the same time, a populism based on national economic and security interests, which also includes resistance to migration as part of a principled opposition to EU supranationalist supremacy, can be very effective in today's Europe. Indeed, the case of Nigel Farage and his United Kingdom Independence Party (UKIP) offered a remarkable case study in this regard. UKIP's wellspring of populist support made it an influential force, to the point that the mainstream conservative Tory Party was obliged to appease its restless backbenchers by offering a campaign platform—the referendum on EU membership that party leader David Cameron never expected to be passed—to the British public. That UKIP could not only get the referendum but see the vote actually pass shocked the European establishment and elated fellow right-wing parties chafing at the bit to win more powers from an aloof and heavy-handed Brussels. The Brexit vote, followed by the even more unexpected victory of Donald Trump in 2016, revitalized all European conservative parties in advance of an election year that could be, many warned, a litmus test for the future viability of the European Union.

Although right-wing parties have typically been dismissed as no match for concentrated leftist forces on a national level, and thus only capable of (possibly) forming only weak or minority governments, they have demonstrated a greater potential to win power on the local level, where they can dedicate more resources to addressing local problems. This was demonstrated by the German AfD's strong showings in local elections during the migrant crisis. This trend will have an impact in the future, considering European governments' decisions, under EU pressure, to accept more migrants and to disperse them throughout countries in order to avoid the formation of yet more urban ghettoes.

In the absence of sweeping changes, the aftershocks of the migrant crisis tempered leftist ambitions, with reality and right-wing agitation pulling them toward the center on national levels. The Norwegian diplomat points out that "even people on the left have started to be more realistic about the future in a scenario of unlimited immigration, and have to some extent supported the more restrictive measures taken by the government." Time, and future elections, will show how the uneasy relationship develops between, and within, a right and left undergoing their own internal transformations.

CHAPTER 8

The Costs of Crisis: Social Impact and the Securitization Ahead

In the aftermath of the migrant crisis, Europe's future is being shaped at the fluid nexus of politics, economy, and public safety; all of these manifest at the level of society, and in its different manifestations and interpretations. The interaction of all of these elements has created a combustible atmosphere in which there will be definite winners (chiefly, politicians, corporations, and those dependent on the white-collar migration economy) and losers (primarily, average European citizens and the migrants and refugees themselves). The media, which has been so influential in creating and sustaining mass public manipulation on all sides of the issue, will be instrumental in determining how European societies process the overall phenomenon. Of course, social media is included here, being an emerging key driver that will increasingly displace "planted" narratives in the mainstream, politically influenced press, as the latter becomes continually a victim of social preferences and business realities. As everywhere else in the digital age, reality becomes increasingly malleable and self-selective, a hostage of what had, in 2016, memorably described as the "postfact era."

While migration has had a sharp effect on state capacities in areas like health care, education, integration measures, and tangible aid infrastructure and matériel, a detailed examination of each sector would require a separate study. In the big picture, even before 2015 migration's perceived cost burden on states had sparked strong European public debate. In Britain, for example, the social welfare expenses associated with immigration have made it a hot-button issue for years. Immigration and state costs was in fact one of the issues that influenced the vote to leave the European Union in June 2016.

European and international analysts alike have tried to gauge the cost–benefit balance of migration, and come to different conclusions—a phenomenon that just shows that the answer is still inconclusive. In general, the heaviest initial costs during the crisis were on social support infrastructure for refugees. Here the preexisting social debate on costs was exacerbated by the inconvenient timing. As migration exploded in Europe, countries like France were suffering from high unemployment, which led to street protests and political instability. The same occurred in Greece, stuck as it was in economic torpor caused by disastrous German-imposed austerity measures meant to save the euro, following Greece's 2009 debt crisis. "Frontline" countries like Italy and Greece simply did not have the public resources to cope with migrants, thus opening the door to large-scale operations by the European Union, aid groups, and international institutions—key players in the general migration economy. And the crisis also exposed internal disputes over budgets, which also had perceived direct impact on security capabilities. For example, when German interior minister Thomas de Maizière called for limiting refugee numbers in 2015, he was criticized for having failed, despite years of warning, to have increased staff and budget for the Federal Office for Migration and Refugees (BAMF).[1]

Hidden well away from the media-driven images of squalid migrant camps, burning shelters, terrorist attacks, marches, and horrific murders, the European Commission was, as usual, quietly crunching numbers. Its spring 2016 economic forecast found that the direct additional fiscal implications for countries most affected by the crisis are "expected to fall in the range of 0.1–0.6 percent of GDP, on a cumulative basis over 2015–2016," according to one official cost–benefit analysis. However, the report adds, "those estimates may prove to be at the low end, depending on how the situation evolves." On the other hand, the European Union expected that "GDP could increase by an additional 0.2% by 2017," and especially for Germany, where simulations pointed to a potential GDP increase of between 0.4–0.8 percent by 2017, "depending on the assumptions made about the skill level of migrants." In other words, the economic gains and losses from migration essentially canceled each other out. And in order for these forecasts to be achieved, the European Union advocated "lowering barriers" to migrant employment, "to facilitate the 'employability' of migrants." This was considered as "essential for their ability to get a regular job and to have a positive impact on growth and public finances in the medium term."[2] This positive projection also presupposed the need for social integration—something that is desirable but hardly guaranteed.

Another prognosis, from the Paris-based intergovernmental Organisation for Economic Co-operation and Development (OECD), also indicated that any cost–benefit analysis of migration remained unclear. At the same time, its generally positive conclusions presupposed the open-door outcomes that, while dear to the powerful globalist leaders, are highly unpopular among many Europeans—and the politicians they elect. Thus, the

OECD predicted that "the effects on host country labour markets should build up only very progressively over time as refugees become better integrated and as they reunite with their family. For refugees to realise their full potential it will be however important to enable them to locate where their skills are the most needed."[3] The likelihood of this "integration" is, however, very much uncertain, given the massive cultural divides between native Europeans and immigrants, fueled further by radically opposed political sentiments.

The European Union also has taken up the Merkel–Schäuble thesis that migration is beneficial because it addresses demographic problems and labor shortages. "The EU's working-age population is expected to decline by some 3.5% by 2020 (assuming zero net migration), and labour supply shortages could become bottlenecks to growth. It will bring demographic challenges in the next decades that could, to some extent, threaten the future growth of the EU economy."[4] The obvious problem with this argument, of course, is that any "assumption" of "zero net migration" is facetious, as the entry of over one million newcomers in 2015 alone abundantly showed. Further, at a time of high unemployment (particularly, youth unemployment) in various EU countries, this argument seemed incomprehensible to many Europeans. Attitudes against migrants tended to harden with each new European initiative to train and fund the newcomers, since European countries already had more than enough social problems to deal with, from unemployment and homelessness to drug abuse and health care. Nevertheless, heading into 2017, EU leaders were still clinging to the beliefs and reasoning of 2015. "We need migration for our economies and for our welfare systems, with the current demographic trend," said foreign affairs commissioner Federica Mogherina at (yet another) EU summit in Malta in early February 2017.[5] Yet discussions of migration from this standpoint were essentially criticized as concealing tacit "racism" or "xenophobia." And the predictable result of this was to alienate populations and increase support for populist groups.

It is no surprise, therefore, that some who would prefer to avoid calculating the economic impact of migration altogether; not only because it is hard to quantify, but also because it tends to inflame public and political discourse. Leftist supporters of migration often support this tactic. "A cost benefit analysis of refugees will inevitably put the spotlight on costs and that will give [Dutch right-wing politician Geert] Wilders' already hysterical hordes more ammunition," argued economist Marcel Canoy in November 2015. "It would be much better to do our utmost to increase the long-term benefits. That would be better for migrants and asylum seekers, better for Europe and better even for disgruntled citizens."[6] Such arguments represent, most basically, the affirmation of positive public relations campaigns for migration, a strategy shared by sympathetic politicians, the charity industry, and supranational blocs like the UN.

Although European governments and media have stigmatized and, in some cases, banned claims that migrants are more prone to violence and crime than native Europeans, the migrant crisis did in fact bring with it a surge in violent crime associated with immigrant populations. This is indisputable. But stuck between lingering political correctness constraints and a desire not to inflame public sentiment, local authorities have had a difficult time in disclosing and responding to violent events. This in turn has sparked further social unrest, as manifested by political protests and counterprotests, as well as the rise of civil-defense movements associated with extremist elements across Europe.

These reactions were largely due to the bumbling responses of government in the wake of migrant-related violence. These responses often have been met with scorn and condemnation. For example, police in Östersund, Sweden, were heavily criticized by local leaders and citizens after they warned women not to venture out alone at night, following a spate of sexual assaults by immigrants in March 2016.[7] This followed the much-derided proposal of a German mayor in January, telling women to keep an "arm's length" from strangers following the mass sexual assaults in Cologne on New Year's Eve. The suggestion quickly became a social media phenomenon in Germany. *Deutsche Welle* reported that "by late evening on Tuesday, #einearmlänge—which translates as 'an arm's length'— was one of Germany's top-trending hashtags."[8] Although the proposal was internalized as a sort of comedic faux pas by society, there was also a sense of simmering anger with authorities perceived as preferring self-repressive measures for domestic society—a tacit admission that foreign cultural norms would be acceptable within European society. And even in politically-correct Sweden, a senior policeman who revealed on Facebook that immigrants were responsible for the vast majority of serious crimes that he dealt with received considerable online support from Swedes in February 2017.[9]

As has been shown, the failure of authorities to control the migrant crisis caused a surge in attacks against the migrants themselves. This was much more the case in the Northern European countries than in the Southern ones, due to cultural differences and specific local realities. For example, in the December 2015 riot, some 2,000 people protested against government plans to build a refugee center in the small Dutch town of Geldermalsen, resulting in clashes with police. Soon after, the January 25, 2016, stabbing of Swedish aid worker Alexandra Mezher by an asylum seeker at a refugee center sparked more violence against immigrants and strengthened far-right groups. In February, angry Germans burned refugee centers and surrounded a bus with incoming migrants. Government statistics revealed that in 2015 "there were about 1,000 such attacks, five times the number reported in 2014."[10] And, inevitably, such events are seen as a call to arms by left-wing anarchists, creating an evermore complex threat matrix for police.

Similar future violent events will result in a moment of reckoning for European society and the politicians it elects. The big question remains as to whether migrants can, or should, be integrated into European society. This presumes the perception, one which many do not share, that immigration is beneficial in the first place. A public opinion study of 10 European countries carried out by Britain's Chatham House published in February 2017 revealed that 55 percent of Europeans opposed any further immigration from Muslim-majority countries. Only 20 percent supported continuing the "open door" policy. Only in Spain did public support for Muslim migration exceed 30 percent, while in Poland and Hungary, support for Muslim immigration stood at roughly 5 percent.[11]

The debate has been particularly fierce in Scandinavia, one of the more liberal corners of Europe. Sweden particularly has become a magnet for migrants owing to its generous welfare provisions, which many argue discriminate against native Swedes (particularly the poor and elderly) when it comes to housing and medical services. The provisions are so generous that many migrants do not even seek work, notes Nima Gholam Ali Pour, a member of the board of education in the city of Malmö. "Those who come to Sweden seem to be seeking a country that provides many entitlements but not many obligations. People seeking success go to the U.K., Canada or the United States, while it often appears as if people who want to break the rules choose to come to Sweden."[12]

Yet other Scandinavian states' policies have become more pragmatic since the 2015 crisis. Norway is a good example. "I do not see us benefiting from immigration, as the average immigrant does not give added value to our country," notes former Norwegian diplomat Carl Schiötz Wibye. "True, many immigrants do find work, but many others also find out how they can best benefit from our welfare system without working. And for those who want to work, the training and/or schooling can be very costly. Furthermore, immigrants tend to have a much shorter working life than the average Norwegian." As a former ambassador to Saudi Arabia and author of a new monograph on Saudi Wahhabism, the retired diplomat has a better view than most on the intercultural aspects of today's migration problems, as well as the prevailing local realities. He notes that pro-immigration Norwegians "are mostly driven by idealistic ideas, such as helping people who are in difficulty, wherever they are in the world. In addition, there is a tiny group of people who run refugee centers and make a lot of money on the new arrivals. But this group does not really have a voice in politics; their immediate interests are too obvious."[13]

In a European future of weak coalition governments and internally divided national populations, ideologically motivated street protests and demonstrations will increase, primarily focusing on issues of economy, education and social policies, and especially as they relate to immigration. This trend has already been witnessed in most European countries, and meeting the challenge will constitute a further chronic strain on local and national security resources, in terms of manpower, matériel, and time.

The European political discourse will be heavily impacted by strong rhetoric from left and right, with each approaching election being treated as a referendum on both morality and security, and as a potential challenge to the "common values" of the Continent. In the bigger picture, the increasing tendency for national agendas and politics to clash, domestically and at EU levels, puts the very future of the European Union in question. In a lucid assessment of February 2016, former Austrian diplomat Stefan Lehne predicted that "the migration challenge could result in one of three scenarios: a looser union, a regrouping of some member states in a smaller, hard-core Schengen, or a revival of integration in this field."[14]

The very fact that alternative "scenarios" are being discussed by serious thinkers today is deeply disconcerting to mainstream Euro-federalists who had always assumed their project was as inevitable as it was virtuous. Indeed, following Brexit and Donald Trump's election in November 2016, an already somber mood among European establishment leaders grew downright morbid. At a November economic conference in Berlin, French prime minister Valls warned that "Europe could die," stressing that France must implement the unpopular economic reforms that had fueled huge street protests against his own government. "A policy of growth cannot be reduced to reducing wage costs and public deficits," Valls stated, while begging for further clarity regarding European consensus on migration policy and society, calling on Europe "to stop being naive in the area of international trade and immigration, and to say more clearly 'who can and cannot enter and stay' in the continent."[15]

The fact that mainstream politics no longer has the answers for social ills in Europe, America, and many other countries has simply tempted these leaders to try a new strategy—change the questions. As European right-wing blocs surged through 2016 (partly by blaming immigration for rising crime and terrorism), this tactic held some appeal for a visibly angst-ridden European left. Major political parties had failed to convince voters that their security policies were viable during the migration crisis. Thus, the parties and think tanks behind them have sought to minimize the security aspect, and indeed distance it from the migration crisis in the broader public discourse. This specific strategy, which is expected to continue in the medium term, is considered by the left as an antidote to right-wing extremism (and general criticism of the left's migration policy).

This strategy of evasion was laid out in a 2016 analysis by Hungarian left-wing strategist Tamás Boros. He wrote that the center-left must acknowledge that "it will be unable to create a social majority for its own politics regarding refugees: it is impossible to win elections with a leftist ideological answer to the refugee crisis. The more the political agenda is dominated by the question of refugees, the more populist parties will gain support, and the more countries they will rise to power in." The solution, according to the Hungarian activist, is to simply avoid the subject and hope for the best. The left should "sustain its pro-refugee stance, but focus all its energies on avoiding this topic in European public life. Leftwing parties can stop populism from gaining even more ground if they divert the political agenda away from topics that are easy for populists to exploit, and if they will be the ones to dictate the criteria for a country's success-ful government . . . the left can regain its old strength if European politics will be about social Europe, about the reduction of social inequality, about higher pay for workers, about improving health and education, and not at all about the question of refugees."[16]

Although this strategy will be attempted, it is unlikely to succeed as counterterrorism operations increase and as the migration crisis rumbles on. Any mainstream politicians who embrace the strategy of evasion will thus be depicted as out of touch with ground realities and citizen concerns. There is simply too much bad news that cannot be ignored. There are too many sensitive crisis zones on Europe's peripheries, all of which contrib-ute to the immigration and security challenges Europe faces. For exam-ple, Belgian interior minister Jan Jambon warned on November 15, 2016, that a "wave" of 3,000 to 5,000 Islamic State jihadists—all originally from European countries—could return to Europe, as the "caliphate" steadily lost territory in Iraq and Syria. "All the intelligence agencies are trying to monitor the situation and exchange information," the minister stated. "If the wave comes, we must be ready."[17] Considering that only a relatively small number of homegrown terrorists had essentially shut down Paris and Belgium in the previous year's terrorist attacks, the security implica-tions of the statement were almost beyond comprehension.

At the same time that European security risks continued to mount, the aggravated complexities of the migrant crisis are leading to the politiciza-tion of security and justice, further exposing internal social and ideological fault lines. The case of Berlin public prosecutor Roman Reusch is telling in this regard. In a 2007 interview, Reusch criticized Germany's lax depor-tation laws, blaming the legal impasse on a "liberal education bourgeoi-sie, which lives in other areas," and was thus ignorant of ground realities. "These people lean back, make great speeches, but do not provide any integration services, which is left up to the subclass [to carry out]." Reusch stated that almost 80 percent of youth perpetrators in Berlin came from "a migration background," with 70 percent being from the Middle East. And even though they were born in Germany, he described the youth criminals as having "a vocabulary of 500 [German-language] words, largely devoid of grammar."[18] The prosecutor was dismissed following these politically incorrect comments.

However, in April 2016, as a member of the new AfD party, Reusch became Berlin's chief state prosecutor. The promotion gave him "authority to cooperate with foreign law enforcement authorities and deport foreign criminals." For the Turkish association of Berlin and Brandenburg (TBB), it was "more than worrying that a leading member of the AfD, which famously employs scorn against refugees and Islam" could be chief prosecutor. A local alliance of defense lawyers also protested. TBB spokeswoman Ayse Demir suggested that the appointment was actually a ploy by the centrist establishment Social Democrats and Christian Democrats, which were being threatened by AfD gains ahead of the city-state's September 2016 parliamentary elections. The TBB warned Berlin Justice Minister Thomas Heilmann (Reusch's appointer) that the move "would not bring any AfD votes."[19]

This kind of negative intervention is especially problematic for Germany; it has often been put under a spotlight due to its history. Similarly, proscriptive methods (such as banning organizations on ideological grounds) tend to be employed first, with more extraordinary means used only in special cases. This policy has been utilized most frequently against neo-Nazi groups. Indeed, the official title of Germany's domestic intelligence service—the *Bundesamt für Verfassungsschutz*, or "Federal Office for the Protection of the Constitution"—indicates the founding principles on which postwar Germany's policing were created. Before becoming Merkel's finance chief, Wolfgang Schäuble had been a tough-minded interior minister who used proscriptive measures frequently. In May 2008, he banned two right-wing groups accused of being "reservoirs of organized Holocaust deniers."[20] In 2009, he banned another far-right group, the Homeland-Faithful German Youth, claiming that it was indoctrinating children with racist and Nazi ideology.[21] Another neo-Nazi group, the "White Wolves Terror Crew" (WWT) was banned in 2016, as a direct result of the migrant crisis.[22]

Germany has proscribed other groups, such as the Frankfurt branch of the Turkish International Humanitarian Relief (IHH), the Islamist charity behind the controversial "Gaza aid flotilla" in 2010. (This was possibly more a favor to the Israeli government, however.) Similarly, during the migrant crisis five years later, de Maizière appeased the Erdoğan government by banning a newspaper published in Germany by the Turkish left-wing extremist group Revolutionary People's Liberation Party (DHKP-C), and ordered actions against the group.[23] However, the leftist group was less of a threat to Germany than to Turkey. The organization, which stems from the 1978 Revolutionary Left (in Turkish, Devrimci Sol or Dev Sol), has historic bases in Belgium, Germany, and Holland. Although the Marxist–Leninist group was once known for professional targeted assassinations of Western officials, Turkish military, and businessmen, it has increasingly targeted Turkey's ruling government in recent years.[24]

The migrant crisis has brought new challenges for the German tactical ban policy, however. Through 2016, hundreds of raids occurred, targeting suspected ISIS supporters. One specific case, though, seemed curious in that it was expansive and yet led to no arrests: the November 15 police action that led to the banning of the "True Religion" extremist group. Police searched 190 mosques, apartments, and offices connected to the organization, which was "ubiquitous" in Germany for handing out free translated copies of the Koran in public places. However, "what on the surface seemed like a legitimate religious organization was also a recruiting operation for the Islamic State, Interior Minister Thomas de Maizière said Tuesday. He added that 140 people affiliated with the group had gone on to fight in Syria."[25] Because no arrests were made, it was unclear whether the police were just gathering intelligence for future purposes, or attempting to strengthen Merkel's image as "tough on terrorism" in advance of 2017 elections; it was probably a bit of both.

Nevertheless, the proscriptive method is not adequate for modern-day realities, as subsequent events revealed. When True Religion was banned, its members simply opened a new group called "We Love Muhammad." Instead of Korans, its activists in Frankfurt started "handing out biographies of Mohammed [sic] and telling passersby to download the group's new smartphone app."[26] Similarly in Switzerland, where authorities began considering a ban on Koran distribution, Islamists were moving on to biographies and Islamic audiobooks for children. Austria too was considering some sort of tougher action. But such blanket bans tend to just attract more visibility for groups, which in any case can easily reach the masses through modern technology. In short, the German state model of proscription created in an earlier context, motivated to keep Adolf Hitler's works out of circulation, was no longer effective for the modern European context.

German authorities have also been hampered by weak security legislation—a factor that evolved in reaction to the Gestapo and Stasi legacies. Wolfgang Schäuble, for one, has always advocated tougher security measures through legislative changes. Preventive detentions, targeted assassinations, and restricted access to Internet and cell phones for terrorist suspects are among the more "muscular" approaches that Schäuble proposed.[27] After the *Charlie Hebdo* attacks in January 2015 in Paris, he and French counterpart Michel Sapin demanded the European Commission pass legislation to help authorities trace financial transactions and freeze terrorist assets in the EU.[28] For his part, Thomas de Maizière proposed a law to replace the identity cards of potential foreign fighters with another form of identification—which again proved controversial among Germany's leftists.[29]

An increasing problem for European law enforcement will be a personnel attrition rate caused by immigration's unfavorable conditions. European governments have often denied that some immigrant neighborhoods have become "no-go areas" for police. Yet, even in 2007, Berlin prosecutor Reusch had spoken of immigrant neighborhoods of Berlin where the youths "consider the police as a foreign occupation," making certain neighborhoods too dangerous to patrol.[30] Indeed, even though "every police chief and interior minister will deny it," said chairman of Germany's largest police union Bernhard Witthaut in 2011, Germany did indeed have no-go areas. These were immigrant-inhabited neighborhoods where female officers particularly were not respected.[31]

In Sweden, as of September 2016, there were more than 50 reportedly no-go areas in which police and even emergency services would be attacked should they try to enter. This had a psychological toll on human resources: a full 80 percent of Swedish police planned to quit, according to one September 2016 report. Up to three officers were quitting per day "as they feel the government isn't giving them the tools to tackle the epidemic of criminality" ravaging the country due to migration, which ranged from migrant sexual assaults to grenade attacks. A sudden epidemic of car burnings was also rocking Sweden, Denmark, and other countries. Swedish police sergeant Peter Larsson told a Norwegian broadcaster that officers had been saying: "We have a major crisis. Many colleagues have chosen to leave. We will not be able to investigate crimes, we have no time to travel to the call-outs we are set to do." In migrant-populated and crime-ridden suburbs like Rinkeby in Stockholm and Gothenburg, shootings and even attacks on journalists have occurred. Sergeant Larsson warned that if the government did not choose "to make a real commitment now, it's going to end in disaster."[32] According to Swedish researcher Ingrid Carlqvist, immigrants "are trying to impose Sharia law in these areas and they are doing a good job."[33]

At the same time in France, police were ambushed by a gang of youths with Molotov cocktails, suffering serious injuries in Paris in October 2016. Morale there has been damaged as well, as police "have complained of being increasingly under attack—from jihadists, ordinary criminals and hooded youths who have clashed with police during recent demonstrations over labour reforms."[34] Throughout the migrant crisis, anarchists and migrant activists—native Europeans who often had migrants intermingled in their ranks—showed an increasing brazenness and disrespect for police across the Continent, both in targeted attacks and at flashpoints such as at borders, migrant centers, and protests. Greek police, for example, had become accustomed for years to attacks by anarchists, and the migration crisis only increased the frequency and severity of such attacks. At the same time, police were being urged to show restraint at all times, causing frustration and a high amortization rate of equipment. (Indeed, as previously cited, a full 40 percent of Macedonian border police equipment was damaged in only a few months of patrolling.)

Given these realities, several developments are likely. Policing will become a major political issue, as countries like Sweden, France, and

Belgium grapple with the political and public security cost of having to use significant force to "recover" immigrant-inhabited neighborhoods. Quite possibly, a lack of strong leadership and limited interest will lead them to take the path of least resistance and accept that certain territorial losses are acceptable. In such scenarios, isolated pockets of urban Europe will become safe-havens for terrorism planners and organized crime groups. As was seen in the Belgian raids in Molenbeek, action is usually only reactive. Unfortunately, it will probably take further terrorist attacks for police to tackle the tougher neighborhoods where few or no native Europeans live anyway.

Other issues are affecting policing in Europe. Back in 2011, German police union chief Witthaut had pointed that police were both underfunded and undermanned: this also had to do with the rise of private-sector security industries. "There are not enough young people to be recruited," he said, since the state was competing with the better-paying private security sector, making "qualified young people scarce." Further, he perceived a disparity in justice system operations regionally, with northern German regions being more lenient on suspects and Bavaria in the south tending to be tougher on crime in general. This did not augur well for the future of a unified German approach, the police union chief predicted.[35] If European countries are unable to enforce justice in a unified manner on national levels, it becomes even less likely that they can do so on an EU-wide level.

Criminologist Gavin Slade expects that "at some stage [there will be] a moral panic about organized crime among new migrants in Europe, which will be framed in the language of territorially minded gangs." According to this British expert, a major security concern is the use of prisons as recruiting centers for jihadists and criminal groups. This will only increase with the arrival of migrants driven to the criminal underworld by a lack of proper employment and nonassimilation. "Ethnically diverse prisons and recruitment into organized crime will be a defining issue for the management of prisons, firstly, but also our understanding of the source of organized criminal authority and power in the future," he attests. Comparing the current case of Europe to the United States, where ethnically and racially divided gangs are especially prominent in prison populations, Slade expects that "similar failures in prison management and rising prison populations" will expedite "the emergence of ethnically based prison gangs that will impact outside the prisons."[36]

As European jails become increasingly full of immigrants, prison costs will rise, leading to state budget issues in some countries. Here, EU legislation will have a major effect and has already created continental imbalances. In April 2016, a landmark European Court of Justice ruling "barred member states from sending prisoners back to their EU countries to finish their prison terms if their human rights are threatened there," according to one British report that cited a massive rise in inmates from other countries in U.K. prisons. "The ruling prevented Germany extraditing suspected criminals to their homes in Romania and Hungary because of fears their fundamental human rights would be put at risk by the condition of the prisons."[37] Given the general absence of migrants from Eastern European countries, the burden of costs will also fall on the heavily inundated countries like Sweden, Germany, and France.

Another and far wider challenge for authorities will be the securitization of public spaces. This will have to be done as inconspicuously as possible, to maintain general public approval while also being adaptive to an ever-increasing range of threats. These range from terrorist attacks, physical assaults, and protests to damage and disruption of vehicles, property, and public works. The migrant crisis shocked Europeans generally accustomed to a peaceful life not only by terrorism, but also by attacks occurring in broad daylight in public parks, at swimming pools, and at well-attended public celebrations. There are no simple solutions for this range of threats. The major security events witnessed since 2014 have shown that almost every place can now be considered a target for one kind of security event or another.

After the Paris and Brussels attacks, several European governments increased their security and counterterrorism budgets. This represented not only much-needed help for local and national security forces, but also a windfall for corporations in the industry. The securitization phenomenon has triggered citizen concerns among those championing privacy and civil liberties; however, the proliferation of sudden and unexpected terrorist attacks since 2015 has slowly inculcated a broader acceptance of such measures as "necessary" for the general public safety, especially in states with high immigrant populations.

There will be a clear economic benefit from the securitization of Europe, but in an increasingly globalized and stratified economy, the riches will not be shared widely. Profit for corporations has increased in direct proportion to the volume increase in migration from 2015 onward. Often, this has been in the more mundane sorts of civilian equipment needed by aid organizations and national governments assisting refugees. But, in other cases, profit has increased for companies providing security solutions for chronic threats. For example, interest has surged in companies that make equipment (such as police riot gear, batons, shields, and so on).

Indeed, among security companies active on the EU level, "there does seem to be a trend towards an increase in the offer for such equipment, but the offer became so big that competition is also important," notes Manuela Tudosia, a government relations professional and researcher specializing in security, defense, and health policies. Regarding future procurement trends for such matériel, she believes that more than any company or companies, "innovation would be the winner. Probably those companies [will benefit most] that can offer the best, most secure, and lightest equipment (imagine the weight that a policeman or soldier has to carry while wearing all this equipment on them). And to provide all this at an acceptable price is a challenge for the industry, and a complex comparison exercise for procurement officers."[38]

Another transformative security development for European society is the greater proliferation of small arms. Unlike the United States, gun ownership has never been a significant issue for most Europeans, but since the beginning of the migrant crisis sales have skyrocketed. "All across Germany, a country with some of the most stringent gun-control laws in Europe, demand is skyrocketing for non-lethal self-defense weapons," reported the Gatestone Institute. These items included "pepper sprays, gas pistols, flare guns, electroshock weapons and animal repellants. Germans are also applying for weapons permits in record numbers." Altogether, the migrant crisis drove the sale of pepper spray alone up by 600 percent in 2015.[39]

Another major economic beneficiary of the migration-security economy in Europe is the technology sector. Research and development will continue to flourish, as governments and supranational organizations procure the latest solutions in everything from police body cameras with artificial intelligence integration to surveillance equipment to network securitization, and advanced encryption/decryption programs for security services. At the local level, this securitization is being driven by public fears over street crime and terrorist attacks. For example, officials in Italy announced they would be installing new cameras and other security systems to guard the Leaning Tower of Pisa at the town's main square. Police and military began patrolling the area 24 hours a day following a foiled jihadist plot against the historic tourist attraction.[40] The Vatican, which is also a major tourist site and target of Islamic radicals, has in recent years increased physical security, surveillance and for the first time, employed a cybersecurity expert.[41]

Even before the Russian annexation of Crimea, NATO had been warning of the threat of "hybrid war" scenarios, which include both tangible and cyber potentials. As has been shown, the migrant crisis itself has represented an ideal example of the former type. Regarding cyberwar, European security planners are worried about the medium-term period, and rushing to catch up. One problem remains that allied and interlinked countries are at different stages of development and have varying levels of network capacity. "Currently in Bulgaria, we have already had some serious DDoS attacks, and all of our government institution found that they were unprepared for this and were completely blocked," notes Martin Konov, an IT manager at telecommunications vendor Intracom Bulgaria. "Now the government developed a new Cyber Security Strategy which should be followed to make the entire network more stable and protected in the next two to three years." Further, regarding the phenomenon of network hijacking for ransom purposes in Europe today, "the numbers are definitely increasing," Konov adds.[42]

As Europe tries to develop new cyber capabilities, patch holes and develop a uniform approach, it is doing so with industry participation, coordinated at the supranational level. On July 5, 2016, the European Commission announced the launch of a new public–private partnership on cybersecurity that was "expected to trigger €1.8 billion of investment by 2020," according to the commission. "This is part of a series of new initiatives to better equip Europe against cyberattacks and to strengthen the competitiveness of its cybersecurity sector."[43] The increasingly sophisticated government and popularly available technology will play in influencing perceptions of the securitization process, and the ability of individuals and groups to participate: with each passing day, industrial capabilities get closer to a convergence point between off-the-shelf technology and that which was previously accessible only to governments and major corporations. At the same time, emerging powers are shaking up the old order; as of June 2016, China had built the world's fastest supercomputer, using all domestically-made processors and thus eliminating any need for American-made parts.[44]

The securitization of Europe in the wake of the migrant crisis is a reality, even though the underlying motives and causes behind that crisis remain only partly known. "The real end game could actually be about control," notes an official with the European Parliament. According to this theory, the European Union was able to use public fear as momentum for passing controversial legislation like the PNR. "Before the crisis, PNR [the Passenger Name Record law] had been stuck for years in parliament, as had airport body screeners (due to perceived health hazards)." The parliamentary official adds that other winners of the European Union's securitization spree include "big data companies—many German, American, and Israeli companies are doing quite well."[45]

Indeed, a provisional PNR deal was reached just weeks after the Paris Attacks—on December 2, 2015—between the European Parliament and Council on an EU directive regulating "the use of Passenger Name Record (PNR) data for the prevention, detection, investigation and prosecution of terrorist offences and serious crime," according to an official EP Justice and Home Affairs Commission statement of June 1, 2016. The directive "will oblige airlines to hand EU countries their passengers' data in order to help the authorities to fight terrorism and serious crime. It would require more systematic collection, use and retention of PNR data on air passengers, and would therefore have an impact on the rights to privacy and data protection."[46] Indeed, due to historic concepts of civil liberties and privacy, the European Union had been a hard nut to crack for corporate lobbyists on this issue, for many years. The securitization of "big data" indeed means a huge opportunity for companies specialized in the field.

However, whether the business of border screening will lead to improved security is a question for the future. The PNR vote was far from unanimous, and it appears that some concessions were promised to dissenters. For example, an internal draft report on fundamental rights and big data (from October 2016) included a nondiscrimination clause that warned that "owing to the intrusiveness of decisions and measures taken by law enforcement authorities in citizens' lives and rights, maximum caution is necessary to avoid unlawful discrimination and the targeting of certain population groups, especially marginalised groups and ethnic and racial minorities."[47] Such language definitely will open the door to future lawsuits from people feeling they have been wrongly singled out, and also will cause practical dilemmas for law enforcement fearful of a codified reprimand if the lines of political correctness are crossed during investigative procedures.

In the big picture, several key factors make the character of securitization in Europe different than in the United States or elsewhere. As in other sectors, this multinational bloc aims to preserve a certain balance in procurement and participation; thus major deals and projects typically involve consortia consisting of companies from multiple nations. Further, "the defense industry in Europe is much less liberal than in the US or the UK. Major groups are owned by the state or are put under its control," says Italian security and defense expert Marco Giulio Barone. "And minor groups serve as subcontractors of the major ones, or compete in subsectors where major groups allow them (or have no interest in)."[48] The European Union also has a strict Transparency Register that affects the relationship with the private sector.[49] Unlike the case of the United States or other countries, there is no corresponding military–industrial lobby in Brussels—though to be sure there are many very interested and active corporations, and a certain degree of "revolving door" positions between private and public sectors.

According to Barone, the European Union is "not cohesive enough for long-term objectives and practical capabilities that could foster strong consistent policies favoring military investment." Therefore, European defense industry companies seeking export markets in regions like the Middle East, North Africa, and Gulf countries "use external procurement to compensate for poor domestic financing. This depends on each single EU member, which jealously guards its sovereignty and position. This is a common feature for all EU countries." Similarly, the Italian expert adds, the lack of an EU-level procurement process has made it "very hard" for the commission to pursue its plan for the European Defense and Technology Industrial Base (EDTIB).[50] In any case, the European defense industry "would much prefer focusing on its core activities (i.e., producing weapons and systems of weapons) rather than adapting what they have to civil tasks."[51]

In the current charged atmosphere of migration, terrorism, and a possible threat from Russia, NATO has been both very active in the securitization of Europe's east and keen to avoid "duplication." This is coming as NATO observes an increasingly ambitious European Union, as with the various security operations that led to the creation of an EU Coast Guard in September 2016. The June 23 Brexit vote will also affect the orientation of of America's trusted ally, which had vetoed past attempts to form a European army separate from NATO. In late June 2016, as the Italian EU external affairs commissioner Federica Mogherini was preparing to release a new EU military strategy paper, NATO chief Jens Stoltenberg warned that "NATO has well established structures that are tested and tried over decades. They are important part of NATO cooperation."[52]

Currently, the European Union and NATO "have a formalized way of interaction with the industry—be it military or not—whereby the expertise of the industry can be required in certain cases," says Manuela Tudosia. "I would qualify it as a necessary dialogue in order to be able to better assess available capabilities and need for further investment." This formalized relationship means that both organizations help coordinate "member states, their interoperability, and—to the extent possible—the avoidance of duplication in procurement or R&D," the Brussels-based expert adds. At present, most of the European Union funding available for security-related policies is in fact "going to R&D (rather than off-the-shelf procurement). Participation of industries from several countries in a consortium is often a prerequisite, and this says a lot about the importance of 'national geographical balance.'"[53]

This delicate balancing of powers and interests between member states, and between NATO and the European Union as separate cooperating entities, has been complicated—while offering a wealth of opportunities—by the three crises that have emerged since 2014. At the NATO 2016 Warsaw Summit, along with a heavy focus on Russia and Eastern Europe, the alliance announced that it was "contributing effectively to addressing the refugee and migrant crisis in the Aegean Sea, and stands ready to consider possible additional support to international efforts in the Mediterranean, in complementarity and cooperation with the European Union."[54] Considering the security risks to Europe stemming from immigration, it should be noted that terrorism is considered a homeland security rather than mutual defense matter. NATO is therefore not involved with all terrorism-related aspects and policies facing Europe. When it occurs, European defense industry interaction with NATO is mainly executed through the NATO Industrial Advisory Group, while the alliance also may organize specific events for particular industries as required.[55]

Thus, since the conditions for "lobbying" in a conventional sense are lacking in the European Union, many companies "just observe the strategic environment around us, make a guess about potential needs based on this observation, then they try to test the extent to which the need is real. It may turn out it is not. A lot can actually be pure speculation," notes Tudosia. And so the events and trends that steer EU migration policy "will determine the potential lobbying trends. An example from another sector would be the financial crisis," the Brussels expert adds. "It was right after—not before—this crisis that many public affairs companies in Brussels [became] specialized in financial regulations. In addition, I would see any policy—including migration—as a continuum, not a given. You continuously learn from past lessons and you continuously adapt."[56]

The biggest long-term securitization achievement to come from the migration crisis—for the European Union as a supranational organization—has probably already occurred. On September 14, 2016, the former external borders security body Frontex became the European Border and Coast Guard Agency, to coordinate the new European Border and Coast Guard (EBCG) that had been supported by a European Council meeting of December 2015. The agency was reborn with a stronger mandate and a goal of creating common standards of external border management, and submit periodic risk analyses regarding vulnerabilities and local needs.[57] Given the many political divisions within both the European Union and its member states, it is unlikely that a greater result (such as a real "EU army") will be realized anytime soon. But the migration crisis did at least bring a coast guard—a goal that the defense industry had been supporting since at least 2010.

In general, the migrant crisis has been beneficial for the largest European defense players (like Italy's Finmeccanica, the U.K.'s BAE Systems, France's Thales, and European multinational Airbus) and their subsidiaries. The interests of the industry in general are promoted by the European Organisation for Security (EOS), which counts the leading contractors among its members, and which produces regular studies while promoting advocacy and hosting working groups for the interests of the European defense industry.[58]

In 2015, *Fortune* reported that "from 2002 to 2013, Airbus, Finmeccanica, and Thales—largely through subsidiaries—have collected the lion's share of 225 million euros to thicken the defenses of 'Fortress Europe' through the development of drones, olfactory sensors, and border patrol robots." According to the study, "border control is already a core piece of these companies' export portfolios. These firms have secured contracts for high-profile and high-tech border security projects in the Middle East and North Africa—in Libya and Saudi Arabia, for instance—worth billions of euros." It added that in the case of Finmeccanica, "rising demand for border security and surveillance has been offsetting losses in traditional military orders" through 2013 alone.[59]

Yet, although this and other media reports have claimed that the migrant crisis provides an opportunity for defense contractors "in their own backyard," the EBCG itself is not likely to be much of a cash cow. The bulk of its equipment depends on existing assets pooled by the member states involved. The agency was allotted an overall budget of 238 million euros in 2016, which is slated to increase to 281 million euros in 2017, and then 322 million euros in 2020. This is a steady increase but not a massive one. In the case of another substantial migrant wave (or two), budgets will have to be reassessed. The EBCG's funds "are so limited, that I don't think any major group could live on it," says Italian expert Marco Giulio Barone "At least half of that budget will be spent on human resources and at least 25 percent of it will go for maintenance and logistics. For military procurement contracts, what's left is just pocket change." And, while the new agency will have, for the first time, the ability to select and procure its own equipment, "the negotiating power of the four bigs (the UK, France, Germany and Italy) overwhelms any other competitor in cases like this."

In the end, a wide gap exists between these supranational, pan-European securitization interests and those of the everyday citizen. In a Europe that ever seeks to be (as the institutional rhetoric says) "at whole and at peace," it is ironic that the big security projects seem to be, despite all their bureaucracy and complex rivalries, much easier to achieve than the small ones. Although the European Union will be able to point to quantitative successes in managing large-scale security processes on external borders and in data management, it is helpless at the local level of the streets, the schools, and public places. The security threats present in real-life local situations predated the migrant crisis of 2015. But it seems it took that crisis to make many Europeans aware of the potential risks to a lifestyle that was previously taken for granted.

CHAPTER 9

The Geopolitics of Migration: National Interests, Europe, and the Globalist Agenda

In early October 2015, an obscure Berlin-based think tank, the European Stability Initiative (ESI), released a detailed plan for solving the migrant crisis. Conspicuously titled "The Merkel Plan," the report proposed that Germany should give asylum to 500,000 Syrian refugees registered in Turkey and provide "safe transport to successful applicants." In return, Turkey should agree to take back new migrants stuck in Greece. Germany would also help Turkey obtain visa-free travel by 2016. A common European asylum system, and more future financial aid were also recommended.[1] As if by magic, Angela Merkel vocalized these ideas in a German television interview days later.

The chancellor's ventriloquism was most exciting for the ESI chairman, Gerald Knaus, an Austrian sociologist and dilettante who had already been flooding European inboxes for years with clever observations and sweeping proposals for the general improvement of Europe, in line with an unfailingly establishment-left worldview. "For a policy to take just three days to go from Knaus's outbox to the mouth of the chancellor was a first" for ESI, noted *Foreign Policy* in a sympathetic feature of September 9, 2016. The U.S. establishment magazine was defending Knaus, following months of criticism in the German and Austrian press. It was a time of intense geopolitical turmoil, too: Turkey was becoming ever more authoritarian, following July's failed coup attempt, and had restored relations with Russia, while the UN's Summit on Refugees (led by U.S. president Barack Obama and prominent representatives from the worlds of philanthropy and business) was fast approaching. Not only solving, but profiting from, the migrant crisis was the new challenge of the day.

In addition to the constant battle for influence and patronage, concerns had emerged over the ESI's excessive "public attention"; such bodies usually attract little public interest, and purposefully so. The public backlash against ESI had included "gross exaggeration in German media outlets (one regional headline proclaimed Knaus the 'man saving Merkel') to angry emails and tweets from members of the far right, who accuse the ESI of tearing apart Germany's cultural fabric by importing foreigners or claim it is driven by American interests (the ESI has twice received funding from George Soros's Open Society Foundations for projects on human rights and Azerbaijan)."[2]

Foreign Policy dutifully depicted Knaus as a sort of shy evangelist for human rights who had undertaken the burden of diplomatic missionary work on behalf of the greater good; despite their concerns about potential criticism when preparing their report, Knaus and his colleagues "felt they had little choice but to roll up their sleeves when they witnessed the EU 'dropping the ball' on implementing their strategy. In its missive laying out the plan, the ESI had argued it was crucial to move quickly, before the situation ballooned out of control and before right-wing groups seized on the chaos for their gain."

This rhetorical iteration of inevitability with a seize-the-day momentum is common among globalists, and the intervention to save ESI was pure public relations. The German public accusations of foreign influence had clearly struck a nerve: after all, it was not beyond plausible explanation that a simple think tank expert would spend months "shuttling between the EU and Turkey to listen, persuade, and cajole policymakers and to rally the European public." But this is precisely the shadow diplomacy that has been employed by a globalist deep state of influencers during the European migrant crisis, through the use of relatively obscure individuals and small groups to relentlessly push policies that they know are deeply unappealing to most Europeans.

The ESI and its director typify the profile of entities used by globalists to influence migration policy. Knaus had worked in universities, NGOs, and for the European Union since the 1990s in places like Ukraine and the Balkans, before becoming a visiting fellow at Harvard and similarly affiliated with the Open Society Foundation of George Soros.[3] As will be seen, Soros was one of the key geopolitical players behind the 2015 European migration crisis. Knaus also became involved with the European Council on Foreign Relations (ECFR), a copycat version of the U.S.-based based Council on Foreign Relations. The Brussels-based policy shop was formed with partial Soros funding in 2007, apparently "inspired by the role American think-tanks played in helping the US move from isolationism to global leadership."[4] Like similar NGOs and think tanks, the ESI helps global interests create consensus through "independent" research and advocacy. ESI has received funding from Soros, the European Commission, major

European governments and development agencies, as well as Belgium's King Baudouin Foundation, the Charles Stewart Mott Foundation, the U.S. Institute of Peace, the German Marshall Fund of the United States, the Rockefeller Brothers Fund, and so on.[5]

When discussing the geopolitics of migration, there are two levels of distinct, yet overlapping, interests: the national and supranational. In the first category are individual countries and nations and in the second, political blocs (chiefly, the European Union) and international organizations, guided by treaties and their own mandates. This distinction is a fundamental one that precedes politics. In today's increasingly divided Europe, the traditional ideological paradigms and differentiations between political blocs are being questioned, and often rejected, by populations that have become increasingly angered at phenomena like governmental corruption and democracy deficit. This trend has been accelerated by the proliferation of new media and technologies that are rapidly replacing the historic gatekeepers of information.

Traditional definitions of political left and right are also being transformed. The new visibility of Russia, the persistence of countries like Hungary, Slovakia, and Macedonia against the European Union on migration, and even the ascent of Iceland's direct-democracy, technophile Pirate Party in 2016 all indicate that new battle lines have been drawn between national and local sovereignty versus neoliberal globalism. In this light, the migration issue is so interesting because it encompasses all of the questions being debated today—politics, economy, security, social dimensions, education, health care, and more—that are intimately involved with the outcomes of migration on local, national, and supranational levels. And, as the crisis of 2015 revealed, migration potentially has the power to break countries and blocs apart due to its social impact.

At the same time, for several decades very strong foundations have been laid for the development of migration as a global project and industry, at the very highest levels of politics, business, academia, and associated fields. The complex interwoven interests at this level will be examined and identified closely in the final part of this chapter. As the example of the ESI "Merkel Plan" revealed, the global interests advocating and implementing these policies are operating a sort of shadow government, working surreptitiously from within the established power structure. However, with the populist uprisings we have seen since 2015, this traditional system is under assault. How the globalists use migration to retrench its position will be a key question for assessing the future of Europe (and the world).

First, however, the geopolitics of migration has an impact at the primary level, that of the state. This comparative assessment of events and trends reveals how the key states have acted and are positioning themselves toward other states and supranational blocs in terms of migration. Fundamentally, it is the actions of individual states that will drive the physical movement and presence of migrants and refugees, and as such drive policy locally and internationally.

The most important country in this regard remains Turkey. As the gatekeeper of millions of migrants from war zones and more distant places, NATO's only Muslim state used its geostrategic position to maximum advantage during the migrant crisis and afterward. Whereas individual Western countries and the European Union had criticized Turkish governments for alleged human rights violations, judicial shortcomings, cracking down on free speech, and persecuting the Kurds, the European bloc was effectively silenced by the reality that its own future existence depended on the good graces of President Erdoğan.

The thought that the viability of the whole European project depended on the whims of one single leader in a highly volatile region was deeply troubling for many European leaders. Yet no one had a better solution than conceding to the Turkish demands for billions in aid money and visa liberalization. The failed coup of July 15, 2016, only redoubled Erdoğan's tendency to crack down on opponents, sacking or arresting over 100,000 persons from all walks of life by November. However, throughout 2016 much of the promised European funds were still frozen up and the visa deal was still unresolved, with many national-level European politicians opposed to it in principle. In the aftermath of more than one million Muslim migrants arriving in the heart of Europe, this was a popular position for politicians seeking local votes, even if it imperiled the larger EU project intended to keep the European Union–Turkey migrant deal alive. And, for Turkish politicians long irritated by European posturing on "common values" issues in public discourse, being the migrant gatekeeper gave additional confidence in their own domestic criticism of the Europeans.

The fact that Turkey got to the point where Europe's security depended on the caprices of one authoritarian ruler reveals a failure in European planning and analysis. In 2003, when Erdoğan's Justice and Development (AKP) party first came to power on promises of fighting corruption and improving the economy, no one really understood how ambitious their goals were—or how Islamist they could become. In hindsight, this should not have been a surprise, as Erdoğan, a former mayor of Istanbul, had always been solidly Islamist. Having emerged from a poor background in urban Istanbul, he had always been oriented toward the people, and he came to power opposed to the secular nationalist elite who were, at that time, upholding the French Republican values of national founding father Mustafa Kemal Atatürk, the creator of modern Turkey in 1922. And the traditional defender of those values, it was understood for decades, was the military.

Modern Turkey thus developed in parallel to, and often with the influence of, Western Europe, thought it kept its own singular identity. For Islamists, the phase change that Erdoğan completed since 2003 has simply been a course correction, hearkening back to an earlier and "purer" Otto-man era in which Islam determined national unity. As with most other populist movements, secular and religious alike, modern Turkish Islamic-nationalism is thus marked by an element of nostalgia. Through "soft power" mechanisms such as films and television soap operas that have influence into the Balkans and beyond, this narrative of a better and truer Turkey—whether it be the 16th century of Sultan Suleiman the Magnifi-cent, or the wistful final days of the Ottoman Balkans—has been pushed heavily for over a decade in popular culture.

On the more tangible policy side, the AKP government's attempts to create a more ambitious foreign policy during a period of constant eco-nomic growth would help create the conditions for the country to become a migrant magnet. The state-owned Turkish Airlines was heavily subsi-dized to increase its connections list to dozens of new cities worldwide, while the country lifted visa requirements for a host of (primarily Muslim) countries in the developing world. The cumulative result of this was that, even before 2015, aspiring economic migrants from distant lands could simply take an inexpensive flight to reach Turkey and continue their asy-lum seeking adventure from there.

Until the Syrian crisis in 2011, Turkey's new foreign policy of "zero problems with neighbors" (one most associated with the former foreign minister, Ahmet Davutoğlu) was successful. Turkey was moving, rela-tively peacefully, toward Erdoğan's goal of becoming leader of the Islamic world while not turning its back on Europe. But the government's fateful turn toward the Middle East would embroil it in conflict. Faced with a decades-long Kurdistan Worker's Party (PKK) in the southeast of Turkey, an autonomous Kurdistan in Iraq, and a potentially breakaway Kurd-ish region of Syria controlled by the YPG militia, Erdoğan supported the proxy war against the Assad regime and the Kurds, allowing the Islamic State to operate unhindered. Contraband business such as oil smuggling enriched prominent Turks, while hospitals were offered to treat wounded ISIS fighters and logistics lines between Turkey and ISIS-held border ter-ritories were kept open.[6]

This complicity also meant that Turkey kept outside parties away from its ever-growing refugee camps. When refugees were eventually pre-vented from working in Turkey, the tendency for them to try their luck in Europe with human traffickers increased. At the same time, Russia's inter-vention in Syria from September 2015 created a dramatic new dynamic for Turkey, which fatefully shot down a Russian fighter jet over Syria and was hit by instant economic retaliation and information warfare from a furious Moscow. Relations would only be restored following the failed July 2016 coup attempt.

By November 2016, the Turkish president was continuing to consolidate his grip on power, making more and more arrests of persons associated with the alleged coup-plotters (U.S.-based cleric Fethullah Gülen and his network), while closing major opposition newspapers. The European Union, while making strong statements of concern, was hardly in a position to dictate terms. The potential for a new migrant wave the following spring could literally destroy the European Union and, with a string of high-profile elections ahead, Brussels did not want to rock the boat. However, in the long run the great purge of 2016 will create a vacuum, diminishing capacities over all sectors in Turkey, as well as encouraging voluntary migration, when possible, of Western- and secular-minded professionals. By October 2016, it had already caused a mass exodus of people associated with the Gülen movement to "safe" countries with a functional local network, in the Balkans and elsewhere in Europe especially.

Throughout the migrant crisis, the European Union and Germany were thoroughly outplayed at every hand by the Turks. The EU Enlargement Commission's scathing report on Turkish reform efforts and handling of the coup attempt was written with the usual robotic detachment from reality that characterizes the worldview of the Brussels bubble.[7] According to the report, Turkey's "anti-terror law is not in line with the acquis [EU norms] with regard to its scope and definitions and its application raises serious fundamental rights concerns." Instatement of the death penalty would be another automatic demerit, according to the European Union. The report was not appreciated by President Erdoğan. His spokesman, İbrahim Kalın, noted ominously that if the EU decides to halt membership negotiations with Turkey, there would be "consequences." Kalın warned that "if they resort to such ways, they will have to live with the results."[8]

What could such consequences entail? In a subsequent interview, President Erdoğan noted that Turkey "is currently hosting three million refuges on its territory . . . if they all marched into Europe, the Europeans would not know what to do with them." He also reminded that of the promised 6 billion euros in aid, "the EU has only given 250–300 million euros to Turkey so far."[9] The implicit threat disturbed Europe, where leaders had repeatedly rushed to reach any stopgap solution they could find to appease public sentiment during the crisis. But in truth, they never had a Plan B for how they would react should Erdoğan activate the "nuclear option" of sending another mass wave of refugees into Greece. Thus, while the EU Enlargement Commission produces such progress reports on an annual basis for all candidate countries, the especially harsh wording of the Turkish report neither phased nor embarrassed a population that has long since stopped trying to appease Brussels. Above all, what Erdoğan's mix of nostalgic nationalism, militarism, and Islamic politics has reinforced is a competing sense of national identity and pride that had been missing for many years. The power of being Europe's migrant gatekeeper has reinforced Turkish independence.

In its new orientation to the world, therefore, Turkey will continue to maintain the age-old balancing act between East and West, but will become more inward-looking and more oriented toward the Middle East and wider Muslim world. It will continue to be the major gatekeeper for the migration issue, and this factor will continue to condition European leaders' reactions toward local leaders and policies. And this will also inspire great trepidation for the European Union, which was again spooked at the end of January 2017, when Turkey threatened to suspend the migrant readmission agreement after Greek leaders decided not to extradite Turkish military members who had escaped to Greece during the July 2016 coup attempt.[10] Brussels seems to have understood that it is not a tenable solution that Turkey's migration policy (and, potentially, the overall stability of a Muslim country of 80 million) is subject to the relative fortune of one unpredictable leader. Yet in reality there is nothing that the European Union can do about the situation except negotiate and hope for the best.

Russia is another major country that had an important national policy regarding the migrant crisis; this unfolded in the context of a new Cold War that, many feared, could easily turn into a hot one through 2016 and into 2017. The 2014 Crimean referendum to join Russia, and the subsequent Syrian intervention that saved the country from Islamic State, shocked and angered Western hawks who predicted military dangers for Europe. The NATO military buildup along Russia's borders that followed the alliance's July 2016 Warsaw Summit re-created the conditions of Soviet times, even seeing Norway break its long-standing treaty with Russia by stationing American troops on its territory. Further, the Baltic states and Poland encouraged the creation of anti-Russian, civil-defense militia groups. Western media coverage of such groups was generally positive, whereas it had been overwhelmingly critical and negative regarding similar groups opposed to migrant violence.

Throughout the overlapping crises, a Western media campaign accused Russia of using the migrant crisis to divide Europe. On March 2, 2016, NATO's supreme commander in Europe claimed that the Russian and Syrian governments were using the migration crisis to deliberately divide Europe. Speaking before the U.S. Senate's Armed Services Committee, General Philip Breedlove claimed that Putin and Assad were "deliberately weaponising migration in an attempt to overwhelm European structures and break European resolve," without offering proof.[11] Around the same time, there were also reported fears among German intelligence that Russia was instrumentalizing the left-wing agitators helping migrants break across the Greek–Macedonian border.[12]

It is unclear to what extent this is true, though it was obvious that Russian media did pay close attention to the crisis, with broadcaster RT often the only source of English-language information on migrant-related events happening in local areas of Europe that were otherwise generally only covered domestically. Whether or not it was Russia's goal to divide Europe through media manipulation, the fact that Russian media covered the migration crisis regularly indicated some degree of national interest.

In light of what it perceived as an increasingly aggressive and dangerous NATO, Russia did seem to regard the migrant issue as one in which it could use existing relationships and exert leverage over countries most affected, in an attempt to achieve national interests. The most important countries to Moscow in this regard have been Germany, France, Greece, and Italy. U.S.-imposed sanctions against Russia have never been popular in Europe, with German industrialists protesting in recent years. President Putin has thanked Greek prime minister Tsipras for his position against sanctions, and relations with Italy have always been warm. Russian diplomatic missions in both Greece and Italy are significant in terms of deployment and intelligence capacities, and it is clear that Moscow has observed the weakness of both countries during the migrant crisis as a point of leverage.

Russia takes a keen interest today in countries with strong right-wing nationalist movements, and especially in France, where Marine Le Pen has been outspoken in her support of President Putin. In February 2016, the Front National treasurer announced it was applying to foreign banks, including Russian ones, for 27 million euros needed for 2017 campaign funding. The French far-right party is notoriously strapped for cash, "as French banks refuse to lend it money," Wallerand de Saint-Just, the Front National's treasurer was reported as saying. Le Pen's party had previously in 2014 secured an 11 million euro Russian bank loan. But Le Pen "denied that financing from a Russian-owned bank would influence the party's policies."[13] In February 2017, two months before pivotal presidential elections, Le Pen reiterated her support for ending sanctions on Russia, describing them as a source of "major problems for the EU."[14]

Russia also sees an opportunity in the case of future political changes in Europe. In recent years, Vladimir Putin has sought to project his vision of the world, one based on state sovereignty, nationalism, and traditional cultural values, as an alternative to globalism and the kind of liberal cultural relativism it promotes. As discussed, this has included both political and religious outreach to Europeans and has implied that Russia is the country doing most to preserve "European values" today. Whether or not this is the case, Western ideological enemies do often tend to oppose right-wing movements in general. With the anticipated future infighting between domestic political parties and violence between extremist groups on the ideological fringes—not to mention future Islamic terrorist attacks—it seems likely that Russia will continue to portray itself as the example for Europeans seeking to preserve their traditional values and culture against perceived external enemies—the migrant/Islamist groups as well as the leftists and globalists in general. But awareness of this more intangible, soft-power objective was largely obscured during the migrant crisis by Western hysteria over alleged Russian plans to invade Europe militarily. The politicization of an alleged "Russian threat" that characterized the 2016 U.S. presidential campaign, and was immediately weaponized by opponents of the new Trump administration, indicated that tensions would not readily be eased. In fact, the first major statements from senior Trump administration officials indicated a continuation of policy of the preceding administration.[15]

Russia is also aware that the longer the migrant crisis continues, the better its opportunities will be to promote this national vision in Europe—though globally speaking, it considers European power and influence declining. Noting the overall turbulence in the region, Russian experts are not convinced that the worst of the migrant crisis is over. At the major annual Kremlin-supported policy conference, the Valdai Discussion Group, migration was a key topic in October 2016. Indeed, Andrei Bystritsky (Board Chairman of the Foundation for Development and Support of the Valdai Discussion Club) noted then that a conference panel entitled *The World after Migration* perhaps "should have been called *The World before Migration*, because the biggest waves of migration and the greatest threats may be still ahead."[16] Such comments indicate Russia's strategic awareness that Europe is not out of the woods yet.

Further, Russia has criticized Europe for losing its values and spiritual compass, while at the same time nominating itself as an interfaith leader and example for the West to follow. Although not a destination for migrants, Russia has a Muslim population of 20 million (15 percent of the population) and has seen upward of 2,500 Chechens go to fight for ISIS in Syria and Iraq. In September 2015, President Putin inaugurated the $15 million Moscow Cathedral Mosque with a speech calling for greater education of youths, in order to avoid extremism. He stated that "terrorists of the so-called Islamic State discredit the great world religion, discredit Islam by sowing hate, killing people . . . destroying the world's cultural heritage in a barbaric way."[17] Such words reflect a larger strategy meant to stifle charges of "Islamophobia" against Russia (though many of the European parties that admire Putin's government are clearly anti-Islamist), while also preserving economic relations with Muslim countries in Asia and Africa.

Among European nations, none had more at stake than Germany with the migrant crisis. Just as Turkey's Erdoğan and Russia's Putin are leaders who oversaw phase changes in their respective nations' identity and political direction, Germany's Angela Merkel also played a major role at a transformative moment in national and European history. However, her story is perhaps even more interesting, in that, unlike the Turkish or Russian leaders, she personifies the connection between Europe's last phase change—the reunification of Germany and launch of the European

Union—and the current one, in which the twin crises of finance (the euro) and migration have contributed to social and political processes leading the Continent into its next incarnation.

Born in 1954 in West Germany, Merkel grew up in the East and began her political career there after the 1989 Revolution, when she was briefly deputy spokesperson for the first democratically elected East German government. After German reunification in 1990, Merkel was elected to the *Bundestag* as representative from the state of Mecklenburg-Vorpommern. An early protégé of Chancellor Helmut Kohl (who referred to her as *mein Mädchen*, or "my girl"), Merkel would hold various ministerial roles. After Kohl's defeat in 1998, she became secretary-general of the Christian Democratic Union (CDU) political party. The new party president, technocrat Wolfgang Schäuble, had been in politics since 1965, representing yet another figure from the golden years of postwar enthusiasm for the "European project." Although toppled in 2000 during a CDU party funding scandal, when he was replaced by Merkel, Schäuble has stuck around as a senior CDU cabinet member. He became infamous during the euro crisis for promoting uncompromising austerity measures.

Unlike many Germans, Merkel supported the American establishment's views on trans-Atlantic trade initiatives and the invasion of Iraq in 2003. In the 2005 federal election, she became chancellor, but only after forming a "grand coalition" with a natural ally (Bavarian sister party Christian Social Union, or CSU), and a less preferable choice (the Social Democratic Party of Germany, or SPD). The cumulative effect of this kind of coalition was a cautious, weak, and consensus-driven government led by conservatives (in theory). Along with austerity measures and migration, this basic fact allowed abundant political space for more right-wing blocs, such as today's AfD, to form in opposition. After winning the 2009 federal election with slightly better numbers, and a different coalition partner, the CDU took elections of 2013 in what was considered a "landslide" at the time. However, Merkel still had to form a coalition with the SPD, once again moderating any conservative policies, with the exception of Schäuble's trademark fiscal discipline.

In October 2010, Merkel made a statement that now seems quite curious. In a speech for CDU youth members, she acknowledged that multiculturalism in Germany had "utterly failed," and voiced skepticism about (but hoped for) immigrant integration. She invoked Germany's Christian heritage as well—something that has become almost unthinkable for a centrist party in Europe today. The general strength of public and media sentiment against immigration, even in 2010, was remarkable, considering the grand welcome that German society would give to migrants in 2015.[18] However, in January 2015, during a Turkish state visit to Germany, Merkel announced that "Islam is part of Germany." Merkel was heavily criticized for this affirmation, even within her own party.[19]

So what happened to Angela Merkel in between these statements? For one, she became an unrelenting globalist. The euro crisis shock and bailout battles with the IMF and Greece certainly had something to do with that, but it also matched her earlier views on neoliberal trade deals. At the 2013 World Economic Forum in Davos, Merkel offered her statistical argument: Europe had only 7 percent of the global population, produced 25 percent of global GDP, and spent almost 50 percent of the global social costs. Increasing competitiveness while cutting social spending was the only solution for Europe, Merkel preached.[20] The *Financial Times* commented that "although Ms. Merkel stopped short of suggesting that a ceiling on social spending might be one yardstick for measuring competitiveness, she hinted as much in the light of soaring social spending in the face of an ageing population."[21]

This explanation for Germany's refugee policy in 2015 seems plausible to one EU official in Brussels, speaking off the record. German labor shortages "could easily be addressed by cherry-picking the very best-qualified Syrians," the official maintains. "They wanted to fix this problem without taking in economic migrants from Turkey and Western Balkan countries, as there is prejudice against these people, who tend to want to stay in Germany and become benefit claimants. On the other hand, taking in somebody qualified and who has gratitude for being received could create another kind of bond or loyalty." This official also noted that simple humanitarian impulses gripped the chancellor, who fancied herself the "Mother Theresa" of Europe.[22]

Despite the CDU's losses in September 2016 Berlin state elections, Merkel remained defiant on migration. "If I could, I would turn back time many, many years to be able to better prepare myself and the whole government and all those in positions of responsibility for the situation that met us rather unprepared in late summer 2015," she said in a press conference.[23] Such statements clearly belie Merkel's 2010 perception of multiculturalism as an "utter failure." In fact, Merkel was essentially lamenting her own failure to have used stealth conditioning of the German government and public toward accepting mass migration. This puts her in the same boat with the dedicated globalists who have been pushing such policies for decades, most often under the radar. Further, as a Christian Democrat who always played down Christianity in favor of nebulous "common values," Merkel remains an enigma.

"Merkel's motives are still a puzzle," says German journalist Karl Peter-Schwartz, in reflecting on the 2015 migrant crisis. "There are several hypotheses and none is really convincing." Aside from the above economic argument for migration (one that Finance Minister Schäuble shared), five arguments were debated most commonly in German society. One was simply political; according to this, Merkel sought "to disarm the leftist opposition by adopting their agenda." Another motive could be more image-driven: "to show a 'nice face' and let the world forget the 'ugly German'" perception from World War II. Third, some suspected Merkel of seeking "a demographic change in order to weaken the national state and to promote EU centralization," or else simply "to show that she commands in Europe." Finally, there was always the possibility, Germans feared, that their chancellor had been blackmailed by a foreign power, like Russia or the United States.[24]

The last possibility arose following former NSA contractor Edward Snowden's 2013 revelations about mass surveillance, among which was the claim that the American spy agency had been listening in on Merkel's personal calls. Although President Obama pledged to stop this practice, the NSA would not promise to block general surveillance in Germany. The exposure embarrassed and angered the German chancellor (and much of the public). Further, another chronic international dispute was simmering, regarding repatriation of German National Bank gold after decades of storage in the U.S. Federal Reserve and other foreign banks.[25] A repatriation program began the next year. (In 2015, 210 tons of German gold was repatriated from Paris, and just under 100 tons from New York, of a total of 674 tons to be repatriated to Frankfurt by 2020.)[26] A final tense situation overlapping with the 2015 migrant crisis the haggling between the European Union and the United States over the ill-fated Trans-Atlantic Trade and Investment Partnership trade deal (TTIP).

The migrant crisis thus occurred in the context of much larger geopolitical events regarding which the general public is unlikely to ever be informed, as most of them were discussed in secret, by closed groups of politicians, bankers, or intelligence agencies. Nevertheless, it is worth keeping these cases in mind when examining the migration crisis in a geopolitical context. In any case, supporting migration in general did align with certain preexisting goals, which will be discussed below, identified and structured by a globalist shadow regime operating through international organizations, corporations, and national governments.

In this respect, the globalist views of Merkel and her right-hand man, Wolfgang Schäuble, also coincided with the strong European federalist agenda shared by these two throwbacks to an earlier and more optimistic time for the "ever closer union" in Europe. A former close adviser to Helmut Kohl, Schäuble had always been a strong advocate of European integration. Back in 1994, Schäuble and fellow lawmaker Karl Lamers called on the EU to adopt an originally French proposal—the principle of "variable geometry." According to this plan, the five core EU countries (Germany, France, and the Benelux) would pursue monetary union, and later, common foreign and defense policies.[27] The two reiterated this call in 2014, when immigration had become a divisive political issue.[28] Schäuble's vision also reportedly includes "turning the Commission over time into a European 'government.'"[29]

At the time, Schäuble urged Germans to welcome migrants by comparing contemporary experience to Germany's *Gastarbeiter* ("guest worker") program of the 1950s and 1960s, in which bilateral treaties were signed with European and other nations; the latter sent (theoretically, temporary) workers to fuel Germany's postwar "economic miracle."[30] Ironically, although German officials were leery about inviting in Muslim Turks, tacit American pressure for geopolitical reasons forced the German government to accept the 1961 treaty with Ankara. Today Germany is home to 4 million Turks, and whereas the first generation assimilated fairly well, the second- and third-generation descendants of the original *Gastarbeiter* laborers have not. Schäuble's anachronistic analogy thus ignored the hugely divergent domestic and international situations of past and present experiences of German immigration. But it was indicative of original federalist thinking that still has tremendous influence in Europe today.

On the level of the European Union, postcrisis migration strategy was being crafted with two factors in mind: rising movements of nationalism and antiglobalism across the Continent, and the pragmatic issue of securing the external border and planning economic expansionism into Africa. The migrant crisis actually gave new impetus for the latter goal, but the realities of Visegrad Group opposition to migrant quotas and the symbolic impact of Brexit forced EU leaders to pause: was the entire European project itself in danger of collapsing?

Gold Mercury International (GMI), a European consultancy established in 1961, has had a long history of working with European leaders. In 2014, GMI undertook a project to give the European Union its own sort of "nation brand." As adviser to the European Union in the 1990s, GMI President Nicolas De Santis was one of the few seasoned experts who cautioned that the pan-European identity, vision, and all-around brand were weak; the bloc's expansion from 12 nations soon compounded the identity diffusion. At the time, he advised the European Union that an "identity vacuum" would reach a breaking point, following the integration of Eastern Europe—with the Brexit vote appearing to confirm that warning.

"Before an EU brand strategy, we need an EU vision," said De Santis in October 2016. "This is what BRAND EU works to develop as part of its efforts. An inclusive vision that puts pluralism at the center to generate 'energy' from the diversity Europe and the world offer. If Europe does not figure out a way to create value out of its diversity and migration, it will not thrive."[31]

However, the hard reality of internal Brussels politics tends to contest such visions. During the migrant crisis, divisions within and between political blocs prevented a unified response—unsurprising considering the multinational composition of the European Union and its varied ideological and cultural worldviews. "Even the German CDU members in the European Parliament's EPP bloc were surprised by Merkel's approach," recalls the EU official cited above. "EPP's cohesion suffered. At the same time, the S&D and ALDE blocs were pro-migrant . . . especially [Guy] Verhofstadt favored a common European response."[32]

However, even some countries led by ALDE-affiliated governments (like the Dutch government led by the VVD party, and Denmark under the Venstre party) closed or controlled their borders at various points. Diverging strategies emerged too regarding how to implement Merkel's plan, with Hungary's Viktor Orbán—whose party, Fidesz, was also in the EPP bloc—pushing for a tough, security-driven response to migration that would eventually be followed to different degrees by Austria, Slovenia, Croatia, and Poland. Representatives of some of the European Union's newer member states were angry for a compelling reason: while they were European, and shared similar values and the culture, their citizens were not allowed to work freely across the European Union. On the other hand, Syrians were being welcomed, without restrictions, documentation, or other proper procedure. Aside from the politicians, "the main stakeholders in designing the migration strategy were the interior ministers of the member states, some with more influence than others—for one example, the Swedish interior minister, Beatrice Ask, and Germany's Thomas de Maizière."[33]

Nevertheless, Brussels insiders maintain that the trend toward nationalism and sovereignty-driven movements is partly the European Union's fault. It failed to take into account the local interests of all member states, affecting the European Union's actual cohesion capacity. The migration crisis and Brexit vote just brought these issues into the open, in real-world scenarios. Now, even the candidate countries and other aspirants are unsympathetic. After the 2014 Ukraine crisis, the Ukrainians hoped to be given some faster track to the European Union, having turned their back on neighbor and historic partner Russia. Instead, they got a notice that it would be at least 20 years before they could think of joining. Turkey, as has been shown, is going its own way. And even the remaining Balkan candidate countries are indifferent. If the European Union could forcibly encourage and promise to train and employ one million migrants from afar in a single year, they ask, why have their own applications been blocked by the Brussels club for over 25 years now? In short, anti-EU sentiment is shared much more widely than it would appear to outside observers, who only read occasional accounts of protests within major EU countries.

There are no easy solutions for these questions. For experts scrutinizing the situation, the deficiencies are more obvious. Thus although there are "three key symbols of European identity" in the ideas of a single market, euro currency, and European citizenship, "the problem is that these symbols are not connected to an emotional narrative that provides a sense of belonging, as they were developed by the elites and handed down to the people," De Santis concedes. "Europe is currently moving backwards to independence movements, protectionism and extreme populist movements because their narrative 'connects' and is highly emotional, while the EU narrative is an elitist one connected to the global elites and not the people . . . BRAND EU must develop a global vision and EU narrative that can include the unity and support of its peoples to make the project survive."[34]

The Brussels official cited agrees that the bloc's PR efforts have failed, but points to additional and harder challenges. "Yes, the EU has to advertise its achievements. Being so technical, citizens fail to see what the EU is actually doing, in areas like ecology, consumer protection, the free market, free movement and so on. But there is also the EU budget. With the UK opting out, it will be even more difficult to keep growing EU own resources. A possible way forward would be introducing an 'EU citizen tax'—but this would only make EU more hated by regular people. So a big dilemma remains concerning where the EU will get all the money it seeks to fulfill its ever-growing ambitions."[35]

One of these ambitions is a gradual expansion of common foreign and economic policy oriented toward developing economies. Particularly with the case of Africa, the migrant crisis actually accelerated these efforts, as the EU was obliged to spend more time and resources on preventive measures for securing external borders while developing programs meant to address the root causes of migration. One key event was the November 2015 Valletta Summit on Migration in Malta, organized by European and African leaders. There they signed an agreement creating an Emergency Trust Fund to help African development, with the European Union also encouraging African countries to repatriate migrants.

This highly organized plan coincided with both an EU economic agenda and programs for improving security and economic conditions to lessen migration from West Africa; both of these goals were primarily executed for EU interests. By October 2016, the European Union was undertaking detailed scenario planning with the help of internal and external experts. This work factored in estimates that Germany could expect to receive 300,000 illegal migrants for the year, even despite the generally successful stopgap deal with Turkey. However, EU planners also feared that the deal's possible breakdown (due to internal turbulence in Turkey or a political impasse) could create conditions for one to two million more refugees and migrants leaving Greece for Turkey, to try their luck on the Balkan Route again. In such a case, Europe would essentially be back to square one, though domestic electorates would be far less forgiving than in 2015.

These estimate numbers were never made public, for obvious reasons. They were provided to the author by Winfried Veit, a German consultant and chief of EU scenario planning for West African migration. The main purpose of Chancellor Merkel's trips to Mali, Ethiopia, and Niger was, he stated, "to convince the governments there to keep their people back . . . In order to do so she offered some financial incentives. One of the main offers concerns the city of Agadez in Niger." Known as the "gate to the Sahara," Agadez is the point "from where most of the West African migrants start their journey to the Mediterranean." West Africa is particularly important to the European Union because it has the fastest-growing population in the world, with numbers set to double by 2050. According to Veit, the European Union was offering, as of November 2016, a project valued at 17 million euros, specifically intended to create alternative employment opportunities for human traffickers. A second project valued at 10 million euros was being earmarked for police equipment and better border control. Third, the European Union was planning to provide support for Agadez's already huge refugee camp—the very existence of which remained completely unknown to Europeans already nervous over migrant floods.[36]

In the same way that Turkey has been the decision maker for migrant streams, Egypt, Libya, and even Morocco are being watched carefully by the European Union. On October 31, 2016, unusually large street protests erupted in Morocco over the accidental death of a fisherman harassed by police.[37] Morocco, along with Algeria, was the only North African country to have prevented an Arab Spring uprising in 2011. Cooperation between Spain and the pro-Western, moderate Moroccan king has traditionally kept the border sealed in the Western Mediterranean. However, future instability in yet another weakly democratic, youth-heavy Muslim state could lead to the overthrow of the Moroccan elite, and create the conditions for a third front in the migration war. The European Union would be unlikely to survive an assault on three fronts, as it would cause security and social breakdowns, along with a populist revolt within Europe.

Along with its multinational efforts with Africa (as seen at the November 2015 Valletta Summit) the European Union has worked bilaterally with African countries on migration. "There are already negotiations going on with Mali, Senegal, Nigeria and Ethiopia on Turkey-like agreements," confirms Winfried Veit. "And Egypt is also asking for money in order to stop migrants leaving their shores. (In all cases, the EU offers support for equipment and training for police forces, in addition to trade incentives, development aid etc.)."[38]

These solutions will be insufficient, however. Leaders like Macedonian president Gjorge Ivanov repeatedly warned through the crisis that Europe was sitting on a ticking time bomb, regarding migrant numbers and future mass extortion of the European Union. In a February 2016 speech at the Munich Security Conference, Ivanov warned that Egypt alone was sitting on five million potential refugees.[39] Worse, the Egyptians learned how to weaponize these migrants for geopolitical (and not merely financial) goals. For example, Egyptian authorities allowed traffickers to increasingly target far-off Italy in the spring of 2016, following a diplomatic row over the opaque murder of an Italian researcher, Giulio Regeni, who had been interacting with trade unions in Cairo. Dark rumors swirled that Regeni had been a spy and was murdered by Egyptian counterintelligence. Although his family and country denied such speculations, Italy briefly recalled its ambassador and the European Union also criticized Egypt over the mysterious murder. Yet Rome and Brussels failed to understand the obvious lesson: that is, migrant-exporting countries can pose asymmetric threats to European cohesion, through both financial and physical means, and for both economic and geopolitical reasons.[40]

Once the European Union promised to open its cash register to Turkey, to the tune of 6 billion euros, all of the migrant-producing countries within its periphery saw the opportunity for mass extortion. "None of these countries want EU training programs, which have always essentially been used to funnel money back to European companies," scoffed one realist British diplomat with Middle East experience. "These countries want cash and only cash. The EU, as usual, is living in its own world."[41] The opportunity for migrant-producing countries to claim billions in preventive "aid" money is just one of the unplanned (but not particularly surprising) side effects of the rushed EU–Turkey deal. Worse, sensing EU internal discord and the pivotal role of Germany, some countries were holding out for other deals: "Egypt wants a special deal with Berlin, not Brussels," noted one senior European security official. "They regard Brussels as disorganized, and Germany as the main actor. They also want their own deal with Italy."[42]

The European Union's adventures in Africa and the Middle East during and after the migrant crisis reaffirm this perceived lack of unity from outside, as well as the depth of its ambitions. But because such overtures are not well publicized, the average Europeean is hardly aware that these ventures are even occurring. Populist sentiment will increase in direct proportion to efforts by an already unpopular and distrusted bloc to expand European activities even further. Right-wing parties like France's Front National, Germany's AfD, and the Sweden Democrats play to a sovereignty-first electorate that seems to be growing across the Continent. As has been seen, hardline federalists from an earlier time, like Wolfgang Schäuble, seek to bolster the core EU countries for a more united future. This ambition is shared by pan-Europeans like Nicolas De Santis, who specifically cites the Ventotene Manifesto of Altiero Spinelli and Ernesto Rossi as the ideological precursor to the EU itself.

"The issue of the EU's future comes down to one thing: the sharing of national sovereign power at the center for the benefit of all its constituent parts," De Santis avers. "The EU is a hybrid between a federation, a confederation and an international organisation. This hybrid has to evolve to a full federation that can take immediate action on big issues such as immigration on a federal level. A more federal EU will also clarify further what the EU project is about, as now it is even unclear for experts to describe this strange animal called the EU. But without the support of its people a full federation will never happen as they have to be the ones that believe that this evolution towards further sharing of sovereign power is the best for all."[43]

Although it is unlikely that such consensus will ever be reached—especially not now, with migration and terrorism topping the list of concerns for Europeans—it is very revealing to note that influential European advisers in 2016 still believed strongly in the almost century-old federalist dream of Spinelli and Coudenhove-Kalergi. Well into the 21st century, Europe's future is still being shaped by two opposing ideologies with roots, ultimately, in 19th-century philosophies of political and social order. These conflicting ideologies are destined to combat one another, on both the level of mainstream politics and in street battles between anarchists and the mobilized forces of the far right. As Europe teeters, and potentially self-destructs amid political infighting, weak coalitions, and the looming specter of constant terrorist attacks associated popularly with migration, one single power is only too happy to fill the vacuum; that is, the globalist deep state that fundamentally organizes and controls the migration issue as a political, social, and economic commodity.

This structure thrives in the shadows of world politics and business, and owes its power to an influence that is both totally dispersed and totally interconnected, which makes it hard to pin down. Its aspirations are unparalleled and unlimited. This parallel government, united by common interests such as migration, has worked to advance its social solutions and financial gain for decades, picking up new adherents and useful figureheads over time. But through it all, the essential operations, structure, methods, and goals remain the same: unleashing a plutocratic and technocratic network to execute a radical reshaping of populations, governance, and public perception, oriented toward solving "big-picture" issues such as population control, climate change, and depletion of natural resources.

The migration issue is thus just one of several interconnected topics that constitute the pillars of this worldview. There is constant overlap with global business, the military–industrial complex, the technology sector, big pharma, the development sector, philanthropy, and more. The migration deep state comprises international organizations (often affiliated with the United Nations, private corporations, and governments). It works to advance its policy laterally through academia, media, and relevant think tanks; as was seen in the case of the "Merkel Plan," these in turn influence politicians in the European Union. The key actors seek to exploit perceived vulnerabilities—particularly, political and social disharmony—to advance their goals. And with the 2015 crisis, this has followed the trademark globalist tendency toward a problem–reaction–solution model—one now being used to fundamentally change Europe, and probably other regions of the world forever.

Of course, the globalists are not without their enemies. The rise of both right- and left-wing Euroskeptic movements, the Brexit vote to leave the European Union, the strong stand of Russia for the principle of state sovereignty, and particularly the election of Donald Trump as president of the United States are just the most major indicators of popular hatred for globalist elites and everything they are believed to stand for. However, despite the occasional setback, their general agenda has slowly kept advancing for decades. Mostly, this is because they operate discreetly, behind the scenes. The globalist deep state thus operates freely and quietly, away from the sound and fury of the protests, wars, and general alienation of polarized political, religious, and ideological groups.

Although populist revolts from right and left, from secular and religious groups alike, all tend to oppose "globalism," they largely fail to stop it due to the relative invisibility of the people and groups making key decisions—though they are hiding in plain sight. While average European citizens could easily name a few prominent persons most associated with a globalist pro-migrant cause—from Angela Merkel to Pope Francis to billionaire philanthropist George Soros—they would have a harder time identifying how such personalities are connected, how they operate, and thus the points where they could be stopped. Even dedicated antiglobalists have currently no capacity for identifying the migration deep state and neutralizing its activities.

Although the migrant cause is becoming an increasingly important one to the globalist shadow government, the key players and their networks are seldom identified by the media. Among the most important figureheads in the globalist migration movement is the proclaimed godfather of globalization, Peter Sutherland. His motives for supporting mass migration have been specifically economic. Presently special representative of the UN secretary general for International Migration, Sutherland may be the most influential European most people have never heard of. Educated at Dublin's elite Jesuit Gonzaga College, Sutherland served as Ireland's attorney general in the early 1980s before joining the EU Commission. Sutherland is also a former director general of the World Trade Organization, former chairman of BP and a Goldman Sachs chairman between 1995 and 2015. He has been intimately involved with other secretive globalist cabals, such as the Bilderberg Group and the Trilateral Commission.

Peter Sutherland's fundamental orientation to migration was determined by his experience with economic competition policy he led for the European Commission from 1985. A 1992 report (now, named after him) on the then–European Economic Community's Internal Market proved influential. After opening up competition across Europe in various key sectors, Sutherland in 1993 led the General Agreement on Tariffs and Trade (GATT), a treaty that became the World Trade Organization. GATT was the world's biggest trade agreement, and in advocating it Sutherland employed the kind of stealth tactics of eliciting broad consensus that had historically been used by supporters of European federalism and globalism, such as Altiero Spinelli and Jean-Claude Juncker: according to one account, Sutherland worked to create "the sense of unstoppable momentum" for the trade deal, by mobilizing "aggressive public relations."[44]

Sutherland became an ideal candidate for advancing the next phase of the global economy—human capital—and then–UN secretary general Kofi Annan reportedly had asked him to become UNHCR head twice before Sutherland finally agreed to take on the lesser role of special representative, in January 2006. Although keeping his day job as a captain of industry and finance, Sutherland thus also found time to promote the UN's new Global Forum on Migration and Development (GFMD). In this capacity, Sutherland was essentially reprising his public relations role from GATT. However, instead of building consensus for a trade deal, the job was to convince countries to accept mass migration for their development goals. The GFMD's work was showcased at a major UN event in September 2006, and since then its activities have only grown, becoming intertwined with a range of political, economic, and development elites seeking to create global migration governance rules.[45]

In a 2012 article coauthored with fellow pro-migration advocate and former EU commissioner, Sweden's Cecilia Malmström, Sutherland argued that the chaotic Arab Spring of the year before had been a lost 'historic opportunity' for the EU "to begin weaving together the two sides of the Mediterranean."[46] Sutherland has also argued that opposition to globalization is "morally indefensible." In the same year, Sutherland bluntly told the British House of Lords that the European Union "should be doing its best to undermine" the "homogeneity" of its member states. Migration was a "crucial dynamic for economic growth" in some EU nations, said Sutherland, lamenting "however difficult it may be to explain this to the citizens of those states."[47]

Such elitist and patronizing rhetoric does not sit well with right-wing groups already deeply suspicious that the globalist migration agenda is essentially a form of cultural genocide targeting Europe's historic populations. An acid critique in the British press following the House of Lords speech concluded that for officials like Sutherland, Europe seemed "not to be a place where Europeans live, but a wholly abstract entity, an entry in a balance sheet."[48] But rather than a deliberate kind of eugenics, what we have seen from UN globalists like Sutherland is essentially a deliberate misinterpretation of basic UN agreements for a covert economic and political purpose. These officials argue that state sovereignty is an "illusion" and that UN-enshrined human rights law allows people to relocate anywhere at any time, regardless of their status or intent. However, as American lawyer and columnist Joseph Klein notes, "The United Nations Charter sets forth the fundamental principle of national sovereignty . . .

Article 2.1 of the UN Charter states that the UN organization is 'based on the principle of the sovereign equality of all its Members.'" UN Charter Article 2.7 reads: "Nothing contained in the present Charter shall authorize the United Nations to intervene in matters which are essentially within the domestic jurisdiction of any state or shall require the Members to submit to such matters to settlement under the present Charter."[49]

Nevertheless, the globalists have been incredibly effective in creating a tacit consensus within media, academia, and governments that unconditional "freedom of movement" is in fact enshrined by the UN, European Union, and other supranational organizations. One effect of this is to build the basis for left-wing support, and to manipulate guilt by false juxtapositions (Klein notes two cases during the migrant crisis in which false analogies between Nazism and opposition to mass migration were spun by Sutherland and François Crépeau, the UN special rapporteur on the human rights of migrants). Yet above all, the globalist migration bodies have defined their mandate so broadly, and have inferred a "human rights" capacity so widely, that almost anything can fall within their remit, leading to a tendency toward maximization of funding and activities. For example, the International Organization for Migration defines a migrant as "any person who is moving or has moved across an international border or within a State away from his/her habitual place of residence, regardless of (1) the person's legal status; (2) whether the movement is voluntary or involuntary; (3) what the causes for the movement are; or (4) what the length of the stay is."[50] This sort of all-inclusive definition is broadly beneficial for declaring a near-universal mandate. This is the inherent worldview of most international migration entities.

Peter Sutherland and his colleagues at the UN and related organizations managed the migrant crisis toward these predetermined ends, back in early May 2015, when it was still largely an "Italian problem." Speaking before the UN Security Council, Sutherland mentioned the ongoing EU security operations against traffickers, but stressed that "an effective strategy to address the crisis, including in the context of a Security Council resolution, begins with the immediate need to save lives. If we do not frame our response in this way, it would represent a moral failure of the first order, one that would undermine international law and security." Further, he averred, "the entire international community must accept a fair share of the refugee burden." All talks of human rights aside, it ultimately came down to the globalist economics argument: "For the doctors, professors, and engineers among them—as well as for the nurses, construction workers, and others with skills our countries need—we could offer labor visas, seasonal visas, and circular migration visas."[51] Just before the September 2016 UN Summit on refugees, Sutherland warned that its conclusions must be adopted, because of the alleged peril of "nativist movements that now threaten decades of progress on human rights and international cooperation."[52]

A close collaborator of Sutherland's, and the second globalist mastermind behind the European migrant crisis of 2015 was George Soros, one of the contemporary world's most controversial characters. The octogenarian investor, hedge-fund billionaire, and operator of a massive network of international foundations, think tanks, universities, and charities has impacted events far more deeply than even his most ardent critics could imagine. And, with a massive fortune, active heirs, and numerous ideological and business partners, the Soros political project will certainly survive beyond its founder's eventual death.[53]

Soros's now-massive Quantum Fund was launched in 1969 by the Swiss banker George C. Karlweis, who was deemed "the brain behind Banque Privee, owned by the late Edmond de Rothschild." In a 2011 feature on Karlweis, Arnaud De Borchgrave wrote that the banker's "biggest claim to fame" was creating Soros and Quantum. "An original $100,000 stake in Soros's fund was worth $150 million by 1994. Between 1970 and 2000, the return was 3,365 percent (for 10 consecutive years it did 42.6 percent per year)."[54]

Although Soros has long been known for making controversial comments about his own perceived genius, his basic business model is really quite simple: to amass financial profit and political influence by exploiting, and when necessary creating, social and economic chaos and division between people. "Soros has proved that with the vast resources of money at his command he has the ability to make the once unthinkable acceptable," noted the *Los Angeles Times* in 2004. "His work as a self-professed 'amoral' financial speculator has left millions in poverty when their national currencies were devaluated, and he pumped so much cash into shaping former Soviet republics to his liking that he has bragged that the former Soviet empire is now the 'Soros Empire.'"[55]

Even critics of his leftist political activities have had to admire the billionaire's investment savvy, though. Once dubbed "the man who broke the Bank of England" for betting against the pound—a move that earned him over $1 billion in 1992—Soros has almost always been on the winning side of business deals. But there is a far darker side to this brilliant business mind, which has been chronicled innumerable times across the world, in terms of projects conducted to gain a political result, often through violent protests and "grassroots" activism against democratically elected governments.

The major focus of Soros activities has been on judiciary, governance, minority, and migration issues, both in America and worldwide. Exploiting such issues and populations has allowed him to divide populations and increase political and financial influence. In Europe, his groups were active in the Ukrainian crisis of 2014, in various Balkan crises, and in "helping" Greece during its financial and migration problems. In Greece, Soros opened a charity running a network of local hubs originally for the poor, crisis-affected Greeks, which came in quite useful during the refugee crisis. It was given the all-purpose name Solidarity Now, years before "solidarity" became the most celebrated motto of the Greek prime minister, the pope, Angela Merkel and other pro-migrant voices. Like Peter Sutherland and other elites, Soros's dream is of a worldwide free trade zone unhindered by borders, national laws, and even nationalities.

Despite his organizations' emphasis on minority rights, the billionaire's animosity to traditional culture and identity are frequently cited. "His name is perhaps the strongest example of those who support anything that weakens nation-states," claimed one of Soros's greatest enemies, Hungarian prime minister Viktor Orbán, discussing Soros and his activist minions in October 2015. "They support everything that changes the traditional European lifestyle." At the time, Soros had just released his six-point plan for solving the migrant crisis and had attacked the Hungarian leader's defensive border fencing policy, which apparently "treats the protection of national borders as the objective and the refugees as an obstacle," said Soros. "Our plan treats the protection of refugees as the objective and national borders as the obstacle."[56]

The Soros plan of September 2015 prefigured the "Merkel Plan" of his follower Gerald Knaus in October, and echoed the May statements of Peter Sutherland. Any European plan for migrants "must be accompanied by a global response, under the authority of the United Nations and involving its member states," decreed Soros. "This would distribute the burden of the Syrian crisis over a larger number of states, while also establishing global standards for dealing with the problems of forced migration more generally." Soros ordered the European Union to accept "at least a million asylum-seekers annually for the foreseeable future," and pay all their costs, while allowing them to go to their country of choice. The billionaire currency speculator stated that Europe could fund this experiment "by issuing long-term bonds using its largely untapped AAA borrowing capacity, which will have the added benefit of providing a justified fiscal stimulus to the European economy."

Under the plan, the European Union would create a single asylum system, override national interests, and send billions of euros to aid countries like Turkey and Jordan, while also creating "special economic zones with preferred trade status in the region, including in Tunisia and Morocco, to attract investment and generate jobs for both locals and refugees." Soros stated that Orbán's own six-point plan "subordinates the human rights of asylum-seekers and migrants to the security of borders, threatens to divide and destroy the EU by renouncing the values on which it was built and violating the laws that are supposed to govern it."[57]

Again, the manipulative recourse to "human rights" in the migration game has been the key focus of the globalist approach to controlling the process; few criticize those claiming to be motivated by humanitarian intentions. The general stratagem not only stigmatizes opponents as "racist" or "isolationist"—it also wins the sympathy of a left that (at least some of which) would otherwise naturally oppose the kind of rampant neoliberal capitalism pushed by the globalists internationale. Indeed, throughout the European migrant crisis, the Soros networks played a key role in influencing both institutions and policy makers, not to mention in harnessing the naive (and not so naive) cadre of the radical left on the ground, who became a sort of shock troop fighting for migrant rights on land and at sea. Soros himself has always been a proponent of radical system change—whether through betting against a financial market or pushing a geopolitical policy—and in the case of the migrant crisis, this was no different.

Yet George Soros's constant invocation of "human rights" in exploiting the migration business was not just the cynical ploy of a motivated moneyman. It was part of a highly organized crusade to transform the European (and, indeed, global) order through advocacy, donations, media manipulation, and the occasional support for violent revolutions. His flagship Open Society Foundations (OSF) have funneled over $13 billion into such projects since opening in 1979, and oversee a labyrinthine network of subsidiaries that work with affiliated NGOs, academia, media, and governments to relentlessly push a corporate globalist left-wing agenda.

As leaked documents in 2016 revealed, Soros's organizations gather precise intelligence on friends and foes in high positions and media and engage in a constant effort to win supporters and discredit enemies. This "mapping" activity identified, in the case of the European Union, each specific European parliamentarian "likely to support Open Society values during the 2014–2019 legislature," according to one review. The "mapping" activity isolated some "11 committees and 26 delegations, as well as the European Parliament's highest decision-making bodies: 226 MEPs who are proven or likely Open Society allies."[58]

By operating in the shadows, and dispersing power laterally through a sometimes seemingly unrelated network of advocacy groups and other partners, the Soros cabal has been able to influence European and world leaders, with a massive increase in influence within the United States as well during the Obama years.[59] Although the November 2016 election of Donald Trump was a setback for George Soros, it merely encouraged him to organize actions and strategies that would put the Democratic Party further under his control. The new president's controversial executive orders on immigration provided an ideal excuse for both protests by Soros-linked groups, and for fundraising to pro-migrant causes. In any case, his networks had already become so firmly integrated into the globalist superstructure that the election was unlikely to derail his ambitions.

Two months before the November 2016 election Soros had adapted his demands for the European Union in light of Brexit; now, he was only ordering the bloc to accept a minimum of 300,000 refugees a year, rather than the one million demanded the year before. But Soros remained determined to implement an agenda that had become not a "six-point" one, but rather a "seven-pillar" platform. After the UN's historic summit on migration in September 2016, which included multi-billion-dollar commitments from the tech-sector plutocracy, Soros announced that he had "earmarked" some $500 million for "social impact initiatives": these would involve funding start-ups and refugee-owned businesses in various sectors. According to Soros, tech would be a major one as it provided "solutions to the particular problems that dislocated people face." In keeping with his usual model, all profits would be owned by his nonprofit foundations programs, which would work closely with the UNHCR, International Rescue Committee, and other humanitarian giants.[60] As such, the general program of wealth recycling and transfer upon which the globalist migrant economy is based would continue.

The whole network of persons and groups involved in the global migration deep state is far too expansive and dispersed to be treated in full, encompassing as it does a wide range of political, ideological, and business actors. But some additional top-level representatives include António Guterres, the former UNHCR director and, previously, Portuguese prime minister, who was elected UN secretary general in October 2016. His Italian successor at UNHCR, Filippo Grandi, previously held high positions within the global body's development and refugee programs. Other people of influence include Barack Obama, the Clintons, IOM director-general William Lacy Swing, a former U.S. ambassador to several African countries, and the former British Labour Party politician David Miliband, who became head of the International Rescue Committee (IRC) charity in 2013. With 12,000 employees and an annual budget of $450 million, IRC is one of the major humanitarian NGOs (Miliband's own personal salary was reported as $600,000 a year).[61] Similar development- and migration-sector charities, like the global powerhouse Save the Children, have trustee boards deeply tied to major corporations across the full range of sectors.[62]

The humanitarian-development complex is a massive and growing multi-billion-dollar industry. It is also forming increasingly symbiotic relationships with governments, which increases the scale and penetration power of the migration deep state. Jason Miko, an American consultant who worked for humanitarian giant Mercy Corps in the Balkans during the 1990s, notes that "there is an incestuous relationship between governments and humanitarian and development NGOs. People regularly go back and forth between working for such groups and the US government." By the very nature of the relationship, he adds, "this creates a bubble, and a certain mindset shared between governments and NGOs." In such an environment, it becomes easy for the kind of "echo chamber" that propagandists for mass migration and other causes seek to foster, especially because of the generally leftist worldview shared by most people involved in the sector.[63]

The purpose of all international organizations and grant-based NGOs is to expand their territory and, if necessary, justify their own existence. The European migration crisis has provided a perfect opportunity for that. The Organization for Security and Cooperation in Europe (OSCE), a lingering remnant of a Cold War peace initiative now mostly known for election monitoring activities, is just one prominent example of organizations that have redefined mandates to benefit from the migration crisis. With an overall mission that is nebulous at best, but also a tremendous bureaucracy to sustain, the OSCE has jumped wholeheartedly into the migration industry; indeed, migration "is increasingly at the centre of the organization's action," the OSCE itself states.[64]

Industry veterans like Miko recall an earlier time in which the convergence between charities, supranational organizations, and governments was less pronounced. In his view, one transformative event that propelled these interests into a closer relationship was Hurricane Mitch, which left 11,000 dead in Central America in 1998. Such natural disasters, along with wars, environmental problems, and migration crises gradually aligned public and private sector interests until they were finely calibrated, with no turning back possible. The nonprofit humanitarian sector embraced a new role in which it would have "a seat at the table," working directly with government policy makers, while also receiving increasingly lavish funding. "Back in the 1990s, more charities had a mandate of helping," Miko attests. "But when they discovered that they could have a seat at the table, and eat from the trough, their appetites became insatiable."[65]

Religious institutions and leaders comprise another, often overlooked, level of the migration industry's shadow structure. In the case of Europe in 2015, none was more important than the liberal Pope Francis. The first Jesuit pope, the Argentine Italian pontiff visited Lampedusa in 2013 to publicize the refugee cause as a specifically moral issue for Europe. He set the example by bringing home Syrian refugees from the Greek island of Lesvos in April 2016. Later, in a September meeting with "hundreds of alumni of Jesuit schools," Francis promised that the Vatican would help "refugees through acts of mercy that promote their integration into the European context and beyond." One month later, the pope visited an increasingly polarized Sweden with the head of the Lutheran World Council, to appeal for European solidarity.[66] The pope is also among those who have depicted the migrant crisis within the context of World War II.

The interrelated nature of this elite has advanced, slowly but surely, a common migration policy that also aids the financial and geopolitical interests of globalists. These interests have generally favored support for unconditional migration, blaming terrorism on social and economic ills and attempting to distance it from religion, particularly, from Islam, an argument fiercely opposed by European populists and nationalists. And this campaign, essentially a public-relations exercise, was ramped up and synchronized in early 2017, as pivotal elections loomed in Holland, France, and Germany.

For example, a joint press release from the International Organization for Migration (IOM) and the UN High Commissioner for Refugees (UNHCR) referring to President Trump's temporary travel ban on seven Muslim-majority countries stated "we strongly believe that refugees should receive equal treatment for protection and assistance, and opportunities for resettlement, regardless of their religion, nationality or race."[67] And speaking in Saudi Arabia just before the February 2017 World Government Summit in Dubai, new UN secretary-general Guterres claimed that "Islamophobia" in national policies and popular discourse causes Islamic terrorist attacks.[68] This controversial theory had been tacitly implied by the previous Obama administration, and general leftist movements at odds with the tougher stance of the Trump administration and most nationalist-leaning political forces in Europe. The fact that Guterres—the former head of the UNHCR—was vocalizing a theory that to many would seem false, or at least incomplete, indicates how migration politics have affected the political agenda of the world's largest international organization.

At the same time, another major pro-migrant globalist, Pope Francis, went so far as to say that "Muslim terrorism does not exist" in a tone-deaf speech aiming to quell populist fears by blaming religious radicalization on inequality and poverty.[69] Speaking just days later at the Munich Security Conference, Angela Merkel called for cooperation with Islamic states, "to convince people that it is not Islam that is the problem, but a falsely understood Islam." The election-year plea came as other German officials were promising that 2017 would see record deportations of failed asylum seekers. However, Merkel added that "the European Union has a responsibility" to take in more migrants.[70] The discrepancy between statements of Merkel and her officials seemed to indicate again that a longer-term globalist commitment to further refugee resettlement was being disguised, if temporarily, by CDU concerns about eroding public support in advance of fall elections.

As was the case with Guterres and other high officials, people do not just wander into the migration-development stratosphere by accident. The new UN secretary-general's successor at UNHCR, Filippo Grandi, had held various high-level positions in various UN aid and refugee agencies since the late 1980s. And long before joining the International Rescue Committee (IRC), David Miliband, the president and CEO of the IRC, was promoting an EU expansionist goal toward the Middle East and North Africa identical to that of Soros, Sutherland, and generations of Euro-federalists, back in 2007, while he was British foreign minister. In his vision, European enlargement would entail a "version of the European Free Trade Association that could gradually bring the countries of the Maghreb, the Middle East and Eastern Europe in line with the single market, not as an alternative to membership, but potentially as a step towards it."[71]

The integration of countries on the southern shores of the Mediterranean Sea into a broader European zone—in essence, a return to the glory days of the Roman Empire—is not a sudden fantasy but has been built up since the 1960s through the German guest workers program. Intergovernmental summits, committees, trust funds, and associations have long been common between European, Arab, and African blocs. The 2015 migrant crisis simply accelerated the integration process, with each new emergency summit resulting in a complementary increase in European taxpayer donations.[72] Some critics have observed that this pattern of activity will lead to increasing religion-focused radicalization and social tension among the common people in Europe, though for the globalists that is not a concern.[73]

The top-level leaders of the migration deep state are united also by shared external networks active in both migration and EU expansionism. UN chief Guterres, for another example, belongs to the Club of Madrid, an informal grouping of former heads of state that promotes global democratization efforts. As of 2016, its projects included a globalist "Shared Societies" program for "overcoming identity-based divisions and building shared societies"—a platform for the migration crisis identical to that of George Soros and his ilk.[74] Another Club of Madrid member, ardent pro-migrant and Euro-federalist MEP Guy Verhofstadt, pushed for reforming the European Union's asylum and migration system in 2015, criticizing David Cameron and François Hollande for opposing the European Commission's Soros- and UN-influenced migrant redistribution plan.[75] Like fellow pro-migrant federalists Angela Merkel and Jean-Claude Juncker, Verhofstadt is a past winner of the Edmond Israel Foundation's Vision for Europe Award, which honors leaders who advance European integration. The Luxembourg-based foundation is named for the late banker who ran Clearstream International, one of the world's most powerful financial institutions.[76]

The global financial system may indeed be the real convergence point for the federalism, globalism, and migration power interests. Peter Sutherland, himself a former head of Ireland's AIB Bank and Goldman Sachs, has also been a dependable Vatican financial adviser, which helps explain his influence on Pope Francis regarding migration. In December 2006, Sutherland was appointed to advise the Vatican Bank, under the appropriately grandiose title Consultor of the Extraordinary Section of the Administration of the Patrimony of the Apostolic See.[77] In July 2013, he was called to a closed-door meeting with the Council of Cardinals over urgent reform measures required for the scandal-plagued bank.[78] Later, Sutherland also became president of the International Catholic Migration Commission (ICMC), which has a governing council of approximately 20 international bishops and Vatican appointees. In 2012—well before the current crisis—the ICMC was lobbying European and American officials to resettle more refugees. In fact, this Catholic group helped launch the "Resettlement Saves Lives" program with Amnesty International, the Churches Commission for Migrants in Europe (CCME), the European Council on Refugees and Exiles (ECRE), the IOM, and the German NGO Save Me.[79]

Another major global Catholic charity, Jesuit Refugee Services (JRS), has benefited in particular from the arrival of Rome's first Jesuit pope: "definitely, having Pope Francis there has gotten us much more attention and helped fundraising," attested one JRS Europe official.[80] In addition to conducting a wide variety of refugee-related activities, it is interesting to note that JRS Europe utilizes the same consensus-building activities that Sutherland used in winning public support for GATT once upon a time; for example, one JRS Europe program involves organizing "national hospitality campaigns in Spain, Portugal and France to raise awareness and to promote hospitality as an explicit rejection of those discourses in the mainstream that fuel hostility and the scapegoating of forced migrants."[81]

One of the great myths of the European migrant crisis was that Greece had been a helpless victim, all but left for dead. What has never been appreciated is the extent to which the migration deep state had already penetrated the country, through preexisting Greek personal and business connections to Soros and Sutherland. Indeed, the role of Greek and Greek American globalists cannot be overstated when outlining the contemporary history of the 2015 crisis. Among the most important was Demetrios Papademetriou, a longtime migration expert and cofounder of the Washington-based Migration Policy Institute (MPI), which was created in 2001 out of the Carnegie Endowment for International Peace's International Migration Policy Program. Papademetriou was simultaneously chairman of Open Society Foundation's International Migration Initiative (IMI), the major Soros organization that "identified" MSI and other groups for migration advocacy with governments and the UN.[82] Papademetriou also led the organization's Brussels-based operation, Migration Policy Institute Europe, which provided the major lobbying push for the globalist migration agenda with leading think tanks (often, Soros-affiliated) and European Parliament structures.

Another major Greek American migration figure during the crisis was Gregory Maniatis, Peter Sutherland's assistant since 2006. Maniatis had been an MPI senior policy expert previously. During and after the European migrant crisis, Maniatis was also codirector of the International Migration Project at the Columbia Global Policy Initiative, and belongs to the elite

Council on Foreign Relations. In 2016, Maniatis shared center stage with George Soros during the latter's keynote speech at the program's Concordia conference. A hacked internal memo from the Soros International Migration Institute, written on May 12, 2016, revealed that the Columbia Global Policy Initiative (CGPI) "hosts the secretariat for Peter Sutherland, the UN Secretary General's Special Representative on International Migration [and] has been able to take advantage of momentum created by the current crisis to shape conversations about rethinking migration governance." Further according to the memo, "IMI provided project support for the drafting of The Sutherland Report, which aims to set the stage for institutional reforms to global migration governance, and to break new ground on protections for migrants outside the asylum system."[83] Essentially, therefore, the trajectory of today's global migration policy ideas has been created by a very small and powerful group of people, who have privately instrumentalized major international organizations and universities for their policy goals.

Oddly enough, yet more Greeks have been intimately involved in this tight network of interests. The Concordia event was founded by the Greek British businessman Nicholas Logothetis, one of several heirs of the shipping tycoon, Michael Logothetis.[84] Through its companies (most notably, the Libra Group) the family successfully diversified globally to include aviation, real estate, hotels, and renewable energy, and remain close to the American Democratic Party and European elite.[85] Even closer within the Soros orbit was another Greek American magnate, Stelios Zavvos, the Athens chairman of the board at Soros's Solidarity Now charity, formed in the wake of the euro-crisis.[86] Under the charity banner, he published an editorial in February 2016 in leading Greek newspaper *Kathimerini*, reiterating the globalist talking points on migration policy, and making a remarkably revealing admission about the Soros institution. "Three years ago, a small group of citizens with the financial assistance of the international philanthropic organization Open Society Foundations and the Norwegian government, created the philanthropic organization SolidarityNow," wrote Zavvos. "Its purpose is to help meet the upcoming migration flows and vulnerable groups facing the financial and social crisis." It would seem remarkably prescient that the two investors had anticipated the migrant crisis by over two years.[87]

As founder and president of the Harvard Business School Club of Greece, Zavvos has hosted Soros on speaking engagements. In a 2011 profile, Zavvos was described as "a well-known investor and power broker on both sides of the Atlantic." His main company, Zeus Capital Partners, was said to be "funded by major financial institutions, sovereign wealth funds, world-famous investors and Greek shipowners."[88] It had carved out a formidable real estate footprint in Southeast Europe. When in September 2013 Soros was married for a third time (to a woman 42 years his junior)

Stelios Zavvos was the best man. In chronicling the wedding, Greek media recalled that his name "became widely known in our country during the infamous meeting between then–Prime Minister George Papandreou with George Soros in 2010."[89]

Indeed, Soros had always been an interested party in Greek finance and its significance for the fate of the euro and general European project. Much earlier, on February 27, 2010, British media hinted that Soros was among "a secretive group of Wall Street hedge fund bosses [said] to be behind a plot to cash in on the decline of the euro." The emerging Greek debt crisis, already affecting other European countries, was damaging the euro even as hedge funds like Soros Fund Management were "placing huge bets on the currency's decline, which could make the speculators hundreds of millions of pounds." Potentially, it was a replay of 1992, when Soros capitalized on the fall of sterling.[90] And Soros himself had injected panic into the public discourse just six days earlier, by noting that the outlook for the euro was bad; its "construction is patently flawed. A fully fledged currency requires both a central bank and a Treasury." Soros noted that, as the euro's creators had anticipated, a European monetary union without a prior political one would prove problematic. But that was what the compromises of the Maastricht Treaty had set for the European Union.[91]

It is one of those strange ironies of modern geopolitics that a billionaire hedge fund manager, a currency speculator, and an ideological philanthropist could establish a beachhead in a specific country due to the crisis of one industry—finance—that would create opportunities for managing a second, later one, with migration. But that is what happened with George Soros in Greece, as it wobbled unsteadily from economic implosion to a humanitarian catastrophe in only five short years.

Nevertheless, that is what happened. And, in the absence of strong governance and unity in a culturally and socially divided Europe, we can expect the geopolitics of the future to be executed more and more by this unelected and unaccountable globalist elite. After all, no group can gain more from all the chaos that the migration waves have brought, and there are no others that can remain immune from the aftershocks of the crisis, than can international institutions, NGOs and other entities of the global migration industry. With an unprecedented opportunity for ever-greater financial gain, territorial expansion of a new and promising industry, there is no reason to think that the masters of migration will stop now. Although all of the pundits and politicians provided the "narratives" (and occasionally, even decisions) during the migration crisis and debt crisis that immediately preceded it, the outcome of events was and will be decided by a hidden globalist elite, as Europe lurches from one disaster to the next.

Epilogue

A single death is a tragedy; a million deaths is a statistic.

—*Joseph Stalin*

The European migrant crisis has proven the cynical Soviet dictator right in every way. At the human level, the level of the single suffering refugee, the story of the crisis was told (and very effectively so) by media, creating the emotional resonance needed to propel a reaction on the industrial scale, the scale of the unknown millions, propelling the general project to heights that neither public comprehension nor interest could ascend. And, in that rarified air, the crisis disappeared, only to reemerge quite transformed. It became the property of bureaucrats, bean counters, statisticians and programmers, corporations, advocates, opinion columnists, and professors.

At the beginning of this book, it was argued that the major difference regarding the events of 2015 was quantitative, not qualitative, thus making the crisis first and foremost a logistics issue. Illegal migration to Europe had been going on for over 25 years already by that point. It was not something new. The concept just needed to become an event, in order to qualify as a historic process upon which Europe's next era could begin. And the constant repetition of rhetoric that described the crisis as "unprecedented since World War II" created the context needed for framing Europe's present within a specific, chosen past.

Europe's current phase change marks the first since the collapse of the empire and ideology that Stalin himself once oversaw, and the moment when a long-deferred European dream finally seemed possible; the ideal of a reunified continent, the "ever closer union" of which the founding fathers had spoken so passionately. Yet if such a union is to be achieved in the future, it will be a more forced one, according to different exigencies, and certainly with some new populations among it.

The migration crisis is not over, and neither are the dramatic political, social, economic, and security challenges it has brought with it. The conflict zones stretching along Europe's southern and eastern flanks— and even beyond this near-abroad—have the potential to re-create the turbulent events of 2015 at any time. At the same time, the fault lines of increasingly polarized left- and right-wing partisan ideologies are already resulting in earthquakes of various sizes, in Europe and around the world. Britain's vote to leave the European Union, although it may take years or be less complete than first imagined, nevertheless shook Europe to its core. Even more so did the election in America of Donald Trump as president, proclaimed as a populist and an archenemy of the globalists, a man who campaigned on defending the interests of the common man—a victory that in turn galvanized other populist movements in Europe. And it was this very populist resurgence that would create, in reaction, a wider and more ideologically driven leftist opposition, one in which migration would become an ever more central issue.

The 2015 migrant crisis can be remembered for many things, and ascribed different sorts of significances. Its meaning and its causality will doubtless be explored by generations of historians. And its effects will continue to shape those who lived through it and were directly affected by it.

However, what is most important to remember about the event, in this author's opinion, is that the migrant crisis represented not only the hard crystallization of an amorphous phenomenon into a historical event, but also the greatest opportunity for money laundering and mass transfers of wealth in human history. In a world that had in only eight years peeked over the precipice of total financial collapse and stepped back, migration was a type of economic rescue bigger than any bank bailout or injection of funds. In the deeper symmetries of global events, the migrant crisis that affected Europe so deeply in 2015 is fundamentally and directly linked to the near-collapse of the global economy seven years earlier. In ways that are not yet fully known or appreciated, it is part of the great, invisible economic recovery of which we are generally unaware, but which surrounds and in some way sustains us.

The sound and fury of Europe's party politics, terrorism, and upheaval will helpfully block attention of most people and institutions from exploring this line of thought further. Both tragedies and statistics are bound to recur and reorient public attention. Nevertheless, future researchers curious about the ultimate origins, identity, and goals of global migration will hopefully find this book to have been at the very least a stepping-stone upon which to reach for these rarified heights, where the migration crisis disappeared into itself.

Notes

INTRODUCTION

1. Jon Henley, Ian Traynor, and Warren Murray, "Paris Attacks: EU in Emergency Talks on Border Crackdown," *The Guardian*, November 20, 2015. Available at: https://www.theguardian.com/world/2015/nov/20/paris-attacks -france-launches-un-push-for-unified-declaration-of-war-on-isis.

CHAPTER 1

1. Edison Kurani, "Albania Has a High Number of Asylum Seekers, UNHCR Report Says," Balkaneu.com, June 21, 2016. Available at: http://www.balkaneu .com/albanian-high-number-asylum-seekers-unhcr-report.

2. Jill Petzinger and Jess Smee, "Greece's Planned Border Fence Is 'an Act of Despair,'" Spiegel Online, January 6, 2011. Available at: http://www.spiegel.de /international/europe/the-world-from-berlin-greece-s-planned-border-fence-is -an-act-of-despair-a-738118.html.

3. Matteo Albertini and Chris Deliso, "Italian Security in the MENA and Balkans, Part 1: Military and Energy Aspects," Balkanalysis.com, July 4, 2016. Available at Central and Eastern European Online Library: https://www.ceeol .com/search/journal-detail?id=1045.

4. "Libya Migrants: Hundreds Feared Drowned in Mediterranean," BBC, April 15, 2015. Available at: http://www.bbc.com/news/world-africa-32311358.

5. Bruno Waterfield, "Greece's Defence Minister Threatens to Send Migrants Including Jihadists to Western Europe," *The Telegraph*, March 9, 2015. Available at: http://www.telegraph.co.uk/news/worldnews/islamic-state/11459675/Greeces -defence-minister-threatens-to-send-migrants-including-jihadists-to-Western -Europe.html.

6. "EU Leaders Agree to Relocate 40,000 Migrants," BBC, June 26, 2015. Available at: http://www.bbc.com/news/world-europe-33276443.

7. Chris Deliso, "Macedonian Migration Policy and the Future of Europe," Balkanalysis.com, December 23, 2015. Available at Central and Eastern European Online Library: https://www.ceeol.com/search/journal-detail?id=1045.

8. "Germany: 'No Limit' to Refugees We'll Take In," Sky News, September 5, 2015. Available at: http://news.sky.com/story/germany-no-limit-to-refugees -well-take-in-10347281.

9. "Migrant Crisis: Germany Starts Temporary Border Controls," BBC, September 14, 2015. Available at: http://www.bbc.com/news/world-europe-34239674.

10. "Slovenia Reinstating Controls at Border with Hungary," *The Slovenia Times*, September 17, 2015. Available at: https://sloveniatimes.com/9574/slovenia -reinstating-controls-at-border-with-hungary.

11. "Migrant Crisis: Why EU Deal on Refugees Is Difficult," BBC, September 25, 2015. Available at: http://www.bbc.com/news/world-europe-34324096.

12. "Migrant Crisis: EU to Begin Seizing Smugglers' Boats," BBC, October 7, 2015. Available at: http://www.bbc.com/news/world-europe-34461503.

13. "Migrant Crisis: Thousands of New Reception Places Agreed," BBC, October 26, 2015. Available at: http://www.bbc.com/news/world-europe-34634214.

14. "Migrant Crisis: Over One Million Reach Europe by Sea," BBC, December 30, 2015. Available at: http://www.bbc.com/news/world-europe-35194360.

15. Jon Henley, Ian Traynor, and Warren Murray, "Paris Attacks: EU in Emergency Talks on Border Crackdown," *The Guardian*, November 20, 2015. Available at: https://www.theguardian.com/world/2015/nov/20/paris-attacks-france -launches-un-push-for-unified-declaration-of-war-on-isis.

16. Chris Deliso, "Macedonian Migration Policy and the Future of Europe," op. cit.

17. David Crouch, "Sweden Slams Shut Its Open-Door Policy towards Refugees," *The Guardian*, November 24, 2015. Available at: https://www.theguardian .com/world/2015/nov/24/sweden-asylum-seekers-refugees-policy-reversal.

18. "Norway: New Ministry Is Created to Address Influx of Migrants," Associated Press, December 16, 2015. Available at: http://www.nytimes.com/2015/12/17 /world/europe/norway-new-ministry-is-created-to-address-influx-of-migrants .html.

19. "Prosecutor: Most Cologne New Year's Suspects Are Refugees," Associated Press, February 15, 2016. Available at: https://apnews.com/article/4d8372a4077 144cdbd67e4f630d23c47.

20. "Turkish President Threatens to Send Millions of Syrian Refugees to EU," *The Guardian*, February 12, 2016. Available at: https://www.theguardian.com /world/2016/feb/12/turkish-president-threatens-to-send-millions-of-syrian -refugees-to-eu.

21. "Bulgaria to Close All External EU Borders, PM Announces," ITV News, February 15, 2016. Available at: http://www.itv.com/news/update/2016-02-15 /bulgaria-to-close-all-external-eu-borders-pm-announces.

22. "Migrant Crisis: Greece Recalls Ambassador from Austria amid EU Rifts," BBC, February 25, 2016. Available at: http://www.bbc.com/news/world-europe -35658776.

23. "Migrant Crisis: Slovenia Moves to 'Shut Down' Balkans Route," BBC, March 9, 2016. http://www.bbc.com/news/world-europe-35760534.

24. "Migrant Crisis: Angela Merkel Condemns Closure of Balkan Route," BBC, March 10, 2016. Available at: http://www.bbc.com/news/world-europe-35772206.

25. Michael S. Schmidt and Sewell Chan, "NATO Will Send Ships to Aegean Sea to Deter Human Trafficking," *New York Times*, February 11, 2016. Available at: http://www.nytimes.com/2016/02/12/world/europe/nato-aegean-migrant -crisis.html.

26. Lara Marlowe, "Calais Residents Protest over 'Economic Catastrophe' of Camp," *The Irish Times*, March 8, 2016. Available at: http://www .irishtimes.com/news/world/europe/calais-residents-protest-over-economic -catastrophe-of-camp-1.2563492.

27. Patrick Kingsley, "Balkan Countries Shut Borders as Attention Turns to New Refugee Routes," *The Guardian*, March 9, 2016. Available at: https://www.theguardian .com/world/2016/mar/09/balkans-refugee-route-closed-say-european-leaders.

28. "Tsipras Reacts to Tusk Statement on Closure of Balkan Route for Migrants," *Kathimerini*, March 10, 2016. Available at: http://www.ekathimerini .com/206840/article/ekathimerini/news/tsipras-reacts-to-tusk-statement -on-closure-of-balkan-route-for-migrants.

29. "Turkey Threatens to Back Out of EU Migrant Deal over Visas," France 24, April 19, 2016. Available at: http://www.france24.com/en/20160419-turkey -migrant-deal-eu-visa-free-travel.

30. Excerpts of March 2016 activist leaflet seen by the author.

31. "Italian Police, Demonstrators Clash in Protest against Austrian Fence," Reuters, May 7, 2016. Available at: http://www.reuters.com/article/us-europe -migrants-border-brenner-idUSKCN0XY07Y.

32. "Hundreds Hurt in Police Clashes at Greece-Macedonia Border," Reuters, April 10, 2015. Available at: https://www.theguardian.com/world/2016/apr/10 /clashes-between-migrants-and-police-at-border-between-greece-and-macedonia.

33. Chris Deliso, "Europe Gets Religion, Again," *The American Interest*, June 9, 2016. Available at: http://www.the-american-interest.com/2016/06/09/europe -gets-religion-again.

34. "Clashes Break Out at Migrants Camp on Greek Island: Police," Reuters, April 26, 2016. Available at: http://www.reuters.com/article/us-europe-migrants -greece-clashes-idUSKCN0XN271.

35. Chiara Palazzo, "Norway Offers to Pay Asylum Seekers £1000 Bonus to Leave the Country," *The Telegraph*, April 26, 2016. Available at: http://www.telegraph .co.uk/news/2016/04/26/norway-to-pay-asylum-seekers-extra-money-to-leave.

36. "Migrant Crisis: EU Plans Penalties for Refusing Asylum Seekers," BBC, May 4, 2016. http://www.bbc.com/news/world-europe-36202490.

37. "Towards a Sustainable and Fair Common European Asylum System," European Commission Press release, May 4, 2016. Available at: https://ec.europa .eu/commission/presscorner/detail/en/IP_16_1620.

38. "Commission Presents Options for Reforming the Common European Asylum System and Developing Safe and Legal Pathways to Europe," European Commission, Press release, April 6, 2016. Available at: http://europa.eu/rapid /press-release_IP-16-1246_en.htm.

39. "Council Conclusions on the External Aspects of Migration," European Council, May 23, 2016. Available at: http://www.consilium.europa.eu/en/press /press-releases/2016/05/23-fac-external-aspects-migration/.

40. "Nigel Farage Tells MEPs: You're Not Laughing Now," BBC, June 28, 2016. Available at: http://www.bbc.com/news/uk-politics-eu-referendum-36651406.

41. Richard Wike, Bruce Stokes, and Katie Simmons, "Europeans Fear Wave of Refugees Will Mean More Terrorism, Fewer Jobs," Pew Global, July 11, 2016. Available at: http://www.pewglobal.org/2016/07/11/europeans-fear-wave-of-refugees-will-mean-more-terrorism-fewer-jobs.

42. Maria-Antoaneta Neag, "'The EU and Turkey Need Each Other': Interview with Ambassador Selim Yenel," Balkanalysis.com, July 20, 2016. Available at Central and Eastern European Online Library: https://www.ceeol.com/search/journal-detail?id=1045.

43. "European Border and Coast Guard: Council Confirms Agreement with Parliament," European Council, June 22, 2016. Available at: http://www.consilium.europa.eu/en/press/press-releases/2016/06/22-border-and-coast-guard.

44. "EUCAP Sahel Niger: Mission Extended, Budget Agreed, Mandate Amended," European Council, July 18, 2016. Available at: http://www.consilium.europa.eu/en/press/press-releases/2016/07/18-fac-sahel-niger.

45. "EUNAVFOR MED Operation Sophia Authorised to Start Two Additional Supporting Tasks," European Council, August 30, 2016. Available at: http://www.consilium.europa.eu/en/press/press-releases/2016/08/30-eunavfor-med-sophia-op-add-supporting-tasks.

46. "European Border and Coast Guard: Final Approval," European Council, September 14, 2016. Available at: http://www.consilium.europa.eu/en/press/press-releases/2016/09/14-european-border-coast-guard.

47. Noah Barkin and Jason Hovit, "EU Leaders Agree to post-Brexit 'Road Map,' but Divided on Refugees," The Globe and Mail, September 16, 2016.

48. "Remarks by President Obama at Leaders Summit on Refugees." White House press briefing, September 20, 2016. Available at: https://www.whitehouse.gov/the-press-office/2016/09/20/remarks-president-obama-leaders-summit-refugees.

49. Data taken from the Fact Sheet provided by the White House press briefing, September 20, 2016. Available at: https://www.whitehouse.gov/the-press-office/2016/09/20/fact-sheet-leaders-summit-refugees.

50. "Facebook, Google, Other Tech Giants Answer Obama's Refugee Plea," CNET.com, September 20, 2016. Available at: https://www.cnet.com/tech/tech-industry/facebook-google-other-tech-giants-answer-obamas-refugee-plea-president-syria.

51. Ivana Kottasova, "George Soros Is Investing $500 Million to Help Refugees," CNN, September 20, 2016. Available at: http://money.cnn.com/2016/09/20/technology/soros-investment-migrants-refugees.

52. "UN Summit Seen as 'Game Changer' for Refugee and Migrant Protection," UNHCR press release, September 6, 2016. Available at: http://www.unhcr.org/news/latest/2016/9/57ceb07e4/un-summit-game-changer-refugee-migrant-protection.html.

53. "Antonio Guterres of Portugal Appointed as Next U.N. Secretary-General," NBC News, October 13, 2016. Available at: http://www.nbcnews.com/news/world/united-nations-appoints-portugal-s-guterres-next-u-n-chief-n665736.

54. "G7 Ise—Shima Leaders' Declaration," Japanese Ministry of Foreign Affairs, May 26–27, 2016. Available at: http://www.mofa.go.jp/files/000160266.pdf.

55. "World Leaders at UN Summit Adopt 'Bold' Plan to Enhance Protections for Refugees and Migrants," UN News Center, September 19, 2016. Available at: https://www.un.org/development/desa/en/news/population/un-summit -adopts-ny-declaration.html.

56. "EU's Tusk Demands Closure of Balkan Route to Refugees 'for Good,'" Deutsche Welle, September 24, 2016. Available at: http://www.dw.com/en/eus -tusk-demands-closure-of-balkan-route-to-refugees-for-good/a-35881684.

CHAPTER 2

1. Nick Squires and Peter Foster, "Renzi, Hollande and Merkel Head to Birth-place of European Project to Map Out Post-Brexit Future," *The Telegraph*, August 22, 2016. Available at: http://www.telegraph.co.uk/news/2016/08/22/renzi -hollande-and-merkel-head-to-birthplace-of-european-project.

2. "Why Brussels Isn't Boring," *The Economist*, September 12, 2002. Available at: http://www.economist.com/node/1325309.

3. Felix Markham, *Napoleon* (New York: Penguin Books USA Inc., 1966), 257.

4. Henry Parker Willis, *A History of the Latin Monetary Union* (Chicago: University of Chicago Press, 1901), 266.

5. John F. Pollard, *Money and the Rise of the Modern Papacy: Financing the Vatican, 1850–1950* (New York: Cambridge University Press, 2005), 39.

6. "Eurozone: A Nightmare Scenario—Latin Lessons," *Financial Times*, September 16, 2011. Available at: https://www.ft.com/content/80094624-e076-11e0 -bd01-00144feabdc0.

7. Théodore de Korwin Szymanowski, *L'avenir économique, social et politique en Europe* (Paris: Ed. H. Marot, 1888). Available at: http://www.msz.gov .pl/pl/ministerstwo/publikacje/biblioteka_jednosci_europejskiej/przyszlosc _europy_w_zakresie_gospodarczym__spolecznym_i_politycznym__l_avenir _economique__social__politique_en_europe.

8. "European Prize for the Chancellor," Office of the German Federal Chancellor, January 13, 2011. Available at: https://www.bundeskanzlerin.de/ContentArchiv /EN/Archiv17/Artikel/_2011/01/2011-01-13-merkel-europapreis_en.html.

9. The group's official website is www.paneuropa.org.

10. "Hungary Marks 1989 Freedom Event," BBC, August 19, 2009. Available at: http://news.bbc.co.uk/2/hi/8209173.stm.

11. Winston S. Churchill, *Never Give In! The Best of Winston Churchill's Speeches* (New York: Hyperion, 2003), 427–430.

12. See Aristide Briand, *Memorandum on the Organization of a System of Federal European Union* (French Ministry of Foreign Affairs, May 1, 1930). Available at: https://www.wdl.org/en/item/11583. See also D. Weigall and P. Stirk, eds., *The Origins and Development of the European Community* (Leicester University Press, 1992), 11–15.

13. See Édouard Herriot, *The United States of Europe* (New York: The Viking Press, 1930).

14. Arthur Salter, *Allied Shipping Control: An Experiment in International Administration* (Oxford: Clarendon Press, 1921).

15. See Antonio Gramsci, *Prison Notebooks, Volumes 1, 2 & 3*, Joseph A. Buttigieg, ed. (New York: Columbia University Press, 2011).

16. Spinelli's 1941 Manifesto of Ventotene is available online at: https://www
.cvce.eu/en/obj/the_manifesto_of_ventotene_1941-en-316aa96c-e7ff-4b9e-b43a
-958e96afbecc.html.

17. Ambrose Evans-Pritchard, "The European Union Always Was a CIA Project, as Brexiteers Discover," *The Telegraph*, April 27, 2016. Available at: http://
www.telegraph.co.uk/business/2016/04/27/the-european-union-always-was
-a-cia-project-as-brexiteers-discover.

18. Richard Aldrich, "OSS, CIA and European Unity: The American Committee on United Europe 1948–60," *Diplomacy & Statecraft*, March 1, 1997. Available
at: http://www2.warwick.ac.uk/fac/soc/pais/people/aldrich/publications/oss
_cia_united_europe_eec_eu.pdf.

19. The group's official website is www.europeanmovement.eu.

20. Rebattet's position in the organization enabled his son to have access to information and glean insights for a doctoral thesis that was sealed for three decades
in an Oxford library. It is particularly useful as historians have noted many of
the original documents surrounding the postwar federalist movement have been
destroyed. See F. X. Rebattet, "The European Movement, 1945–1953: A Study in
National and International Non-government Organisations Working for European
Unity," PhD thesis, Oxford University, 1963.

21. See "The Establishment of the European Movement," cvce.eu. Available
at: http://www.cvce.eu/en/recherche/unit-content/-/unit/04bfa990-86bc-402f
-a633-11f39c9247c4/272166ae-84b2-466b-9cfa-4df511389208.

22. Somewhat ironically, considering Europe's modern-day turbulence, the
European Commission eulogizes these founding fathers by claiming that "without
their energy and motivation we would not be living in the sphere of peace
and stability that we take for granted." See "History of the EU," European
Commission. Available at: https://european-union.europa.eu/principles-countries
-history/history-eu_en.

23. See "Solemn Declaration on European Union," European Council, June 19,
1983. Available at: http://aei.pitt.edu/1788.

24. Hugh Wilford, *The CIA, the British Left and the Cold War: Calling the Tune?*
(London: Routledge, 2003), 46–47.

25. See Michael Burgess, *Federalism and European Union: The Building of Europe,
1950–2000* (London: Routledge, 2000). The 1984 treaty itself is available at:
http://www.cvce.eu/obj/draft_treaty_establishing_the_european_union_14
_february_1984-en-0c1f92e8-db44-4408-b569-c464cc1e73c9.html.

26. The official text of the agreement is available online. See "The Schengen
Acquis—Agreement between the Governments of the States of the Benelux Economic Union, the Federal Republic of Germany and the French Republic on the
Gradual Abolition of Checks at Their Common Borders." Available at: http://eur-lex
.europa.eu/legal-content/EN/ALL/?uri=CELEX:42000A0922(01).

27. "The Schengen Area and Cooperation," European Commission. Available
at: http://eur-lex.europa.eu/legal-content/EN/TXT/?uri=URISERV%3Al33020.
See also "Schengen, Borders and Visas," European Commission. Available at:
http://ec.europa.eu/dgs/home-affairs/what-we-do/policies/borders-and-visas
/index_en.htm.

28. Andrea Dernbach, "Germany suspends Dublin agreement for Syrian
refugees," Euractiv, August 26, 2015. Available at: https://www.euractiv.com
/section/economy-jobs/news/germany-suspends-dublin-agreement-for-syrian
-refugees.

29. "The Universal Declaration of Human Rights," United Nations. Available at: https://www.un.org/en/about-us/universal-declaration-of-human-rights.

30. The ICCPR was put into practice in 1976, a decade after being introduced. As of April 2014, it had 76 signatories.

31. "Free Movement of Persons," European Parliament. Available at: http://www.europarl.europa.eu/atyourservice/en/displayFtu.html?ftuId=FTU_2.1.3.html.

32. These comments were made to the author by a German parliamentarian during an international conference, in February 2016.

33. Martin Banks, "Guy Verhofstadt Appointed as European Parliament's Brexit Negotiator," *The Parliament Magazine*, September 9, 2016. Available at: https://www.theparliamentmagazine.eu/articles/news/guy-verhofstadt-appointed-european-parliaments-brexit-negotiator.

34. The group has an official website. See: https://thespinelligroup.eu.

CHAPTER 3

1. Jon Henley, Harriet Grant, Jessica Elgot, Karen McVeigh, and Lisa O'Carroll, "Britons Rally to Help People Fleeing War and Terror in Middle East," *The Guardian*, September 3, 2016. Available at: https://www.theguardian.com/uk-news/2015/sep/03/britons-rally-to-help-people-fleeing-war-and-terror-in-middle-east.

2. "Remarks by President Obama at Leader's Summit on Refugees," White House press release, September 20, 2016. Available at: https://obamawhitehouse.archives.gov/the-press-office/2016/09/20/remarks-president-obama-leaders-summit-refugees.

3. Patrick Donahue, "Merkel Confronts Facebook's Zuckerberg over Policing Hate Posts," Bloomberg, September 26, 2015.

4. This German organization, known as FSM, bills itself as a "non-profit association responsible for protection of minors in the Internet." Given this mandate, it is not clear why this organization would be teamed with Facebook to fight general "xenophic" commenting, nor who its funders are. FSM did not reply to a query for clarification by the author. For more information, see the FSM's official website: https://www.fsm.de/en.

5. Patrick Donahue, "Merkel Confronts Facebook's Zuckerberg Over Policing Hate Posts," op. cit.

6. Samuel Gibbs, "Facebook Apologises for Psychological Experiments on Users," *The Guardian*, July 2, 2014. Available at: https://www.theguardian.com/technology/2014/jul/02/facebook-apologises-psychological-experiments-on-users.

7. Lia Steakley, "How Social Media Can Affect Your Mood," Stanford Medicine, October 3, 2014. Available at: http://scopeblog.stanford.edu/2014/10/03/how-social-media-can-affect-your-mood.

8. Laura Hautala, "Social Media's Echo Chamber Fuels Migrant Backlash in Sweden and Finland," August 27, 2016, cnet.com. Available at: https://www.cnet.com/news/refugee-crisis-europe-social-media-impact-on-sweden-finland.

9. Although not a finalized document at time of writing, this draft was broadly representative of EU thinking on the subject. See "Draft Report on Fundamental Rights Implications of Big Data: Privacy, Data Protection, Non-discrimination, Security and Law-Enforcement (2016/2225(INI))," European Parliament Committee on Civil Liberties, Justice and Home Affairs, October 19, 2016.

10. Lily Rothman and Liz Ronk, "This Is What Europe's Last Major Refugee Crisis Looked Like," *Time*, September 11, 2015. Available at: http://time.com/4029800/world-war-ii-refugee-photos-migrant-crisis.

11. See Anthony Faiola, "A Global Surge in Refugees Leaves Europe Struggling to Cope," *Washington Post*, April 21, 2015. Available at: https://www.washingtonpost.com/world/europe/new-migration-crisis-overwhelms-european-refugee-system/2015/04/21/3ab83470-e45c-11e4-ae0f-f8c46aa8c3a4_story.html. See also Patrick Boehler and Sergio Peçanha, "The Global Refugee Crisis, Region by Region," *New York Times*, August 26, 2015. Available at: http://www.nytimes.com/interactive/2015/06/09/world/migrants-global-refugee-crisis-mediterranean-ukraine-syria-rohingya-malaysia-iraq.html?_r=0. See also "Europe Faces Worst Migration Crisis 'since World War II,'" CBS News, September 3, 2015. Available at: http://www.cbsnews.com/videos/europe-faces-worst-migration-crisis-since-world-war-ii-2.

12. "World Leaders' Neglect of Refugees Condemns Millions to Death and Despair," Amnesty International, June 15, 2015. Available at: https://www.amnesty.org/en/latest/news/2015/06/world-leaders-neglect-of-refugees-condemns-millions-to-death-and-despair.

13. "Irregular Migrant, Refugee Arrivals in Europe Top One Million in 2015: IOM," International Organisation on Migration press release, December 22, 2015. Available at: https://www.iom.int/news/irregular-migrant-refugee-arrivals-europe-top-one-million-2015-iom.

14. See Euan McKirdy, "UNHCR Report: More Displaced Now Than after WWII," CNN, June 20, 2016. Available at: http://edition.cnn.com/2016/06/20/world/unhcr-displaced-peoples-report. The report is referring to the official report of the UNHCR released contemporaneously, "Global Forced Displacement Hits Record High," UNHCR communication, June 20, 2016. Available at: http://www.unhcr.org/news/latest/2016/6/5763b65a4/global-forced-displacement-hits-record-high.html.

15. The organization's website at the time was http://www.refugeesarewelcome.org.

16. Dimitris Avramopoulos, "A European Response to Migration: Showing Solidarity and Sharing Responsibility," European Commission official speech, August 14, 2015. Available at: http://europa.eu/rapid/press-release_SPEECH-15-5498_en.htm.

17. "European Response to Dire Refugee Crisis Urgently Needed," Party of European Socialists, September 4, 2015. Available at: http://www.pes.eu/eu_response_to_dire_refugee_crisis_urgently_needed.

18. Karl Vick and Simon Shuster, "Chancellor of the Free World," *Time*, December 9, 2015. Available at: http://time.com/time-person-of-the-year-2015-angela-merkel.

19. Jeffrey K. Olick and Andrew J. Perrin, *Guilt and Defense* (Cambridge, MA: Harvard University Press, 2010), 24–25.

20. Jeffrey K. Olick, "The Guilt of Nations?" *Ethics & International Affairs*, September 2003, 17.

21. This theme is explored in Janine N. Clark, *Serbia in the Shadow of Milosevic: The Legacy of Conflict in the Balkans* (London: I. B. Taurus, 2008).

22. Fischer relied on previously neglected documents from the World War I era in making his case. His key work in this field was published in German in 1961.

For the English translation, see Fritz Fischer, *Germany's Aims in the First World War* (New York: W. W. Norton, 1968).

23. Anna Sauerbrey, "Will Germany Succumb to Hate?" *New York Times*, September 2, 2015. Available at: http://www.nytimes.com/2015/09/03/opinion/will-germany-succumb-to-hate.html.

24. "Testing the Limits: How Many Refugees Can Germany Handle?" Spiegel Online, July 30, 2015. Available at: http://www.spiegel.de/international/germany/germany-being-tested-by-huge-refugee-influx-a-1045560.html.

25. Author interview with German official, October 11, 2015.

26. Author interview with EU official, January 2016.

27. Justin Huggler, "'Cover-Up' over Cologne Sex Assaults Blamed on Migration Sensitivities," *The Telegraph*, January 6, 2015. Available at: http://www.telegraph.co.uk/news/worldnews/europe/germany/12085182/Cover-up-over-Cologne-sex-assaults-blamed-on-migration-sensitivities.html.

28. "Swedish Police Probe 'Cover-Up of Migrant Sex Assaults,'" BBC, January 11, 2016. Available at: http://www.bbc.com/news/world-europe-35285086.

29. "Swedish Police Officer Causes Controversy with Facebook Post," *The Local*, February 8, 2017. Available at: http://www.thelocal.se/20170208/swedish-police-officer-causes-controversy-with-facebook-post.

30. Nick Thorpe, "Migrant Crisis: Hungary Denies Fuelling Intolerance in Media," BBC, December 22, 2015. Available at: http://www.bbc.com/news/world-europe-35162515.

31. "NATO Commander: Russia Uses Syrian Refugees as 'Weapon' against West," Deutsche Welle, March 2, 2016. Available at: http://www.dw.com/en/nato-commander-russia-uses-syrian-refugees-as-weapon-against-west/a-19086285.

32. Geoff Dyer, "Biden Hints at US Cyber Revenge on Russia," *Financial Times*, October 16, 2016. Available at: https://www.ft.com/content/2d9c73fa-935b-11e6-a80e-bcd69f323a8b.

33. Michael Ertl, "German Refugees Use Advertising to Target Anti-immigration YouTube Videos," BBC, April 20, 2016. Available at: http://www.bbc.com/news/world-europe-36095659.

34. "The Role of Social Media in Europe's Migrant Crisis," Channel 4 News, January 15, 2015. Available at: http://www.channel4.com/news/role-of-social-media-in-europe-migrant-crisis.

35. The Germany-based activist group has operated a variety of websites, such as www.w2eu.info.

36. See Jonathan Samuel, "Sky Finds 'Handbook' for EU-Bound Migrants," Sky News, September 13, 2015. Available at: http://news.sky.com/story/sky-finds-handbook-for-eu-bound-migrants-10346437.

37. "Code of Conduct on Countering Illegal Hate Speech Online," European Commission, May 31, 2016. Available at: https://commission.europa.eu/strategy-and-policy/policies/justice-and-fundamental-rights/combatting-discrimination/racism-and-xenophobia/eu-code-conduct-countering-illegal-hate-speech-online_en.

38. Soeren Kern, "European Union Declares War on Internet Free Speech," Gatestone Institute, June 3, 2016. Available at: https://www.gatestoneinstitute.org/8189/social-media-censorship.

39. "Code of Conduct on Countering Illegal Hate Speech Online," op. cit.

CHAPTER 4

1. Brief press statements were recorded at the time. See "President Tusk Meets Presidents of Serbia and FYR of Macedonia," European Council, December 16, 2015. The official video summary is available at: https://tvnewsroom.consilium.europa .eu/video/president-tusk-meets-presidents-of-serbia-and-fyr-of-macedonia.

2. Author interview with Macedonian President Gjorge Ivanov, October 17, 2016.

3. Chris Deliso, "Safeguarding Europe's Southern Borders: Interview with Klaus Roesler, Director of Operations Division, Frontex," Balkanalysis.com, September 23, 2011. Available at Central and Eastern European Online Library: https://www.ceeol.com/search/journal -detail? id=1045.

4. Ioannis Michaletos and Chris Deliso, "The Hellenic Coast Guard: Greece's First Line of Maritime Defense," Balkanalysis.com, June 8, 2015. Available at Central and Eastern European Online Library: https://www.ceeol.com/search /journal-detail?id=1045.

5. From a Greek policeman's comments for the author at Eidomeni, October 5, 2015.

6. Chris Deliso, "Mistrust and Different Priorities Vex EU-Macedonian Security Cooperation," Balkanalysis.com, May 27, 2016. Available at Central and Eastern European Online Library: https://www.ceeol.com/search/journal -detail?id=1045.

7. Author interview with Karl-Peter Schwartz, November 6, 2016.

8. Based on author interviews with senior European officials, February, May, and October 2016.

9. Chris Deliso, "Exclusive: Germany's BND Investigating Migration Risks and Russian Influence in Greece," Balkanalysis.com, March 7, 2016. Available at Central and Eastern European Online Library: https://www.ceeol.com/search /journal-detail?id=1045.

10. Author interview with Phillip Ingram, October 24, 2016.

11. Selina Sykes, "Four Teenage Girls Arrested for Planning Bataclan-Style Attack on a Concert Hall in Paris," *Express*, March 11, 2016. Available at: http:// www.express.co.uk/news/world/651953/Paris-terror-attacks-Bataclan.

12. Hui Min Neo, "German Police Arrest Algerian Suspects over 'Berlin IS Plot,'" AFP, February 4, 2016.

13. "France Dijon: Driver Targets City Pedestrians," BBC, December 21, 2014. Available at: http://www.bbc.com/news/world-europe-30571911.

14. Patrick Martin, "History of Lone-Wolf Vehicle Attacks Suggests Risk of Emulation Is Very Real," *The Globe and Mail*, July 15, 2016. Available at: http:// www.theglobeandmail.com/news/world/history-of-lone-wolf-vehicle-attacks -suggests-risk-of-emulation-is-very-real/article30933070.

15. Elisa Sguaitamatti and Chris Deliso, "New Information Surfaces on Killed Terrorist Anis Amri, as Italian Investigation Continues," Balkanalysis.com, December 24, 2016. Available at Central and Eastern European Online Library: https://www.ceeol.com/search/journal-detail?id=1045.

16. "Delivery Driver Plotted to Kill U.S. Soldiers in Britain," Reuters, April 1, 2016. Available at: http://www.reuters.com/article/us-britain-security-usa-plot -idUSKCN0WY4U6.

17. Larissa Kennelly, "Brussels Jewish Museum Reopens: 'An End to Inno-cence,'" BBC, September 14, 2014. Available at: http://www.bbc.com/news/blogs -eu-29164962.

18. Author interview with Yossi Melman, October 20, 2016.

19. Author interview with Ioannis Michaletos, October 21, 2016.

20. Fatjona Mejdini, "Albanian Police Arrest 'Terror Attack' Suspect," Balkan Insight, August 16, 2016. Available at: http://www.balkaninsight.com/en/article /albania-police-charge-a-man-from-kosovo-with-terrorism-08-18-2016.

21. Laura Smith-Spark and Greg Botelho, "Suspect Detained after Behead-ing, Explosion in France," CNN, June 26, 2015. Available at: http://edition.cnn .com/2015/06/26/europe/france-attack/index.html.

22. "French Police Chief's Killer 'Claimed Allegiance to IS,'" BBC, June 14, 2016. Available at: http://www.bbc.com/news/world-europe-36524094.

23. Author interview with Ioannis Michaletos, op. cit.

24. Author interview with Marco Giulio Barone, October 23, 2016.

25. Jamie Crawford, "U.S. Soldier Helps Foil Plot to Blow Up School," CNN, April 21, 2016. Available at: http://edition.cnn.com/2016/04/21/politics/us-soldier -saves-denmark-school/index.html.

26. Greg Botelho, "7 Alleged ISIS Charged for Plotting Terror in Moscow, St. Petersburg," CNN, February 17, 2016. Available at: http://edition.cnn.com /2016/02/17/europe/russia-isis-charges-terror-plot.

27. Chris Deliso, "Turkey's Developing Role in Africa: Interview with Mehmet Ozkan and Birol Akgun," Balkanalysis.com, January 1, 2011. Available at Central and Eastern European Online Library: https://www.ceeol.com/search/journal -detail?id=1045.

28. This aspect comes up in numerous media reports; in his own field research in 2015 and 2016, the present author has spoken with over 30 people from various African countries in migrant camps, who stated they originally reached Turkey on Turkish Airlines flights before making the sea crossing. None of them were war refugees.

29. This center was the result of a politically decided agreement between U.S. president Barack Obama and Albanian left-wing premier Edi Rama. It is in line with long-standing U.S. policy to favor the "Albanian factor" over other Balkan countries. As such, it is not likely to contribute much to overall trust or regional intelligence sharing, though it will be a mark of prestige for the Tirana govern-ment. As of February 2017, a local security expert had said to this author that the center was still not well organized nor staffed.

30. Colin Freeman, "Inside Kacanik, Kosovo's Jihadist Capital," The Telegraph, August 23, 2015. Available at: http://www.telegraph.co.uk/news/worldnews /europe/kosovo/11818659/Inside-Kacanik-Kosovos-jihadist-capital.html.

31. Violeta Hyseni Kelmendi, "Kosovo Mobilizes to Fight Religious Radical-ism and Terrorism," Osservatorio Balcani e Caucaso, August 25, 2014. Available at: http://www.balcanicaucaso.org/eng/Areas/Kosovo/Kosovo-mobilizes-to-fight -religious-radicalism-and-terrorism-155153.

32. Una Hajdari, "Kosovo to Jail Fighters in Foreign Conflicts," Balkan Insight, March 13, 2015. Available at: http://www.balkaninsight.com/en/article/kosovo-law-to-punish-fighting-in-foreign-conflicts.

33. Carlotta Gall, "How Kosovo Was Turned into Fertile Ground for ISIS," *New York Times*, May 21, 2016. Available at: http://www.nytimes.com/2016/05/22/world/europe/how-the-saudis-turned-kosovo-into-fertile-ground-for-isis.html?_r=0.

34. Labinot Leposhtica, "Kosovo Jails Hard-line Imam for 10 Years," Balkan Insight, May 20, 2016. Available at: http://www.balkaninsight.com/en/article/kosovo-hard-line-imam-sentenced-to-10-years-in-prison-05-20-2016.

35. Adrian Shtuni, "Ethnic Albanian Foreign Fighters in Iraq and Syria," Combating Terrorism Center at West Point. Available at: https://ctc.westpoint.edu/ethnic-albanian-foreign-fighters-in-iraq-and-syria.

36. Aleksandra Bogdani, "Albanian Villages Ponder Local Spike in ISIS Recruits," Balkan Insight, April 25, 2016. Available at: http://www.balkaninsight.com/en/article/albanian-villages-ponder-local-spurt-of-isis-recruits-04-22-2016.

37. Joby Warrick, "In Albania, Concerns over the Islamic State's Emergence," *Washington Post*, June 11, 2016.

38. Sinisa Jakov Marusic, "Macedonian Police Targets ISIS Suspects," Balkan Insight, August 6, 2015. Available at: http://www.balkaninsight.com/en/article/macedonia-launches-anti-terror-busts-08-06-2015.

39. Sinisa Jakov Marusic, "Macedonia Arrests Nine ISIS Suspects," Balkan Insight, August 7, 2015. Available at: http://www.balkaninsight.com/en/article/macedonia-arrests-nine-isis-suspects-08-07-2015.

40. Matteo Albertini, "Italy and Kosovo Intensify Actions against Another ISIS-Linked Group," Balkanalysis.com, December 6, 2015. Available at Central and Eastern European Online Library: https://www.ceeol.com/search/journal-detail?id=1045.

41. Author interview with Ioannis Michaletos, op. cit.

42. Aurelien Breeden, "Four in France, Including 16-Year-Old Girl, Are Held in Bomb Plot," *New York Times*, February 10, 2017. Available at: https://www.nytimes.com/2017/02/10/world/europe/france-arrest-montpellier.html?_r=0.

43. Henry Samuel, "'Religious Tensions' Spark Gunfight in French Migrant Camp," *The Telegraph*, January 27, 2016.

44. Laurens Cerulus, "The Cost of the Brussels Lockdown: €51.7 Million a Day," Politico, November 30, 2015. Available at: http://www.politico.eu/article/brussels-lockdown-financial-damage-52-million-vrt-terrorism-business.

45. See Tino Sanandaji, "Islamists Caused Overwhelming Majority of Terrorist Deaths in Europe during Last Decade," February 20, 2011. Available at: http://tino.us/2011/02/islamists-caused-overwhelming-majority-of-terrorist-deaths-in-europe-during-last-decade. This analysis critiqued claims made in Europol's official report, EU Terrorism Situation and Trend Report TE-SAT, 2007–2009.

46. Emma Luxton, "Is Terrorism in Europe at a Historical High?" World Economic Forum, March 24, 2016. Available at: https://www.weforum.org/agenda/2016/03/terrorism-in-europe-at-historical-high.

47. Caelainn Barr, "'Terrorism Threat Is Waning': Figures Put Europe's Summer of Violence in Context," *The Guardian*, July 28, 2016. Available at: https://www .theguardian.com/world/2016/jul/28/there-is-less-of-a-terrorism-threat-now -experts-put-europes-summer-of-violence-in-context.

48. See chapter 5.3, titled "The Hamburg Contingent," in the U.S. government's official report on the terrorist attacks of September 11, 2001. Available at: https://9 -11commission.gov/report/911Report_Ch5.htm.

49. Author interview with Phillip Ingram, op. cit.

50. Author interview with Ioannis Michaletos, op. cit.

51. Author interview with Phillip Ingram, op. cit.

52. Author interview with Marco Giulio Barone, op. cit.

53. Edward N. Luttwak, "Doing Counterterrorism Right," Nikkei Asia Review, November 30, 2015. Available at: http://asia.nikkei.com/Viewpoints/Viewpoints /Doing-counterterrorism-right.

54. Matt Zuvela, "German Police Arrest Three Syrian Refugees Suspected of 'IS' Connections," Deutsche Welle, September 13, 2016. Available at: http:// www.dw.com/en/german-police-arrest-three-syrian-refugees-suspected-of-is -connections/a-19546768.

55. "ISIS Sleepers 'May Have Arrived as Refugees' in Germany, Ready for Action—Top Intel Official," RT, August 11, 2016. Available at: https://www.rt.com /news/355587-refugees-isis-sleepers-germany.

56. Joshua Posaner, "German Intelligence Warns of ISIL 'Hit Squads' Among Refugees," *Politico*, August 11, 2016. Available at: http://www.politico.eu/article /german-intelligence-warns-of-is-hit-squads-among-refugees.

57. Author interview with Phillip Ingram, op. cit.

58. Author interview with Yossi Melman, op. cit.

59. Author interview with Phillip Ingram, op. cit.

60. Author interview with Bulgarian DANS officer, September 29, 2016.

61. John Goetz and Bob Drogin, "'Curveball' Speaks, and a Reputation as a Dis-information Agent Remains Intact," *Los Angeles Times*, June 18, 2008. Available at: http://www.latimes.com/world/middleeast/la-na-curveball18-2008jun18-story .html.

62. Author interview with Ioannis Michaletos, op. cit.

63. Observations based on author field research throughout 2016.

CHAPTER 5

1. Author field research at Greek migrant camp, August 2016.

2. The comment by a senior European intelligence officer was made to the author in October 2016.

3. Quotation and figures are from a Europol press release of October 12, 2016.

4. "Migrant Smuggling in the EU," Europol Public Information, February 2016. Available at: https://www.europol.europa.eu/publications-events/publications /migrant-smuggling-in-eu.

5. Ibid.

6. "Human Trafficking Focus of INTERPOL Conference," Interpol, October 20, 2016.

7. Author interview with Ioannis Michaletos, October 25, 2016.

8. The 22-page internal EEAS report, written on January 29, 2016, was uploaded on the WikiLeaks website. See "'EUNAVFOR MED—Operation SOPHIA'—Six Monthly Report: June, 22nd to December, 31st 2015." Available at: https://wikileaks.org/eu-military-refugees.

9. See "Adopting Resolution 2240 (2015), Security Council Authorizes Member States to Intercept Vessels off Libyan Coast Suspected of Migrant Smuggling," United Nations, October 9, 2015. Available at: http://www.un.org/press/en/2015/sc12072.doc.htm.

10. See "'EUNAVFOR MED—Operation SOPHIA'—Six Monthly Report: June, 22nd to December, 31st 2015," op. cit.

11. Ibid.

12. Author interview with Ioannis Michaletos, op. cit.

13. Lindita Arapi, "Balkan Route to Western Europe for Yugoslavia Guns," Deutsche Welle, December 5, 2015. Available at: http://www.dw.com/en/the-balkan-route-to-western-europe-for-yugoslavia-guns/a-18896280.

14. Adrian Shtuni, "Black Market Supply and Demand: The Flow of Illegal Weapons from the Western Balkans to Islamist Militants in Western Europe," *Jane's Terrorism & Insurgency*, March 25, 2016.

15. "Weapons and Explosives Seized in INTERPOL-Led Operation," Interpol press release, April 21, 2016. Available at: https://www.interpol.int/en/News-and-Events/News/2016/Weapons-and-explosives-seized-in-INTERPOL-led-operation.

16. "Drug Money and Opiate Trafficking on the Balkan Route, Focus of New UNODC Report," UNODC press release, November 26, 2015. Available at: https://www.unodc.org/unodc/en/frontpage/2015/November/drug-money-and-opiate-trafficking-on-the-balkan-route--focus-of-new-unodc-report.html.

17. Comments by Phil Evans for the author, October 31, 2016.

18. Fiona Rose-Greenland, "How Much Money Has ISIS Made Selling Antiquities? More Than Enough to Fund Its Attacks," *Washington Post*, June 3, 2016. Available at: https://www.washingtonpost.com/posteverything/wp/2016/06/03/how-much-money-has-isis-made-selling-antiquities-more-than-enough-to-fund-its-attacks/?utm_term=.f892c73cf65e.

19. Chris Deliso, "Smugglers and Legends Complicate Fight against Antiquities Theft (Part 1)," Balkanalysis.com, November 16, 2005. Available at Central and Eastern European Online Library: https://www.ceeol.com/search/journal-detail?id=1045.

20. Mark Vlasic, "Mark Vlasic: Illicit Trade in Looted Antiquities Helps Finance ISIS Terror Network," *National Post*, September 15, 2014. Available at: https://nationalpost.com/opinion/mark-vlasic-illicit-trade-in-looted-antiquities-helps-finance-isis-terror-network.

21. The University of Chicago project is called Modeling the Antiquities Trade in Iraq and Syria (MANTIS), and more information about it is available at: https://oi.uchicago.edu/research/projects/mantis. The venture is itself funded by an external nonprofit organization, The Antiquities Coalition. See https://theantiquitiescoalition.org.

22. "Dutch Journalist Easily Buys Fake Syrian Passport, Says Terrorists Can Do It Too," RT, September 16, 2015. Available at: https://www.rt.com/news/315591-fake-syrian-passport-journalist.

23. "Migrant Smuggling in the EU," op. cit.

24. Thomas Siebert, "Der Handel mit syrischen Pässen blüht," *Der Tagesspiegel*, September 8, 2015. Available at: http://www.tagesspiegel.de/politik/fluechtlinge- -der-handel-mit-syrischen-paessen-blueht/12290592.html.

25. "Migrant Smuggling in the EU," op. cit.

26. For more information on the general system, see Mohammed El Qorchi, Samuel Munzele Maimbo, and John F. Wilson, "Informal Funds Transfer Systems an Analysis of the Informal Hawala System," August 18, 2003. This Joint IMF–World Bank paper is available at: http://www.imf.org/external/pubs/nft/op/222.

27. The full report is available on the official website. See "The Trafficking in Human Beings Financial Business Model," Europol, October 1, 2015. Available at: https://www.europol.europa.eu/content/trafficking-human-beings-financial -business-model.

28. Author interview with Dr. Gergana Yordanova, October 31, 2016.

29. Anton Troianovski, Manuela Mesco, and Simon Clark, "The Growth of Refugee Inc.," *Wall Street Journal*, September 14, 2015. Available at: http://www.wsj .com/articles/in-european-refugee-crisis-an-industry-evolves-1442252165.

30. Author interview with Gavin Slade, November 11, 2016.

31. Ibid.

32. Author interview with Ioannis Michaletos, op. cit.

33. Vickiie Oliphante, "Mafia V Migrants: Mafia Bosses Declare War after Immigration Levels in Sicily Soar," *Express*, April 23, 2016. Available at: http://www .express.co.uk/news/world/663657/Mafia-bosses-declare-war-man-shot-as -immigration-levels-in-Sicily-rise.

34. Annalisa Merelli, "The Center of Sicily's Biggest City Was Emptied by the Mafia. Now It's Being Reclaimed by Migrants," Quartz, June 21, 2016. Available at: http://qz.com/704320/migrants-are-bringing-back-to-life-palermos-historical -center-which-the-mafia-had-ravaged.

35. "Migrant Smuggling in the EU," op. cit.

36. Jamie Dettmer, "Europe's Migration Crisis a Boon for Organized Crime," VOA News, September 8, 2015. Available at: http://www.voanews.com/a /europe-migration-crisis-a-boon-for-organized-crime/2952482.html.

37. Mark Townsend, "Child Migrants in Sicily Must Overcome One Last Obstacle —The Mafia," *The Observer*, July 24, 2016. Available at: https://www.theguardian .com/world/2016/jul/23/child-migrants-in-sicily-must-overcome-mafia -obstacle.

38. Author interview with former embassy worker in Athens, August 2016.

39. Milos Mitrovic, "Migrants in Serbia Spend 6 Million EUR per Day," Balkaneu.com, August 11, 2015. Available at: http://www.balkaneu.com/migrants -serbia-spend-6-million-eur-day.

40. Bill Donahue, "Meet the Two Brothers Making Millions Off the Refugee Crisis in Scandinavia," Bloomberg, January 6, 2016. Available at: http://www .bloomberg.com/features/2016-norway-refugee-crisis-profiteers.

41. Anton Troianovski, Manuela Mesco, and Simon Clark, "The Growth of Refugee Inc.," op. cit.

42. See the program description on the newspaper's website. Available at: https://www.theguardian.com/global-development/conflict-and-development.

43. For the official description of "content funding" models for migration articles, see https://www.theguardian.com/info/2016/jan/25/content-funding.

44. The homepage of this project is: http://edition.cnn.com/specials/world/freedom-project.

45. Nina Elbagir, "How Children Are Trafficked into Europe," CNN, June 16, 2015. Available at: http://edition.cnn.com/2015/06/15/europe/freedom-project-misery-trail-children.

46. The foundation is named in honor of the Obaid family's deceased patriarch. Founder Tarek Obaid heads the family's PetroSaudi oil firm. Executive Vice President Karim Obaid is also the administrator of Swiss-based Edelweiss Capital. And foundation CEO Nawaf Obaid is a Visiting Fellow at Harvard's Kennedy School of Government, while remaining an intimate diplomatic adviser to Saudi royals. He served as an adviser to Prince Turki Al Faisal, Saudi Ambassador to the U.K. and then United States during the Bush administration. However, he was briefly sidelined followed a November 2006 newspaper column, in which he warned that if the United States pulled out of Iraq, "one of the first consequences will be massive Saudi intervention to stop Iranian-backed Shiite militias from butchering Iraqi Sunnis." Coincidence or not, this precise outcome occurred in 2014 with the creation of ISIS. In July 2016, Obaid tried to argue that Saudi support for terrorism in Iraq was just "a myth." See Nawaf Obaid, "Stepping into Iraq," *Washington Post*, November 29, 2006. Available at: http://www.washingtonpost.com/wp-dyn/content/article/2006/11/28/AR2006112801277.html. See also Nawaf Obaid, "The Myth of Saudi Support for Terrorism," *Washington Times*, July 21, 2016. Available at: http://www.washingtontimes.com/news/2016/jul/21/the-myth-of-saudi-support-for-terrorism.

47. Chris Deliso, "Macedonian Migration Policy and the Future of Europe," op. cit.

48. Chris Deliso, "Mistrust and Different Priorities Vex EU-Macedonian Security Cooperation," Balkanalysis.com, May 27, 2016. Available at: http://www.balkanalysis.com/blog/2016/05/27/mistrust-and-different-priorities-vex-eu-macedonian-security-cooperation.

49. See Tamar Lewin, "As Interest Fades in the Humanities, Colleges Worry," *New York Times*, October 30, 2013. Available at: http://www.nytimes.com/2013/10/31/education/as-interest-fades-in-the-humanities-colleges-worry.html?ref=education.

50. Victor Davis Hanson, "The Death of the Humanities," Hoover Institution, January 28, 2014. Available at: http://www.hoover.org/research/death-humanities.

51. See "CEU Offers More Than a Dozen Courses Related to Migration," CEU website, October 8, 2015. Available at: https://www.ceu.edu/article/2015-10-08/ceu-offers-more-dozen-courses-related-migration.

52. For example, a website on human rights jobs noted new courses in three different British universities, offering degrees under departments of social sciences, law, and even psychoanalysis. See "4 Master Programs on Refugee and Migration Studies," http://www.humanrightscareers.com/4-master-programs-on-refugee-and-migration-studies.

53. Alison Abbott, "The Mental-Health Crisis among Migrants," *Nature*, October 10, 2016. Available at: http://www.nature.com/news/the-mental-health-crisis-among-migrants-1.20767.

54. "EPA Position Paper on Psychiatric Care of Refugees in Europe: Current Situation of Refugees Arriving in Europe," European Psychiatric Association, November 2015. Available at: http://www.europsy.net/wp-content/uploads/2015/11/EPA-statement-on-Refugees-20151102_FINAL.pdf.

CHAPTER 6

1. Virginia Hale, "Huge Spike in 'New French': Report Suggests Govt Rushing Citizenship before 2017 Election," Breitbart.com, October 7, 2016. Available at: http://www.breitbart.com/london/2016/10/07/french-govt-rushing-citizenship.

2. Ingrid Melander, "'Crumbling' French Left Battles over Who Should Run in 2017 Election," Reuters, October 30, 2016. Available at: https://www.reuters.com/article/france-politics-socialists-idINKBN12U0SP.

3. Adrian Valbray, "Hamon's Victory Confirms 'Corbynisation' of French Left," EurActiv, January 30, 2017. Available at: http://www.euractiv.com/section/elections/news/hamons-victory-confirms-corbynisation-of-french-left.

4. Jason Cowley, "Emmanuel Macron: A Populist Eruption from the Liberal Centre," *New Statesman*, February 23, 2017. Available at: http://www.newstatesman.com/politics/uk/2017/02/emmanuel-macron-populist-eruption-liberal-centre.

5. Nick Miller, "French Elections: The Hollywood Candidate, Emmanuel Macron, Is Gaining Ground," *Sydney Morning Herald*, February 11, 2017. Available at: http://www.smh.com.au/world/french-elections-the-hollywood-candidate-emmanuel-macron-is-gaining-ground-20170207-gu7v5a.html.

6. Jean-Marc LeClerc, "Manuel Valls veut doubler le nombre de naturalizations," *Le Figaro*, August 29, 2013. Available at: http://www.lefigaro.fr/actualite-france/2013/08/28/01016-20130828ARTFIG00452-manuel-valls-veut-plus-de-naturalisations.php.

7. Régis Soubrouillard, "Hollande inverse la courbe des naturalizations," *Causeur*, October 6, 2016. Available at: http://www.causeur.fr/hollande-naturalisations-manuel-valls-40398.html.

8. Official statistics on the French government's website. Available at: http://www.immigration.interieur.gouv.fr/Info-ressources/Statistiques/Tableaux-statistiques/L-acces-a-la-nationalite-francaise.

9. Sanya Khetani, "93 Percent of French Muslims Voted for Hollande," *Business Insider*, May 8, 2012. Available at: http://www.businessinsider.com/muslims-hollande-france-sarkozy-2012-5?IR=T.

10. Soeren Kern, "Muslim Voters Change Europe," Gatestone Institute, May 17, 2012. Available at: https://www.gatestoneinstitute.org/3064/muslim-voters-europe.

11. Dan Bilefsky, "More Migrants Storm Fence to Enter Ceuta, Spanish Enclave in Africa," *New York Times*, February 20, 2017. Available at: https://www.nytimes.com/2017/02/20/world/europe/ceuta-morocco-border-migrants.html?_r=0.

12. Conn Hallinan, "Socialist Meltdown in Spain; Right-Wing Will Take Government," People's World, October 11, 2016. Available at: http://www.peoplesworld.org/article/socialist-meltdown-in-spain-right-wing-will-take-government.

13. Sam Jones, "Pedro Sánchez Insists He Is Still in Charge of Spanish Socialist Party," *The Guardian*, September 29, 2016. Available at: https://www.theguardian.com/world/2016/sep/29/pedro-sanchez-insists-still-charge-spanish-socialist-party.

14. Owen Jones, "Spain Can Halt Europe's Slide to the Populist Right," *The Guardian*, November 3, 2016. Available at: https://www.theguardian.com /commentisfree/2016/nov/03/spain-halt-europes-slide-populist-right-podemos.

15. Conn Hallinan, "Socialist Meltdown in Spain; Right-Wing Will Take Government," op cit.

16. "Rajoy Congratulates New PSOE Administrator as Polls Suggest Socialists Could Be Hit Hard at a Third Election," The Spain Report, October 3, 2016. Available at: https://www.thespainreport.com/articles/935-161003183659-rajoy -congratulates-new-psoe-administrator-as-polls-suggest-socialists-could-be-hit -hard-at-a-third-election.

17. "PSOE Implosion a Gift to Rajoy and Podemos, the Spain Report," September 29, 2016. Available at: https://www.thespainreport.com/articles/922 -160929193618-psoe-implosion-a-gift-to-rajoy-and-podemos.

18. Tobias Buck, "Madrid Considers 'Nuclear Option' to Halt Catalan Referendum," *Financial Times*, February 23, 2017. Available at: https://www.ft.com /content/c9bf1ce0-f9b0-11e6-bd4e-68d53499ed71.

19. Dick Nichols, "After Congress Win, Podemos's Iglesias Promises 'Return to the Streets,'" GreenLeft, February 24, 2017. Available at: https://www .greenleft.org.au/content/after-congress-win-podemoss-iglesias-promises -return-streets.

20. Alejandro López, "Huge Demonstration in Barcelona in Defence of Refugees and Open Borders," World Socialist Website, February 20, 2017. Available at: https://www.wsws.org/en/articles/2017/02/20/barc-f20.html.

21. "More Than 150,000 Join Pro-refugee Protest in Barcelona." France24, February 19, 2017. Available at: http://www.france24.com/en/20170218-over-150000 -join-pro-migrant-protest-barcelona.

22. Yanis Papadimitriou, "Greece's Left-Wing Syriza Party in the Midst of Change," *Deutsche Welle*, October 13, 2016. Available at: http://www.dw.com/en /greeces-left-wing-syriza-party-in-the-midst-of-change/a-36035991.

23. "Swedish PM Going to Saudi Arabia," Sverige Radio, October 20, 2016. Available at: https://sverigesradio.se/sida/artikel.aspx?programid=2054&arti kel=6544416.

24. Emma Henderson, "Swedish Police Banned from Describing Criminals Anymore in Case They Sound Racist," *The Independent*, January 14, 2016. Available at: http:// www.independent.co.uk/news/world/europe/swedish-police-are-not-allowed -to-give-descriptions-of-alleged-criminals-so-as-not-to-sound-racist-a6810311.html.

25. Heather Saul, "Refugee Crisis: Sweden's Deputy Prime Minister Asa Romson Cries as She Announces Asylum Policy U-turn," *The Independent*, November 26, 2015. Available at: http://www.independent.co.uk/news/people/refugee -crisis-sweden-deputy-prime-minister-cries-as-she-announces-u-turn-on-asylum -policy-a6749531.html.

26. Larry Elliott and Jill Traynor, "Dutch PM Says Refugee Crisis Could Shut Down Europe's Open Borders for Good," *The Guardian*, January 21, 2016. Available at: https://www.theguardian.com/world/2016/jan/21/dutch-pm-says-refugee -crisis-could-shut-down-europes-open-borders-for-good.

27. Jenny Hill, "Could This Man Be the Next Chancellor of Germany?" BBC, February 24, 2017. Available at: http://www.bbc.com/news/world-europe-39067413.

28. Jefferson Chase, "Integration Commissioner Plans a Multicultural Germany," *Deutsche Welle*, February 14, 2017. Available at: http://www.dw.com/en/integration-commissioner-plans-a-multicultural-germany/a-37546826.

29. See Liam Deacon, "Green Politico: It's Time to Learn Arabic and Stop Worrying about Migration," Breitbart, October 18, 2016. Available at: http://www.breitbart.com/london/2016/10/18/green-politician-tells-germans-learn-arabic-stop-worrying-mass-migration. See also Tom Parfitt, "Drug Scandal: Top MP Forced to Resign after Being 'Caught with Crystal Meth,'" *Express*, March 4, 2016. Available at: http://ww.express.co.uk/news/world/649715/Volker-Beck-crystal-meth-Germany-Green-Party-politics-drugs.

30. Chris Deliso, "Potential for Convergence of Anarchist and Migration Activist Interests in Greece," Balkanalysis.com, December 12, 2015. Available at Central and Eastern European Online Library: https://www.ceeol.com/search/journal-detail?id=1045.

31. John Brady Kiesling, *Greek Urban Warriors: Resistance & Terrorism, 1967–2014* (Athens: Lycabettus Press, 2014), 352.

32. Ioannis Michaletos, "Left-Wing Terrorist Attacks and Organized Violence in Greece, 2008–2012," Balkanalysis.com, February 14, 2013. Available at Central and Eastern European Online Library: https://www.ceeol.com/search/journal-detail?id=1045.

33. Ioannis Michaletos, "In First Nine Months of 2016, Urban Violence and Crime Rise in Greece," Balkanalysis.com, October 11, 2016. Available at Central and Eastern European Online Library: https://www.ceeol.com/search/journal-detail?id=1045.

34. Author observations from discussions with Greek anarchists and other participants, August 2016.

35. Conn Hallinan, "Spain's Turmoil and Europe's Crisis," Foreign Policy in Focus, October 10, 2016. Available at: http://fpif.org/spains-turmoil-europes-crisis.

CHAPTER 7

1. John Henley, "Anders Breivik's Human Rights Violated in Prison, Norway Court Rules," *The Guardian*, April 20, 2016. Available at: https://www.theguardian.com/world/2016/apr/20/anders-behring-breiviks-human-rights-violated-in-prison-norway-court-rules.

2. Sasha Polakow-Suransky, "The Ruthlessly Effective Rebranding of Europe's New Far Right," *The Guardian*, November 1, 2016. Available at: https://www.theguardian.com/world/2016/nov/01/the-ruthlessly-effective-rebranding-of-europes-new-far-right.

3. Ibid.

4. Stephanie Kirchgaessner, "Top Official in Italy's M5S Increases Call for Referendum on Euro," *The Guardian*, December 8, 2016. Available at: https://www.theguardian.com/world/2016/dec/08/top-official-in-italys-m5s-increases-calls-for-referendum-on-euro.

5. Author interview with Karl-Peter Schwartz, November 7, 2016.

6. Kai Arzheimer, "The AfD's Second Place in Mecklenburg-West Pomerania Illustrates the Challenge Facing Merkel in 2017," London School of Economics Blog,

September 5, 2016. Available at: http://blogs.lse.ac.uk/europpblog/2016/09/05/afd-mecklenburg-west-pomerania-merkel.

7. Kate Brady, "Almost Two Thirds of Germans Believe Islam 'Does Not Belong in Germany,' Poll Finds," *Deutsche Welle*, May 12, 2016. Available at: http://www.dw.com/en/almost-two-thirds-of-germans-believe-islam-does-not-belong-in-germany-poll-finds/a-19251169.

8. Alison Smale, "Germany's Embrace of Migrants Spawns Rise of Far-Right Leader," *New York Times*, March 9, 2016. Available at: http://www.nytimes.com/2016/03/10/world/europe/germanys-embrace-of-migrants-spawns-rise-of-far-right-leader.html.

9. Ibid.

10. Peter Walker, "Germany's Anti-migrant AfD Party Slumps to Worst Poll Results in Seven Months," *The Independent*, February 23, 2017. Available at: http://www.independent.co.uk/news/world/europe/germany-afd-party-polls-frauke-petry-anti-immigration-latest-a7595221.html.

11. Author interview with Karl-Peter Schwartz, op. cit.

12. Ibid.

13. Angelique Chrisafis, "Front National Wins Opening Round in France's Regional Elections," *The Guardian*, December 7, 2015. Available at: https://www.theguardian.com/world/2015/dec/06/front-national-wins-opening-round-in-frances-regional-elections.

14. Satjayit Das, "Marine Le Pen Has More of an Appeal to Left Wing Voters Than Pollsters Would Like to Admit," *The Independent*, February 26, 2017. Available at: http://www.independent.co.uk/voices/marine-le-pen-macron-fillion-french-elections-who-will-win-a7600206.html.

15. Sasha Polakow-Suransky, "The Ruthlessly Effective Rebranding of Europe's New Far Right," op. cit.

16. Alissa J. Rubin, "France's Far-Right National Front Gains in Regional Elections," *New York Times*, December 6, 2015. Available at: http://www.nytimes.com/2015/12/07/world/europe/frances-far-right-national-front-gains-in-regional-elections.html.

17. David Crouch, "The Rise of the Anti-immigrant Sweden Democrats: 'We Don't Feel at Home Any More, and It's Their Fault,'" *The Guardian*, December 14, 2014. Available at: https://www.theguardian.com/world/2014/dec/14/sweden-democrats-flex-muscles-anti-immigrant-kristianstad.

18. "The Ultimate Guide to Sweden's Party Leaders," *The Local*, September 11, 2015. Available at: http://www.thelocal.se/20150427/ultimate-guide-to-whos-who-in-swedish-politics-2015.

19. Johan Carlstrom, Niklas Magnusson, and Amanda Billner, "Biggest Opposition Party Ready to Topple Swedish Government," Bloomberg, January 19, 2017. Available at: https://www.bloomberg.com/news/articles/2017-01-19/biggest-opposition-party-ready-to-topple-swedish-government.

20. Sara Malm, "Sweden: Home of IKEA, Meatballs, ABBA and . . . Racism? How the Swedish Right-Wing Went from a Joke to a Big Political Player in Just Seven Years," *The Daily Mail*, January 6, 2016. Available at: http://www.dailymail.co.uk/news/article-3349890/Sweden-Home-IKEA-meatballs-ABBA-racism-Swedish-right-wing-went-joke-big-political-player-just-seven-years.html.

21. Ian Black, "Far Right Comes Second in Dutch Poll," *The Guardian*, May 16, 2002. Available at: https://www.theguardian.com/world/2002/may/16/eu.thefarright.

22. Elizabeth Kolbert, "Beyond Tolerance," *The New Yorker*, September 9, 2002. Available at: http://www.newyorker.com/magazine/2002/09/09/beyond-tolerance.

23. Samuel Osborne, "Geert Wilders: Far-Right Dutch PM Frontrunner Says 'Islam and Freedom Are Not Compatible,'" *The Independent*, February 22, 2017. Available at: http://www.independent.co.uk/news/world/europe/geert-wilders-dutch-pm-frontrunner-far-right-islamophobic-freedom-a7593466.html.

24. Yoruk Bahceli, "Wilders Tells Dutch Parliament Refugee Crisis Is 'Islamic Invasion,'" Reuters, September 10, 2015. Available at: https://www.reuters.com/article/us-europe-migrants-netherlands-idUSKCN0RA0WY20150910.

25. Toby Sterling, "Dutch Politician Wilders Will Face Trial on Charges of Inciting Racial Hatred," Reuters, October 14, 2016. Available at: http://www.reuters.com/article/us-netherlands-wilders-discrimination-idUSKBN12E0IB.

26. "Riot in Dutch Town over Plan for Asylum-Seeker Centre," Reuters, December 17, 2015. Available at: https://www.reuters.com/article/uk-europe-migrants-netherlands-idUKKBN0TZ2ZD20151217.

27. Author interview with Carl Schiötz Wibye, October 21, 2016.

28. David Crouch and Patrick Kingsley, "Danish Parliament Approves Plan to Seize Assets from Refugees," *The Guardian*, January 26, 2016. Available at: https://www.theguardian.com/world/2016/jan/26/danish-parliament-approves-plan-to-seize-assets-from-refugees.

29. Comments made to the author by a Sinn Fein adviser, September 23, 2016.

30. See "What Is the SNP's Policy on Immigration?" SNP official Website. Available at: http://www.snp.org/pb_what_is_the_snp_s_policy_on_immigration.

31. Honor Mahony, "Flanders Tells Moroccan Migrants How to Behave," EU Observer, May 15, 2012. Available at: https://euobserver.com/news/116274.

32. This has increased Euroskepticism among some right-wing party supporters, who see the perpetuation of the Coudenhove-Kalergi Prize (famously won by Angela Merkel, among other prominent European leaders) as a proof that the EU establishment is trying to destroy traditional Europe. The count's work was extensive and written in a now-archaic form of German, and there are few English translations of his work in more than excerpt form. One complete text in English is *Europe Must Unite*, which calls for a Swiss-style federation. Unverifiable claims have been made by critics that some of his works are banned from republication in Germany owing to their explosive nature. For the BNP criticism, see the British National Party website: http://bnp.org.uk/news/national/european-union%E2%80%99s-coudenhove-kalergi-plan-%E2%80%94part-1. For the Greek Golden Dawn criticism, see a supporter website: http://golden-dawn-international-newsroom.blogspot.mk/2013/01/the-coudenhove-kalergi-plan-genocide-of.html.

33. Mathew Day, "EU Parliament Head Refuses to Apologise Over 'Coup' Comment after Polish PM Request," *The Telegraph*, December 15, 2015. Available at: http://www.telegraph.co.uk/news/worldnews/europe/poland/12051752/EU-parliament-head-refuses-to-apologise-over-coup-comment-after-Polish-PM-request.html.

34. Nic Robertson, Antonia Mortensen, and Wojciech Treszczynski, "Poland's Militias 'Ready for Anything' Amid Rising Tensions with Russia," CNN, October 27, 2016. Available at: http://edition.cnn.com/2016/10/27/europe/poland-militias-russia-tension.

35. See Meike Dülffer, Carsten Luther, and Zacharias Zacharakis, "Caught in the Web of the Russian Ideologues," Zeit Online, February 7, 2015. Available at: http://www.zeit.de/politik/ausland/2015-02/russia-greece-connection-alexander-dugin-konstantin-malofeev-panos-kammeno.

36. See "Metropolitan Hilarion Compares Europe with the Atheistic Soviet Union." Pravmir.com, April 19, 2016. Available at: http://www.pravmir.com/metropolitan-hilarion-compares-europe-with-the-atheistic-soviet-union.

37. Jennifer Newton, "A Society That Can't Defend Its Children Has No Tomorrow: Putin Condemns Europe's Handling of Migrants and Says the Child Rape in Austria Shows 'a Dilution of National Values,'" The Daily Mail, November 3, 2016. Available at: http://www.dailymail.co.uk/news/article-3900748/A-society-t-defend-children-no-tomorrow-Putin-condemns-Europe-s-handling-migrants-says-child-rape-Austria-shows-dilution-national-values.html.

38. "Soldiers of Odin's Secret Facebook Group: Weapons, Nazi Symbols and Links to MV Lehti," YLE, March 16, 2016. Available at: https://yle.fi/a/3-8749308.

39. "Police Commissioner: Street Patrols Have 'No Special Rights,'" YLE, January 5, 2016. Available at: https://yle.fi/a/3-8573593.

40. Stefan Lisinski and Lasse Wierup, "Nazistledare gripen för vapenbrott," Dagens Nyheter, November 25, 2003. Available at: http://www.dn.se/nyheter/sverige/nazistledare-gripen-for-vapenbrott/.

41. Jake Wallis Simons, "Finland-Based Soldiers of Odin Are Neo-Nazi White Supremacist Led Vigilantes," The Daily Mail, February 4, 2016. Available at: http://www.dailymail.co.uk/news/article-3426685/Nazi-daggers-SS-hats-hangman-s-noose-night-patrol-Soldiers-Odin-neo-Nazi-led-vigilantes-vowing-Europe-s-women-safe-migrant-sex-attacks.html.

42. Anthony Faiola, "Soldiers of Odin: The Far-Right Groups in Finland 'Protecting Women' from Asylum Seekers," The Independent, February 1, 2016. Available at: http://www.independent.co.uk/news/world/europe/soldiers-of-odin-the-far-right-groups-in-finland-protecting-women-from-asylum-seekers-a6846341.html.

43. "Soldiers of Odin Are Now Present in These Countries," Speisa.com, http://speisa.com/modules/articles/index.php/item.2734/soldiers-of-odin-are-now-present-in-these-countries.html.

44. Liz Alderman, "Greece Arrests Senior Members of Far-Right Party," New York Times, September 28, 2013. Available at: http://www.nytimes.com/2013/09/29/world/europe/greece-cracks-down-on-golden-dawn-with-arrests.html.

45. The Bloc Identitaire had an official website (in French), which no longer operates.

46. "The Strategic Provocation of Bloc Identitaire and an Interview with Fabrice Robert," March 29, 2012. Note that this interview was available at its original Web address at time of writing, but not at time of publication.

47. Haydn Rippon, "Occupy Le Mosque: France's New Radical Nativism," The Conversation via Boston University, November 2, 2012. Available at: https://theconversation.com/occupy-le-mosque-frances-new-radical-nativism-10368.

48. "The Strategic Provocation of Bloc Identitaire and an Interview with Fabrice Robert," op. cit.

49. The BI's official NovoPress.info website was no longer available at time of publication.

50. Jan Erk, "From Vlaams Blok to Vlaams Belang: The Belgian Far-Right Renames Itself," West European Politics, May 2005, 493–502. Available at: http://media.leidenuniv.nl/legacy/Jan%20Erk%20-%20From%20Vlaams%20Blok%20to%20Vlaams%20belang.pdf.

51. Chris Tomlinson, "Left-Wing Extremists Leave 'Identitarian' Populist Activist in Coma," Breitbart, June 14, 2016. Available at: http://www.breitbart.com/london/2016/06/14/identitarian-put-coma-left-extremists.

52. See the critical review of young Identitarian Markus Willinger's Generation Identity: A Declaration of War against the '68er, for one example. James Heiser, "Mistaken Identity: The Ideological Confusion of 'Generation Identity,'" The New American, April 17, 2015. Available at: http://www.thenewamerican.com/reviews/books/item/20682-mistaken-identity-the-ideological-confusion-of-generation-identity.

53. Sasha Polakow-Suransky, "The Ruthlessly Effective Rebranding of Europe's New Far Right," op. cit.

54. Parties member to the group were updated on its official EU parliamentary Web page (http://www.menleuropa.eu/national-delegation). No longer operational at time of publication.

55. Author interview with Karl-Peter Schwartz, February 13, 2017.

56. Author interview with Karl-Peter Schwartz, November 7, 2016.

57. Author interview with Carl Schiötz Wibye, op. cit.

CHAPTER 8

1. Noah Barkin, "Loyal Merkel Ally in Firing Line over Refugee Crisis," Reuters, September 17, 2015. Available at: http://www.reuters.com/article/us-europe-migrants-germany-minister-idUSKCN0RH2BV20150917.

2. "An Economic Take on the Refugee Crisis: Macro-Economic Assessment for the EU," Institutional Paper 033, European Commission, July 2016. Available at: http://ec.europa.eu/economy_finance/publications/eeip/pdf/ip033_en.pdf.

3. "How Will the Refugee Surge Affect the European Economy?" Organization for Economic Cooperation and Development, November 2015. Available at: https://www.oecd.org/migration/How-will-the-refugee-surge-affect-the-European-economy.pdf.

4. "Economic Take on the Refugee Crisis: Macro-Economic Assessment for the EU," op. cit.

5. "Ageing Europe Needs Migrants: EU's Mogherini." Press TV, February 9, 2017. Available at: http://www.presstv.ir/Detail/2017/02/09/509751/EU-Mogherini-ageing-population-immigrants-economy.

6. Marcel Canoy, "A Cost-Benefit Analysis of Refugees Will Only Fuel Hysteria," Dutchnews.nl, November 9, 2015. Available at: http://www.dutchnews.nl/features/2015/11/a-cost-benefit-analysis-of-refugees-will-only-fuel-hysteria.

7. "Police Defend Warning for Solo Women in Northern Sweden," The Local, March 8, 2016. Available at: http://www.thelocal.se/20160308/backlash-begins-after-swedish-women-told-not-to-go-out-alone.

8. "Twitter Storm as Cologne Mayor Suggests Women Stay at 'Arm's Length' from Strangers," *Deutsche Welle*, January 5, 2016. Available at: http://www.dw.com /en/twitter-storm-as-cologne-mayor-suggests-women-stay-at-arms-length-from -strangers/a-18962430.

9. Lizzie Stromme, "Swedes Rally to Defend Officer Facing Probe for 'Migrants to Blame for Serious Crime' Rant," *The Local*, February 10, 2017. Available at: http://www.express.co.uk/news/world/765613/Swedes-rally-defend-police -probe-migrants-blame-for-serious-crime-rant.

10. Jenny Hill, "Migrant Attacks Reveal Dark Side of Germany," BBC, February 22, 2016. Available at: http://www.bbc.com/news/world-europe-35633318.

11. Matthew Goodwin, Thomas Raines, and David Cutts, "What Do Europeans Think About Muslim Immigration?" Chatham House, February 7, 2017. Available at: https://www.chathamhouse.org/expert/comment/what-do-europeans -think-about-muslim-immigration.

12. Nima Gholam Ali Pour, "Welcome to Sweden, Eldorado for Migrants!" Gatestone Institute, February 18, 2017. Available at: https://www.gatestoneinstitute .org/9901/sweden-migrants-costs.

13. Author interview with Carl Schiötz Wibye, October 21, 2016.

14. Stefan Lehne, "How the Refugee Crisis Will Reshape the EU," Carnegie Europe, February 4, 2016. Available at: http://carnegieeurope.eu/2016/02/04/how -refugee-crisis-will-reshape-eu-pub-62650.

15. "Europe Could Die, French PM Manuel Valls Warns in Berlin," RT, November 17, 2016. Available at: https://www.rt.com/news/367241-europe -collapse-valls-berlin.

16. Tamás Boros, "Populism and Migration: Challenges for the Left," Das Progressive Zentrum, March 15, 2016. Available at: http://www.progressives -zentrum.org/populism-and-migration-challenges-for-the-left/?lang=en.

17. Liam Deacon, "Belgium Minister: Europe Must Prepare for 5,000 Returning Islamic State Jihadists," Breitbart, November 15, 2016. Available at: http:// www.breitbart.com/london/2016/11/15/belgium-minister-europe-must-prepare -5000-returning-islamic-state-jihadist.

18. Ulrike Demmer and Markus Verbeet, "Das Problem explodiert," Spiegel Online, May 7, 2007. Available at: http://www.spiegel.de/spiegel/a-481413 .html.

19. Ben Knight, "Berlin Promotes AfD Member to Top Prosecutor," *Deutsche Welle*, April 25, 2016. Available at: http://www.dw.com/en/berlin-promotes -afd-member-to-top-prosecutor/a-19213936.

20. "Germany Launches Nationwide Crackdown on Neo-Nazi Youth Group," *Haaretz*, October 9, 2008. Available at: http://www.haaretz.com/news/germany -launches-nationwide-crackdown-on-neo-nazi-youth-group-1.255222.

21. "Germany Bans Group Preaching Nazi Ideology to Children," *Haaretz*, March 31, 2009. Available at: http://www.haaretz.com/jewish/2.209/germany -bans-group-preaching-nazi-ideology-to-children-1.273246.

22. Madeline Chambers, "Germany Bans Neo-Nazi Group as Fears of Far-Right Grow," Reuters, March 16, 2016. Available at: http://www.reuters.com/article/us -germany-neonazis-idUSKCN0WI24W.

23. "Germany Bans Extremist Turkish Paper, Conducts Raids," AP, May 6, 2015. Available at: http://www.hurriyetdailynews.com/germany-bans-extremist -turkish-paper-conducts-raids.aspx?pageID=238&nID=82022&NewsCatID=351.

24. "Double Bomb Attack in Ankara Targets 'Resolution Process': Turkish PM Erdoğan," *Hurriyet Daily News*, March 20, 2013. Available at: http://www .hurriyetdailynews.com/double-bomb-attack-in-ankara-targets-resolution -process-turkish-pm-erdogan.aspx?pageID=238&nID=43362&NewsCatID=338.

25. Anthony Faiola, "Germany Launches Raids across 60 Cities, Bans Group on Suspicion of Islamic State Recruiting," *Washington Post*, November 15, 2016. Available at: https://www.washingtonpost.com/world/germany-launches-raids -across-60-cities-bans-radical-islamist-group/2016/11/15/0353ef76-1649-4216 -89c6-ef4a916b922e_story.html.

26. Virginia Hale, "Switzerland Considers Ban on Koran Distribution," Breitbart, November 17, 2016. Available at: http://www.breitbart.com/london/2016/11/17 /swiss-consider-ban-koran-distribution.

27. Mark Landler, "Germans Weigh Civil Rights and Public Safety," *New York Times*, July 13, 2007. Available at: http://www.nytimes.com/2007/07/13/world /europe/13germany.html.

28. Harriet Torry, "Germany, France Urge EU to Clamp Down on Terrorist Financing," *Wall Street Journal*, March 31, 2015. Available at: http://www.wsj.com/articles /germany-france-urge-eu-to-clamp-down-on-terrorist-financing-1427814952.

29. Rainer Buergin and Arne Delfs, "Germany Clamps Down on Flow of Fighters to Islamic State," Bloomberg, October 17, 2014. Available at: http://www .bloomberg.com/news/articles/2014-10-17/germany-clamps-down-on-flow-of -fighters-to-islamic-state.

30. Ulrike Demmer and Markus Verbeet, "Das Problem explodiert," op. cit.

31. Dietmar Seher, "In Problemvierteln fürchtet sich sogar die Polizei," WAZ, August 1, 2011.

32. Chris Tomlinson, "80 Percent of Swedish Police Consider Quitting over Migrant Danger," Breitbart, September 20, 2016. Available at: http://www.breitbart .com/london/2016/09/20/80-per-cent-swedish-police-consider-quitting-due -danger.

33. "Migrants Want Sharia Law in Swedish No-Go Zones," RT, September 26, 2016. Available at: https://www.rt.com/op-edge/360675-sweden-migrants-police -zones.

34. "French Police in Life-Threatening Condition after Molotov Cocktail Attack," France 24, October 9, 2016. Available at: http://www.france24.com /en/20161009-french-police-injured-molotov-cocktail-attack-paris-suburb.

35. Dietmar Seher, "In Problemvierteln fürchtet sich sogar die Polizei," op. cit.

36. Author interview with Gavin Slade, November 11, 2016.

37. Marco Giannangeli, "Britain's Prisons See Huge Rise in EU Convicts at £150 Million Cost to Taxpayer," *Express*, April 10, 2016. Available at: http://www .express.co.uk/news/uk/659620/Britain-prison-huge-rise-EU-convicts-150 million-taxpayer.

38. Author interview with Manuela Tudosia, October 22, 2016.

39. Soeren Kern, "Germans Stock Up on Weapons for Self-Defense," Gatestone Institute, December 21, 2015. Available at: https://www.gatestoneinstitute.org/7088/germany-weapons.

40. Thomas D. Williams, "Italy Deports Jihadist Suspected of Plotting Attack on Leaning Tower of Pisa," Breitbart, August 13, 2016. Available at: http://www.breitbart.com/national-security/2016/08/13/italy-deports-jihadist-suspected-plotting-attack-leaning-tower-pisa.

41. See Matteo Albertini and Chris Deliso, *The Vatican's Challenges in the Balkans: Bolstering the Catholic Church in 2015 and Beyond*, Balkanalysis.com: 2015. Kindle edition. Available at: https://www.amazon.com/dp/B00S30A7BQ.

42. Author interview with Martin Konov, October 27, 2016.

43. "Commission Signs Agreement with Industry on Cybersecurity and Steps Up Efforts to Tackle Cyber-threats," European Commission, July 5, 2016. Available at: https://ec.europa.eu/commission/presscorner/detail/en/IP_16_2321.

44. Agam Shah, "China's Secretive Mega Chip Powers the World's Fastest Computer," PCWorld, June 20, 2016. Available at: http://www.pcworld.com/article/3086107/hardware/chinas-secretive-super-fast-chip-powers-the-worlds-fastest-computer.html.

45. Author interview with European Parliament official, November 10, 2016.

46. "EU Passenger Name Record (PNR) Directive: An Overview," European Parliament, June 1, 2016. Available at: http://www.europarl.europa.eu/news/en/news-room/20150123BKG12902/eu-passenger-name-record-(pnr)-directive-an-overview.

47. See "Draft Report on Fundamental Rights Implications of Big Data: Privacy, Data Protection, Non-discrimination, Security and Law-Enforcement (2016/2225(INI))," European Parliament Committee on Civil Liberties, Justice and Home Affairs, October 19, 2016.

48. Author interview with Marco Giulio Barone, October 23, 2016.

49. The official website of the EU Transparency Register is available at: http://ec.europa.eu/transparencyregister/public.

50. For more information about this initiative, see the website of the European Defence Agency (EDA): https://eda.europa.eu.

51. Author interview with Marco Giulio Barone, op. cit.

52. Julian E. Barnes, "NATO Head Warns against EU Duplicating Capabilities," *Wall Street Journal*, June 28, 2016. Available at: http://www.wsj.com/articles/nato-head-warns-against-eu-duplicating-capabilities-1467128167.

53. Author interview with Manuela Tudosia, op. cit.

54. See Warsaw Declaration on Transatlantic Security, NATO, July 9, 2016. Available at: https://www.nato.int/cps/en/natohq/official_texts_133168.htm.

55. Official information on the NATO Industrial Advisory Group is available at: https://diweb.hq.nato.int/niag/Pages_Anonymous/Default.aspx.

56. Author interview with Manuela Tudosia, op. cit.

57. For full official documentation, see "European Border and Coast Guard: Final Approval," European Council, September 14, 2016. Available at: http://www.consilium.europa.eu/en/press/press-releases/2016/09/14-european-border-coast-guard.

58. The official EOS website is available at: http://www.eos-eu.com.

59. Keith Proctor, "Europe's Migrant Crisis: Defense Contractors Are Poised to Win Big," *Fortune*, September 10, 2015. Available at: http://fortune .com/2015/09/10/europe-migrant-crisis-defense-contractors.

CHAPTER 9

1. The ESI October 2015 report is available at: http://www.esiweb.org/pdf /ESI%20-%20The%20Merkel%20Plan%20-%20Compassion%20and%20 Control%20-%204%20October%202015.pdf.

2. Sumi Somaskanda, "Can This Man Save the Europe-Turkey Migrant Deal?" *Foreign Policy*, September 9, 2016. Available at: http://foreignpolicy.com/2016/09/09 /can-this-man-save-the-europe-turkey-migrant-deal-gerald-knaus-esi-refugees.

3. See official biographical information, available at: http://www.esiweb.org /index.php?lang=en&id=279&person_ID=1.

4. For general information, see the ECFR website, available at: http://www.ecfr .eu/about.

5. The full list of ESI donors is available at: http://www.esiweb.org/index .php?lang=en&id=65.

6. Among many other accounts on this controversial topic see David L. Phillips, "Research Paper: ISIS-Turkey Links," *Huffington Post*, November 9, 2014. Available at: http://www.huffingtonpost.com/david-l-phillips/research-paper -isis-turke_b_6128950.html.

7. For the full text, see "Turkey 2016 Report," European Commission, November 9, 2016. Available at: http://ec.europa.eu/enlargement/pdf/key_documents /2016/20161109_report_turkey.pdf.

8. "Ankara Rebuffs EU's Harsh Progress Report," *Hurriyet Daily News*, November 9, 2016. Available at: http://www.hurriyetdailynews.com/ankara-rebuffs-eus -harsh-progress-report.aspx?PageID=238&NID=105914&NewsCatID=510.

9. "Erdogan Says Europe Not Ready to Face 3mn Refugees as EU-Turkey Deal Collapse Looms," RT, November 11, 2016. Available at: https://www.rt.com /news/366513-erdogan-threatens-europe-refugees.

10. "Turkey Threatens to Cancel Greece Migration Deal in Soldiers' Extradition Row," Reuters, January 27, 2017. Available at: http://www.reuters.com/article /us-turkey-security-greece-military-idUSKBN15B0SC.

11. "Migrant Crisis: Russia and Syria 'Weaponising' Migration," BBC, March 2, 2016. Available at: http://www.bbc.com/news/world-europe-35706238.

12. Chris Deliso, "Exclusive: Germany's BND Investigating Migration Risks and Russian Influence in Greece," op. cit.

13. Ivo Oliveira, "National Front Seeks Russian Cash for Election Fight," *Politico*, February 19, 2016. Available at: http://www.politico.eu/article/le-pen-russia -crimea-putin-money-bank-national-front-seeks-russian-cash-for-election-fight.

14. Lucy Pasha Robinson, "Marine Le Pen Backs Vladimir Putin and Denies Invasion of Crimea," *The Independent*, February 7, 2017. Available at: http://www .independent.co.uk/news/world/europe/marine-le-pen-front-national-russian -kremlin-putin-invasion-annexation-crimea-ukraine-2014-a7566196.html.

15. For example, in mid-February 2017, the new U.S. secretary of state Rex Tillerson pressed his Russian counterpart, Sergei Lavrov, on Ukraine, while

the new defense secretary, James Mattis, indicated that the U.S. commitment to NATO would remain strong, while claiming that Russia had "interfered" in the 2016 U.S. elections—a talking point of the Hilary Clinton campaign that has not been proven and which the Trump team has consistently denied. See David M. Herszenhorn, "Mattis Says He Expects NATO Allies to Step Up," *Politico*, February 16, 2017. Available at: http://www.politico.eu/article/james-mattis-says-he-expects-eu-nato-allies-to-step-up.

16. Comment made from event transcript. See "Meeting of the Valdai International Discussion Club," Official Russian President's website, October 27, 2016. Available at: http://en.kremlin.ru/events/president/news/53151.

17. Gabriela Baczynska, "Putin Opens Moscow's Largest Mosque, Warns against Extremists," Reuters, September 23, 2015. Available at: http://www.reuters.com/article/us-russia-mosque-idUSKCN0RN1UD20150923.

18. See "Merkel Says German Multicultural Society Has Failed," BBC, October 17, 2010. See also Stephen Evans, "Germany's Charged Immigration Debate," BBC, October 17, 2010. Available at: http://www.bbc.com/news/world-europe-11532699.

19. "Gehört der Islam zu Deutschland? Kauder widerspricht Merkel," Idea.de, January 19, 2015. Available at: http://www.idea.de/politik/detail/gehoert-der-islam-zu-deutschland-kauder-widerspricht-merkel-89332.html.

20. "Bundesregierung Rede von Bundeskanzlerin Merkel beim Jahrestreffen 2013 des World Economic Forum," January 24, 2013. Available at: https://www.bundesregierung.de/ContentArchiv/DE/Archiv17/Reden/2013/01/2013-01-24-merkel-davos.html.

21. Quentin Peel, "Merkel Warns on Cost of Welfare," *Financial Times*, December 16, 2012. Available at: https://www.ft.com/content/8cc0f584-45fa-11e2-b7ba-00144feabdc0.

22. Author interview with EU official, November 4, 2016.

23. Anton Troianovski, "Merkel Says Germany Won't Stop Accepting Refugees, Muslims," *Wall Street Journal*, September 19, 2016. Available at: http://www.wsj.com/articles/merkel-says-germany-wont-stop-accepting-refugees-muslims-1474288469.

24. Author interview with Karl-Peter Schwartz, November 7, 2016.

25. Sven Böll and Anne Seith, "Why Germany Wants to See Its US Gold," Spiegel Online, October 30, 2012. Available at: http://www.spiegel.de/international/germany/german-politicians-demand-to-see-gold-in-us-federal-reserve-a-864068.html.

26. Ronan Manly, "Update on Bundesbank Gold Repatriation 2015," Bullionstar.com, January 27, 2016. Available at: https://www.bullionstar.com/blogs/ronan-manly/update-on-bundesbank-gold-repatriation.

27. Stephen Kinzer, "German Plan for Phased Union of Europe Provokes Controversy," *New York Times*, September 4, 1994. Available at: http://www.nytimes.com/1994/09/04/world/german-plan-for-phased-union-of-europe-provokes-controversy.html.

28. Paul Taylor, "Twenty Years on, Schaeuble Pleads again for Core Europe," Reuters, September 1, 2014. Available at: https://www.reuters.com/article/us-eu-schaeuble-idUSKBN0GW1XR20140901.

29. Hans-Edzard Busemann, "Germany's Schaeuble Wants to Rebalance EU Commission's Role," Reuters, July 30, 2015. Available at: http://www.reuters.com/article/us-europe-commission-germany-idUSKCN0Q41DW20150730.

30. Madeline Chambers, "Germany Needs Immigration, Finance Minister Says after Anti-asylum Rallies," Reuters, December 27, 2014. Available at: http://uk .reuters.com/article/uk-german-immigration-schaeuble-idUKKBN0K50AT20141227.

31. Author interview with Nicolas De Santis, October 17, 2016.

32. Author interview with EU official, op. cit.

33. Ibid.

34. Author interview with Nicolas De Santis, op. cit.

35. Author interview with EU official, op. cit.

36. Author interview with Winfriend Veit, November 7, 2016.

37. Aida Alami, "Protests Erupt in Morocco over Fish Vendor's Death in Garbage Compactor," *New York Times*, October 30, 2016. Available at: http://www .nytimes.com/2016/10/31/world/middleeast/protests-erupt-in-morocco-over -fish-vendors-death-in-garbage-compactor.html?_r=0.

38. Author interview with Winfriend Veit, op. cit.

39. "Macedonia cannot be a traffic light to regulate refugees"—President Ivanov at the panel discussion entitled "Towards further Euro-Atlantic Integration of Southeast Europe within the 52nd Munich Security Conference," Macedonian President's Office, February 13, 2016. Available at: http://www.president.gov .mk/en/media-centre/speeches/3626-msc2016.html.

40. Matteo Albertini and Chris Deliso, "Italian Security in the MENA and Balkans, Part 1: Military and Energy Aspects." Balkanalysis.com, July 4, 2016. Available at Central and Eastern European Online Library: https://www.ceeol .com/search/journal-detail?id=1045.

41. Author interview with British diplomat, September 22, 2016.

42. Author interview with senior European security official, February 7, 2017.

43. Author interview with Nicolas De Santis, op. cit.

44. Craig VanGrasstek, *The History and Future of the World Trade Organization* (Geneva: World Trade Organization, 2013), 70.

45. The official GFMD website is available at: http://www.gfmd.org.

46. Peter Sutherland and Cecilia Malmstrom, "Europe's Immigration Challenge," Project Syndicate, July 20, 2012. Available at: https://www.project-syndicate .org/commentary/europe-s-immigration-challenge?barrier=true.

47. Brian Wheeler, "EU Should 'Undermine National Homogeneity' Says UN Migration Chief," BBC, June 21, 2012. Available at: http://www.bbc.com/news/uk -politics-18519395.

48. Sebastian Shakespeare, "The Questions Peter Sutherland, the Globe's Grandee, Was NOT Asked by the Lords EU Subcommittee," *The Daily Mail*, June 27, 2012. Available at: http://www.dailymail.co.uk/debate/article-2165584 /Peter-Sutherland-globes-grandee.html#ixzz4Q4pMt800.

49. Joseph Klein, "UN Officials Mocks National Sovereignty," FrontPageMag .com, October 28, 2015. Available at: http://www.frontpagemag.com/fpm /260584/un-officials-mock-national-sovereignty-joseph-klein.

50. See "Who Is a Migrant?" International Organization for Migration. Available at: http://www.iom.int/who-is-a-migrant.

51. "Remarks by Peter D. Sutherland, UN Special Representative for International Migration before the United Nations Security Council," United Nations, May 11, 2015.

52. Peter Sutherland, "Migration's Private-Sector Problem-Solvers," Project Syndicate, September 12, 2016. Available at: https://www.project-syndicate.org/commentary/private-sector-migration-solutions-by-peter-sutherland-2016-09.

53. According to one media report, the Soros charity empire, led by his Open Society Foundations, has been "quietly preparing for a post-George era by creating a stronger governance and management structure to guide a professionalized foundation for decades to come—one that is likely to absorb the bulk of the Soros fortune. (That fortune, as we've pointed out, will likely grow even larger in coming years, judging by Soros's investing track record of late. He's more than tripled his wealth since 2005.)" See Ade Adeniji, "Like Father, Like Son: Alexander Soros's Emerging Social Justice Mission," Insidephilanthropy.com, January 14, 2016. Available at: http://www.insidephilanthropy.com/home/2016/1/14/like-father-like-son-alexander-soros-emerging-social-justice.html.

54. Arnaud De Borchgrave, "Commentary: Big Gnome: Financial Situation Can't Last," UPI, April 16, 2011. Available at: http://www.upi.com/Commentary-Big-Gnome-Financial-situation-cant-last/17111303816102.

55. Rachel Ehrenfeld and Shawn Macomber, "George Soros: The 'God' Who Carries Around Some Dangerous Demons," *Los Angeles Times*, October 4, 2004. Available at: http://articles.latimes.com/2004/oct/04/opinion/oe-ehrenfeld4.

56. Andras Gergely, "Orban Accuses Soros of Stoking Refugee Wave to Weaken Europe," Bloomberg, October 30, 2015. Available at: http://www.bloomberg.com/news/articles/2015-10-30/orban-accuses-soros-of-stoking-refugee-wave-to-weaken-europe.

57. George Soros, "Rebuilding the Asylum System," Project Syndicate, September 26, 2015. Available at: https://www.georgesoros.com/essays/rebuilding-the-asylum-system.

58. Tyler Durden, "Soros Hack Reveals Plot Behind Europe's Refugee Crisis; Media Manipulation; Cash for 'Social Justice,'" Zerohedge.com, August 16, 2016. Available at: http://www.zerohedge.com/news/2016-08-16/soros-hack-reveals-plot-behind-europes-refugee-crisis-media-funding-and-manipulation?page=3.

59. Indeed, as one of the Wikileaks e-mails from former Hillary Clinton campaign director John Podesta revealed, in 2003 a Soros-linked "progressive" master organization had been created to focus on American politics. At a September 2007 meeting with Democratic Party donors, Podesta—then the president of the Soros-funded Center for American Progress—presented a long-term strategy "to control public discourse, change American demographics and divide the electorate by categories such as race, gender and age," as one review described it. The classic Soros strategy of divide and conquer was thus fully integrated into the Obama agenda, as future events would abundantly show. See Peter Hasson, "REVEALED: Liberal Money's Longterm Strategy to Control Public Opinion and Secure 'Advantageous' Demographics," The Daily Caller, November 2, 2016. Available at: http://dailycaller.com/2016/11/02/revealed-liberal-moneys-longterm-strategy-to-control-public-opinion-and-secure-advantageous-demographics/#ixzz4PzMPM2SY.

60. Remarks made by George Soros at the 2016 Concordia Summit's Private Sector Forum on Migration and Refugees, September 20, 2016. The official website is available at: http://www.concordia.net/the-summit-2016.

61. Sebastian Shakespeare, "Revealed—David Miliband Is Paid a Staggering £425,000 as Boss of New York–Based Refugee Charity," *The Daily Mail*, December 31, 2015. Available at: http://www.dailymail.co.uk/news/article-3379572 /SEBASTIAN-SHAKESPEARE-Revealed-David-Miliband-paid-staggering -425-000-boss-New-York-based-refugee-charity.html.

62. See the relevant Web page of Save the Children, available at: https://www .savethechildren.org/us/about-us/leadership-and-trustees.

63. Author interview with Jason Miko, November 3, 2016.

64. See the relevant page on the OSCE's website, see: http://www.osce.org /secretariat/migration.

65. Author interview with Jason Miko, op. cit.

66. Thomas D. Williams, "Pope Francis, Lutheran Chief, Urge Christians to 'Defend the Rights of Refugees,'" Breitbart, November 1, 2016. Available at: http://www.breitbart.com/london/2016/11/01/pope-francis-lutheran-chief -urge-christians-defend-rights-refugees.

67. "Joint IOM-UNHCR Statement on President Trump's Refugee Order," International Organization for Migration, January 28, 2017. Available at: https://www.unhcr.org/news/news-releases/joint-iom-unhcr-statement -president-trumps-refugee-order.

68. Sarah Lee, "UN Secretary General: Islamophobia Leads to Terrorism," *The Blaze*, February 12, 2017. Available at: http://www.theblaze.com/news /2017/02/12/un-secretary-general-islamophobia-leads-to-terrorism.

69. The pope claimed that no religions lead to terrorism, but made his argument based on social issues, rather than theological doctrine, thus ignoring the main argument European populists have used when criticizing Islam. See the official speech, Pope Francis, "Message of His Holiness Pope Francis on the Occasion of the World Meetings of Popular Movements in Modesto (California)," February 10, 2017. Available at: http://w2.vatican.va/content/francesco/en/messages/pont-messages/2017/docu ments/papa-francesco_20170210_movimenti-popolari-modesto.html.

70. Jack Montgomery, "Merkel: Europe Must Take More Migrants, Islam Is Not the Source of Terrorism," Breitbart, February 18, 2017. Available at: http://www .breitbart.com/london/2017/02/18/merkel-europe-must-take-more-migrants -and-islam-is-not-the-cause-of-terrorism.

71. "EU 'Should Expand beyond Europe,'" Liveleak.com, November 16, 2007. Available at: http://www.liveleak.com/view?i=eca_1195230031.

72. See, for example, "The EU Emergency Trust Fund for Africa." European Commission/International Cooperation and Development. Available at: https:// trust-fund-for-africa.europa.eu/our-mission-p_en.

73. The most influential modern investigation has been the Eurabia theory of researcher Bat Ye'or, based on an assessment of official European and Arab cooperation since 1973. According to this, a long-term outcome will be the domination of Islamic immigrant society in Europe. The theory has been cited by both supporters and critics. See Bat Ye'or, *Eurabia: The Euro-Arab Axis* (Madison, NJ: Fairleigh Dickinson University Press, 2005).

74. This project is described on the group's official website: https://clubmadrid .org/work/programmes/shared-societies-project.

75. Guy Verhofstadt, "Face à la situation des migrants, l'UE a besoin de leadership, pas d'ériger des murs," *Huffington Post* (France), August 20, 2015. Available

at: http://www.huffingtonpost.fr/guy-verhofstadt/politique-immigration-union
-europeenne_b_8007656.html.

76. See "Short Biography of Edmond Israel," Cvce.eu. Available at: http://
www.cvce.eu/content/publication/2011/1/17/1e1f8045-ee84-4a48-a1ff
-a151c29a97c9/publishable_en.pdf.

77. Jane Martinson, "OK, He Chairs BP, but Really He Wants to Run Europe," *The Guardian*, January 19, 2007. Available at: https://www.theguardian.com/business
/2007/jan/19/oilandpetrol.news.

78. Nick Webb, "Pope Drafts in Peter Sutherland after Vatican Bank Hit by Scandals," *Irish Independent*, June 8, 2014. Available at: http://www.independent.ie
/business/irish/pope-drafts-in-peter-sutherland-after-vatican-bank-hit-by-scandals
-30336625.html.

79. See the relevant ICMC Web page at: https://www.icmc.net/programs
/advocating-for-increased-resettlement-places-for-syrian-refugees. See also the official 'Resettlement Saves Lives 2020' Web page at: http://www.resettlement
.eu/page/resettlement-saves-lives-2020-campaign.

80. Comments made to the author by a JRS Europe official in Brussels, December 3, 2015.

81. This was listed as part of the "Communities of Hospitality" project on the JRS website: https://jrseurope.org/en/project/communities-of-hospitality.

82. Peter Hasson, "Leaked Soros Memo: Refugee Crisis 'New Normal,' Gives 'New Opportunities' for Global Influence," The Daily Caller, August 15, 2016. Available at: http://dailycaller.com/2016/08/15/leaked-soros-memo-refugee-crisis
-new-normal-gives-new-opportunities-for-global-influence/#ixzz4Q0pkAlDl.

83. William F. Jasper, "Hacked Docs Expose Soros-Obama-UN Refugee Invasion Network," *The New American*, August 19, 2016. Available at: https://
thenewamerican.com/us/immigration/hacked-docs-expose-soros-obama-un
-refugee-invasion-network.

84. Logothetis and Maniatis opened the Concordia 2016 event, which was co-organized with the Columbia University's Global Policy Initiative. The agenda is available at: http://globalpolicy.columbia.edu/sites/default/files/private_sector
_forum_on_migration_and_refugees_agenda.pdf.

85. See the Libra Group official website, available at: https://www.libra.com
/about-us.

86. See the Solidarity Now official website, available at: http://www.solidaritynow
.org/solidarity-now-en/advisory-board-en.html.

87. Stelios Zavvos, "Migration Flows, Europe and Greece," *Kathimerini*, February 14, 2016. Available at: https://www.solidaritynow.org/en/migration
-flows-europe-greece.

88. Antonis Diamataris, "Greek-American Investor and Power Broker Stelios Zavvos," The National Herald, December 15, 2011.

89. Vasilis Goulas, "Τζορτζ Σόρος: Τρίτο στεφάνι στα 83 του, με Έλληνα κουμπάρο," *Proto Thema*, September 27, 2013. Available at: http://www.protothema.gr
/stories/article/314320/tzortz-sorostrito-stefani-sta-83-toume-ellina-koubaro-.

90. Karl West, "Man Who Broke the Bank of England, George Soros, 'at Centre of Hedge Funds Plot to Cash in on Fall of the Euro,'" *The Daily Mail*, February

27, 2010. Available at: http://www.dailymail.co.uk/news/article-1253791/Is-man -broke-Bank-England-George-Soros-centre-hedge-funds-betting-crisis-hit-euro .html#ixzz4Q1FZqgzv.

91. George Soros, "The Euro Will Face Bigger Tests Than Greece," *Financial Times*, February 21, 2010. Available at: https://www.ft.com/content/88790e8e -1f16-11df-9584-00144feab49a.

Bibliography

ARTICLES WITHOUT NAMED AUTHORS

"Adopting Resolution 2240 (2015), Security Council Authorizes Member States to Intercept Vessels off Libyan Coast Suspected of Migrant Smuggling." United Nations, October 9, 2015. Available at: http://www.un.org/press/en/2015/sc12072.doc.htm.

"Ankara Rebuffs EU's Harsh Progress Report." *Hurriyet Daily News*, November 9, 2016. Available at: http://www.hurriyetdailynews.com/ankara-rebuffs-eus-harsh-progress-report.aspx?PageID=238&NID=105914&NewsCatID=510.

"Antonio Guterres of Portugal Appointed as Next U.N. Secretary-General." NBC News, October 13, 2016. Available at: http://www.nbcnews.com/news/world/united-nations-appoints-portugal-s-guterres-next-u-n-chief-n665736.

"Bulgaria to Close All External EU Borders, PM Announces." ITV News, February 15, 2016. Available at: http://www.itv.com/news/update/2016-02-15/bulgaria-to-close-all-external-eu-borders-pm-announces.

"Bundesregierung Rede von Bundeskanzlerin Merkel beim Jahrestreffen 2013 des World Economic Forum," January 24, 2013. Available at: https://www.bundesregierung.de/ContentArchiv/DE/Archiv17/Reden/2013/01/2013-01-24-merkel-davos.html.

"CEU Offers More Than a Dozen Courses Related to Migration." CEU.com, October 8, 2015. Available at: https://www.ceu.edu/article/2015-10-08/ceu-offers-more-dozen-courses-related-migration.

"Clashes Break Out at Migrants Camp on Greek Island: Police." Reuters, April 26, 2016. Available at: http://www.reuters.com/article/us-europe-migrants -greece-clashes-idUSKCN0XN271.

"Code of Conduct on Countering Illegal Hate Speech Online." European Commission, May 31, 2015. Available at: https://commission.europa.eu/strategy-and-policy /policies/justice-and-fundamental-rights/combatting-discrimination/racism -and-xenophobia/eu-code-conduct-countering-illegal-hate-speech-online_en.

"Commission Presents Options for Reforming the Common European Asylum System and Developing Safe and Legal Pathways to Europe." European Commission, Press release, April 6, 2016. Available at: http://europa.eu /rapid/press-release_IP-16-1246_en.htm.

"Commission Signs Agreement with Industry on Cybersecurity and Steps Up Efforts to Tackle Cyber-threats." European Commission, July 5, 2016. Available at: https://ec.europa.eu/commission/presscorner/detail/en /IP_16_2321.

"Council Conclusions on the External Aspects of Migration." European Council, May 23, 2016. Available at: http://www.consilium.europa.eu/en/press /press-releases/2016/05/23-fac-external-aspects-migration/.

"Delivery Driver Plotted to Kill U.S. Soldiers in Britain." Reuters, April 1, 2016. Available at: http://www.reuters.com/article/us-britain-security-usa-plot -idUSKCN0WY4U6.

"Double Bomb Attack in Ankara Targets 'Resolution Process': Turkish PM Erdoğan." *Hurriyet Daily News*, March 20, 2013. Available at: http:// www.hurriyetdailynews.com/double-bomb-attack-in-ankara-targets -resolution-process-turkish-pm-erdogan.aspx?pageID=238&nID=43362& NewsCatID=338.

"Draft Report on Fundamental Rights Implications of Big Data: Privacy, Data Protection, Non-discrimination, Security and Law-enforcement (2016/2225(INI))." European Parliament Committee on Civil Liberties, Justice and Home Affairs, October 19, 2016.

"Drug Money and Opiate Trafficking on the Balkan Route, Focus of New UNODC Report." UNODC press release, November 26, 2015. Available at: https:// www.unodc.org/unodc/en/frontpage/2015/November/drug-money-and -opiate-trafficking-on-the-balkan-route--focus-of-new-unodc-report.html.

"Dutch Journalist Easily Buys Fake Syrian Passport, Says Terrorists Can Do It Too." RT, September 16, 2015. Available at: https://www.rt.com/news /315591-fake-syrian-passport-journalist.

"An Economic Take on the Refugee Crisis: Macro-Economic Assessment for the EU," Institutional Paper 033, European Commission, July 2016. Available at: http://ec.europa.eu/economy_finance/publications/eeip/pdf/ip033 _en.pdf.

"EPA Position Paper on Psychiatric Care of Refugees in Europe: Current Situation of Refugees Arriving in Europe," European Psychiatric Association, November 2015. Available at: http://www.europsy.net/wp-content /uploads/2015/11/EPA-statement-on-Refugees-20151102_FINAL.pdf.

"Erdogan Says Europe Not Ready to Face 3mn Refugees as EU-Turkey Deal Collapse Looms." RT, November 11, 2016. Available at: https://www.rt.com /news/366513-erdogan-threatens-europe-refugees.

"The Establishment of the European Movement." cvce.eu. Available at: http://
     www.cvce.eu/en/recherche/unit-content/-/unit/04bfa990-86bc-402f
     -a633-11f39c9247c4/272166ae-84b2-466b-9cfa-4df511389208.
"The EU Emergency Trust Fund for Africa." European Commission/International
     Cooperation and Development. Available at: http://ec.europa.eu/europeaid
     /regions/africa/eu-emergency-trust-fund-africa_en.
"EU Leaders Agree to Relocate 40,000 Migrants." BBC, June 26, 2015. Available at:
     http://www.bbc.com/news/world-europe-33276443.
"EU Passenger Name Record (PNR) Directive: An Overview." European Parlia-
     ment, June 1, 2016. Available at: http://www.europarl.europa.eu/news
     /en/news-room/20150123BKG12902/eu-passenger-name-record-(pnr)
     -directive-an-overview.
"EU Should Expand beyond Europe." Liveleak.com, November 16, 2007. Available
     at: http://www.liveleak.com/view?i=eca_1195230031.
"EUCAP Sahel Niger: Mission Extended, Budget Agreed, Mandate Amended."
     European Council, July 18, 2016. Available at: http://www.consilium
     .europa.eu/en/press/press-releases/2016/07/18-fac-sahel-niger.
"EUNAVFOR MED Operation Sophia Authorised to Start Two Additional Sup-
     porting Tasks." European Council, August 30, 2016. Available at: http://
     www.consilium.europa.eu/en/press/press-releases/2016/08/30-eunavfor
     -med-sophia-op-add-supporting-tasks.
"'EUNAVFOR MED—Operation SOPHIA'—Six Monthly Report: June, 22nd
     to December, 31st 2015." Available at: https://wikileaks.org/eu-military
     -refugees.
"Europe Could Die, French PM Manuel Valls Warns in Berlin." RT, November
     17, 2016. Available at: https://www.rt.com/news/367241-europe-collapse
     -valls-berlin.
"Europe Needs Migrants: EU's Mogherini." Press TV, February 9, 2017. Available at:
     http://www.presstv.ir/Detail/2017/02/09/509751/EU-Mogherini-ageing
     -population-immigrants-economy.
"European Border and Coast Guard: Council Confirms Agreement with Parlia-
     ment." European Council, June 22, 2016. Available at: http://www.consilium
     .europa.eu/en/press/press-releases/2016/06/22-border-and-coast-guard.
"European Border and Coast Guard: Final Approval." European Council, September
     14, 2016. Available at: http://www.consilium.europa.eu/en/press/press
     -releases/2016/09/14-european-border-coast-guard.
"European Prize for the Chancellor." Office of the German Federal Chancellor, Janu-
     ary 13, 2011. Available at: https://www.bundeskanzlerin.de/ContentArchiv
     /EN/Archiv17/Artikel/_2011/01/2011-01-13-merkel-europapreis_en.html.
"European Response to Dire Refugee Crisis Urgently Needed." Party of Euro-
     pean Socialists, September 4, 2015. Available at: http://www.pes.eu/eu
     _response_to_dire_refugee_crisis_urgently_needed.
"Eurozone: A Nightmare Scenario—Latin Lessons." Financial Times, Septem-
     ber 16, 2011. Available at: https://www.ft.com/content/80094624-e076
     -11e0-bd01-00144feabdc0.
"EU's Tusk Demands Closure of Balkan Route to Refugees 'for Good.'"
     Deutsche Welle, September 24, 2016. Available at: http://www.dw.com/

en/eus-tusk-demands-closure-of-balkan-route-to-refugees-for-good/a
-35881684.

"Facebook, Google, Other Tech Giants Answer Obama's Refugee Plea." CNET
.com, September 20, 2016. Available at: https://www.cnet.com/tech/tech
-industry/facebook-google-other-tech-giants-answer-obamas-refugee
-plea-president-syria.

"Fact Sheet on the Leaders' Summit on Refugees." White House Press releases
September 20, 2016. Available at: https://www.whitehouse.gov/the
-press-office/2016/09/20/fact-sheet-leaders-summit-refugees.

"France Dijon: Driver Targets City Pedestrians." BBC, December 21, 2014. Available at: http://www.bbc.com/news/world-europe-30571911.

"Free Movement of Persons." European Parliament. Available at: http://www.europarl
.europa.eu/atyourservice/en/displayFtu.html?ftuId=FTU_2.1.3.html.

"French Police Chief's Killer 'Claimed Allegiance to IS.'" BBC, June 14, 2016. Available at: http://www.bbc.com/news/world-europe-36524094.

"French Police in Life-Threatening Condition after Molotov Cocktail Attack."
France 24, October 9, 2016. Available at: http://www.france24.com/en
/20161009-french-police-injured-molotov-cocktail-attack-paris-suburb.

"G7 Ise—Shima Leaders' Declaration." Japanese Ministry of Foreign Affairs, May
26–27, 2016. Available at: http://www.mofa.go.jp/files/000160266.pdf.

"Gehört der Islam zu Deutschland? Kauder widerspricht Merkel." Idea.de, January 19, 2015. Available at: http://www.idea.de/politik/detail/gehoert-der
-islam-zu-deutschland-kauder-widerspricht-merkel-89332.html.

"Germany Bans Extremist Turkish Paper, Conducts Raids." AP, May 6, 2015.
Available at: http://www.hurriyetdailynews.com/germany-bans-extremist
-turkish-paper-conducts-raids.aspx?pageID=238&nID=82022&NewsCa
tID=351.

"Germany Bans Group Preaching Nazi Ideology to Children." Haaretz, March
31, 2009. Available at: http://www.haaretz.com/jewish/2.209/germany
-bans-group-preaching-nazi-ideology-to-children-1.273246.

"Germany Launches Nationwide Crackdown on Neo-Nazi Youth Group." Haaretz,
October 9, 2008. Available at: http://www.haaretz.com/news/germany
-launches-nationwide-crackdown-on-neo-nazi-youth-group-1.255222.

"Germany: 'No Limit' to Refugees We'll Take In." Sky News, September 5, 2015.
Available at: http://news.sky.com/story/germany-no-limit-to-refugees
-well-take-in-10347281.

"How Will the Refugee Surge Affect the European Economy?" Organization for
Economic Cooperation and Development, November 2015. Available at:
https://www.oecd.org/migration/How-will-the-refugee-surge-affect-the
-European-economy.pdf.

"Human Trafficking Focus of INTERPOL Conference." Interpol, October 20, 2016.

"Hundreds Hurt in Police Clashes at Greece-Macedonia Border." Reuters, April 10,
2015. Available at: https://www.theguardian.com/world/2016/apr/10
/clashes-between-migrants-and-police-at-border-between-greece-and
-macedonia.

"Hungary Marks 1989 Freedom Event." BBC, August 19, 2009. Available at: http://
    news.bbc.co.uk/2/hi/8209173.stm.
"Irregular Migrant, Refugee Arrivals in Europe Top One Million in 2015: IOM."
    International Organisation on Migration press release, December 22, 2015.
    Available at: https://www.iom.int/news/irregular-migrant-refugee-arrivals
    -europe-top-one-million-2015-iom.
"ISIS Sleepers 'May Have Arrived as Refugees' in Germany, Ready for Action—Top
    Intel Official." RT, August 11, 2016. Available at: https://www.rt.com/news
    /355587-refugees-isis-sleepers-germany.
"Italian Police, Demonstrators Clash in Protest against Austrian Fence." Reuters,
    May 7, 2016. Available at: http://www.reuters.com/article/us-europe
    -migrants-border-brenner-idUSKCN0XY07Y.
"Joint IOM–UNHCR Statement on President Trump's Refugee Order,"
    International Organization for Migration, January 28, 2017. Available at:
    https://www.unhcr.org/news/news-releases/joint-iom-unhcr-statement
    -president-trumps-refugee-order.
"Libya Migrants: Hundreds Feared Drowned in Mediterranean." BBC, April 15,
    2015. Available at: http://www.bbc.com/news/world-africa-32311358.
"Merkel Says German Multicultural Society Has Failed." BBC, October 17, 2010.
    Available at: http://www.bbc.com/news/world-europe-11559451. See also
    Stephen Evans, "Germany's Charged Immigration Debate," BBC, October
    17, 2010. Available at: http://www.bbc.com/news/world-europe-11532699.
"Metropolitan Hilarion Compares Europe with the Atheistic Soviet Union."
    Pravmir.com, April 19, 2016. Available at: http://www.pravmir.com
    /metropolitan-hilarion-compares-europe-with-the-atheistic-soviet-union.
"Migrant Crisis: Angela Merkel Condemns Closure of Balkan Route." BBC,
    March 10, 2016. Available at: http://www.bbc.com/news/world-europe
    -35772206.
"Migrant Crisis: EU Plans Penalties for Refusing Asylum Seekers." BBC, May 4,
    2016. Available at: http://www.bbc.com/news/world-europe-36202490.
"Migrant Crisis: EU to Begin Seizing Smugglers' Boats." BBC, October 7, 2015.
    Available at: http://www.bbc.com/news/world-europe-34461503.
"Migrant Crisis: Germany Starts Temporary Border Controls." BBC, September 14,
    2015. Available at: http://www.bbc.com/news/world-europe-34239674.
"Migrant Crisis: Greece Recalls Ambassador from Austria amid EU Rifts." BBC,
    February 25, 2016. Available at: http://www.bbc.com/news/world-europe
    -35658776.
"Migrant Crisis: Over One Million Reach Europe by Sea." BBC, December 30, 2015.
    Available at: http://www.bbc.com/news/world-europe-35194360.
"Migrant Crisis: Russia and Syria 'Weaponising' Migration." BBC, March 2, 2016.
    Available at: http://www.bbc.com/news/world-europe-35706238.
"Migrant Crisis: Slovenia Moves to 'Shut Down' Balkans Route." BBC, March 9,
    2016. Available at: http://www.bbc.com/news/world-europe-35760534.
"Migrant Crisis: Thousands of New Reception Places Agreed." BBC, October 26,
    2015. Available at: http://www.bbc.com/news/world-europe-34634214.
"Migrant Crisis: Why EU Deal on Refugees Is Difficult." BBC, September 25, 2015.
    Available at: http://www.bbc.com/news/world-europe-34324096.
"Migrant Smuggling in the EU." Europol Public Information, February, 2016. Available
    at: https://www.europol.europa.eu/publications-events/publications
    /migrant-smuggling-in-eu.

"Migrants Want Sharia Law in Swedish No-Go Zones." RT, September 26, 2016. Available at: https://www.rt.com/op-edge/360675-sweden-migrants -police-zones.

"More Than 150,000 Join Pro-Refugee Protest in Barcelona." France24, February 19, 2017. Available at: http://www.france24.com/en/20170218-over -150000-join-pro-migrant-protest-barcelona.

"NATO Commander: Russia Uses Syrian Refugees as 'Weapon' against West." Deutsche Welle, March 2, 2016. Available at: http://www.dw.com/en /nato-commander-russia-uses-syrian-refugees-as-weapon-against -west/a-19086285.

"Nigel Farage Tells MEPs: You're Not Laughing Now." BBC, June 28, 2016. Available at: http://www.bbc.com/news/uk-politics-eu-referendum-36651406.

"Norway: New Ministry Is Created to Address Influx of Migrants." Associated Press, December 16, 2015. Available at: http://www.nytimes.com /2015/12/17/world/europe/norway-new-ministry-is-created-to -address-influx-of-migrants.html.

"Police Commissioner: Street Patrols Have 'No Special Rights.'" YLE. January 5, 2016. Available at: https://yle.fi/a/3-8573593.

"Police Defend Warning for Solo Women in Northern Sweden." The Local, March 8, 2016. Available at: http://www.thelocal.se/20160308/backlash -begins-after-swedish-women-told-not-to-go-out-alone.

"President Tusk Meets Presidents of Serbia and FYR of Macedonia." European Council, December 16, 2015. The official video summary is available at: https://tvnewsroom.consilium.europa.eu/video/president-tusk-meets -presidents-of-serbia-and-fyr-of-macedonia.

"Prosecutor: Most Cologne New Year's Suspects Are Refugees." Associated Press, February 15, 2016. Available at: https://apnews.com/article /4d8372a4077144cdbd67e4f630d23c47.

"PSOE Implosion a Gift to Rajoy and Podemos." The Spain Report, September 29, 2016. Available at: https://www.thespainreport.com/articles/922 -160929193618-psoe-implosion-a-gift-to-rajoy-and-podemos.

"Rajoy Congratulates New PSOE Administrator as Polls Suggest Socialists Could Be Hit Hard at a Third Election." The Spain Report, October 3, 2016. Available at: https://www.thespainreport.com/articles/935-161003183659-rajoy -congratulates-new-psoe-administrator-as-polls-suggest-socialists-could -be-hit-hard-at-a-third-election.

"Remarks by Peter D. Sutherland, UN Special Representative for International Migration before the United Nations Security Council." United Nations, May 11, 2015.

"Remarks by President Obama at Leader's Summit on Refugees," White House press release, September 20, 2016. Available at: https://obamawhitehouse .archives.gov/the-press-office/2016/09/20/remarks-president-obama -leaders-summit-refugees.

"Riot in Dutch Town over Plan for Asylum-Seeker Centre." Reuters, December 17, 2015. Available at: https://www.reuters.com/article/uk-europe -migrants-netherlands-idUKKBN0TZ2ZD20151217.

"The Role of Social Media in Europe's Migrant Crisis." Channel 4 News, January 15, 2015. Available at: http://www.channel4.com/news/role-of-social-media-in-europe-migrant-crisis.

"The Schengen Area and Cooperation." European Commission. Available at: http://eur-lex.europa.eu/legal-content/EN/TXT/?uri=URISERV%3Al33020. See also "Schengen, Borders and Visas," European Commission. Available at: http://ec.europa.eu/dgs/home-affairs/what-we-do/policies/borders-and-visas/index_en.htm.

"Slovenia Reinstating Controls at Border with Hungary." *The Slovenia Times*, September 17, 2015. Available at: https://sloveniatimes.com/9574/slovenia-reinstating-controls-at-border-with-hungary.

"Soldiers of Odin Are Now Present in These Countries." Speisa.com. Available at: http://speisa.com/modules/articles/index.php/item.2734/soldiers-of-odin-are-now-present-in-these-countries.html.

"Soldiers of Odin's Secret Facebook Group: Weapons, Nazi Symbols and Links to MV Lehti." YLE, March 16, 2016. Available at: https://yle.fi/a/3-8749308.

"Solemn Declaration on European Union." European Council, June 19, 1983. Available at: http://aei.pitt.edu/1788.

"The Strategic Provocation of Bloc Identitaire and an Interview with Fabrice Robert." March 29, 2012. Available at: http://www.bloc-identitaire.com/actualite/2380/the-strategic-provocation-of-bloc-identitaire-an-interview-with-fabrice-robert.

"Swedish PM Going to Saudi Arabia." Sverige Radio, October 20, 2016. Available at: https://sverigesradio.se/sida/artikel.aspx?programid=2054&artikel=6544416.

"Swedish Police Officer Causes Controversy with Facebook Post," *The Local*, February 8, 2017. Available at: http://www.thelocal.se/20170208/swedish-police-officer-causes-controversy-with-facebook-post.

"Swedish Police Probe 'Cover-Up of Migrant Sex Assaults.'" BBC, January 11, 2016. Available at: http://www.bbc.com/news/world-europe-35285086.

"Testing the Limits How Many Refugees Can Germany Handle?" Spiegel Online, July 30, 2015. Available at: http://www.spiegel.de/international/germany/germany-being-tested-by-huge-refugee-influx-a-1045560.html.

"Towards a Sustainable and Fair Common European Asylum System." European Commission Press release, May 4, 2016. Available at: https://ec.europa.eu/commission/presscorner/detail/en/IP_16_1620.

"The Trafficking in Human Beings Financial Business Model." Europol, October 1, 2015. Available at: https://www.europol.europa.eu/content/trafficking-human-beings-financial-business-model.

"Tsipras Reacts to Tusk Statement on Closure of Balkan Route for Migrants." *Kathimerini*, March 10, 2016. Available at: http://www.ekathimerini.com/206840/article/ekathimerini/news/tsipras-reacts-to-tusk-statement-on-closure-of-balkan-route-for-migrants.

"Turkey 2016 Report." European Commission, November 9, 2016. Available at: http://ec.europa.eu/enlargement/pdf/key_documents/2016/20161109_report_turkey.pdf.

"Turkey Threatens to Back Out of EU Migrant Deal over Visas." France 24, April 19, 2016. Available at: http://www.france24.com/en/20160419 -turkey-migrant-deal-eu-visa-free-travel.

"Turkey Threatens to Cancel Greece Migration Deal in Soldiers' Extradition Row." Reuters, January 27, 2017. Available at: http://www.reuters.com/article /us-turkey-security-greece-military-idUSKBN15B0SC.

"Turkish President Threatens to Send Millions of Syrian Refugees to EU." *The Guardian*, February 12, 2016. Available at: https://www.theguardian.com /world/2016/feb/12/turkish-president-threatens-to-send-millions-of -syrian-refugees-to-eu.

"Twitter Storm as Cologne Mayor Suggests Women Stay at 'Arm's Length' from Strangers." *Deutsche Welle*, January 5, 2016. Available at: http://www .dw.com/en/twitter-storm-as-cologne-mayor-suggests-women-stay-at -arms-length-from-strangers/a-18962430.

"The Ultimate Guide to Sweden's Party Leaders." *The Local*, September 11, 2015. Available at: http://www.thelocal.se/20150427/ultimate-guide-to-whos -who-in-swedish-politics-2015.

"UN Summit Seen as 'Game Changer' for Refugee and Migrant Protection." UNHCR press release, September 6, 2016. Available at: http://www.unhcr .org/news/latest/2016/9/57ceb07e4/un-summit-game-changer-refugee -migrant-protection.html.

"The Universal Declaration of Human Rights." United Nations. Available at: https://www.un.org/en/about-us/universal-declaration-of-human -rights.

"Warsaw Declaration on Transatlantic Security," NATO, July 19, 2016. Available at: https://nato.usmission.gov/warsaw-declaration-transatlantic-security.

"Weapons and Explosives Seized in INTERPOL-led Operation." Interpol press release, April 21, 2016. Available at: https://www.interpol.int/en/News-and-Events /News/2016/Weapons-and-explosives-seized-in-INTERPOL-led-operation.

"What Is the SNP's Policy on Immigration?" SNP official website. Available at: http://www.snp.org/pb_what_is_the_snp_s_policy_on_immigration.

"Why Brussels Isn't Boring." *The Economist*, September 12, 2002. Available at: http://www.economist.com/node/1325309.

"World Leaders at UN Summit Adopt 'Bold' Plan to Enhance Protections for Refugees and Migrants." UN News Center, September 19, 2016. Available at: https://www.un.org/development/desa/en/news/population/un -summit-adopts-ny-declaration.html.

"World Leaders' Neglect of Refugees Condemns Millions to Death and Despair." Amnesty International, June 15, 2015. Available at: https://www .amnesty.org/en/latest/news/2015/06/world-leaders-neglect-of-refugees -condemns-millions-to-death-and-despair.

ARTICLES AND BOOKS WITH NAMED AUTHORS

Abbott, Alison. "The Mental-Health Crisis among Migrants." *Nature*, October 10, 2016. Available at: http://www.nature.com/news/the-mental-health -crisis-among-migrants-1.20767.

Adeniji, Ade. "Like Father, Like Son: Alexander Soros' Emerging Social Justice Mission." Insidephilanthropy.com, January 14, 2016. Available at: http://www.insidephilanthropy.com/home/2016/1/14/like-father-like-son-alexander-soros-emerging-social-justice.html.

Alami, Aida. "Protests Erupt in Morocco over Fish Vendor's Death in Garbage Compactor." *New York Times*, October 30, 2016. Available at: http://www.nytimes.com/2016/10/31/world/middleeast/protests-erupt-in-morocco-over-fish-vendors-death-in-garbage-compactor.html?_r=0.

Albertini, Matteo. "Italy and Kosovo Intensify Actions against Another ISIS Linked Group." Balkanalysis.com, December 6, 2015. Available at Central and Eastern European Online Library: https://www.ceeol.com/search/journal-detail?id=1045.

Albertini, Matteo, and Chris Deliso. "Italian Security in the MENA and Balkans, Part 1: Military and Energy Aspects." Balkanalysis.com, July 4, 2016. Available at Central and Eastern European Online Library: https://www.ceeol.com/search/journal-detail?id=1045.

Albertini, Matteo, and Chris Deliso. *The Vatican's Challenges in the Balkans: Bolstering the Catholic Church in 2015 and beyond*, Balkanalysis.com: 2015. Available at: https://www.amazon.com/dp/B00S30A7BQ.

Alderman, Liz. "Greece Arrests Senior Members of Far-Right Party." *New York Times*, September 28, 2013. Available at: http://www.nytimes.com/2013/09/29/world/europe/greece-cracks-down-on-golden-dawn-with-arrests.html.

Aldrich, Richard. "OSS, CIA and European Unity: The American Committee on Untied Europe 1948–60." *Diplomacy & Statecraft*, March 1, 1997. Available at: http://www2.warwick.ac.uk/fac/soc/pais/people/aldrich/publications/oss_cia_united_europe_eec_eu.pdf.

Arapi, Lindita. "Balkan Route to Western Europe for Yugoslavia Guns." *Deutsche Welle*, December 5, 2015. Available at: http://www.dw.com/en/the-balkan-route-to-western-europe-for-yugoslavia-guns/a-18896280.

Arzheimer, Kai. "The AfD's Second Place in Mecklenburg-West Pomerania Illustrates the Challenge Facing Merkel in 2017." London School of Economics Blog, September 5, 2016. Available at: http://blogs.lse.ac.uk/europpblog/2016/09/05/afd-mecklenburg-west-pomerania-merkel.

Avramopoulos, Dimitris. "A European Response to Migration: Showing Solidarity and Sharing Responsibility." European Commission official speech, August 14, 2015. Available at: http://europa.eu/rapid/press-release_SPEECH-15-5498_en.htm.

Baczynska, Gabriela. "Putin Opens Moscow's Largest Mosque, Warns against Extremists." Reuters, September 23, 2015. Available at: http://www.reuters.com/article/us-russia-mosque-idUSKCN0RN1UD20150923.

Bahceli, Yoruk. "Wilders Tells Dutch Parliament Refugee Crisis Is 'Islamic Invasion.'" Reuters, September 10, 2015. Available at: https://www.reuters.com/article/us-europe-migrants-netherlands-idUSKCN0RA0WY20150910.

Banks, Martin. "Guy Verhofstadt Appointed as European Parliament's Brexit Negotiator." *The Parliament Magazine*, September 9, 2016. Available at: https://www.theparliamentmagazine.eu/articles/news/guy-verhofstadt-appointed-european-parliaments-brexit-negotiator.

Barkin, Noah. "Loyal Merkel Ally in Firing Line over Refugee Crisis." Reuters, September 17, 2015. Available at: http://www.reuters.com/article/us-europe-migrants-germany-minister-idUSKCN0RH2BV20150917.

Barkin, Noah, and Jason Hovit. "EU Leaders Agree to post-Brexit 'Road Map,' but Divided on Refugees." *The Globe and Mail*, September 16, 2016.

Barnes, Julian E. "NATO Head Warns against EU Duplicating Capabilities." *Wall Street Journal*, June 28, 2016. Available at: http://www.wsj.com/articles/nato-head-warns-against-eu-duplicating-capabilities-1467128167.

Barr, Caelainn. "'Terrorism Threat Is Waning': Figures Put Europe's Summer of Violence in Context." *The Guardian*, July 28, 2016. Available at: https://www.theguardian.com/world/2016/jul/28/there-is-less-of-a-terrorism-threat-now-experts-put-europes-summer-of-violence-in-context.

Bilefsky, Dan. "More Migrants Storm Fence to Enter Ceuta, Spanish Enclave in Africa." *New York Times*, February 20, 2017. Available at: https://www.nytimes.com/2017/02/20/world/europe/ceuta-morocco-border-migrants.html?_r=0.

Black, Ian. "Far Right Comes Second in Dutch Poll." *The Guardian*, May 16, 2002. Available at: https://www.theguardian.com/world/2002/may/16/eu.thefarright.

Boehler, Patrick, and Sergio Peçanha. "The Global Refugee Crisis, Region by Region." *New York Times*, August 26, 2015. Available at: http://www.nytimes.com/interactive/2015/06/09/world/migrants-global-refugee-crisis-mediterranean-ukraine-syria-rohingya-malaysia-iraq.html?_r=0. See also "Europe Faces Worst Migration Crisis 'since World War II,'" CBS News, September 3, 2015. Available at: http://www.cbsnews.com/videos/europe-faces-worst-migration-crisis-since-world-war-ii-2.

Bogdani, Aleksandra. "Albanian Villages Ponder Local Spike in ISIS Recruits." Balkan Insight, April 25, 2016. Available at: http://www.balkaninsight.com/en/article/albanian-villages-ponder-local-spurt-of-isis-recruits-04-22-2016.

Böll, Sven, and Anne Seith. "Why Germany Wants to See Its US Gold." Spiegel Online, October 30, 2012. Available at: http://www.spiegel.de/international/germany/german-politicians-demand-to-see-gold-in-us-federal-reserve-a-864068.html.

Boros, Tamás. "Populism and Migration: Challenges for the Left." Das Progressive Zentrum, March 15, 2016. Available at: http://www.progressives-zentrum.org/populism-and-migration-challenges-for-the-left/?lang=en.

Botelho, Greg. "7 Alleged ISIS Charge for Plotting Terror in Moscow, St. Petersburg." CNN, February 17, 2016. Available at: http://edition.cnn.com/2016/02/17/europe/russia-isis-charges-terror-plot.

Brady, Kate. "Almost Two Thirds of Germans Believe Islam 'Does Not Belong in Germany,' Poll Finds." *Deutsche Welle*, May 12, 2016. Available at: http://www.dw.com/en/almost-two-thirds-of-germans-believe-islam-does-not-belong-in-germany-poll-finds/a-19251169.

Breeden, Aurelien. "Four in France, Including 16-Year-Old Girl, Are Held in Bomb Plot." *New York Times*, February 10, 2017. Available at: https://www

.nytimes.com/2017/02/10/world/europe/france-arrest-montpellier.
html?_r=0.

Briand, Aristide. *Memorandum on the Organization of a System of Federal European Union*. French Ministry of Foreign Affairs, May 1, 1930. Available at: https://www.wdl.org/en/item/11583. See also D. Weigall and P. Stirk, eds., *The Origins and Development of the European Community*. Leicester University Press, 1992, 11–15.

Buck, Tobias. "Madrid Considers 'Nuclear Option' to Halt Catalan Referendum." *Financial Times*, February 23, 2017. Available at: https://www.ft.com/content/c9bf1ce0-f9b0-11e6-bd4e-68d53499ed71.

Buergin, Rainer, and Arne Delfs. "Germany Clamps Down on Flow of Fighters to Islamic State." Bloomberg, October 17, 2014. Available at: http://www.bloomberg.com/news/articles/2014-10-17/germany-clamps-down-on-flow-of-fighters-to-islamic-state.

Burgess, Michael. *Federalism and European Union: The Building of Europe, 1950–2000*. London: Routledge, 2000. The 1984 treaty itself is available at: http://www.cvce.eu/obj/draft_treaty_establishing_the_european_union_14_february_1984-en-0c1f92e8-db44-4408-b569-c464cc1e73c9.html.

Busemann, Hans-Edzard. "Germany's Schaeuble Wants to Rebalance EU Commission's Role." Reuters, July 30, 2015. Available at: http://www.reuters.com/article/us-europe-commission-germany-idUSKCN0Q41DW20150730.

Canoy, Marcel. "A Cost-Benefit Analysis of Refugees Will Only Fuel Hysteria." Dutchnews.nl, November 9, 2015. Available at: http://www.dutchnews.nl/features/2015/11/a-cost-benefit-analysis-of-refugees-will-only-fuel-hysteria.

Carlstrom, Johan, Niklas Magnusson, and Amanda Billner. "Biggest Opposition Party Ready to Topple Swedish Government." Bloomberg, January 19, 2017. Available at: https://www.bloomberg.com/news/articles/2017-01-19/biggest-opposition-party-ready-to-topple-swedish-government.

Cerulus, Laurens. "The Cost of the Brussels Lockdown: €51.7 Million a Day." Politico, November 30, 2015. Available at: http://www.politico.eu/article/brussels-lockdown-financial-damage-52-million-vrt-terrorism-business.

Chambers, Madeline. "Germany Bans Neo-Nazi Group as Fears of Far-Right Grow." Reuters, March 16, 2016. Available at: http://www.reuters.com/article/us-germany-neonazis-idUSKCN0WI24W.

Chambers, Madeline. "Germany Needs Immigration, Finance Minister Says after Anti-asylum Rallies." Reuters, December 27, 2014. Available at: http://uk.reuters.com/article/uk-german-immigration-schaeuble-idUKKBN0K50AT20141227.

Chase, Jefferson. "Integration Commissioner Plans a Multicultural Germany." *Deutsche Welle*, February 14, 2017. Available at: http://www.dw.com/en/integration-commissioner-plans-a-multicultural-germany/a-37546826.

Chassany, Anne-Sylvaine. "French Right Calls for François Hollande's Impeachment." *Financial Times*, November 7, 2016. Available at: https://www.ft.com/content/caac17c2-a4d6-11e6-8b69-02899e8bd9d1.

Chrisafis, Angelique. "Front National Wins Opening Round in France's Regional Elections." *The Guardian*, December 7, 2015. Available at: https://www.theguardian.com/world/2015/dec/06/front-national-wins-opening-round-in-frances-regional-elections.

Churchill, Winston S. *Never Give In! The Best of Winston Churchill's Speeches*. New York: Hyperion, 2003, 427–430.

Clark, Janine N. *Serbia in the Shadow of Milosevic: The Legacy of Conflict in the Balkans*. London: I. B. Taurus, 2008.

Cowley, Jason. "Emmanuel Macron: A Populist Eruption from the Liberal Centre." *New Statesman*, February 23, 2017. Available at: http://www.newstatesman .com/politics/uk/2017/02/emmanuel-macron-populist-eruption-liberal -centre.

Crawford, Jamie. "U.S. Soldier Helps Foil Plot to Blow Up School." CNN, April 21, 2016. Available at: http://edition.cnn.com/2016/04/21/politics/us -soldier-saves-denmark-school/index.html.

Crouch, David. "The Rise of the Anti-immigrant Sweden Democrats: 'We Don't Feel at Home Any More, and It's Their Fault." *The Guardian*, December 14, 2014. Available at: https://www.theguardian.com/world/2014/dec/14 /sweden-democrats-flex-muscles-anti-immigrant-kristianstad.

Crouch, David. "Sweden Slams Shut Its Open-Door Policy towards Refugees." *The Guardian*, November 24, 2015. Available at: https://www.theguardian.com /world/2015/nov/24/sweden-asylum-seekers-refugees-policy-reversal.

Crouch, David, and Patrick Kingsley. "Danish Parliament Approves Plan to Seize Assets from Refugees." *The Guardian*, January 26, 2016. Available at: https://www.theguardian.com/world/2016/jan/26/danish-parliament -approves-plan-to-seize-assets-from-refugees.

Das, Satjayit. "Marine Le Pen Has More of an Appeal to Left Wing Voters Than Pollsters Would Like to Admit." *The Independent*, February 26, 2017. Available at: http://www.independent.co.uk/voices/marine-le-pen-macron -fillion-french-elections-who-will-win-a7600206.html.

Day, Matthew. "EU Parliament Head Refuses to Apologise over 'Coup' Comment after Polish PM Request." *The Telegraph*, December 15, 2015. Available at: http://www.telegraph.co.uk/news/worldnews/europe/poland /12051752/EU-parliament-head-refuses-to-apologise-over-coup-comment -after-Polish-PM-request.html.

De Borchgrave, Arnaud. "Commentary: Big Gnome: Financial Situation Can't Last." UPI, April 16, 2011. Available at: http://www.upi.com /Commentary-Big-Gnome-Financial-situation-cant-last/17111303816102.

Deacon, Liam. "Belgium Minister: Europe Must Prepare for 5,000 Returning Islamic State Jihadists." Breitbart, November 15, 2016. Available at: http:// www.breitbart.com/london/2016/11/15/belgium-minister-europe-must -prepare-5000-returning-islamic-state-jihadist.

Deacon, Liam. "Green Politico: It's Time to Learn Arabic and Stop Worrying about Migration." Breitbart, October 18, 2016. Available at: http://www .breitbart.com/london/2016/10/18/green-politician-tells-germans-learn -arabic-stop-worrying-mass-migration.

Deliso, Chris. "Europe Gets Religion, Again." *The American Interest*, June 9, 2016. Available at: http://www.the-american-interest.com/2016/06/09/europe -gets-religion-again.

Deliso, Chris. "Exclusive: Germany's BND Investigating Migration Risks and Russian Influence in Greece." Balkanalysis.com, March 7, 2016. Available at Central and Eastern European Online Library: https://www.ceeol.com /search/journal-detail?id=1045.

Deliso, Chris. "Macedonian Migration Policy and the Future of Europe." Balkanalysis.com, December 23, 2015. Available at Central and Eastern European Online Library: https://www.ceeol.com/search/journal -detail?id=1045.

Deliso, Chris. "Mistrust and Different Priorities Vex EU-Macedonian Security Cooperation." Balkanalysis.com, May 27, 2016. Available at Central and Eastern European Online Library: https://www.ceeol.com/search /journal-detail?id=1045.

Deliso, Chris. "Potential for Convergence of Anarchist and Migration Activist Interests in Greece." Balkanalysis.com, December 12, 2015. Available at Central and Eastern European Online Library: https://www.ceeol.com /search/journal-detail?id=1045.

Deliso, Chris. "Safeguarding Europe's Southern Borders: Interview with Klaus Roesler, Director of Operations Division, Frontex." Balkanalysis.com, September 23, 20111. Available at Central and Eastern European Online Library: https://www.ceeol.com/search/journal-detail?id=1045.

Deliso, Chris. "Smuggler and Legends Complicate Fight against Antiquities Theft (Part 1)." Balkanalysis.com, November 16, 2005. Available at Central and Eastern European Online Library: https://www.ceeol.com/search /journal-detail?id=1045.

Deliso, Chris. "Turkey's Developing Role in Africa: Interview with Mehmet Ozkan and Birol Akgun." Balkanalysis.com, January 1, 2011. Available at Central and Eastern European Online Library: https://www.ceeol.com/search /journal-detail?id=1045.

Demmer, Ulrike, and Markus Verbeet. "Das Problem Explodiert." Spiegel Online, May 7, 2007. Available at: http://www.spiegel.de/spiegel/a-481413.html.

Dernbach, Andrea. "Germany suspends Dublin agreement for Syrian refugees," Euractiv, August 26, 2015. Available at: https://www.euractiv.com /section/economy-jobs/news/germany-suspends-dublin-agreement-for -syrian-refugees.

Dettmer, Jamie. "Europe's Migration Crisis a Boon for Organized Crime." VOA News, September 8, 2015. Available at: http://www.voanews.com/a /europe-migration-crisis-a-boon-for-organized-crime/2952482.html.

Diamataris, Antonis. "Greek-American Investor and Power Broker Stelios Zavvos." The National Herald, December 15, 2011.

Donahue, Bill. "Meet the Two Brothers Making Millions Off the Refugee Crisis in Scandinavia." Bloomberg, January 6, 2016. Available at: http://www .bloomberg.com/features/2016-norway-refugee-crisis-profiteers.

Donahue, Patrick. "Merkel Confronts Facebook's Zuckerberg over Policing Hate Posts." Bloomberg, September 26, 2015.

Dülffer, Meike, Carsten Luther, and Zacharias Zacharakis. "Caught in the Web of the Russian Ideologues." Zeit Online, February 7, 2015. Available at: http://www.zeit.de/politik/ausland/2015-02/russia-greece-connection -alexander-dugin-konstantin-malofeev-panos-kammeno.

Durden, Tyler. "Soros Hack Reveals Plot behind Europe's Refugee Crisis; Media Manipulation; Cash for 'Social Justice.'" Zerohedge.com, August 16, 2016. Available at: http://www.zerohedge.com/news/2016-08-16/soros-hack

-reveals-plot-behind-europes-refugee-crisis-media-funding-and-mani
   pulation?page=3.
Dyer, Geoff. "Biden Hints at US Cyber Revenge on Russia." *Financial Times*,
   October 16, 2016. Available at: https://www.ft.com/content/2d9c73fa
   -935b-11e6-a80e-bcd69f323a8b.
Ehrenfeld, Rachel, and Shawn Macomber. "George Soros: The 'God' Who Car-
   ries Around Some Dangerous Demons." *Los Angeles Times*, October 4,
   2004. Available at: http://articles.latimes.com/2004/oct/04/opinion/oe
   -ehrenfeld4.
El Qorchi, Mohammed, Samuel Munzele Maimbo, and John F. Wilson. "Informal
   Funds Transfer Systems: An Analysis of the Informal Hawala System."
   August 18, 2003. A Joint IMF–World Bank paper. Available at: http://
   www.imf.org/external/pubs/nft/op/222.
Elbagir, Nina. "How Children Are Trafficked into Europe." CNN, June 16, 2015.
   Available at: http://edition.cnn.com/2015/06/15/europe/freedom-project
   -misery-trail-children.
Elliott, Larry, and Jill Traynor. "Dutch PM Says Refugee Crisis Could Shut Down
   Europe's Open Borders for Good." *The Guardian*, January 21, 2016. Avail-
   able at: https://www.theguardian.com/world/2016/jan/21/dutch-pm
   -says-refugee-crisis-could-shut-down-europes-open-borders-for-good.
Erk, Jan. "From Vlaams Blok to Vlaams Belang: The Belgian Far-Right Renames
   Itself." *West European Politics*, May 2005, 493–502. Available at: http://
   media.leidenuniv.nl/legacy/Jan%20Erk%20-%20From%20Vlaams%20
   Blok%20to%20Vlaams%20belang.pdf.
Ertl, Michael. "German Refugees Use Advertising to Target Anti-immigration
   YouTube Videos." BBC, April 20, 2016. Available at: http://www.bbc.com
   /news/world-europe-36095659.
Evans-Pritchard, Ambrose. "The European Union Always Was a CIA Project, as
   Brexiteers Discover." *The Telegraph*, April 27, 2016. Available at: http://
   www.telegraph.co.uk/business/2016/04/27/the-european-union-always
   -was-a-cia-project-as-brexiteers-discover.
Faiola, Anthony. "A Global Surge in Refugees Leaves Europe Struggling to Cope."
   Washington Post, April 21, 2015. Available at: https://www.washingtonpost
   .com/world/europe/new-migration-crisis-overwhelms-european-refugee
   -system/2015/04/21/3ab83470-e45c-11e4-ae0f-f8c46aa8c3a4_story.html.
Faiola, Anthony. "Germany Launches Raids Across 60 Cities, Bans Group on
   Suspicion of Islamic State Recruiting." *Washington Post*, November 15,
   2016. Available at: https://www.washingtonpost.com/world/germany
   -launches-raids-across-60-cities-bans-radical-islamist-group/2016
   /11/15/0353ef76-1649-4216-89c6-ef4a916b922e_story.html.
Faiola, Anthony. "Soldiers of Odin: The Far-Right Groups in Finland 'Protecting
   Women' from Asylum Seekers." *The Independent*, February 1, 2016. Available at: http://www.independent.co.uk/news/world/europe/soldiers
   -of-odin-the-far-right-groups-in-finland-protecting-women-from-asylum
   -seekers-a6846341.html.
Freeman, Colin. "Inside Kacanik, Kosovo's Jihadist Capital." *The Telegraph*, August
   23, 2015. Available at: http://www.telegraph.co.uk/news/worldnews
   /europe/kosovo/11818659/Inside-Kacanik-Kosovos-jihadist-capital.html.

Gall, Carlotta. "How Kosovo Was Turned into Fertile Ground for ISIS." *New York Times*, May 21, 2016. Available at: http://www.nytimes.com/2016/05/22/world/europe/how-the-saudis-turned-kosovo-into-fertile-ground-for-isis.html?_r=0.

Gergely, Andras. "Orban Accuses Soros of Stoking Refugee Wave to Weaken Europe." Bloomberg, October 30, 2015. Available at: http://www.bloomberg.com/news/articles/2015-10-30/orban-accuses-soros-of-stoking-refugee-wave-to-weaken-europe.

Gholam Ali Pour, Nima. "Welcome to Sweden, Eldorado for Migrants!" Gatestone Institute, February 18, 2017. Available at: https://www.gatestoneinstitute.org/9901/sweden-migrants-costs.

Giannangeli, Marco. "Britain's Prisons See Huge Rise in EU Convicts at £150 Million Cost to Taxpayer." *Express*, April 10, 2016. Available at: http://www.express.co.uk/news/uk/659620/Britain-prison-huge-rise-EU-convicts-150million-taxpayer.

Gibbs, Samuel. "Facebook Apologises for Psychological Experiments on Users." *The Guardian*, July 2, 2014. Available at: https://www.theguardian.com/technology/2014/jul/02/facebook-apologises-psychological-experiments-on-users.

Goetz, John, and Bob Drogin. "'Curveball' Speaks, and a Reputation as a Disinformation Agent Remains Intact." *Los Angeles Times*, June 18, 2008. Available at: http://www.latimes.com/world/middleeast/la-na-curveball18-2008jun18-story.html.

Goodwin, Matthew, Thomas Raines, and David Cutts. "What Do Europeans Think About Muslim Immigration?" Chatham House, February 7, 2017. Available at: https://www.chathamhouse.org/expert/comment/what-do-europeans-think-about-muslim-immigration.

Goulas, Vasilis. "Τζορτζ Σόρος:Τρίτο στεφάνι στα 83 του, με Ελληνα κουμπάρο" ["George Soros: Third Crown at 83, with a Greek Godfather"]. *Proto Thema*, September 27, 2013. Available at: http://www.protothema.gr/stories/article/314320/tzortz-sorostrito-stefani-sta-83-toume-ellina-koubaro- [in Greek].

Gramsci, Antonio. *Prison Notebooks, Volumes 1, 2 & 3*. Joseph A. Buttigieg, ed. New York: Columbia University Press, 2011.

Hajdari, Una. "Kosovo to Jail Fighters in Foreign Conflicts." Balkan Insight, March 13, 2015. Available at: http://www.balkaninsight.com/en/article/kosovo-law-to-punish-fighting-in-foreign-conflicts.

Hale, Virginia. "Huge Spike in 'New French': Report Suggests Govt Rushing Citizenship before 2017 Election." Breitbart, October 7, 2016. Available at: http://www.breitbart.com/london/2016/10/07/french-govt-rushing-citizenship.

Hale, Virginia. "Switzerland Considers Ban on Koran Distribution." Breitbart, November 17, 2016. Available at: http://www.breitbart.com/london/2016/11/17/swiss-consider-ban-koran-distribution.

Hallinan, Conn. "Socialist Meltdown in Spain; Right-Wing Will Take Government." People's World, October 11, 2016. Available at: http://www.peoplesworld.org/article/socialist-meltdown-in-spain-right-wing-will-take-government.

Hallinan, Conn. "Spain's Turmoil and Europe's Crisis." Foreign Policy in Focus, Octo-
    ber 10, 2016. Available at: http://fpif.org/spains-turmoil-europes-crisis.
Hanson, Victor Davis. "The Death of the Humanities." Hoover Institution, Jan-
    uary 28, 2014. Available at: http://www.hoover.org/research/death
    -humanities.
Hasson, Peter. "Leaked Soros Memo: Refugee Crisis 'New Normal,' Gives 'New
    Opportunities' for Global Influence." The Daily Caller, August 15, 2016.
    Available at: http://dailycaller.com/2016/08/15/leaked-soros-memo-refugee
    -crisis-new-normal-gives-new-opportunities-for-global-influence/#ixzz
    4Q0pkAlDl.
Hasson, Peter. "Revealed: Liberal Money's Longterm Strategy to Control Public
    Opinion and Secure 'Advantageous' Demographics." The Daily Caller,
    November 2, 2016. Available at: http://dailycaller.com/2016/11/02/revealed
    -liberal-moneys-longterm-strategy-to-control-public-opinion-and-secure
    -advantageous-demographics/#ixzz4PzMPM2SY.
Hautala, Laura. "Social Media's Echo Chamber Fuels Migrant Backlash in Sweden
    and Finland." August 27, 2016, CNET.com. Available at: https://www.cnet
    .com/news/refugee-crisis-europe-social-media-impact-on-sweden-finland.
Heiser, James. "Mistaken Identity: The Ideological Confusion of 'Generation
    Identity.'" The New American, April 17, 2015. Available at: http://www
    .thenewamerican.com/reviews/books/item/20682-mistaken-identity
    -the-ideological-confusion-of-generation-identity.
Henderson, Emma. "Swedish Police Banned from Describing Criminals Anymore
    in Case They Sound Racist." The Independent, January 14, 2016. Available
    at: http://www.independent.co.uk/news/world/europe/swedish-police
    -are-not-allowed-to-give-descriptions-of-alleged-criminals-so-as-not-to
    -sound-racist-a6810311.html.
Henley, John. "Anders Breivik's Human Rights Violated in Prison, Norway Court
    Rules." The Guardian, April 20, 2016. Available at: https://www.theguardian
    .com/world/2016/apr/20/anders-behring-breiviks-human-rights-violated
    -in-prison-norway-court-rules.
Henley, Jon, Ian Traynor, and Warren Murray. "Paris Attacks: EU in Emergency
    Talks on Border Crackdown." The Guardian, November 20, 2015. Available
    at: https://www.theguardian.com/world/2015/nov/20/paris-attacks
    -france-launches-un-push-for-unified-declaration-of-war-on-isis.
Henley, Jon, Harriet Grant, Jessica Elgot, Karen McVeigh, and Lisa O'Carroll.
    "Britons Rally to Help People Fleeing War and Terror in Middle East."
    The Guardian, September 3, 2016. Available at: https://www.theguardian
    .com/uk-news/2015/sep/03/britons-rally-to-help-people-fleeing-war
    -and-terror-in-middle-east.
Herriot, Édouard. The United States of Europe. New York: The Viking Press, 1930.
Herszenhorn, David M. "Mattis Says He Expects NATO Allies to Step Up."
    Politico, February 16, 2017. Available at: http://www.politico.eu/article
    /james-mattis-says-he-expects-eu-nato-allies-to-step-up.
Hill, Jenny. "Could This Man Be the Next Chancellor of Germany?" BBC, February
    24, 2017. Available at: http://www.bbc.com/news/world-europe-39067413.
Hill, Jenny. "Migrant Attacks Reveal Dark Side of Germany." BBC, February 22,
    2016. Available at: http://www.bbc.com/news/world-europe-35633318.

Huggler, Justin. "'Cover-Up' over Cologne Sex Assaults Blamed on Migration Sensitivities." *The Telegraph*, January 6, 2015. Available at: http://www.telegraph.co.uk/news/worldnews/europe/germany/12085182/Cover-up-over-Cologne-sex-assaults-blamed-on-migration-sensitivities.html.

Jasper, William F. "Hacked Docs Expose Soros-Obama-UN Refugee Invasion Network." *The New American*, August 19, 2016. Available at: https://thenewamerican.com/us/immigration/hacked-docs-expose-soros-obama-un-refugee-invasion-network.

Jones, Owen. "Spain Can Halt Europe's Slide to the Populist Right." *The Guardian*, November 3, 2016. Available at: https://www.theguardian.com/commentisfree/2016/nov/03/spain-halt-europes-slide-populist-right-podemos.

Jones, Sam. "Pedro Sánchez Insists He Is Still in Charge of Spanish Socialist Party." *The Guardian*, September 29, 2016. Available at: https://www.theguardian.com/world/2016/sep/29/pedro-sanchez-insists-still-charge-spanish-socialist-party.

Kelmendi, Violeta Hyseni. "Kosovo Mobilizes to Fight Religious Radicalism and Terrorism." *Osservatorio Balcani e Caucaso*, August 25, 2014. Available at: http://www.balcanicaucaso.org/eng/Areas/Kosovo/Kosovo-mobilizes-to-fight-religious-radicalism-and-terrorism-155153.

Kennelly, Larissa. "Brussels Jewish Museum Reopens: 'An End to Innocence.'" BBC, September 14, 2014. Available at: http://www.bbc.com/news/blogs-eu-29164962.

Kern, Soeren. "European Union Declares War on Internet Free Speech." Gatestone Institute, June 3, 2016. Available at: https://www.gatestoneinstitute.org/8189/social-media-censorship.

Kern, Soeren. "Germans Stock Up on Weapons for Self-Defense." Gatestone Institute, December 21, 2015. Available at: https://www.gatestoneinstitute.org/7088/germany-weapons.

Kern, Soeren. "Muslim Voters Change Europe." Gatestone Institute, May 17, 2012. Available at: https://www.gatestoneinstitute.org/3064/muslim-voters-europe.

Khetani, Sanya. "93 Percent of French Muslims Voted for Hollande." Business Insider, May 8, 2012. Available at: http://www.businessinsider.com/muslims-hollande-france-sarkozy-2012-5?IR=T.

Kiesling, John Brady. *Greek Urban Warriors: Resistance & Terrorism, 1967–2014*. Athens: Lycabettus Press, 2014, 352.

Kingsley, Patrick. "Balkan Countries Shut Borders as Attention Turns to New Refugee Routes." *The Guardian*, March 9, 2016. Available at: https://www.theguardian.com/world/2016/mar/09/balkans-refugee-route-closed-say-european-leaders.

Kinzer, Stephen. "German Plan for Phased Union of Europe Provokes Controversy." *New York Times*, September 4, 1994. Available at: http://www.nytimes.com/1994/09/04/world/german-plan-for-phased-union-of-europe-provokes-controversy.html.

Kirchgaessner, Stephanie. "Top Official in Italy's M5S Increases Call for Referendum on Euro." *The Guardian*, December 8, 2016. Available at: https://www.theguardian.com/world/2016/dec/08/top-official-in-italys-m5s-increases-calls-for-referendum-on-euro.

Klein, Joseph. "UN Officials Mocks National Sovereignty." FrontPageMag
    .com, October 28, 2015. Available at: http://www.frontpagemag.com
    /fpm/260584/un-officials-mock-national-sovereignty-joseph-klein.
Knight, Ben. "Berlin Promotes AfD Member to Top Prosecutor." *Deutsche
    Welle*, April 25, 2016. Available at: http://www.dw.com/en/berlin
    -promotes-afd-member-to-top-prosecutor/a-19213936.
Kolbert, Elizabeth. "Beyond Tolerance." *The New Yorker*, September 9, 2002. Avail-
    able at: http://www.newyorker.com/magazine/2002/09/09/beyond
    -tolerance.
Kottasova, Ivana. "George Soros Is Investing $500 Million to Help Refugees." CNN,
    September 20, 2016. Available at: http://money.cnn.com/2016/09/20
    /technology/soros-investment-migrants-refugees.
Kurani, Edison. "Albania Has a High Number of Asylum Seekers, UNHCR Report
    Says." Balkaneu.com, June 21, 2016. Available at http://www.balkaneu
    .com/albanian-high-number-asylum-seekers-unhcr-report.
Landler, Mark. "Germans Weigh Civil Rights and Public Safety." *New York Times*,
    July 13, 2007. Available at: http://www.nytimes.com/2007/07/13/world
    /europe/13germany.html.
LeClerc, Jean-Marc. "Manuel Valls veut doubler le nombre de naturaliza-
    tions." *Le Figaro*, August 29, 2013. Available at: http://www.lefigaro.fr
    /actualite-france/2013/08/28/01016-20130828ARTFIG00452-manuel
    -valls-veut-plus-de-naturalisations.php.
Lee, Sarah. "UN Secretary General: Islamophobia Leads to Terrorism." The
    Blaze, February 12, 2017. Available at: http://www.theblaze.com
    /news/2017/02/12/un-secretary-general-islamophobia-leads-to-terrorism.
Lehne, Stefan. "How the Refugee Crisis Will Reshape the EU." Carnegie Europe,
    February 4, 2016. Available at: http://carnegieeurope.eu/2016/02/04/how
    -refugee-crisis-will-reshape-eu-pub-62650.
Leposhtica, Labinot. "Kosovo Jails Hard-line Imam for 10 Years." Balkan Insight,
    May 20, 2016. Available at: http://www.balkaninsight.com/en/article
    /kosovo-hard-line-imam-sentenced-to-10-years-in-prison-05-20-2016.
Lewin, Tamar. "As Interest Fades in the Humanities, Colleges Worry." *New
    York Times*, October 30, 2013. Available at: http://www.nytimes.com
    /2013/10/31/education/as-interest-fades-in-the-humanities-colleges
    -worry.html?ref=education.
Lisinski, Stefan, and Lasse Wierup. "Nazistledare gripen för vapenbrott." *Dagens
    Nyheter*, November 25, 2003. Available at: http://www.dn.se/nyheter
    /sverige/nazistledare-gripen-for-vapenbrott/.
López, Alejandro. "Huge Demonstration in Barcelona in Defence of Refugees and
    Open Borders." World Socialist Web Site, February 20, 2017. Available at:
    https://www.wsws.org/en/articles/2017/02/20/barc-f20.html.
Luttwak, Edward N. "Doing Counterterrorism Right." Nikkei Asia Review,
    November 30, 2015. Available at: http://asia.nikkei.com/Viewpoints
    /Viewpoints/Doing-counterterrorism-right.
Luxton, Emma. "Is Terrorism in Europe at a Historical High?" World Eco-
    nomic Forum, March 24, 2016. Available at: https://www.weforum.org
    /agenda/2016/03/terrorism-in-europe-at-historical-high.

Mahony, Honor. "Flanders Tells Moroccan Migrants How to Behave." EU Observer, May 15, 2012. Available at: https://euobserver.com/news/116274.

Malm, Sara. "Sweden: Home of IKEA, Meatballs, ABBA and . . . Racism? How the Swedish Right-Wing Went from a Joke to a Big Political Player in Just Seven Years." *The Daily Mail*, January 6, 2016. Available at: http://www.dailymail.co.uk/news/article-3349890/Sweden-Home-IKEA-meatballs--ABBA-racism-Swedish-right-wing-went-joke-big-political-player-just-seven-years.html.

Manly, Ronan. "Update on Bundesbank Gold Repatriation 2015." Bullionstar.com, January 27, 2016. Available at: https://www.bullionstar.com/blogs/ronan-manly/update-on-bundesbank-gold-repatriation.

Markham, Felix. *Napoleon*. New York: Penguin Books USA Inc., 1966, 257.

Marlowe, Lara. "Calais Residents Protest over 'Economic Catastrophe' of Camp." *The Irish Times*, March 8, 2016. Available at: http://www.irishtimes.com/news/world/europe/calais-residents-protest-over-economic-catastrophe-of-camp-1.2563492.

Martin, Patrick. "History of Lone-Wolf Vehicle Attacks Suggests Risk of Emulation Is Very Real." *The Globe and Mail*, July 15, 2016. Available at: http://www.theglobeandmail.com/news/world/history-of-lone-wolf-vehicle-attacks-suggests-risk-of-emulation-is-very-real/article30933070.

Martinson, Jane. "OK, He Chairs BP, but Really He Wants to Run Europe." *The Guardian*, January 19, 2007. Available at: https://www.theguardian.com/business/2007/jan/19/oilandpetrol.news.

Marusic, Sinisa Jakov. "Macedonia Arrests Nine ISIS Suspects." Balkan Insight, August 7, 2015. Available at: http://www.balkaninsight.com/en/article/macedonia-arrests-nine-isis-suspects-08-07-2015.

Marusic, Sinisa Jakov. "Macedonian Police Targets ISIS Suspects." Balkan Insight, August 6, 2015. Available at: http://www.balkaninsight.com/en/article/macedonia-launches-anti-terror-busts-08-06-2015.

McKirdy, Euan. "UNHCR Report: More Displaced Now Than after WWII." CNN, June 20, 2016. Available at: http://edition.cnn.com/2016/06/20/world/unhcr-displaced-peoples-report. The report is referring to the official report of the UNHCR released contemporaneously. "Global Forced Displacement Hits Record High." UNHCR communication, June 20, 2016. Available at: http://www.unhcr.org/news/latest/2016/6/5763b65a4/global-forced-displacement-hits-record-high.html.

Mejdini, Fatjona. "Albanian Police Arrest 'Terror Attack' Suspect." Balkan Insight, August 16, 2016. Available at: http://www.balkaninsight.com/en/article/albania-police-charge-a-man-from-kosovo-with-terrorism-08-18-2016.

Melander, Ingrid. "'Crumbling' French Left Battles over Who Should Run in 2017 Election." Reuters, October 30, 2016. Available at: https://www.reuters.com/article/france-politics-socialists-idINKBN12U0SP.

Merelli, Annalisa. "The Center of Sicily's Biggest City Was Emptied by the Mafia. Now It's Being Reclaimed by Migrants." Quartz, June 21, 2016. Available at: http://qz.com/704320/migrants-are-bringing-back-to-life-palermos-historical-center-which-the-mafia-had-ravaged.

Michaletos, Ioannis. "In First Nine Months of 2016, Urban Violence and Crime Rise in Greece." Balkanalysis.com, October 11, 2016. Available at Central and Eastern European Online Library: https://www.ceeol.com/search/journal-detail?id=1045.

Michaletos, Ioannis. "Left-wing Terrorist Attacks and Organized Violence in Greece, 2008–2012." Balkanalysis.com, February 14, 2013. Available at Central and Eastern European Online Library: https://www.ceeol.com /search/journal-detail?id=1045.

Michaletos, Ioannis, and Chris Deliso. "The Hellenic Coast Guard: Greece's First Line of Maritime Defense." Balkanalysis.com, June 8, 2015. Available at Central and Eastern European Online Library: https://www.ceeol.com /search/journal-detail?id=1045.

Miller, Nick. "French Elections: The Hollywood Candidate, Emmanuel Macron, Is Gaining Ground." *Sydney Morning Herald*, February 11, 2017. Available at: http://www.smh.com.au/world/french-elections-the-hollywood -candidate-emmanuel-macron-is-gaining-ground-20170207-gu7v5a.html.

Mitrovic, Milos. "Migrants in Serbia Spend 6 Million EUR per Day." Balkaneu. com, August 11, 2015. Available at: http://www.balkaneu.com/migrants -serbia-spend-6-million-eur-day.

Montgomery, Jack. "Merkel: Europe Must Take More Migrants, Islam Is Not the Source of Terrorism." Breitbart, February 18, 2017. Available at: http:// www.breitbart.com/london/2017/02/18/merkel-europe-must-take -more-migrants-and-islam-is-not-the-cause-of-terrorism.

Neag, Maria-Antoaneta. "'The EU and Turkey Need Each Other': Interview with Ambassador Selim Yenel." Balkanalysis.com, July 20, 2016. Available at Central and Eastern European Online Library: https://www.ceeol.com /search/journal-detail?id=1045.

Neo, Hui Min. "German Police Arrest Algerian Suspects over 'Berlin IS Plot.'" AFP, February 4, 2016.

Newton, Jannifer. "'A Society That Can't Defend Its Children Has No Tomorrow': Putin Condemns Europe's Handling of Migrants and Says the Child Rape in Austria shows 'a Dilution of National Values.'" *The Daily Mail*, November 3, 2016. Available at: http://www.dailymail.co.uk/news /article-3900748/A-society-t-defend-children-no-tomorrow-Putin -condemns-Europe-s-handling-migrants-says-child-rape-Austria-shows -dilution-national-values.html.

Nichols, Dick. "After Congress Win, Podemos's Iglesias Promises 'Return to the Streets.'" GreenLeft, February 24, 2017. Available at: https:// www.greenleft.org.au/content/after-congress-win-podemoss-iglesias -promises-return-streets.

Olick, Jeffrey K. "The Guilt of Nations?" *Ethics and International Affairs*. September 2003, 17.

Olick, Jeffrey K., and Andrew J. Perrin. *Guilt and Defense*. Harvard University Press, 2010, 24–25.

Oliphante, Vickiie. "Mafia V Migrants: Mafia Bosses Declare War after Immigration Levels in Sicily Soar," *Express*, April 23, 2016. Available at: http://www.express.co.uk/news/world/663657/Mafia-bosses-declare -war-man-shot-as-immigration-levels-in-Sicily-rise.

Oliveira, Ivo. "National Front Seeks Russian Cash for Election Fight." *Politico*, February 19, 2016. Available at: http://www.politico.eu/article/le

-pen-russia-crimea-putin-money-bank-national-front-seeks-russian
-cash-for-election-fight.

Osborne, Samuel. "Geert Wilders: Far-right Dutch PM Frontrunner Says 'Islam and Freedom Are Not Compatible.'" *The Independent*, February 22, 2017. Available at: http://www.independent.co.uk/news/world/europe/geert-wilders-dutch-pm-frontrunner-far-right-islamophobic-freedom-a7593466.html.

Palazzo, Chiara. "Norway Offers to Pay Asylum Seekers £1000 Bonus to Leave the Country." *The Telegraph*, April 26, 2016. Available at: http://www.telegraph.co.uk/news/2016/04/26/norway-to-pay-asylum-seekers-extra-money-to-leave.

Papadimitriou, Yanis. "Greece's Left-Wing Syriza Party in the Midst of Change." *Deutsche Welle*, October 13, 2016. Available at: http://www.dw.com/en/greeces-left-wing-syriza-party-in-the-midst-of-change/a-36035991.

Parfitt, Tom. "Drug Scandal: Top MP Forced to Resign after Being 'Caught with Crystal Meth.'" *Express*, March 4, 2016. Available at: http://ww.express.co.uk/news/world/649715/Volker-Beck-crystal-meth-Germany-Green-Party-politics-drugs.

Peel, Quentin. "Merkel Warns on Cost of Welfare." *Financial Times*, December 16, 2012. Available at: https://www.ft.com/content/8cc0f584-45fa-11e2-b7ba-00144feabdc0.

Petzinger, Jill, and Jess Smee. "Greece's Planned Border Fence Is 'an Act of Despair.'" Spiegel Online, January 6, 2011. Available at: http://www.spiegel.de/international/europe/the-world-from-berlin-greece-s-planned-border-fence-is-an-act-of-despair-a-738118.html.

Phillips, David L. "Research Paper: ISIS–Turkey Links." *Huffington Post*, November 9, 2014. Available at: http://www.huffingtonpost.com/david-l-phillips/research-paper-isis-turke_b_6128950.html.

Polakow-Suransky, Sasha. "The Ruthlessly Effective Rebranding of Europe's New Far Right." *The Guardian*, November 1, 2016. Available at: https://www.theguardian.com/world/2016/nov/01/the-ruthlessly-effective-rebranding-of-europes-new-far-right.

Pollard, John F. *Money and the Rise of the Modern Papacy: Financing the Vatican, 1850–1950*. New York: Cambridge University Press, 2005, 39.

Pope Francis. "Message of His Holiness Pope Francis on the Occasion of the World Meetings of Popular Movements in Modesto (California)." The Vatican, February 10, 2017. Available at: http://w2.vatican.va/content/francesco/en/messages/pont-messages/2017/documents/papa-francesco_20170210_movimenti-popolari-modesto.html.

Posaner, Joshua. "German Intelligence Warns of ISIL 'Hit Squads' Among Refugees." *Politico*, August 11, 2016. Available at: http://www.politico.eu/article/german-intelligence-warns-of-is-hit-squads-among-refugees.

Proctor, Keith. "Europe's Migrant Crisis: Defense Contractors Are Poised to Win Big." *Fortune*, September 10, 2015. Available at: http://fortune.com/2015/09/10/europe-migrant-crisis-defense-contractors.

Rippon, Haydn. "Occupy Le Mosque: France's New Radical Nativism." The Conversation via Boston University, November 2, 2012.

Available at: https://theconversation.com/occupy-le-mosque-frances-new-radical-nativism-10368.

Robinson, Lucy Pasha. "Marine Le Pen Backs Vladimir Putin and Denies Invasion of Crimea." *The Independent*, February 7, 2017. Available at: http://www.independent.co.uk/news/world/europe/marine-le-pen-front-national-russian-kremlin-putin-invasion-annexation-crimea-ukraine-2014-a7566196.html.

Robertson, Nic, Antonia Mortensen, and Wojciech Treszczynski. "Poland's Militias 'Ready for Anything' Amid Rising Tensions with Russia." CNN, October 27, 2016. Available at: http://edition.cnn.com/2016/10/27/europe/poland-militias-russia-tension.

Rose-Greenland, Fiona. "How Much Money Has ISIS Made Selling Antiquities? More Than Enough to Fund Its Attacks." *Washington Post*, June 3, 2016. Available at: https://www.washingtonpost.com/posteverything/wp/2016/06/03/how-much-money-has-isis-made-selling-antiquities-more-than-enough-to-fund-its-attacks/?utm_term=.f892c73cf65e.

Rothman, Lily, and Liz Ronk. "This Is What Europe's Last Major Refugee Crisis Looked Like." *Time*, September 11, 2015. Available at: http://time.com/4029800/world-war-ii-refugee-photos-migrant-crisis.

Rubin, Alissa J. "France's Far-Right National Front Gains in Regional Elections." *New York Times*, December 6, 2015. Available at: http://www.nytimes.com/2015/12/07/world/europe/frances-far-right-national-front-gains-in-regional-elections.html.

Salter, Arthur. *Allied Shipping Control: An Experiment in International Administration.* Oxford: Clarendon Press, 1921.

Samuel, Henry. "'Religious Tensions' Spark Gunfight in French Migrant Camp." *The Telegraph*, January 27, 2016.

Samuel, Jonathan. "Sky Finds 'Handbook' for EU-Bound Migrants." Sky News, September 13, 2015. Available at: http://news.sky.com/story/sky-finds-handbook-for-eu-bound-migrants-10346437.

Sanandaji, Tino. "Islamists Caused Overwhelming Majority of Terrorist Deaths in Europe during Last Decade." February 20, 2011. Available at: http://tino.us/2011/02/islamists-caused-overwhelming-majority-of-terrorist-deaths-in-europe-during-last-decade. This analysis critiqued claims made in Europol's official report, "EU Terrorism Situation and Trend Report TE-SAT, 2007–2009."

Sauerbrey, Anna. "Will Germany Succumb to Hate?" *New York Times*, September 2, 2015. Available at: http://www.nytimes.com/2015/09/03/opinion/will-germany-succumb-to-hate.html.

Saul, Heather. "Refugee Crisis: Sweden's Deputy Prime Minister Asa Romson Cries as She Announces Asylum Policy U-turn." *The Independent*, November 26, 2015. Available at: http://www.independent.co.uk/news/people/refugee-crisis-sweden-deputy-prime-minister-cries-as-she-announces-u-turn-on-asylum-policy-a6749531.html.

Schmidt, Michael S., and Sewell Chan. "NATO Will Send Ships to Aegean Sea to Deter Human Trafficking." *New York Times*, February 11, 2016. Available at:

http://www.nytimes.com/2016/02/12/world/europe/nato-aegean-migrant
-crisis.html.

Seher, Dietmar. "In Problemvierteln fürchtet sich sogar die Polizei." WAZ, August
1, 2011.

Sguaitamatti, Elisa, and Chris Deliso. "New Information Surfaces on
Killed Terrorist Anis Amri, as Italian Investigation Continues."
Balkanalysis.com, December 24, 2016. Available at Central and Eastern
European Online Library: https://www.ceeol.com/search/journal
-detail?id=1045.

Shah, Agam. "China's Secretive Mega Chip Powers the World's Fastest Computer." PCWorld, June 20, 2016. Available at: http://www.pcworld.com
/article/3086107/hardware/chinas-secretive-super-fast-chip-powers-the
-worlds-fastest-computer.html.

Shakespeare, Sebastian. "Revealed—David Miliband Is Paid a Staggering £425,000
as Boss of New York-Based Refugee Charity." The Daily Mail, December
31, 2015. Available at: http://www.dailymail.co.uk/news/article-3379572
/SEBASTIAN-SHAKESPEARE-Revealed-David-Miliband-paid
-staggering-425-000-boss-New-York-based-refugee-charity.html.

Shakespeare, Sebastian. "The Questions Peter Sutherland, the Globe's Grandee,
Was NOT Asked by the Lords EU Sub-committee." The Daily Mail, June 27,
2012. Available at: http://www.dailymail.co.uk/debate/article-2165584
/Peter-Sutherland-globes-grandee.html#ixzz4Q4pMt800.

Shtuni, Adrian. "Black Market Supply and Demand: The Flow of Illegal Weapons
from the Western Balkans to Islamist Militants in Western Europe." Jane's
Terrorism and Insurgency, March 25, 2016.

Shtuni, Adrian. "Ethnic Albanian Foreign Fighters in Iraq and Syria." Combating
Terrorism Center at West Point. Available at: https://ctc.westpoint.edu
/ethnic-albanian-foreign-fighters-in-iraq-and-syria.

Siebert, Thomas. "Der Handel mit syrischen Pässen blüht." Der Tagesspiegel, September 8, 2015. Available at: http://www.tagesspiegel.de/politik/fluechtlinge
-der-handel-mit-syrischen-paessen-blueht/12290592.html.

Simons, Jake Wallis. "Finland-Based Soldiers of Odin Are Neo-Nazi White Supremacist Led Vigilantes." The Daily Mail, February 4, 2016. Available at: http://
www.dailymail.co.uk/news/article-3426685/Nazi-daggers-SS-hats
-hangman-s-noose-night-patrol-Soldiers-Odin-neo-Nazi-led-vigilantes
-vowing-Europe-s-women-safe-migrant-sex-attacks.html.

Smale, Alison. "Germany's Embrace of Migrants Spawns Rise of Far-Right
Leader." New York Times, March 9, 2016. Available at: http://www.nytimes
.com/2016/03/10/world/europe/germanys-embrace-of-migrants
-spawns-rise-of-far-right-leader.html.

Smith-Spark, Laura, and Greg Botelho. "Suspect Detained after Beheading, Explosion in France." CNN, June 26, 2015. Available at: http://edition.cnn.com
/2015/06/26/europe/france-attack/index.html.

Somaskanda, Sumi. "Can This Man Save the Europe-Turkey Migrant Deal?"
Foreign Policy, September 9, 2016. Available at: http://foreignpolicy.com

/2016/09/09/can-this-man-save-the-europe-turkey-migrant-deal-gerald
-knaus-esi-refugees/.

Soros, George. "Rebuilding the Asylum System," Project Syndicate, September
26, 2015. Available at: https://www.georgesoros.com/essays/rebuilding
-the-asylum-system.

Soros, George. "The Euro Will Face Bigger Tests Than Greece," *Financial
Times*, February 21, 2010. Available at: https://www.ft.com/content
/88790e8e-1f16-11df-9584-00144feab49a.

Soubrouillard, Régis. "Hollande inverse la courbe des naturalizations." Causeur,
October 6, 2016. Available at: http://www.causeur.fr/hollande-naturalisations
-manuel-valls-40398.html.

Spinelli, Altiero. *Manifesto of Ventotene*. N.p., 1941. Available at: http://www.cvce
.eu/obj/the_manifesto_of_ventotene_1941-en-316aa96c-e7ff-4b9e-b43a
-958e96afbecc.html.

Squires, Nick, and Peter Foster. "Renzi, Hollande and Merkel Head to Birthplace
of European Project to Map Out Post-Brexit Future." *The Telegraph*, August
22, 2016. Available at: http://www.telegraph.co.uk/news/2016/08/22
/renzi-hollande-and-merkel-head-to-birthplace-of-european-project.

Steakley, Lia. "How Social Media Can Affect Your Mood." Stanford Medicine,
October 3, 2014. Available at: http://scopeblog.stanford.edu/2014/10/03
/how-social-media-can-affect-your-mood/.

Sterling, Toby. "Dutch Politician Wilders Will Face Trial on Charges of Inciting
Racial Hatred." Reuters, October 14, 2016. Available at: http://www.reuters
.com/article/us-netherlands-wilders-discrimination-idUSKBN12E0IB.

Stromme, Lizzie. "Swedes Rally to Defend Officer Facing Probe for 'Migrants to
Blame for Serious Crime' Rant." *The Local*, February 10, 2017. Available
at: http://www.express.co.uk/news/world/765613/Swedes-rally-defend
-police-probe-migrants-blame-for-serious-crime-rant.

Sutherland, Peter. "Migration's Private-Sector Problem-Solvers." Project Syndicate, September 12, 2016. Available at: https://www.project-syndicate
.org/commentary/private-sector-migration-solutions-by-peter
-sutherland-2016-09.

Sutherland, Peter, and Cecilia Malmstrom. "Europe's Immigration Challenge."
Project Syndicate, July 20, 2012. Available at: https://www.project
-syndicate.org/commentary/europe-s-immigration-challenge?barrier=true.

Sykes, Selina. "Four Teenage Girls Arrested for Planning Bataclan-Style Attack
on a Concert Hall in Paris." *Express*, March 11, 2016. Available at: http://
www.express.co.uk/news/world/651953/Paris-terror-attacks-Bataclan.

Szymanowski, Théodore de Korwin. *L'avenir économique, social et politique en
Europe*. Paris: Ed. H. Marot, 1888. Available at: http://www.msz.gov.pl/pl
/ministerstwo/publikacje/biblioteka_jednosci_europejskiej/przyszlosc
_europy_w_zakresie_gospodarczym__spolecznym_i_politycznym__l
_avenir_economique__social___politique_en_europe.

Taylor, Paul. "Twenty Years on, Schaeuble Pleads again for Core Europe." Reuters,
September 1, 2014. Available at: https://www.reuters.com/article/us-eu
-schaeuble-idUSKBN0GW1XR20140901.

Thorpe, Nick. "Migrant Crisis: Hungary Denies Fuelling Intolerance in Media."
BBC, December 22, 2015. Available at: http://www.bbc.com/news/world
-europe-35162515.

Tomlinson, Chris. "80 Percent of Swedish Police Consider Quitting over Migrant Danger." Breitbart, September 20, 2016. Available at: http://www.breitbart.com/london/2016/09/20/80-per-cent-swedish-police-consider-quitting-due-danger.

Tomlinson, Chris. "Left-Wing Extremists Leave 'Identitarian' Populist Activist in Coma.'" Breitbart, June 14, 2016. Available at: http://www.breitbart.com/london/2016/06/14/identitarian-put-coma-left-extremists.

Torry, Harriet. "Germany, France Urge EU to Clamp Down on Terrorist Financing." Wall Street Journal, March 31, 2015. Available at: http://www.wsj.com/articles/germany-france-urge-eu-to-clamp-down-on-terrorist-financing-1427814952.

Townsend, Mark. "Child Migrants in Sicily Must Overcome One Last Obstacle—The Mafia." The Observer, July 24, 2016. Available at: https://www.theguardian.com/world/2016/jul/23/child-migrants-in-sicily-must-overcome-mafia-obstacle.

Troianovski, Anton. "Merkel Says Germany Won't Stop Accepting Refugees, Muslims." Wall Street Journal, September 19, 2016. Available at: http://www.wsj.com/articles/merkel-says-germany-wont-stop-accepting-refugees-muslims-1474288469.

Troianovski, Anton, Manuela Mesco, and Simon Clark. "The Growth of Refugee Inc." Wall Street Journal, September 14, 2015. Available at: http://www.wsj.com/articles/in-european-refugee-crisis-an-industry-evolves-1442252165.

Valbray, Adrian. "Hamon's Victory Confirms 'Corbynisation' of French Left," EurActiv, January 30, 2017. Available at: http://www.euractiv.com/section/elections/news/hamons-victory-confirms-corbynisation-of-french-left.

Van Grasstek, Craig. The History and Future of the World Trade Organization. Geneva: World Trade Organization, 2013, 70.

Verhofstadt, Guy. "Face à la situation des migrants, l'UE a besoin de leadership, pas d'ériger des murs." Huffington Post (France), August 20, 2015. Available at: http://www.huffingtonpost.fr/guy-verhofstadt/politique-immigration-union-europeenne_b_8007656.html.

Vick, Karl, and Simon Shuster. "Chancellor of the Free World." Time, December 9, 2015. Available at: http://time.com/time-person-of-the-year-2015-angela-merkel.

Vlasic, Mark. "Mark Vlasic: Illicit Trade in Looted Antiquities Helps Finance ISIS Terror Network." National Post, September 15, 2014. Available at: https://nationalpost.com/opinion/mark-vlasic-illicit-trade-in-looted-antiquities-helps-finance-isis-terror-network.

Walker, Peter. "Germany's Anti-Migrant AfD Party Slumps to Worst Poll Results in Seven Months." The Independent, February 23, 2017. Available at: http://www.independent.co.uk/news/world/europe/germany-afd-party-polls-frauke-petry-anti-immigration-latest-a7595221.html.

Warrick, Joby. "In Albania, Concerns over the Islamic State's Emergence." Washington Post, June 11, 2016.

Waterfield, Bruno. "Greece's Defence Minister Threatens to Send Migrants Including Jihadists to Western Europe." The Telegraph, March 9, 2015. Available at: http://www.telegraph.co.uk/news/worldnews/islamic-state/11459675

/Greeces-defence-minister-threatens-to-send-migrants-including-jihadists
-to-Western-Europe.html.

Webb, Nick. "Pope Drafts in Peter Sutherland after Vatican Bank Hit by Scandals."
Irish Independent, June 8, 2014. Available at: http://www.independent.ie
/business/irish/pope-drafts-in-peter-sutherland-after-vatican-bank-hit
-by-scandals-30336625.html.

West, Karl. "Man Who Broke the Bank of England, George Soros, 'at Centre of
Hedge Funds Plot to Cash in on Fall of the Euro.'" *The Daily Mail*, February 27, 2010. Available at: http://www.dailymail.co.uk/news/article
-1253791/Is-man-broke-Bank-England-George-Soros-centre-hedge-funds
-betting-crisis-hit-euro.html#ixzz4Q1FZqgzv.

Wheeler, Brian. "EU Should 'Undermine National Homogeneity' Says UN Migration Chief." BBC, June 21, 2012. Available at: http://www.bbc.com/news
/uk-politics-18519395.

Wike, Richard, Bruce Stokes, and Katie Simmons. "Europeans Fear Wave of
Refugees Will Mean More Terrorism, Fewer Jobs." Pew Global, July
11, 2016. Available at: http://www.pewglobal.org/2016/07/11/europeans
-fear-wave-of-refugees-will-mean-more-terrorism-fewer-jobs.

Wilford, Hugh. *The CIA, the British Left and the Cold War: Calling the Tune?* London:
Routledge, 2003, 46–47.

Williams, Thomas D. "Italy Deports Jihadist Suspected of Plotting Attack on
Leaning Tower of Pisa." Breitbart, August 13, 2016. Available at: http://
www.breitbart.com/national-security/2016/08/13/italy-deports-jihadist
-suspected-plotting-attack-leaning-tower-pisa.

Williams, Thomas D. "Pope Francis, Lutheran Chief, Urge Christians to 'Defend
the Rights of Refugees.'" Breitbart, November 1, 2016. Available at:
http://www.breitbart.com/london/2016/11/01/pope-francis-lutheran
-chief-urge-christians-defend-rights-refugees.

Willinger, Markus. *Generation Identity: A Declaration of War against the '68er*. London:
Arktos, 2013.

Willis, Henry Parker. *A History of the Latin Monetary Union*. Chicago: University of
Chicago Press, 1901, 266.

Zavvos, Stelios. "Migration Flows, Europe and Greece." Kathimerini, February 14,
2016. Available at: https://www.solidaritynow.org/en/migration-flows
-europe-greece.

Zuvela, Matt. "German Police Arrest Three Syrian Refugees Suspected of 'IS' Connections." *Deutsche Welle*, September 13, 2016. Available at: http://www
.dw.com/en/german-police-arrest-three-syrian-refugees-suspected-of-is
-connections/a-19546768.

Index

About the Author

CHRISTOPHER DELISO is an American writer, analyst and historian. An Oxford-trained Byzantinist, he has reported from Southeast Europe since 2002, covering Balkan geopolitics for The Economist Intelligence Unit from 2004–17 and for the Jane's Group from 2008–10 and 2019–20, while also consulting for political risk and due diligence firms in the UK and EU. He has spoken often for US government agencies such as the INR, DIA and NSC, as well as at international conferences and European defense ministries on regional security issues. He has traveled widely in Europe, the Caucasus and Eastern Mediterranean while authoring books in fields ranging from history and security to travel and current events. He is the author and co-author of numerous articles for major media, as well as books, including *The History of Croatia and Slovenia* (Greenwood, 2020). Read more about his work at www.christopherdeliso.com.

www.ingramcontent.com/pod-product-compliance
Lightning Source LLC
Chambersburg PA
CBHW060153280326
41932CB00012B/1749